GRAVEYARD
OF THE
LAKES

Donald E. Morey
246 Shady Tree Lane
Howes Cave, NY 12092
518-296-8962

GRAVEYARD
OF THE
LAKES

MARK L. THOMPSON

WAYNE STATE UNIVERSITY PRESS • DETROIT

Great Lakes Books

*A complete listing of the books in this series
can be found online at http://wsupress.wayne.edu*

Philip P. Mason, Editor
Department of History, Wayne State University

Dr. Charles K. Hyde, Associate Editor
Department of History, Wayne State University

Front cover: Painting of the *Phoenix* burning by William J. Koelpin. Courtesy of the Wisconsin Maritime Museum, Manitowac, Wisconsin.

Back cover: Waves crashing over the deck of the *S.S. Buckeye*. (Dave Cook)

Cover design by Mary Primeau

Copyright © 2000 by Wayne State University Press, Detroit, Michigan 48201. First paperback printing 2004. All rights are reserved. No part of this book may be reproduced without formal permission. Manufactured in the United States of America.

08 07 06 05 04   5 4 3 2 1

Library of Congress Cataloging-in-Publication Data

Thompson, Mark L., 1945–
      Graveyard of the lakes / Mark L. Thompson
          p. cm. — (Great Lakes books)
      Includes bibliographical references and index.
      ISBN 0-8143-2889-X (alk. paper)
      ISBN 0-8143-3226-9 (pbk: alk. paper)
      1. Shipwrecks—Great Lakes. I. Title. II. Series.
      G525.T475   2000
      977—dc21   00-008710

To the memory of my father,

Charles A. Thompson

The boats were just a part of the

rich heritage he left us

CONTENTS

PREFACE

THIS IS MY FOURTH BOOK ABOUT THE GREAT LAKES shipping industry . . . and it's a book I never intended to write. My other books filled gaps I thought existed in the recent literature about the industry. *Steamboats and Sailors of the Great Lakes* (Detroit: Wayne State University Press, 1991) traced the historical development of the industry and provided an overview of contemporary shipping activity and the changes that have taken place since the shipping recession of the 1980s. *Queen of the Lakes* (Detroit: Wayne State University Press, 1994) featured vignettes about the longest ships that have sailed the lakes and showed how the art and science of shipbuilding has changed over the years. *A Sailor's Logbook* (Detroit: Wayne State University Press, 1999) documented what it was like to work and live aboard lake freighters during the shipping season of 1996. While I intended to write another book about the industry, I had a strong intellectual bias against doing a "shipwreck book."

Since my first book came out, there have been quite a number of books written that fall under the general classification of "Great Lakes shipping." The overwhelming majority of those have been about shipwrecks. While I like a good shipwreck story as much as the next person, it seemed to me that the subject verged on being overdone.

The more I thought about it, though, the more I began to think that another book about shipwrecks *was* needed. As a historian, my greatest disappointment with shipwreck literature has been the almost universal failure of the authors to put the wrecks they write about into any sort of historical context. In *Steamboats and Sailors,* I commented that a shipwreck is *not* "an isolated, exclusive event that occurs to one unlucky ship and its equally hapless crew."[1] Unfortunately, that's precisely the impression you're left with after reading the shipwreck literature.

You don't have to study many wrecks, though, before you're likely to notice some distinct patterns emerging. Those patterns are the result of historical factors that have influenced both the number and nature of wrecks. They include the size of the fleet operating on the lakes, the level of technological development, the status of governmental regulation, and the attitudes and behaviors of those within the industry—the human factor. Without examining those historical elements, you can't possibly reach an in-depth understanding of why a particular shipwreck occurred. Each and every wreck has occurred as a result of the confluence of a general set of historical conditions and the specific circumstances involved in the vessel casualty. The historical conditions can be viewed as setting the stage for a shipwreck which is then played out against that backdrop as a result of the specific situation that arises.

If authors of shipwreck books were the only ones who have failed to grasp the significance of those preexisting historical conditions, it would be of little consequence in the overall scheme of things. Unfortunately, that's not the case. Generations of sailors, shipping company managers, and government officials in both the United States and Canada have shown a pervasive reluctance to look beyond the specifics of any given shipwreck. As a result, conditions and behaviors that had a direct impact on both the number and severity of vessel casualties have been allowed to persist for long periods of time.

It was that oversight in the shipwreck literature that finally convinced me that another book on the subject was warranted. This will not be a traditional shipwreck book, however. While it contains the stories of many shipwrecks, it's purpose is not just to entertain readers, but to enlighten them as well . . . and, hopefully, to correct the historical record.

My interest in shipwrecks, and my perspective on them, can undoubtedly be attributed to my own life experiences. I was a thirteen-year-old junior high school student in Rogers City, Michigan, when the *Carl D. Bradley* sank in a violent November storm on Lake Michigan in 1958. Thirty-three sailors died that terrible night, almost all of them from Rogers City, home port for the *Bradley*. I knew most of those who died, and I knew their wives, mothers and fathers, sons, daughters, brothers, and sisters. One young crewmember had been our paperboy just a few months earlier. Another was my aunt's younger brother. Five were the fathers of kids I had grown up with. For those of us who lived in Rogers City in 1958, it was a tragedy of almost indescribable proportions.

Sadly, the loss of the *Bradley* was not the last maritime tragedy that the people of Rogers City had to endure. In the spring of 1966, another boat from Rogers City—the steamer *Cedarville*—sank in the Straits of Mackinac after colliding with a Norwegian freighter. Ten more Rogers City sailors were lost. Half of them were the fathers of friends of mine. They were men I had known all my life . . . men I still think about today.

The losses of the *Bradley* and *Cedarville* had a profound effect on me. Like almost everyone in Rogers City, I became painfully aware of the enormous human tragedy that results when a ship is lost. I've seen the

1. The author's worn and torn copy of a special edition of the *Presque Isle County Advance* honoring the thirty-three sailors who died in the November 18, 1958, sinking of the *Carl D. Bradley* during a Lake Michigan storm. Most of the dead were from Rogers City, Michigan, and other small communities in Presque Isle County on the northwest shore of Lake Huron. Rogers City was the home port for ships of the Bradley Transportation Line. Only two crewmembers survived the sinking of the *Bradley,* which was later attributed to structural failure. (Author's Collection)

rivers of tears, the lives ripped apart, and the smoldering anger kindled by the needless loss of life.

My inclination to look beyond the specific circumstances of any particular maritime disaster and search for preexisting conditions and patterns of behavior that set the stage for the shipwreck was greatly influenced by my association with Captain James A. Wilson, U.S.C.G. (Ret.). Captain Wilson had a distinguished career as a marine inspection officer for the Coast Guard and was one of three officers assigned to the marine casualty board that investigated the 1975 sinking of the *Edmund Fitzgerald.* In our numerous and lengthy discussions about the loss of the *Fitzgerald,* Jim freely admitted that even though he and his colleagues on the board conducted one of the most detailed casualty investigations in the annals of American maritime history, it was impossible for them to determine with certainty why the *Fitz* sank. What *was* clear, though, was that the Great Lakes shipping industry was dangerously lax when it came to safety. "Complacency" was the exact term the Coast Guard board used to describe industry attitudes regarding vessel safety. In this book, you'll discover that *complacency* is a term that could have been used many times in the long history of shipwrecks on the Great Lakes . . . and it's likely to be used again in the future, after the loss of some as-yet-to-be-determined ship and its ill-fated crew.

Jim Wilson is just one of many people who need to be thanked publicly for the contributions they've made to this book. At the top of the list is my family. They're always supportive, and tolerant of the months I spend away on the boats and the long days in self-imposed sequestration while I'm working on a book.

No individual made a greater contribution to this book than my friend Ralph Roberts. He supplied many of the photos I've used, and his comments on an early draft of my manuscript were indispensable. I've also been greatly inspired by Ralph's commitment to document and preserve the history of the Great Lakes shipping industry.

Finally, I need to admit to you that this book is in many respects a collaborative undertaking. My collaborators are all the writers, researchers, and maritime historians who have documented the stories of shipwrecks on the Great Lakes. I have borrowed extensively from their works in preparing this book, and I owe each of them a deep debt of gratitude. In fairness, I also need to make it clear that their collaboration in this enterprise has been totally involuntary and they should be held blameless for any errors I have made in drawing from their works.

INTRODUCTION:
A River of Tears

Eternal Father strong to save,
Whose arm hath bound the restless wave,
Who bidd'st the mighty ocean deep
Its own appointed limits keep:
O hear us when we cry to Thee
For those in peril on the sea.

Mariners' Hymn

O N THE MORNING OF NOVEMBER 11, 1975, PASTOR Richard W. Ingalls of Mariners' Church in Detroit slowly tolled his church's "brotherhood bell" twenty-nine times. He did so in memory of the twenty-nine crewmen on the freighter *Edmund Fitzgerald* who had been lost the previous evening when their ship sank in a fierce storm on Lake Superior. Tolling the bell once for each mariner lost on the Great Lakes was a tradition Pastor Ingalls had been carrying out privately since shortly after becoming rector of the historic church in 1965.

That particular morning, Pastor Ingalls had an audience, however. Several Detroit reporters who were working on stories about the *Fitzgerald*'s sinking had heard the tolling of the bell and showed up, uninvited, at the old church on the banks of the Detroit River. Ingalls explained to them that he had begun the practice of tolling the bell for lost mariners because his church had a unique mission to minister to and care for merchant seamen that dated back to the consecration of the Gothic structure in 1849.

Many of the media reports about the sinking of the *Fitzgerald* that came out of Detroit later that day mentioned the mournful tolling of the bell at Mariners' as a sidelight.[1] The following year, Canadian singer Gordon Lightfoot released a song entitled "The Wreck of the *Edmund Fitzgerald*," which soared to the top of the pop music charts. The final verse of the haunting ballad included these lines:

In a musty old hall in Detroit they prayed
in the maritime sailors' cathedral

the church bell chimed 'til it rang twenty-nine times
for each man on the *Edmund Fitzgerald*.[2]

Lightfoot's "maritime sailors' cathedral" was, of course, Pastor Ingalls's church, although Mariners' is far from a "musty old hall." Nonetheless, almost overnight Mariners' Church, and Pastor Ingalls's previously private practice of tolling the church's bell for the souls of lost sailors, became part of the shipwreck lore of the lakes, and literally known around the world. Many of the people who have heard the song over the years are not aware, however, that the "maritime sailors' cathedral" actually exists, or that its pastor did, in fact, toll the bell for the crew of the *Fitzgerald* that morning in 1975. Even within the Great Lakes shipping community, there are many who think the poignant events mentioned in Lightfoot's ballad never really happened. On the other hand, some believe the bell at Mariners' has *always* been tolled for lost seamen.

Actually, Mariners' Church didn't have a bell to toll until the bell tower was added to the church in 1957, more than a hundred years after the church was constructed. If the practice of ringing the bell once for each seaman lost on the lakes had dated back to the construction of the church in 1849, the slow tolling of the bell would have been a familiar sound to residents of Detroit. They would have heard it thousands of times over the years . . . because the dog-eared pages in the history of Great Lakes shipping are filled with the names of thousands of dead sailors and lost ships.

The first entry in the roll of shipwrecks on the Great Lakes was made in 1679, before the first settlers had even found their way to what would eventually become Detroit. On August 7, 1679, the *Griffon* sailed out of the headwaters of the Niagara River, the first ship to operate above the majestic falls that separate Lake Ontario from Lake Erie and the upper lakes. The small vessel, only about sixty feet long, had been built along the banks of the Niagara for Robert Cavalier—Sieur de la Salle—a French aristocrat and explorer who had been commissioned by his monarch to search for a passage through North America to China. His aide, Henry de Tonty, the Franciscan friar Louis Hennepin, and thirty-one crewmembers of varying nationalities accompanied la Salle on the maiden voyage of the *Griffon*. The ship's pilot was Lucas, a Dane, who reportedly stood seven feet tall.[3]

It took three days for the *Griffon* to cross Lake Erie and begin the slow, meandering trip up the Detroit and St. Clair Rivers. Not long after reaching the waters of Lake Huron, the little *Griffon* was briefly battered by a storm, probably one of the squall lines that typically beat their way across the lakes during the summer months. After anchoring for a short time in a bay in the Straits of Mackinac to escape another storm front, *Griffon* finally sailed on to Green Bay on northern Lake Michigan, where la Salle bartered with the local Indians, trading trinkets for furs.[4]

By mid-September, the *Griffon* was heavily laden with valuable pelts. La Salle decided to send the ship back down the lakes with a small crew, while he and the rest of his party continued their search for a route to China.[5] *Griffon* departed Green Bay under the command of Lucas, with a crew of only five seamen. Father Hennepin's journal reports that a few days after its departure from Green Bay, local Indians spotted *Griffon* anchored close to shore in northern Lake Michigan. They supposedly warned Lucas to steer a course along the shore and not venture out into the middle of the lakes. According to Father Hennepin, however, "[Lucas] was dissatisfied, and would steer as he pleased, without hearkening to the advice of the savages." After the *Griffon* weighed anchor and sailed through the Straits of Mackinac and onto the waters of Lake Huron, the lakes were swept by an early fall storm that lasted four days. According to Father Hennepin, "The ship was hardly a league [two to four miles] from the coast when it was tossed up by a violent storm in such a manner that our men were never heard of since, and it is supposed that the ship struck upon a sand[bar] and was there buried."[6] The Great Lakes had claimed their first ship.

There is little documentation available about the *Griffon* and many of the other early shipwrecks on the lakes. The earliest known shipwreck on Lake Superior was recorded in 1816, when the schooner *Invincible* was driven ashore and wrecked near Whitefish Point during a November storm. Those aboard supposedly managed to make it safely to shore, but the little ship was a total loss. The *Invincible* had been operated by the Northwest Company to supply their trading headquarters at Fort William, located on the north shore of the lake at what is now Thunder Bay, Ontario.[7]

The first shipwreck on Lake Michigan seems to have occurred off Chicago in 1818 when the schooner *Hercules* was wrecked with all hands. Some days later, Indians found the wreckage and bodies strewn along the beach. By then, bears and wolves had gnawed on most of the bodies.[8]

That fall of 1818 was clearly a hazardous one for shipping on the lakes. On September 27 the famed passenger steamer *Walk-in-the-Water* was badly damaged when she was driven ashore near Buffalo, New York, during a gale on Lake Erie. Less than a month later, the schooners *Eagle*

2. Launched at Buffalo, New York, in 1818, the 135-foot *Walk-in-the-Water* was the first steamboat to operate above Niagara Falls. Seen here in a drawing by marine artist Samuel Ward Stanton, the pioneering passenger steamer was driven ashore near Buffalo during a violent gale that fall. Just three years later, *Walk-in-the-Water* was caught in another Lake Erie storm. After anchoring off Buffalo, the wood-hulled paddle wheeler began leaking badly, and Captain Jebediah Rogers decided to hoist the anchors and let his ship drift onto the beach. The passengers and crew were able to struggle ashore, but the ship was a total loss. (Author's Collection)

and *Commodore Perry* were reported ashore near Buffalo during a storm on October 21. On November 15 the schooner *Independence* capsized and wrecked during a storm off Black River, near Buffalo, and the crew drowned. The same storm drove the schooners *Paulina* and *Wasp* on the beach along the south shore of Lake Erie, put the British brig *Lord Wellington* on the beach at Point Abino, just northwest of Buffalo, and seriously damaged the schooner *Boxer*. Three days later, the schooner *General Brown* was driven ashore at the eastern end of Lake Erie, near Buffalo, and severely damaged.

Ships operating on Lake Erie weren't the only ones to sail in harm's way that fall of 1818. The final vessel casualty recorded during the 1818 season occurred on December 26 when the schooner *Dolphin* was wrecked by heavy ice just east of Rochester, New York, on Lake Ontario.[9]

In retrospect, the devastating toll taken on shipping during 1818 wasn't all that unusual. One authority has reported that of 199 steamships that operated on the lakes between 1818 and 1853, 54—an astonishing 27 percent—became casualties. Of those, 4 exploded, 14 burned, and 36 were otherwise "wrecked," probably as the result of founderings or groundings during storms.[10]

By 1838, the alarming number of accidents involving passenger steamers had attracted the attention of some members of Congress. They passed legislation that year which required steamboats to be inspected and licensed before they could carry passengers.[11] Since then, commercial ships on the Great Lakes have been forced to operate under an ever-increasing burden of statutes and regulations, all aimed at preventing shipwrecks and deaths.

The number of ships operating on the lakes grew almost geometrically during the middle years of the eighteenth century. There were only 10 ships on the lakes in 1810. By 1845 there were 493, and by 1860 the size of the Great Lakes fleet had swelled to 1,457. Over the next ten years almost a thousand ships were added—an increase of 68 percent—bringing the total to 2,455.[12] Unfortunately, the number of shipwrecks seemed to keep pace with the dramatic growth in the size of the Great Lakes fleet.

During 1860, reported to have been "a mild season" on the lakes, 377 wrecks were recorded, resulting in the loss of 594 lives. In 1871, a ship reporter from Detroit who kept a detailed listing of Great Lakes shipwrecks during the season documented a total of 591 founderings, collisions, groundings, and explosions—57 percent more than in 1860.[13]

There were 1,662 sailing ships, 682 steamboats, and 131 barges operating on the lakes in 1871, a total of 2,475 vessels.[14] That means that there was one accident for about every four ships in the Great Lakes fleet. In other words, there was a 25 percent chance that any given ship would be involved in an accident during the season. That's not a statistic that would have been reassuring to crewmembers and passengers traveling on the lakes.

The most thorough record of shipwrecks on any of the lakes has been developed by Dr. Julius F. Wolff, Jr., of the University of Minnesota, Duluth. Over a thirty-year period, Dr. Wolff gathered information on more than 1,350 marine casualties on Lake Superior in which damage exceeded $1,000 or resulted in the loss of life. According to Dr. Wolff, over 350 of the ships were total losses.[15]

If you plotted the locations of the 1,350 casualties documented by Dr. Wolff on a map, you would find that while Lake Superior is dotted with wrecks, there are particularly heavy concentrations at several locations. The area around Isle Royale, for example, has clearly been one of the most hazardous spots on the lake. Isle Royale is a long, narrow island that is the largest of a group of islands that parallels the Canadian shore for more than forty-five miles. It has been the site of at least forty-eight shipwrecks, and probably more. In fact, many of the island's coastal features have been named for ships that went aground there, including Harlem Reef, Bransford Reef, Cumberland Point, and Congdon Shoal, just to name a few (see Chapter 1).

Another place on Lake Superior where there has been an extraordinarily heavy concentration of shipwrecks is the Keweenaw Peninsula, which juts sixty miles out into the lake from the Upper Peninsula of Michigan, opposite Isle Royale. The first wreck recorded on the Keweenaw took place on September 21, 1844, when the brig *John Jacob Astor* blew onto the rocks near Copper Harbor at the northern tip of the peninsula. The *Astor* was operated by its namesake's American Fur Company. It was in the process of unloading supplies for the U.S. Army garrison at nearby Fort Wilkins when a gale came up out of the north. The little ship's anchor wouldn't hold, and the *Astor* was blown ashore. Winter storms later smashed the hull to pieces, but the crew salvaged much of the valuable rigging and equipment.[16]

The loss of the *Astor* was the first of almost 170 shipwrecks that have been documented in the waters around the Keweenaw Peninsula. Nearly 150 of those wrecks involved groundings similar to that of the *Astor*, as vessels were driven aground in storms or accidentally fetched up on the rocky shores during fog or snowstorms. Several wrecks were even attributed to heavy smoke from forest fires that obscured visibility along the shore.[17]

To the east of Isle Royale and the Keweenaw Peninsula are two more of Lake Superior's infamous death traps for ships—Whitefish Bay and Whitefish Point. Whitefish Bay forms the headwaters of the St. Marys River, which connects Lake Superior with Lake Huron. Between the loss of Northwest Company's schooner *Invincible*, which was driven onto Whitefish Point in a November storm in 1816, and the sinking of the *Edmund Fitzgerald* in a killer storm on November 10, 1975, the area around Whitefish Point has claimed a total of at least 240 ships, and probably more.[18] As with Isle Royale and the Keweenaw, the fact that Whitefish Point juts out into Lake Superior has made its sandy, scrub-lined beaches a magnet for ships straying off course, particularly when weather conditions limit visibility. Since Whitefish Bay is also a narrow, meandering funnel through which the heavy shipping traffic in and out

3. Map of the Great Lakes.

of the St. Marys River must pass, it has been an even more hazardous area than Isle Royale or the Keweenaw Peninsula.

Places like Isle Royale, the Keweenaw Peninsula, Whitefish Point, and Whitefish Bay soon came to be regarded as "graveyards" for ships. Their beaches, shoals, and reefs were littered with the broken bones of vessels that stood in mute testimony to the dangers of those shores. Like Lake Superior, each of the Great Lakes has its own all-too-familiar graveyards.

On Lake Ontario, Prince Edward Point has been a death trap for generations of sailors and ships running along the north shore of the lake. Long Point, Point aux Pins, Southeast Shoal, Point Pelee, Pelee Island, and the mouth of the Detroit River have similarly plagued those navigating Lake Erie.

Continuing up the lakes, we find Lake Huron ringed with the grave-yards of ships. One of the worst is the area from Thunder Bay to Presque

Isle Point, along the lake's northwest shore. At least 124 ships have wrecked near Thunder Bay, Thunder Bay Island, Middle Island, False Presque Isle, and Presque Isle Point, and on the many smaller islands, shoals, and reefs scattered along that stretch of shore. At least twenty-seven ships have been seriously damaged when they ran aground in the shallow waters, usually due to fog or navigational error, while other vessels have been driven ashore during storms or sunk in collisions.[19]

South of Thunder Bay are the expansive waters of Saginaw Bay, site of at least 187 shipwrecks. Saginaw Bay was an important center for the lumber industry around the turn of the century, and many of the ships that operated in that now-vanished trade were built of wood cut from Michigan's virgin forests. Those wooden ships were always highly susceptible to fire, often ignited by overturned kerosene lamps or sparks from their own smokestacks. We know, for example, that at least fifty ships burned in Saginaw Bay and the Saginaw River over the years.[20] Another eighty ships ran aground in the dangerous shoals and reefs that surround the tip of Michigan's "thumb" at the southeastern boundary of the bay. Jutting out into Lake Huron, the broad peninsula has snagged many ships that strayed from the shipping lanes while traveling down the lake or running in and out of Saginaw Bay.[21]

South of Saginaw Bay are the headwaters of the St. Clair River at the twin cities of Port Huron, Michigan, and Sarnia, Ontario. The waters north of Port Huron and Sarnia are a funnel for vessel traffic entering or leaving the busy St. Clair River, gateway to Detroit and the bustling ports on Lake Erie and Lake Ontario. Many of the wrecks in the area resulted from collisions between ships traveling in and out of the St. Clair River. Other ships were wrecked when they left the sheltered waters of the river and ventured out into storms on Lake Huron.

Midway up the Canadian shore of Lake Huron is the Bruce Peninsula and the chain of islands that extends to the north and west to form Georgian Bay and the North Channel. The largest "bay" on the Great Lakes, it stretches for more than two hundred miles from Collingwood, Ontario, in the south to the mouth of the St. Marys River in the north. It, too, is an infamous graveyard, the site of at least 213 shipwrecks.[22] Like Saginaw Bay on the western shore of the lake, Georgian Bay was an important center for the timber industry and fleets of wood-hulled "lumber hookers," attested to by the fact that eighty-four of the ships wrecked there were victims of fire.

At the head of Lake Huron, where its waters mix with those of Lake Michigan, are the Straits of Mackinac, which separate Michigan's upper and lower peninsulas. The scenic Straits are a navigator's nightmare of pine-covered islands, peninsulas, and shoal waters lying in wait to rip the bottoms out of passing ships. Like Whitefish Bay and the headwaters of the St. Clair River, the narrow, congested waters also increase the prospects for collisions between ships funneling in and out. At least 152 ships have wrecked around the Straits of Mackinac. Of those, we know that 34 grounded and another 21 were wrecked in collisions.[23]

Traveling down the east shore of Lake Michigan, ships soon come upon another notorious graveyard—the disarmingly picturesque Manitou Passage between the Manitou Islands and the towering sand dunes and bluffs along the Michigan mainland. Information on the total number of wrecks is sketchy, but we know that the broken hulls of thirty-five ships still rest on the sandy bottom of the passage.[24] More than fifty vessels are known to have wrecked around the Manitous, and that probably represents only a small percentage of the actual total.[25]

West of the Manitous is Green Bay, the Lake Michigan equivalent of Georgian Bay. The long, narrow bay is formed by the Door Peninsula and a chain of islands that stretches from the cities of Green Bay and Kewaunee, Wisconsin, to the Garden Peninsula in Michigan's Upper Peninsula. A number of ports are located on Green Bay, including the Wisconsin cities of Green Bay, Sturgeon Bay, and Marinette. Near the top of the bay are the Michigan ports of Menominee and Escanaba. The many islands and shoals around the bay have always created a hazard for shipping. Early French explorers aptly named the most dangerous spot *Porte des Mortes*—Death's Door. The islands around the narrow Death's Door passage, main entrance to Green Bay from Lake Michigan, have claimed countless ships over the years, including eight schooners during a seven-day period in 1872.[26]

While various areas have experienced extraordinarily high numbers of shipwrecks—familiar "graveyards" like Green Bay, Georgian Bay, Saginaw Bay, Whitefish Bay, and the others—they actually account for only a small percentage of the total number of wrecks on the lakes. In his 1899 *History of the Great Lakes*, J. B. Mansfield included detailed data on shipwrecks for the twenty-year period from 1878 through 1897, based on information supplied to him by E. T. Chamberlain, U.S. Commissioner of Navigation. The data show that an almost incomprehensible total of 5,999 ships were wrecked during that period, ranging from a low of 208 in 1879 to a high of 367 in 1892. Between 1,754 and 4,051 crewmembers and 66 to 1,607 passengers were involved in wrecks *each year*, and a total of 1,166 lives were lost over the twenty years.

Of the 5,999 ships involved in wrecks between 1878 and 1897, 1,093 were listed as total losses. The number of total losses ranged from a low of 35 vessels in 1897 to a high of 79 in 1894. Since ships operated only about eight months of the year in those days, an average of one or two ships were lost *each week* during the shipping season.[27] Since there were between 2,455 and 3,018 commercial vessels operating on the lakes during each of the twenty years, an average of about 10 percent of the ships fell victim to a casualty of one sort or another each season.[28]

Of course, the numbers of shipwrecks recorded in Mansfield's seminal work cover only a very short span of the industry's long history. While records are sketchy, research indicates that from the 1679 loss of the *Griffon* to the present, more than 3,500 *major casualties* can be documented on the five Great Lakes.[29] The *total number of casualties* that have occurred over the more than three hundred years of shipping can only be guessed at, but a careful examination of trends in the numbers of wrecks suggests that it could easily be in excess of 25,000.

It's unlikely that there is a shipping industry anywhere in the world, with the possible exception of Great Britain, that has experienced more shipwrecks than the staggering toll recorded on North America's inland seas. In a way, it's misleading to label places like Green Bay, Georgian Bay, Isle Royale, and Whitefish Bay as "graveyards." The grim reality is that the five lakes and the rivers that connect them are one watery graveyard—the *Graveyard of the Lakes*—the final resting place for broken hulls and the moldering bones of the unfortunate souls who died with the ships.

Unfortunately, we have only limited information on most of the shipwrecks that took place on the Great Lakes. Not until 1936 were marine casualty boards impaneled to investigate shipping casualties and issue formal reports of their findings. Information on shipwrecks prior to that time tends to be sketchy, and marine historians and researchers often have to rely on incomplete, inaccurate, exaggerated, and often contradictory accounts in newspapers.

Efforts to determine why any given shipwreck occurred are further confounded by the fact that many ships simply disappeared—sailed into oblivion. In the days prior to radio communications, it was quite common—particularly during a storm—for a vessel to go down without anyone knowing about it until the ship was overdue at its next port, or until someone reported finding debris from its wreck. In the vernacular of the lakes, they had "gone missing," or "sailed through a crack in the lake," or simply "sailed away."

On August 18, 1861, for example, Mrs. E. Bowen was walking along the dock near the west pier of Cleveland's Cuyahoga River when she found a corked bottle floating at the water's edge. The bottle contained a note: "On board schooner *Amelia*, August 12, off Grand River, schooner lost foremast, also mainsail, leaking badly, cargo iron. Must go down. All hands must be lost. C. S. Brace, Capt." A gale that had swept over Lake Erie on August 12 had claimed the little schooner, but its fate remained the subject of speculation until Mrs. Bowen found the captain's hurriedly scribbled note.[30]

Similarly, a short article in a Muskegon, Michigan, newspaper on Monday, October 18, 1880, noted: "Grave apprehensions are entertained for the safety of the steamer *Alpena*, which left this port Friday afternoon for Chicago. Nothing has been seen or heard of it. This morning, a gentleman informed us that a ladder and pail marked '*Alpena*' had been found on the beach at Holland." Two days later, the bodies of two of the *Alpena*'s passengers were found washed up on the beach south of Holland. Five other bodies later washed ashore on the sandy Lake Michigan beaches, along with fire buckets, a piano with its lid torn off, part of a stairway, cabin doors, life preservers, and even a five- by ten-foot flag with the name *Alpena* appliquéd on it in large letters.[31] The ship had been carrying several railroad car loads of apples when it left Muskegon, and for weeks after its disappearance apples bobbed about in the surf off Holland.

A water-soaked note was eventually found among the debris. "This is terrible," it said. "The steamer is breaking up fast. I am aboard from Grand Haven to Chicago." It was signed "George Conner," or "George Connell." It was difficult to decipher the signature on the water-soaked note.

Under the command of Captain Nelson W. Napier, the 175-foot passenger and freight steamer *Alpena* had cleared Grand Haven, Michigan, bound for Chicago, on the evening of Friday, October 15. Thirty-five passengers and a crew of twenty-two men were aboard.[32] It had been a typical Indian-summer day, with warm temperatures and sunny skies, but the barometer was plummeting as the *Alpena* cleared the long pier at Grand Haven and pointed its nose westward. The rapid fall of the barometer indicated that a storm was moving toward the lakes, but Captain Napier decided to sail anyway. We don't know why, and we'll never know why, but it was probably a combination of the fact that when the *Alpena* was loaded and ready to depart the weather was gorgeous and, besides, it was only a short dash across the lake to Chicago.

Wind speeds increased rapidly and reached storm intensity just a few hours after the *Alpena* departed Grand Haven. Winds continued to blow ferociously throughout Saturday and Sunday, whipping the waters of Lake Michigan into towering waves. Sometime Saturday evening, the *Alpena* was sighted by another ship that had been caught out in the blow, but she didn't appear to be experiencing any difficulties. That was the last time the *Alpena* was ever seen. Either Saturday night or Sunday night, the ship broke up and sank. It's almost certain that the wreck happened at night, because most of the bodies later found were wearing nightclothes. Unfortunately, none of those aboard survived to tell us what happened.[33]

In the aftermath of the disaster, the ship's owner, Captain A. E. Goodrich, told reporters that he thought Captain Napier might have held his westerly course too long, then found it impossible to bring his ship about in the high seas. Trapped in the trough formed by the giant waves, the *Alpena* would have rolled violently, possibly damaging its paddle wheels or tearing its engine apart. Other "marine men" thought the debris that floated ashore from the *Alpena* showed signs that its boiler had blown up. Still others disagreed with both those theories, arguing instead that the ship had probably gotten trapped in the trough of the seas and rolled over because of its heavy superstructure.[34]

The *Alpena* wasn't the only casualty of the storm of October 15–17, 1880. Ninety ships caught out on the lakes were damaged during the storm.[35] Nelson Napier wasn't the only captain who ignored his barometer.

Around the turn of the century, another ship that mysteriously disappeared in a Lake Michigan storm became the subject of a song that was popular in communities around the lower lakes. One verse went:

> Here's a sigh for the *Chicora*, for the broken, sad *Chicora*;
> Here's a tear for those who followed her beneath the tossing wave.

The poignant ballad recounts the 1895 loss of the *Chicora*, another of Lake Michigan's many passenger and freight vessels. It disappeared on January 21, 1895, after departing Milwaukee on a cross-lake trip to St. Joseph, Michigan. As in the case of the *Alpena*, the barometer was falling when the *Chicora* left Milwaukee. A storm was definitely brewing, but Captain Edward Stein of the *Chicora* went out anyway. He was later said to have been ill and in a hurry to get to his doctor in St. Joseph. Soon after Captain Stein took his ship out of the harbor at Milwaukee, a severe storm bore down on the lakes.

Several days later, spars and other wreckage from the *Chicora* drifted

4. The 217-foot passenger and freight steamer *Chicora* is one of many Great Lakes ships that have disappeared during storms. She sank on January 21, 1895, after departing Milwaukee, Wisconsin, on a cross-lake run to St. Joseph, Michigan. While twenty-four crewmembers and one passenger were lost with the ship, there is one report that the ship's dog was found wandering along the beach near St. Joseph a few days later. (Ralph Roberts Collection)

ashore between South Haven and Saugatuck, Michigan. Rescue vessels braved thick ice floes and bitterly cold temperatures to search the lake for survivors, but none were ever found. Captain Stein, twenty-three crewmembers, and a solitary passenger—a friend of one of the ship's officers—went down with the ship in the icy waters of Lake Michigan. Most felt it was the violent storm that sank the *Chicora*, but others preferred to believe the heavy ice had stove in her hull.[36] Regardless, Captain Stein's illness proved to be fatal.

On November 21, 1902, the Canadian freighter *Bannockburn* left Port Arthur, Ontario, with a load of wheat and sailed into the teeth of a late-season Lake Superior storm. She was sighted during the night by two passing ships, then disappeared mysteriously. None of her twenty crewmembers was ever found.[37]

The wood-hulled schooner *Rouse Simmons* left Manistique, Michigan, in late November 1912, bound for Chicago with a load of freshly cut Christmas trees. It was later seen off Kewaunee, Wisconsin, flying a distress signal, but then disappeared to become the famed "Christmas tree ship" of the Great Lakes. Captain Herman Scheunemann and his crew of sixteen vanished with their ship.[38] It was reported that the forty-four-year-old schooner was in "a dangerous condition" when it had sailed from Chicago a few days earlier. In fact, a superstitious crewmember by the name of Hogan Hoganson quit just before the ship left the dock, saying that he'd seen rats leaving the ship.[39]

On September 10, 1929, the semi-whaleback freighter *Andaste* was steaming to Chicago from its home port at Grand Haven, Michigan, with a load of stone when it got caught in a fall gale. Bodies and wreckage from the 247-foot workhorse began to drift ashore near Grand Haven several days later. Among the debris was a plank with a plaintive note scribbled on it: "Worst storm I have ever been in. Can't stay up much longer. Hope to God we're saved." It was signed with the initials "A.L.A." The *Andaste*'s captain was Albert L. Anderson. He and twenty-four crewmembers died with their ship.[40]

Only two weeks after the sinking of the *Andaste*, a member of the Coast Guard station at South Haven, Michigan, found a messenger tube floating near the beach. In the sealed tube was a note: "*S.S. Milwaukee,* Oct. 22, '29, 6:30 P.M. Ship taking water fast. We have turned and headed for Milwaukee. Pumps are all working, but the sea-gate is bent and won't keep water out. Flickers are flooded. Seas are tremendous. Things look bad. Crew roll about same as last payday. A. R. Sadon, Purser." It was confirmation of the tragic loss of the *Milwaukee,* one of the ferries that carried railroad cars across Lake Michigan for the Grand Trunk Railroad. The ship had left Milwaukee in the midst of a severe storm on October 22, bound for Muskegon with a load of twenty-seven boxcars. Gone with the ship were Purser Sadon and fifty-one other crewmembers.[41]

If the *Milwaukee* had been part of the Ann Arbor Railroad's fleet of car ferries, her crew might have been able to summon assistance before their ship disappeared beneath the waters of Lake Michigan. In 1906 the Ann Arbor Railroad had equipped their ferries with radiotelegraph sets. From 1903 on, government agencies like the U.S. Life-Saving Service and Steamboat Inspection Service had been urging shipping companies to install radios on their vessels so they could call for help if they were threatened with sinking. On the lakes, however, most captains and shipping executives were opposed to equipping their ships with radios. Captains feared that radios would allow office personnel to interfere in the daily operations of their ships. Company officials felt radios were unnecessary on the Great Lakes and didn't want to incur the expenses of equipping their ships and hiring radio operators. The attitude of many within the Great Lakes shipping industry was made clear in 1907 in a statement by Harry Coulby, president of the giant Pittsburgh Steamship Company: "The boats of the Pittsburgh Steamship Company are not and never will be equipped with wireless," Coulby told the *Cleveland Plain Dealer.*[42]

Despite Coulby's terse statement, the value of having ship-to-shore radios was clearly demonstrated on September 9, 1910, when the car ferry *Pere Marquette 18* foundered in a Lake Michigan storm. Before sinking, she radioed a message to her sister ship, the *Pere Marquette 17,* which was nearby. While many lives were still lost in the sinking, thirty-five persons were saved when the *Pere Marquette 17* altered course and raced to the scene. If the Pere Marquette Railroad hadn't voluntarily equipped its ships with radios, surely all aboard the *Pere Marquette 18* would have died.[43]

Even after all commercial ships on the Great Lakes were equipped with radios, though, there were still mysterious disappearances. After the 600-foot steamer *Daniel J. Morrell* hadn't been heard from for more than thirty-six hours during a severe storm in late November 1966, officials from Bethlehem Steel finally reported their ship missing. A massive search was immediately launched. A few hours later, the crew of a Coast Guard helicopter searching the shoreline along Michigan's thumb found the *Morrell*'s life raft washed up on the beach. On the raft was Dennis Hale, who would prove to be the only survivor from the crew of twenty-nine.

Hale told his rescuers that the *Morrell* had broken in half and sunk at about 2 A.M. the previous day. Coast Guard investigators would later conclude that the electrical lines that supplied power for the ship's radios had been torn apart when the ship broke in half, making it impossible for those aboard to broadcast a distress call. As a result of the lesson learned from the sinking of the *Morrell,* Coast Guard regulations were changed to require every shipboard radio to be equipped with an emergency power supply (see Chapter 4).[44]

Even that change didn't totally eliminate cases of mysterious sinkings, however. In the hours before the *Edmund Fitzgerald*'s loss on November 10, 1975, Captain Ernest McSorley and the mates on watch in the ship's pilothouse were in regular communications with officers on the freighter *Arthur M. Anderson,* which was following them across Lake Superior in a furious storm. At 3:30 in the afternoon, Captain McSorley told the captain of the *Anderson* that the "*Fitz*" had taken on a list after suffering damage to two vents and that he had his ballast pumps on. To those in the *Anderson*'s pilothouse, McSorley didn't sound too concerned.

On seven more instances that afternoon and evening, personnel on the *Fitzgerald* talked by radio with the *Anderson,* the Coast Guard, and the U.S. pilot on a Swedish ship anchored in Whitefish Bay. At no time did anyone in the *Fitzgerald*'s pilothouse offer any additional details about the damage they had sustained. The last radio communication with the injured freighter was at 7:10 P.M. During that conversation, the mate on the *Anderson* asked, "Oh, by the way, how are you making out with your problem?" The word coming back from the *Fitzgerald* was, "We are holding our own."

Ten minutes later, those in the *Anderson*'s pilothouse noticed that the *Fitzgerald* had disappeared from their radar screen. They could see three ships—the saltwater freighters *Avafors, Nanfri,* and *Benfri*—that were leaving Whitefish Bay to head up the lake, but no *Fitzgerald.* Within minutes, they were struck by the horrible realization that the *Fitzgerald* had sunk (see Chapter 5).[45]

Despite the fact that the captain and mates on the *Fitzgerald* had eight radio conversations with Coast Guard personnel and officers on other ships during the afternoon and early evening hours of November 10, we still don't know what caused the ship to sink. Captain McSorley and his mates didn't offer any detailed information about what was happening aboard their ship . . . and the individuals they talked to didn't press for any particulars.

While having radios aboard the *Morrell* and *Fitzgerald* didn't provide much help to us in understanding why those ships were lost, the development of radio communications in the maritime industry has been a significant factor in reducing shipwrecks and deaths on the lakes. The invention of radio is, however, just one of many changes that have affected the industry over the years.

From the launching of the *Griffon* in 1679 until today, the shipping industry has undergone a steady metamorphosis. The number of ships on the Great Lakes grew at a snail's pace after the *Griffon.* In 1833, more than 150 years later, there were only about 200 boats. From the 1830s on, however, the number of ships increased almost exponentially, until it reached a high of 3,018 vessels in 1893.[46] Since then, the size of the Great Lakes fleet has steadily dwindled until there are only about 188 ships in the combined U.S. and Canadian fleets today. Less than 70 of those are owned by U.S. shipping companies.

While the *Griffon* and the other early ships on the lakes were European-style, square-rigged sailing ships, they were found to be poorly suited to conditions on the lakes. Square-rigged barks and brigs were still being built in the 1830s, but schooners became far more popular with shipowners. Because the sails of the schooners were rigged fore-and-aft, they were much more maneuverable than square-rigged vessels, an important factor in a system where ships have to move through many miles of narrow river channels. Schooners also required fewer crewmembers to tend their sails. By 1870, square-rigged ships had almost disappeared from the lakes. Interestingly, schooners were also on a slow voyage toward extinction by then, although it's questionable whether anyone could have envisioned it at the time.

The gradual demise of sailing ships was due to the shift to steam propulsion. The *Frontenac*, the first steamboat on the lakes, had been launched at Kingston, Ontario, in 1816. Others followed in its wake, but slowly at first. In 1833 there were only 11 steamboats, but the fleet of steamers on the lakes grew rapidly after the 1830s. By 1872 there were 682 steamboats, compared to 1,654 sailing ships. Most of the steamers were propelled by large paddle wheels that stuck out from the sides of the hull, outboard of the engine room that was located amidships.[47]

In addition to the 682 steamboats that were operating in 1872, another 216 steamboats that had been built between the appearance of the *Frontenac* in 1816 and the end of the 1871 shipping season were no longer in service. Captain J. W. Hall, who ran a marine reporting service in Detroit during much of the early era of steamboats, maintained detailed records on the dispositions of those vessels. More than half of the 216 steamers that had disappeared from the lakes before the 1872 shipping season were lost in casualties. According to Hall, 69 of the ships had foundered or been wrecked in groundings, resulting in 136 deaths. Another 34 burned, killing 700 of those aboard. Collisions resulted in the destruction of only 12 vessels, but claimed a staggering 601 lives. Of the other 101 steamers, Hall listed 60 as having "went to decay," while 41 were reportedly converted to other uses, primarily as unpowered barges.[48]

When the *Frontenac* and the other early steamers came out, they carried essentially the same cargoes that were then being hauled by sailing vessels—passengers and freight of all descriptions. The steamers proved to be extremely popular with passengers, however, and they rapidly dominated that lucrative trade. Passenger accommodations on the first steamers were below the main deck, just like they were on sailing ships, but in the process of adapting to better serve the passenger trade, the design of the steamers was modified in 1833 by the addition of cabins on the main deck level. In 1839 passenger capacity was further increased by adding a second tier of cabins. Freight continued to be carried in the cargo hold, located below the main deck.

While even the passenger quarters on the pioneering *Frontenac* were considered luxurious in comparison to those found aboard sailing ships, by the 1830s the steamers were nothing short of opulent. As steamboat lines competed for passengers, they began to build "palace steamers" that were outfitted as sumptuously as the finest hotels in the world.

Much of the appeal of the early steamboats was undoubtedly their novelty, but passengers quickly found that they were also more comfortable and more dependable than sailing ships. Other than when the wind was on their sterns, sailing ships always heeled over, away from the direction of the wind. Their decks were seldom level, and passengers often found it difficult to stand or move around. A steamboat, on the other hand, always ran along on an even keel, so passengers could easily move about the ship while it was under way. That was obviously more comfortable, and greatly relieved the tedium that was generally associated with traveling by boat.

The steamers were also quite good at operating on regular schedules. With fair winds, most sailing ships were actually faster than steamers like the *Frontenac,* which could only make about seven miles an hour. Like the tortoise and the hare, however, the steamers could run at a steady seven miles an hour all day and all night, while sailing ships would have bursts of speed when the winds were right but at other times would be becalmed or experience delays by having to tack back and forth into headwinds. As steam engines were continually improved, the steamers were eventually able to operate at speeds that could seldom be equaled by even the fastest schooners.

With a tremendous influx of immigrants coming into the Great Lakes region, the passenger trade was so lucrative that the owner of a steamboat could often recoup its construction costs in a single season of operations. Unfortunately, the boom in the passenger trade didn't last long. By the 1850s railroad lines served all the urban areas along the lower lakes, and many travelers opted to go by train. Trains were faster and less expensive than traveling by ship, and they had the added advantage of being able to operate year-round, while most ships were limited to a season of only eight or nine months.

Even though the popularity of the passenger and freight steamers dropped off markedly during the 1850s, they continued to be vital to communities on the northern lakes that were not yet served by railroads. As a result, many of the shipping lines remained viable until railroads and highways were eventually extended to the northern frontiers. By shifting their emphasis to more tourist-oriented routes, some companies running passenger steamers managed to remain in business until the 1960s.

Because passengers generally preferred to ride on steamboats after 1816, sailing ships were quickly relegated to the freight business, which was growing, but less profitable. While sail-powered vessels would often carry any cargo that was available, many eventually carved out a lucrative niche for themselves hauling bulk cargoes, like grain and coal, that could be dumped into their holds through the unobstructed hatches on their decks. Because the decks of the passenger and freight steamers were covered with cabins, cargo had to be loaded and unloaded through gangways in the side of their hulls. They weren't well suited to handling bulk cargo, because everything had to be wheeled aboard or carried aboard. Many sailing ships also found work in the rapidly growing timber industry, transporting sawn lumber from the mill towns around the northern lakes to urban centers like Chicago, Detroit, Cleveland, and Buffalo. Not only would the holds of the sailing vessels be filled with lumber, but their decks would be stacked high with boards as well.

Starting about 1845, the owners of some sailing ships attempted to increase their efficiency by having them towed through the Detroit and St. Clair Rivers by steam-powered tugs. The sight of five to eight schooners being towed along behind a smoke-belching steam tug soon became a common sight along the rivers. In time, thirty-two tugs were providing towing services.

The sailing fleet got a big break in 1859, when the first trestle-type ore dock was built at Marquette, Michigan. Railroad cars would be pulled out onto the top of the twenty-five-foot-high trestle, and their cargoes of ore would be dumped into hoppers just below the tracks. Chutes at the bottom of the hoppers could then be lowered into the hold of a ship moored at the dock, and by opening a trapdoor the ore would slide down the chute and drop into the ship. The ore dock was a timesaving invention of the first order, particularly when you consider that prior to their development men pushing wheelbarrows full of the heavy ore loaded ships.

Some ore had been carried down the lakes in the holds of passenger and freighter steamers prior to 1859. After all, if you had to load a ship by hand it really didn't make any difference whether you were pushing your wheelbarrow onto the deck of a sailing ship or through the gangway of a steamer. After the construction of the ore dock at Marquette, however, it was unusual for the steamers to haul much ore. For the next ten years, the sailing ships were able to dominate the iron ore trade between Lake Superior and the receiving ports on Lake Erie. The red rivers of iron ore being shipped down the lakes increased so fast during the Civil War, 1860–65, that there were times when there weren't enough ships to carry it all. That pushed freight rates up, to as much as five dollars a ton, double the usual rate, and put smiles on the faces of many owners of sailing ships.

In 1869, Captain Elihu M. Peck, a highly respected shipbuilder in Cleveland, attempted to capitalize on the growing bulk shipments by designing and building a ship specifically for that trade. Launched on November 16, 1869, the 208-foot *R. J. Hackett* was truly unique. While it was powered by a 390-horsepower steam engine, the ship had an open deck like a schooner. Down the center of the deck was a row of hatches spaced on twenty-four-foot centers, so they would line up perfectly with the chutes on the ore docks.

While passenger steamers had their engine rooms amidships, the engine room of Captain Peck's creation was all the way at the stern. On the main deck above the engine room was a cabin that housed the galley and some quarters for crewmembers. The pilothouse was all the way forward at the bow, with additional crew quarters below it. Because of its "two-island" design, the odd-looking *Hackett* had a single, immense cargo hold that could easily be filled at the chute dock at Marquette. In the *Hackett*, Peck had combined the best features of the steamboats and sailing ships into a genuinely new type of vessel. Referred to initially as a "steam barge," Captain Peck's creation was the prototype for hundreds of similarly configured ships that would dominate bulk shipping on the lakes for the next one hundred years—the "Great Lakes bulk freighters."

The year after Captain Peck launched the landmark *Hackett*, he built another pioneering vessel. The *Forest City* was virtually a twin to the *Hackett*, but it had no engine. It was a barge, designed to be towed by the *Hackett*. Steam engines were expensive in those days, but by having the *Hackett* tow the unpowered barge, Peck could substantially increase the return on his investment. The practice that began with Peck's launching of the *Hackett* and *Forest City* started a trend that continued well into the twentieth century.

In the 1880s, iron and steel ships began to supersede wood-hulled freighters like the *Hackett*, but they still followed the design that had been pioneered by Eli Peck. The switch to iron and steel construction allowed builders to turn out much larger ships than they could using wood, however. The first iron bulk freighter, the *Onoko* of 1882, was 302 feet long—the longest ship on the lakes at the time. The first steel-hulled ship, the *Spokane*, was launched in 1886. When the size of the fleet on the lakes reached its peak of 3,018 ships in 1893, the latest class of steel-hulled

5. The *Forest City* (*right*) was launched in 1870 as an unpowered schooner-barge that was towed by the steamer *R. J. Hackett*, the pioneering bulk freighter that had gone into service the previous year. The practice of having steamers tow barges eventually became common on the lakes. In 1872 a steam engine was installed on the *Forest City*, and she is shown here with her own schooner-barge consort (*left*) as the two vessels prepare to enter the original lock at Sault Ste. Marie, Michigan. (Author's Collection)

freighters measured 378 feet in length. Of the 3,018 total vessels, 1,731 were steam-powered, 1,205 were sailing ships, and 82 were barges.[49]

Steamboats had become the predominant type of ship on the lakes in 1886. In that year there were 1,280 steamers, compared to 1,235 sailing ships.[50] The number of sailing ships continued the steady decline that had begun, interestingly enough, in 1869—the year that the *R. J. Hackett* had been launched. The last sailing ship in the freight trades on the lakes was the schooner *Our Son*, which foundered in a 1930 storm on Lake Michigan. Long before the loss of the fifty-five-year-old vessel, sailing ships had ceased to be a viable force in the shipping industry on the lakes.

During the 1893 shipping season, when the size of the Great Lakes fleet was at its zenith, 325 ships were wrecked on the lakes, including 51 that were total losses. Those wrecks resulted in the deaths of 102 passengers and crewmembers.[51] It's a sad commentary, but 1893 was actually a relatively safe year. Based on the best information now available, the worst year for marine accidents was 1914. A total of 702 vessel casualties were recorded that season, including 16 total losses, even though there were only about 875 ships operating on the lakes that year. Quite amazingly, the 702 wrecks resulted in only 16 deaths.[52] The following year, more than 800 people would die in a single accident when the passenger steamer *Eastland* rolled over and sank at its dock in Chicago (see Chapter 4).[53]

It is in stark contrast to those dismal figures that the last total loss of a ship on the lakes was the tanker *Jupiter*, which exploded and burned in 1990, claiming the life of a single crewmember (see Chapter 2). Perhaps even more remarkable is the fact that no ship has been lost in a Great Lakes storm since the 1975 sinking of the *Fitzgerald* (see Chapter 5). The last ship lost in a collision was the *Sidney E. Smith, Jr.* in 1972 (see Chapter 3), and not a single commercial ship has been lost as the result of grounding since the *Frontenac* in 1979 (see Chapter 1). There have been casualties since the losses of the *Jupiter, Fitzgerald, Smith,* and *Frontenac*—groundings, collisions, fires, and some storm damage—but for the most part they have been relatively minor.

One purpose of this book is to attempt to arrive at a clear understanding of the primary causes of both the various types of shipwrecks and their resulting fatalities. It's a fairly standard practice to divide shipwrecks on the lakes into four major categories—strandings and groundings, fires and boiler explosions, collisions, and founderings—and that convention has largely been followed in organizing the succeeding chapters, with one notable exception. Chapter 4 covers founderings, the vast majority of which occurred during storms, but it also includes the stories of a

6. The fifty-five-year-old wood-hulled schooner *Our Son* was well past its prime when it lost its sails and began taking on water during a storm on Lake Michigan on September 26, 1930. It is seen here flying the U.S. flag upside down as a distress signal. The small crew of the aging sailboat was rescued by the steamer *William Nelson*, which was able to work itself alongside *Our Son*. Moments later the vessel that is generally regarded as the last working sailing ship on the Great Lakes plummeted to the bottom. (Ralph Roberts Collection)

number of ships that grounded during storms, even though they did not technically founder. Their inclusion is necessary, however, in order to give readers an accurate understanding of the true scope of destruction that can be caused by storms on the lakes.

Besides, use of the four categories of shipwrecks is nothing more than an artificial construct, and one that can be extremely misleading. The *categories* of shipwrecks—strandings and groundings, fires and boiler explosions, collisions, and founderings—differentiate between *types* of casualties, not their *causes*. A grounding, for example, could have been caused by navigational error, an equipment malfunction, poor visibility, a storm, human error . . . or, most likely, some combination of those factors. Similarly, a foundering could result from storm damage, ice damage, overloading or improper loading, equipment failure, hull failure, human error . . . or some combination of those factors.

To say that a ship sank because it got caught out in a storm is no more adequate an explanation than saying that a person who had arteriosclerosis, cancer, bubonic plague, or AIDS died from *cardiac arrest*—a stoppage of the heart. To understand *why* shipwrecks have occurred, we have to look beyond the easy, superficial explanations.

A second purpose of this book is to attempt to arrive at an understanding of why the numbers of shipwrecks and shipwreck-related deaths have declined so dramatically. Dana Thomas Bowen, the author of several popular shipwreck books, credited the shipping industry itself for the reduction in casualties. In his 1952 *Shipwrecks of the Lakes,* he wrote: "Almost all of the disasters recounted could not have happened even a few years later than they actually did occur." "Shipping," he proffered, "quickly turns its losses into lessons. Careful study by many separate agencies of each marine disaster always follows. What happened? Why did it happen? If at all possible these answers are found. Then ways and means and laws are made to prevent the same thing from again happening." Bowen goes on to say that "a government book of rules and regulations has been formulated based on marine experiences covering years of navigation. Most men believe that if this book is followed to the letter there would be very few major ship disasters, or minor ones either."[54]

While Bowen's argument may seem persuasive, there are actually several other possible explanations for the decline in marine casualties. It's reasonable to assume, for example, that technological developments might also have played some role. It's not difficult to imagine how the installation of aids to navigation, the transition to iron and steel ships, advancements in navigational equipment, and shipboard radio communications might have led to fewer ships being wrecked.

It could also be argued that the decline in the number of shipwrecks and resulting deaths was to some extent merely a natural consequence of the reduction in the number of ships operating on the lakes: fewer ships meant fewer shipwrecks. Basic probability theory would tell us there's potentially some truth to that argument.

In fact, it may be safe to assume that the declining number of shipwrecks and deaths on the lakes was actually a result of all three factors—government regulation of shipping, technological developments, and the downsizing of the Great Lakes fleet. On the other hand, whether one factor might have been of greater significance than the others remains as much of a mystery as what happened to the *Alpena, Chicora, Andaste,* and *Edmund Fitzgerald.*

If there are discernible answers to the questions of what caused shipwrecks and why their frequency has declined, they undoubtedly lie buried somewhere in the litany of maritime disasters that have occurred on the Great Lakes in the 350 years since the loss of the *Griffon.* The search for answers will take us on a long journey, from the fog-shrouded shores of Lake Superior's Isle Royale, to a blazing inferno on Lake Erie, to the unexpected meeting of two sisters on a quiet evening on Lake Huron, to an evil hurricane on Lake Michigan that littered the sandy shore with the bodies of dead sailors.

>>1<<

BEACHED WHALES:
Groundings

ROM THE MID-1800S UNTIL THE 1950S, ISLE ROYALE was populated from April until November each year by scores of commercial fishermen and their families. Most were of Scandinavian descent, with names like Anderson, Bjorlin, Gilbertson, Johnson, Olson, Rasmussen, and Sivertson. For three or four generations, those families fished the clear, cold waters around Lake Superior's largest island, providing a supply of fresh fish for the ever-increasing number of Scandinavian immigrants who settled in Minnesota and northern Wisconsin.

None of the Isle Royale fishermen ever got rich, but most years they did manage to net a reasonable living from the waters off their rugged island paradise. If a ship happened to accidentally fetch up on the island's rocky shore, or on one of the too-numerous-to-count shoals and reefs that lie just offshore, the fishing families often augmented their meager incomes by scavenging from the wreck.[1]

Scavenging from stranded ships has been a timeless, if not always completely honorable, tradition, not just on the lakes, but in coastal waters around the world. As one marine historian noted, "There is an old story telling of a New England preacher who, during the Sunday sermon, called on God to protect the sailors on the sea, but begged that in the event of a disaster the wreck would come ashore on his parish coast!"[2] It's likely that the fishing families of Isle Royale would have shared that pragmatic logic.

Whether they ever enlisted divine intervention in hopes that wrecks would happen along the shores of their island, we'll never know. If they did, their prayers were definitely answered, and quite regularly too, for there seemed to be a steady supply of wrecked ships on the coasts of Isle Royale.

Centurion, 1895

In the early-morning darkness of October 28, 1895, the captain of the 360-foot freighter *Centurion* attempted to guide his ship into the shelter of Siskiwit Bay on the south shore of the island to escape the fury of a powerful northwest gale that was accompanied by heavy snows. Even on a clear day, negotiating the cramped, reef-lined entrance into Siskiwit Bay calls for careful navigation, and with the combination of darkness and driving snow obscuring his vision, it's easy to understand how the captain of the *Centurion* could have gotten slightly off course. Instead of sliding into the sheltered waters of the bay, the big freighter, just over two years old, drove hard and fast onto one of the many unmarked reefs that guard the entrance. By the time the hapless ship ground to a halt, its midship section straddled the reef and its bow had been lifted more than twenty inches up in the water.

A quick check of the cargo hold showed that while the bottom of the ship had been badly damaged by its grinding ride over the rocky shoal, the inner hull was still watertight. The *Centurion*'s hold was filled with 600 tons of copper ingots and 27,000 sacks and barrels of flour. The crew knew that if they could remove enough of the cargo, their lightened ship would probably float free of the shoal. A number of the island's fishermen soon congregated at the site of the wreck, and the *Centurion*'s captain enlisted them to help his crew jettison some of the cargo. They set about the slow, arduous task of hoisting the copper and flour out of the hold and dumping it overboard to lighten the stranded ship. The cargo was valuable, but not nearly as valuable as the *Centurion.*[3]

The crewmen and the contingent of Isle Royale fishermen worked around the clock to lighten the *Centurion.* After most of the copper ingots had been dumped unceremoniously into the shallow waters along the reef, the just-launched steamer *Penobscot* arrived at the scene. Traveling up the lake light, the captain of the *Penobscot* was able to maneuver his 351-foot ship alongside the *Centurion* to take off some of her cargo.

Just over two days after the freighter had run aground, a stout towing hawser was strung between the two ships and the *Penobscot* began trying to pull the *Centurion* off the reef. After twelve hours of constant tugging, and amidst a boisterous cheer from the crewmen and fishermen on the deck of the *Centurion,* the damaged freighter was finally freed at 7 P.M. on October 30. She immediately headed for a shipyard to be repaired. Just over a month later, the stalwart freighter was back in service.[4]

Even before the *Centurion* was worked free from her perch on the reef, eager salvagers had shown up to retrieve the cargo that had been dumped overboard. No wonder, the shallow depths around the reef were littered with copper valued at $100,000 and flour that had been worth $40,000.[5] B. B. Inman and Company of Duluth was hired by the shipowners to salvage the copper for 10 percent of its value. W. H. Singer Company was contracted to salvage what they could of about one thousand barrels of flour that had been scuttled. For their work, the company would receive 50 percent of the value of the flour.[6] Many of the bags and barrels of flour that had been thrown overboard were still floating, and when the Isle Royale fishermen were leaving the *Centurion,* the thankful captain told them to help themselves to any they wanted.

The fishermen pulled a sack of flour out of the water, expecting that it would be completely waterlogged. When they broke it open, however, they found that the wet outer layer of flour had formed a mushy skin, protecting the inside from the water. Most of the flour was just as dry as it had been when it came out of the grinding mill. With that discovery, the fishermen enthusiastically began retrieving sacks of flour from the water. By the time they headed for home, their boats were loaded to the gunwales. They weren't sure what they would do with the hundreds of pounds of flour, but they weren't about to turn down an unexpected gift.

The quandary over what to do with all the flour was quickly solved by the enterprising wife of one of the fishermen. Dora Sivertson offered to turn the salvaged flour into freshly baked bread and rolls for only 50 cents a hundred-pound sack. It goes without saying, she was kept busy at her woodstove for the balance of the time they were on the island that year. In fact, demand was such that she eventually raised her price to 75 cents a sack.[7] Still a bargain, to be sure.

The *Centurion* was far from the first ship to be wrecked around Isle Royale, of course. That took place in 1840. In the fall of that year, the schooner *Siskawit* anchored off the American Fur Company's station at Siskiwit Bay to pick up fifty of the company's employees and transport them to La Pointe in the Apostle Islands, where they would spend the winter. While the little ship was being loaded, a typically violent fall storm came up and threatened to drive the ship ashore. The *Siskawit*'s captain cut his anchor chain and tried to make a dash for open water, but the wind and seas drove the schooner onto a reef.[8]

Storms played a role in many, but certainly not all, of the shipwrecks around Isle Royale. During the summer of 1875, for example, Lake Superior Navigation Company's 205-foot *Cumberland* ran on the Rock of Ages, a dangerous reef off the western end of the island that is covered by only six feet of water. While the reef had long been clearly marked on U.S. navigational charts, it wasn't shown on the Canadian chart being used on the little passenger and freight steamer. Wreckage from the ship drifted ashore on what has since been known as Cumberland Point.[9]

Harlem, 1898

In 1898 the steamer *Harlem* came ashore on Isle Royale near where the *Centurion* had grounded three years earlier. The 288-foot *Harlem* was built at the Detroit Drydock Company at Wyandotte, Michigan, in 1888 for the New York Central Railroad's Western Transit Company. In November 1898 the combination passenger and freight steamer was running for cover in a gale that spawned twenty-foot waves when she accidentally impaled herself on an unnamed shoal off Siskiwit Bay. Although all the crew managed to get off safely, the *Harlem* remained abandoned on the shoal all winter, providing a virtual treasure trove for the island's fishing families. The steamer was salvaged the following spring, but the shoal was known as Harlem Reef from then on.[10]

As in the cases of the *Centurion* and *Harlem*, fall storms and limited visibility often combined to cause shipwrecks around Isle Royale. During the Great Storm in November of 1905, for example, the 434-foot steel steamer *Bransford* was blown onto a reef off the east shore of the island. When high seas almost miraculously lifted her off the rocks a short time later, the 1902-built W. A. Hawgood Company vessel was able to limp on to Superior, Wisconsin.

The *Bransford* had a second run-in with the big island on November 16, 1909. During a gale and blinding blizzard, she ran aground on another of Siskiwit Bay's dangerous shoals. On navigational charts, the shallow spot was soon named for the wreck, but misspelled as "Brandsford Reef."

While Isle Royale claimed the *Bransford* twice, it couldn't kill her. Following her second grounding, she was salvaged and returned to service. Converted to a crane ship by American Steel and Wire and renamed *Clifford F. Hood* in 1943, she operated on the lakes until the 1971 season, and was finally scrapped in Spain in 1974.[11] Not all ships that ran afoul of Isle Royale were as lucky as the *Bransford*, though. One of the unlucky visitors to Isle Royale was the passenger and freight steamer *Monarch*.

Monarch, 1906

In the last light of the day on December 6, 1906, the wood-hulled *Monarch* was preparing to depart Port Arthur, Ontario, for her home port of Sarnia,

Ontario. Her holds had been filled with 85,000 bushels of hard Canadian wheat, valued at $125,000. She also carried cases of succulent canned salmon from the Pacific Northwest and barrels of flour that had been milled in Fort William, just across the river from Port Arthur. Heavy snow was falling as the last of the *Monarch's* twelve passengers hurried aboard, bundled against the biting cold.[12] From the open-air flying bridge atop the wheelhouse, Captain Edward Robertson sounded one blast on the ship's steam whistle, the signal for the deckhands waiting on the dock to cast off the mooring lines. Despite the blustery weather, the deckhands were in a jovial mood as they threw off the heavy lines and hurriedly climbed aboard the ship, which immediately began backing slowly down the dock.

The mood among the crewmembers on the *Monarch* was exceptionally lighthearted, and for good reason. Officials in the Sarnia offices of Northern Navigation Company had told Captain Robertson that this would be the ship's last trip of the 1906 season. After she unloaded her cargo at Sarnia, the *Monarch* would be going into layup for the winter. From captain to coal passers, everyone aboard the 240-foot flagship of the Northern Navigation fleet moved a little faster than usual and went about their familiar tasks with increased enthusiasm, buoyed by the knowledge that in a few short days the long shipping season would be behind them and they would be home with their families.

As the little ship passed the rocky crags of Welcome Island and Pie Island at the mouth of Thunder Bay and headed out onto Lake Superior, the wind was freshening noticeably and the heavy snowfall had reduced visibility to near zero. A less experienced captain might have thought seriously of returning to the shelter of Thunder Bay, but Ed Robertson had spent thirty-five years on the lakes, much of it on the run between Sarnia and Port Arthur. He knew the courses down the lake better than he knew the backyard of his home in Sarnia. Besides, he wanted to get the last trip of the season behind him just as badly as any of his crew.

As the *Monarch* pressed on across Superior at full speed, Captain Robertson passed the word to Chief Engineer Sam Beatty to run out the ship's taffrail log.[13] The log was a small, torpedo-shaped device that was towed behind the ship at the end of a wire. At the trailing end of the log was a propeller that turned as the device was towed through the water. Revolutions of the propeller registered on a counter aboard the *Monarch,* giving them a fairly accurate record of how far the ship had traveled. The combination of the readings from the log and the headings shown on the ship's magnetic compass allowed Captain Robertson to "dead reckon" the

7. The 240-foot passenger and freight steamer *Monarch*, launched in 1890, was one of many ships that have wrecked around Isle Royale over the years. While running at full speed in a Lake Superior snowstorm on December 6, 1906, the wood-hulled ship was driven off course and ran onto the rocks of Blake Point, at the eastern tip of the island. All but one of the forty-four passengers and crewmembers made it safely ashore. They were rescued four days later, after the lighthouse keeper on nearby Passage Island spotted their fires. (Ralph Roberts Collection)

position of the *Monarch* with a fair degree of accuracy. When visibility made it impossible for a captain to see the shore, dead reckoning was the only way he could navigate his ship. It was either that, or go to anchor.

There was still one major obstacle to be negotiated before the *Monarch* was safely out into the open waters of Lake Superior. About twenty-five miles out of Thunder Bay, the ship would have to pick its way through the narrow channel between Passage Island and the northwest tip of Isle Royale. When Captain Robertson thought enough time had passed so that they should be nearing Passage Island, he sent his second mate aft to check the readings on the log. Minutes later, the mate came racing back to the bridge. Almost out of breath, he told Captain Robertson that the taffrail log had iced up, apparently not too long after they had left Thunder Bay. It registered only ten miles.

Unsure of how close they were to Passage Island, and with a gale running and snow limiting visibility to no more than a dozen yards,

Captain Robertson and the mate huddled in the biting cold of the flying bridge, hoping to see a flash of light from the lighthouse on the island or to hear its powerful foghorn. The watchman had also been posted as a lookout at the bow. None of the three saw or heard anything that would indicate where they were.

The *Monarch*'s normal running time from Thunder Bay to Passage Island was two hours and twenty minutes. When Captain Robertson's pocket watch indicated that they should be at the passage, he shouted down to the wheelsman to bring the *Monarch* over onto the course for Whitefish Point. A few minutes later, Robertson shouted down again, telling the wheelsman to come over a couple of degrees to the west. Robertson thought the northwest wind had probably set them a little bit to the east of the usual courseline, and he wanted to correct for that.[14] From the shelter of the enclosed wheelhouse, the wheelsman called out that he thought he had seen a flash of light off to starboard. Captain Robertson and the mate looked in the direction indicated by the wheelsman, but they couldn't see a thing.

Only minutes later, Captain Robertson and the mate were almost thrown off the flying bridge as the *Monarch* drove hard aground on an ice-covered, rocky shore, its bow rammed high up on the rocks until the decks were at almost a forty-five-degree angle. Glancing aft, Captain Robertson saw that the midship section of the *Monarch* had crumbled from the impact and it looked as though the stern could break loose at any moment. Descending quickly to the main deck, Robertson rapidly surveyed the hull of his ship. It was immediately obvious to him that there was a good chance that the *Monarch*'s wood bottom had been seriously damaged. That fear was confirmed minutes later when word was passed that water was flooding into the engine room at the stern.

Fearing that his ship would slide off the rocks and sink in the frigid waters of the lake, Captain Robertson sent word for the chief engineer to keep the engine running full ahead to hold the *Monarch* in place. The captain wanted to get a mooring line ashore as soon as possible, and he ordered one of his mates to hurriedly launch a lifeboat and try to pass a mooring line around a large rock that projected from the shore about twenty-five feet ahead of the ship.

Despite the strenuous efforts of those in the lifeboat, they were unable to land on the rocky shore in the pounding surf. As the passengers and most of the crew crowded together near the *Monarch*'s tilted bow, the snowfall tapered off a little. In the faint light, Captain Robertson surveyed the shore around his crippled ship. It wasn't Passage Island that they'd run on, that was obvious. It looked to him as though they might be on Blake's Point at the northeast tip of Isle Royale, well south of the Passage Island channel he had been steering for. They might as well have been on the moon. The commercial fishermen and their families had already left the island for the year, leaving it populated only by wolves, moose, and other assorted species of wildlife.

Motivated by fear that the ship would slide back into the lake and carry them all to a watery grave, someone came up with an innovative plan for getting a line ashore. A rope was tied securely around the waist of J. D. McCullum, a young watchman who was the brother of one of the *Monarch*'s mates. McCullum then crawled over the gunwale near the bow and was lowered on the rope until just above the pounding surf. Crewmen holding the rope then began to swing McCullum like a pendulum. Gradually, McCullum's arc lengthened as he was swung through the cold air. When he finally swung over the top of a large rock along the shore, those holding the line let go and McCullum dropped to the rock like a sack of mud. Though he clawed at the ice-covered rock with his fingernails in an attempt to hold on, McCullum slid off and fell into the frigid water. Towed back to the side of the ship, the sopping wet crewman was hoisted clear of the surging waves and those on deck again began to swing him back and forth. When he was over the rock, they let go of the line. McCullum again dropped onto the rock, and again he slipped off into the water. On the third attempt, the line broke just as McCullum was over the target. Dropping heavily, the single-minded McCullum was finally able to grab hold. In seconds he had scrambled onto the narrow strip of beach.

A heaving line was thrown to McCullum, then a ladder was sent across so he could make his way up the steep bluff directly ahead of the *Monarch*. Once McCullum had scaled the bluff, the end of a stout mooring line was tied onto the heaving line and the young man pulled it ashore and snaked it securely around a large boulder. Crewmen on the *Monarch* then drew the mooring line tight and laid it down over a bit on the bow of the ship.

One at a time, the crewmen and passengers then began to make their way hand-over-hand across the hawser to the relative safety of the bluff. Captain Robertson ordered the men in the engine room to leave their flooded stations and abandon ship with the rest of the crew and passengers. When about half those on the *Monarch* had managed to cross safely to Isle Royale, the deck suddenly shook and to the sound of cracking timbers and the loud hiss of cold lake water hitting the hot boilers, the stern broke away and slid beneath the water. In terror, a watchman still aboard the shaking *Monarch* grabbed the end of a line and leaped over the side. Unfortunately, the other end of the line wasn't secured and he dropped like a rock into the frenzied waves alongside the ship. The watchman immediately disappeared beneath the water, never to be seen again.

The rest of the crewmembers speedily crossed the line to the top of the bluff, leaving only Captain Robertson aboard the wrecked *Monarch*. Ashore, the survivors gathered firewood and built a large bonfire, both to warm themselves and to provide a signal that might be seen by a passing ship. Throughout the day they kept a vigil along the edge of the bluff, but the lake continued to be churned by the gale and no ships were sighted.

Captain Robertson spent that first night aboard the *Monarch*, and he was probably more comfortable than those huddled around the bonfire on the shore of Blake's Point. With only a windbreak made from a sail salvaged from their ship as shelter, and with only a meager amount of food, it was an interminably long, cold night on the remote tip of Isle Royale. With the coming of the gray dawn, they began to be concerned that the bow section of the *Monarch* was also going to slide off into the deep water and sink. After much urging from both passengers and crewmembers, Captain Robertson finally agreed to leave his ship and join those on the beach.

Four crewmen hiked through the fresh snow to Tobin Harbor, a small fishing settlement a dozen miles down the rugged south shore of the island. There they found that the fishing families had left a few provisions behind when they left the island for the winter. Those supplies were hauled back to Blake's Point and added to the survivors' dwindling stock of flour and canned salmon that had floated ashore from the wreck. Although the gale and snow had subsided, the island was now shrouded in heavy fog that would make it impossible for the wreck or their bonfire to be seen from passing ships. Cold and exhausted, the survivors knew that they faced another bitter night on the forsaken shores of Isle Royale.

At about midnight the fog gradually lifted, and over on nearby Passage Island the lighthouse keeper climbed to the top of the light tower to have a look around. Through the thin haze that hung over the lake, he could make out a glow in the sky over Blake's Point. Well aware that the area around Blake's Point should have been uninhabited, he quickly surmised that some unfortunate ship had run on the beach during the storm.

The lighthouse keeper intended to have one of his crew row over to Isle Royale in the morning to investigate, but the giant swells that continued to roll across Superior in the aftermath of the gale made the four-mile trip across the open water too hazardous. As those shipwrecked at Blake's

Point began to fear that they might not be found until it was too late, the lighthouse keeper paced atop his tower, his eyes constantly fixed on the reassuring light of the bonfire on the island.

The lake was a little calmer the following morning, December 9, and shortly after dawn the assistant lighthouse keeper set out for Isle Royale in a small rowboat. The choppy water made it rough going, and the solitary occupant of the rowboat was soon shrouded in ice from the spray of the waves. When he reached the site of the shipwreck, the heavy surf made it impossible for him to beach the little boat. As the lighthouse tender held his tossing boat into the seas, the *Monarch*'s purser, a man named Beaumont, volunteered to swim out to the rowboat through the bitterly cold water. In minutes, he had crossed the raging stretch of water and pulled himself up and into the rowboat. Shivering from the cold, Beaumont quickly explained how the ship had gone aground and the desperate straits the survivors were in.

Knowing that it would be impossible to ferry all of the survivors to the lighthouse in the dangerous seas, Beaumont and the assistant lighthouse keeper decided to row out into the shipping channel in hopes that they could flag down a passing vessel. After drifting about in the shipping channel for many hours, they were finally able to hail the steamer *Edmonton,* sailing out of Port Arthur on its downbound voyage. The *Edmonton* immediately turned around and headed back for Port Arthur at full speed, arriving there at 2 A.M. on December 10. By 6 A.M. the tugs *James Whalen* and *Laura Grace* were on their way to Blake's Point with two doctors, medical supplies, food, blankets, and heavy rescue gear aboard.

When the tugs arrived at Blake's Point at about 10 A.M., the seas were still too rough to make a landing on the rocky shore. The captain on the *Whalen* signaled to those on shore that he was going to steam around to the lee side of the island where the water would be calmer. There he landed a rescue party that began helping the exhausted and frostbitten survivors board the two boats for the trip back to Port Arthur.

There is no record that anyone ever questioned Captain Robertson's decision to continue steaming toward Passage Island in the face of a worsening gale and near-zero visibility without an accurate log reading to show how far his ship had traveled. Such wrecks were still a common and accepted aspect of shipping on the Great Lakes in 1906. In fact, the passengers who had been aboard the *Monarch* weren't even compensated for their personal losses as a result of the shipwreck, although Northern Navigation magnanimously agreed to cover the costs of their passage down the lake on another ship.

The wreck of the *Monarch* marked the end of Captain Ed Robertson's long career. There had been some talk after the grounding that Robertson was getting too old for the demanding job of commanding a ship on the lakes. We have no way of knowing whether that criticism influenced his decision or not, but Captain Robertson retired before the start of the 1907 shipping season.[15] The lessons of the wreck of the *Monarch*, particularly the inherent danger in trying to navigate through a narrow passage by dead reckoning, were apparently soon forgotten.

Chester A. Congdon, 1918

A dozen years later, the 535-foot *Chester A. Congdon* departed Fort William, Ontario, before dawn on the morning of November 6, 1918, her cavernous cargo holds filled with 390,000 bushels of wheat. When the *Congdon* had gone as far as the mouth of the bay, Captain Charlie Autterson discovered that a storm was blowing out on Lake Superior, so he turned the *Congdon* around and went to anchor in the shelter of Thunder Bay. Captain Autterson didn't want to tangle with a November storm.

The storm seemed to die out several hours later, and at midmorning the *Congdon's* crew weighed anchor and again headed out onto the lake. Although the winds had tapered off, the waves were still high enough to rock the big freighter as it left Thunder Bay and headed on down the lake, but they were of no real concern to the crew. What was of concern was the heavy fog that had rolled in as soon as the winds blew out.

Fog will often cling to the shorelines of the upper lakes because of the difference in temperature between the relatively warm landmasses and the cool waters of the lake, so Captain Autterson decided to continue on, hoping to eventually run out of the fog. He figured that if the fog didn't lift by the time they had run for a couple hours, he would drop the hook and wait for it to clear. Like Captain Robertson before him, Captain Autterson set a dead-reckoning course for Passage Island, the gateway to the open waters of Lake Superior.

By midday the *Congdon* was still running along in a thick fogbank, and Captain Autterson knew they had to be nearing Passage Island. He and the mate on watch listened intently for the sound of the fog signal at the lighthouse on the island. They heard no foghorn, but shortly after 1 P.M. the *Congdon* ran aground on a shoal just off Isle Royale, well south of the deepwater courseline Captain Autterson was trying to steer.

Within two days after the grounding, salvers had removed about

8. The hull of the 535-foot bulk freighter *Chester A. Congdon* broke in half after the ship ran aground on a shoal off Isle Royale while trying to find its way through the passage at the eastern end of the island in a heavy fog. The ship and its cargo of wheat were valued at more than $1 million at the time. Today, the rocky outcropping that claimed the big freighter is known as Congdon Shoal. Many of the island's geographic features are named for ships that wrecked on Lake Superior's largest island. (Ralph Roberts Collection)

30,000 bushels of wheat from the *Congdon*. They had hoped they would eventually be able to remove enough cargo to float the ship free of the shoal, but on November 8 a storm with winds of fifty-five miles an hour roared onto Superior and drove the salvage crew off the wreck. When they were finally able to return to the *Congdon* on November 10, they found that the wind and seas had broken the ship in half between number 6 and 7 hatches. They removed 50,000 more bushels of wheat that fall, but with her back broken, the *Congdon* was declared a total loss.[16]

The *Congdon* and the more than 300,000 bushels of wheat that remained in her holds were valued at over $1 million. Even though the ship was only eleven years old, just barely broken in by Great Lakes standards, the cargo was actually worth more than the hull. With World War I raging across Europe, wheat was selling for $2.35 a bushel, so the cargo left to rot in the broken *Congdon* was worth over $728,000, a sizable fortune in 1918.

The rocky outcropping that claimed Captain Autterson's ship is known yet today as Congdon Shoal, although the two halves of the broken freighter slid off into deep water during the winter of 1918–19.[17] Like

Captain Robertson before him, Captain Autterson had learned the hard way that navigating around Isle Royale in fog or snowstorms could be extremely hazardous . . . and expensive. It was a lesson that just didn't seem to register with the shipping companies and the men who sailed their ships.

George M. Cox, 1933

On May 27, 1933, the 259-foot passenger steamer *George M. Cox* went aground on the Rock of Ages reef off the southwest tip of Isle Royale. At the time, she was running at full speed in a blanket of thick fog that hung low over the lake. Built in 1901, the *Cox* had recently been purchased by the Isle Royale Transportation Company and completely reconditioned as a cruise ship. In fact, it was her first voyage since being refitted, and she was bound for Port Arthur and Fort William to pick up Canadian passengers on their way to the World's Fair at Chicago. There were 125 passengers and crewmembers aboard the *Cox* when it went on the Rock of Ages, including her namesake, George M. Cox, president of the shipping company.

First Mate Art Kronk had been on watch in the *Cox*'s pilothouse when the ship rounded the southwest tip of Isle Royale and headed toward Thunder Bay, and he had supposedly plotted a course that would keep them well clear of the numerous reefs and shoals off the end of the island. After making the turn, Kronk and Captain George Johnson could hear the throaty roar of the foghorn at the Rock of Ages lighthouse, but they felt that the course they were steering would keep them a couple miles west of the shoal waters marked by the light. Captain Johnson was so sure that they had nothing but deep water under their keel that he kept his ship running at full lake speed, scooting through the water at around nineteen miles an hour, even though that violated the navigation and pilot rules that had been in effect for many years.[18] The rules of the road required ships to operate at "moderate speed" when visibility was limited.[19]

As the ship sped along, the first mate thought for an instant that the foghorn sounded awfully close, but he didn't say anything to Captain Johnson. Kronk had been sailing long enough to know that fog had a bad habit of distorting sound. Something that sounded close could well be miles away . . . or it could be even closer than it sounded.

Without any warning, the *Cox* crashed at full speed onto a shoal off the Rock of Ages, striking with such force that her engines and boilers were

9. The bow of the passenger steamer *George M. Cox* was left high and dry after it wrecked on Rock of Ages reef at the west end of Isle Royale on May 27, 1933. The 259-foot vessel was running at full speed in heavy fog when the accident happened, even though navigational rules called for ships to operate at "moderate speed" whenever visibility was limited. All those aboard the *Cox* were able to abandon the precariously perched ship in lifeboats and rafts, and a passing steamer rescued them. (Ralph Roberts Collection)

torn loose from their mountings. Sitting amidships on the rocky shoal, the *Cox*'s bow was jutting into the air, well clear of the surface of the lake. Tons of water immediately began flooding into the ship through a large hole that had been ripped in the port side of the hull. Since the stern section was lower in the water than the bow, the water quickly filled the stern and it listed to port and submerged, leveraging the *Cox*'s bow even higher out of the water.

While most of those aboard the white-hulled steamer had been thrown to the decks by the force of the impact, only three persons were injured. Fearing that his ship might slip off the reef and sink in deep water, Captain Johnson passed the order to abandon ship. Crewmen hurriedly launched the five portside lifeboats and a number of life rafts that were stowed atop the cabin, and within minutes of running aground, all 125 passengers and crewmembers had safely evacuated the ship.

Despite the pea-soup fog that hung over Lake Superior, there was actually a witness to the wreck of the *Cox*. From his vantage point atop the Rock of Ages lighthouse, less than a mile from the scene of the wreck, the lighthouse keeper John Soldenski could see the twin masts of the passenger steamer sticking up through the low-hanging fog. From the extreme rake of the masts, he knew the ship had to be aground. In minutes, Soldenski was racing to the scene in the lighthouse's gasoline-powered boat.

When he reached the scene, Soldenski attached lines to the life rafts and towed them back to the lighthouse, while the lifeboats followed along behind. Back at the lighthouse, he radioed the steamer *Morris S. Tremaine,* which was then passing the island on its way down the lake. The *Tremaine* immediately altered course toward the Rock of Ages. Soldenski took the three injured crewmen, the *Cox*'s nurse, and George M. Cox out to the *Tremaine,* which hove to as close as it could safely get to the Rock of Ages. Once they were aboard, the steamer set a course for Port Arthur, the closest port where assistance was available for the injured crewmen. Other vessels quickly set out from Port Arthur and Fort William to pick up the rest of the *Cox*'s crew and passengers.[20]

The investigation into the grounding of the *Cox* led to the conclusion that First Mate Art Kronk had given the wheelsman the wrong course to steer, off by three degrees. Although Kronk denied making an error, he was censured by the steamboat inspectors. Captain Johnson's confidence was shattered by the casualty, and he retired to his home in Traverse City, Michigan, never to sail again.[21]

We can learn a great deal about groundings and strandings on the Great Lakes simply by studying those that occurred in the waters around Isle Royale. For example, most of the more than twenty-five ships that wrecked at Isle Royale over the years blindly wandered into the hazardous shoal waters during fog, snowstorms, or heavy rains that hid the shores of the island until it was too late for the vessels to avoid grounding. From the beginning of commerce on the lakes until radar became available after World War II, limited visibility was the most common reason for groundings. It is reasonable to conclude that, during the period late in the eighteenth century when the number of ships operating on the lakes was at its zenith, groundings were virtually a daily occurrence. In most cases, however, the ships were traveling slow enough that no serious damage was done, and they either worked themselves off or were pulled off by other vessels.

The incidence of groundings on the lakes is in part a function of the geography of America's expansive inland waterway. As big as the lakes are, vessels are seldom far from shore, there are countless islands, peninsulas, shoals, and reefs just off the heavily traveled shipping lanes, and the big ships are regularly called on to negotiate serpentine rivers.

For the earliest generations of sailors, something as common as a black, overcast night could easily result in a grounding. Until the 1850s, the charts used for navigation on the lakes were privately drawn and often so crude and inaccurate that they could not be relied on in close quarters. The limitations of the charts were compounded by the fact that until after World War I the only navigational instruments available on ships were a magnetic compass, a chip log or taffrail log to measure the distance traveled, and a lead line used to measure water depth. Using these together, a navigator could dead reckon the position of his ship and make sure that it was not straying into shallow waters. Of course, the accuracy of the dead-reckoned positions depended on the competence of the navigator and the accuracy of his compass and log. If the compass or log was off, and that was often the case, or if the ship was being pushed around by high winds and waves, there was no way that even the most proficient navigator could plot the vessel's position with any significant degree of reliability.

When the weather was clear enough, shipboard personnel often didn't navigate at all. Instead, they "piloted" their ship, judging their position by familiar landmarks along the shore. Experienced captains and mates used points of land, islands, bays, hills, structures, and even tall trees along the shore to determine exactly where their ship was. As communities grew up along the shores of the lakes, they were added to the charts as references. The lights of the towns and villages were an especially useful navigational aid at night, when they could often be seen from far out on the lakes.

In 1804 the Canadian government built the first Great Lakes lighthouse near the mouth of the Niagara River at the west end of Lake Ontario. The first U.S. lights on the Great Lakes were erected on busy Lake Erie in 1818. Two years later, the first U.S. light on Lake Ontario went into service on Galloo Island at the headwaters of the St. Lawrence River. In 1825 the first light on Lake Huron was built at Fort Gratiot, on the north side of what is today Port Huron, Michigan, at the confluence of Lake Huron and the St. Clair River. Chicago got its first light in 1832,[22] shortly after the first light on Lake Michigan went into operation at St. Joseph, Michigan.[23] The first lights constructed on Lake Superior went into operation in 1849 at Whitefish Point and Copper Harbor.[24] By 1837 lightships were also in use to mark offshore shoals, reefs, and channels where lighthouses could not easily be constructed. The first Great Lakes lightship was moored in the Straits of Mackinac, while others quickly followed at Spectacle Reef on northern Lake Huron and at Stannard Rock on Lake Superior. Twelve lightships were eventually stationed around the Great Lakes. By 1865 there were seven lighthouses on Lake Ontario, twelve on Lake Huron, and twenty-six on Lake Michigan.[25]

The British conducted the first survey of the lakes in 1815. Information from the survey was used to draw fifty navigational charts, covering the waters from Montreal to the St. Marys River.[26] Congress authorized the first U.S. survey of the lakes in 1841 when $15,000 was appropriated to fund the project. The first chart based on the survey was engraved in 1849, but none of the new charts were issued to captains until 1852.[27] The first series of U.S. charts issued that year covered Lake Erie, including Kelleys Island and the Bass Islands group, and was made available at no charge to the masters of both U.S. and Canadian ships.[28]

While the growing number of lighthouses at key locations provided a great aid to navigation when the weather was clear, they were of little use when visibility fell to near-zero in fog, snow, or rain, weather conditions that are common on the lakes. Snowstorms are frequent during the spring, fall, and early winter months, and heavy rainstorms are likely to sweep over the lakes just about anytime during the middle of the season. Fog obscures the shipping lanes during much of the year, generally as a result of differences between air temperatures and the temperature of the lakes. Spring and fall fog are common hazards for mariners throughout the northern latitudes. In the spring, large bodies of water warm more slowly than the air masses above them. In the fall, the reverse is true. Both situations produce fog. Temperature differentials are particularly pronounced on Lake Superior and northern Lakes Huron and Michigan during the spring. As air temperatures warm over the cold waters of those lakes, which seldom reach a temperature of much over sixty degrees, moisture in the air condenses out as advection fog as it comes in contact with the relatively cold waters of the lakes. The situation commonly lasts until late June when air and water temperatures begin to equalize, but heavy fog is regularly encountered on the northern lakes throughout the summer months.

The Detroit, St. Clair, and St. Marys Rivers and many of the harbors around the lakes are also commonly plagued by radiation fog during much of the shipping season. When skies are clear at night, the land around the rivers and harbors tends to cool rapidly, creating a temperature differential between the ground and the air above it. Radiation fog is common on the lakes from midsummer through September or early October.

Yet another form of fog encountered on the lakes is steam fog, sometimes referred to as evaporation fog, Arctic fog, or sea smoke. Steam fog occurs late in the shipping season, during periods of bitterly cold air temperatures on the northern lakes. The cold, dry air causes moisture to be drawn out of the significantly warmer waters of the lake and results in fog. If the moisture in the air comes in contact with the cold hull of a ship, it will freeze and encase the ship in an eerie layer of hoarfrost, like an ominous white burial shroud. Frozen fog is just another of the weather phenomena that make navigation a tricky business on the lakes.

Logic tells us that the combination of lighthouses, lightships, and detailed and accurate charts undoubtedly prevented many strandings and groundings. It's interesting to note, however, that the number of groundings actually *increased* during the second half of the nineteenth century. Some of the increase can be attributed to the growing number of ships operating on the lakes, but the truth of the matter is that lighthouses, lightships, and good charts simply weren't of much use when you couldn't see from the bow to the stern of the ship you were on. When vessel owners and masters made the decision to continue operating their vessels when fog, snow, or rain limited visibility, they knew that ships were going to go aground—the historical record is clear on that. Combine limited visibility with even a minor navigational error or equipment malfunction, and there was a good chance a ship would end up on a beach, reef, or shoal.

If the ship was operating at full speed when it grounded, and the cases of the *Congdon* and *Cox* suggest that this was often the case, damage was obviously going to be more extensive. That's one reason why the government enacted navigation rules in 1863 that required ships to reduce speed during periods of limited visibility. Those rules were in effect when the *Congdon* and *Cox* groundings occurred, yet both ships were running at full speed when they grounded. It's unlikely they were the only two ships on the lakes that regularly violated that navigation rule.

The wrecks of the *Siskawit* and *Bransford* suggest another reason why the number of groundings didn't go down after the development of charts, lighthouses, and lightships: many sailing ships and steamers were driven ashore during storms. Given the wind and sea conditions, there just wasn't any way for them to stay out in deep water. That was the situation in the 1854 grounding of the schooner *Conductor* on Lake Erie.

Conductor, 1854

On a late-November morning in 1854, the *Conductor* departed Amherstburg, Ontario, near the mouth of the Detroit River, with a cargo of 10,000 bushels of corn bound for Toronto. The wind blew fresh out of the southwest throughout the day, and the little schooner sliced briskly through the choppy waters of Lake Erie. By late afternoon, however, the winds had increased to hurricane conditions and the shallow waters of the lake were being whipped into a frenzy of huge waves and biting spray. Captain Henry Hackett ordered his crew to reef in the mainsails before the winds blew them away, and the crew hunkered down in their heavy oilskins for what they knew would be an unpleasant night.

Around midnight the furious winds and driving snow tore away the *Conductor*'s topsails, and walls of water rolled across the deck and carried away the lifeboat and everything else that wasn't securely tied down. About 4 A.M., Captain Hackett and the others on watch thought they saw the flashing beacon of Long Point Light off to their port side through the snow and darkness. The light stood at the very tip of the long, narrow peninsula, so it appeared that they would easily clear the sandy shoal waters off its end. Unknown to those aboard the *Conductor*, the flash of light they had seen wasn't Long Point Light, but a floating light that marked the entrance to a canal that cut through the base of the peninsula. That put them somewhere between the cut and the tip of the peninsula, and they were rapidly bearing down on the storm-swept shores of Long Point.

Half an hour later, Captain Hackett and his crew were startled when they suddenly saw land directly ahead of their ship. For an instant, Hackett thought of putting the helm hard over and trying to turn back out into the lake. In the condition the ship was in, though, she probably wouldn't have come around too well, and there was a definite chance that she would wallow in the troughs of the giant seas and swamp or roll over. On second thought, running aground was probably a safer course of action. Minutes later, with Captain Hackett and his crew braced for the impact they knew was inevitable, the *Conductor* ran hard aground about half a mile offshore, the keel of their ship driving deep into the sandy bottom. In that exposed position, all aboard knew it was only a matter of time before the waves began to tear their little ship apart. Without a lifeboat, it would also be only a matter of time for them.

Nearby on the shore of Long Point was the shanty of Heremiah Becker, a trapper, and his twenty-three-year-old wife, Abigail, later described as "tall and comely, well knit and physically developed[,] a woman of the lakes and woods, and thoroughly imbued with that dauntless spirit that makes for heroines." As was always his habit in late November, Becker had gone by boat to Port Rowan on the mainland to sell the pelts he had accumulated and buy supplies to get himself and his wife through the approaching months of winter. Unsure of when to expect her husband to return, Abigail Becker had been troubled when the storm had rolled in and riled the waters between their home and the mainland. She didn't sleep well that night, lying in bed and listening to the shriek of the winds and the sound of the waves crashing ashore. At dawn, she dressed warmly and went out to the beach.

In the first dirty light of the stormy day, Abigail Becker could see the *Conductor*. Waves were breaking over the little schooner, and in the bitter November cold, thick ice was already building on the hull and spars. She knew that the ship and its crew were in dire straits. Her first instinct was to build a roaring bonfire on the beach as a beacon to let those on the little ship know they had been sighted.

She could see the crewmen huddled on the deck of the schooner, and it was obvious to her that as precarious as their position was, they had no intention of attempting to come ashore in the crashing breakers. But Abigail Becker knew the waters off the Becker shanty well, and she knew they could safely make it ashore. Without hesitation, she marched into the frenzied surf and waded out as far as she could. Each time one of the huge green waves rolled toward her, she allowed it to lift her from the bottom, knowing that as soon as it rolled under her it would gently set her down again. When she could go no farther, Abigail motioned frantically for the men on the schooner to walk toward her.

It was a terrifying prospect for those on the *Conductor*, but Captain Hackett knew that he and his small crew were going into the lake that day, either by choice or by circumstance. He hesitated only a minute before climbing over the side and dropping into the churning water. Half swimming and half walking, he moved slowly toward the figure of the woman. When he finally reached her, she grabbed his arm and led him through the surf to the safety of the sandy shore. By then another crewman had leapt into the water, and Abigail went back out through the maelstrom and helped him to the beach. One by one, she led them across the shoal, until all eight were safely ashore.

Captain Hackett and his crew spent four days in the Becker shanty before the storm finally broke and Heremiah Becker was able to return home and ferry them to Port Rowan. When they left, each of the shipwrecked sailors expressed his gratitude to Mrs. Becker, and they all apologized that they weren't able to suitably reward her for her bravery.

While Abigail Becker and her husband soon settled back into their familiar routines, there was no way she could have known that she was rapidly becoming famous around the lakes, and beyond. As Captain

Hackett and his crew told and retold the story of how she had saved them all from certain death, newspapers began proclaiming Abigail Becker as "the heroine of Long Point."

To Abigail's surprise, the merchants and sailors of Buffalo presented her with "a substantial purse" the following spring as a tribute for having saved the crew of the *Conductor*. The American Humane Association also awarded her their gold medal for bravery, which she proudly wore around her neck for many years. What she is said to have prized most, however, was the brief, personal note she received from another woman of merit, someone far from the crude Becker shanty on the remote shores of Long Point—Queen Victoria of England.[29]

While the powerful beacons of lighthouses like the one at the end of Long Point often helped mariners avoid being shipwrecked, Captain Henry Hackett of the *Conductor* would have been one of the first to testify that precisely when they were needed most, they were often of the least value. The lighthouses, lightships, and other navigational aids all helped reduce casualties and deaths to some extent, but there were many times when those aboard the ships were strictly on their own.

Superior, 1856

The crewmembers and passengers on the steamer *Superior* certainly felt very much alone on October 29, 1856. The 184-foot passenger and freight steamer was struck by bitter winds, driven snow, and high seas shortly after it left the sanctuary of Whitefish Point and steamed out onto Lake Superior. In time, the *Superior* lost its rudder and smokestack, then the cargo shifted, and the vessel began taking on water. Helpless before the onslaught of the storm, the steamer was driven ashore just west of the Pictured Rocks. In a matter of only about fifteen minutes, the powerful seas destroyed the ship. Sixteen passengers and crewmembers managed to make it ashore in the torrential surf.

The huddled mass of wet and cold survivors watched helplessly as Captain Hiram Jones drowned while trying to swim ashore in a heavy buffalo coat. Eight other crewmen had climbed onto the vessel's big paddle wheels, but one by one they lost their grip and fell to their deaths in the swirling waters.

The survivors set off toward the west, some hiking through the deep snow along the shore while others rowed offshore in the *Superior*'s lifeboat. It was an arduous trip, and two of those who had survived the wreck died along the way. Eventually the bedraggled group found refuge at the cabin of a trader, near the present site of Munising, Michigan.

At least fifty passengers and crewmembers died as a result of the wrecking of the *Superior.* In terms of loss of life, it ranks yet today as the single worst shipwreck on Lake Superior.[30] Lake Superior, with the reputation of being the most dangerous of the Great Lakes, actually lags far behind Lake Huron, Lake Michigan, and Lake Erie when it comes to the number of shipwrecks and numbers of wreck-related deaths. In fact, only Lake Ontario has had fewer shipwrecks.

There have been fewer shipwrecks on Lake Superior only because fewer ships have operated there over the years. Until the first locks were built at Sault Ste. Marie in 1855, the lake was quite literally cut off from the lower lakes by the rapids of the St. Marys River. Even after the locks were built, though, there was still less vessel traffic on Lake Superior than on Lakes Michigan, Huron, and Erie, and that holds true yet today. With the urban and industrial centers like Buffalo, Cleveland, Detroit, Milwaukee, and Chicago located around the lower lakes, it's logical that the greatest vessel traffic would also occur there. If data were available to examine the number of shipwrecks in proportion to the amount of vessel traffic, however, it's altogether possible that Lake Superior would live up to its reputation as the most dangerous of the inland seas.

Jupiter and *Saturn*, 1872

On the morning of November 27, 1872, the side-wheel steamer *John A. Dix* departed the ore docks at Marquette under the command of Captain Joseph Waltman and headed out onto Lake Superior. The *Dix* was towing the schooner-barges *Jupiter* and *Saturn*, a practice begun a few years earlier when Captain Eli Peck built the steamer *R. J. Hackett* and its barge consort, the *Forest City*. Winds and seas on Lake Superior continued to build as the convoy moved east toward Whitefish Point and the entrance to the St. Marys River. By suppertime, the three boats found themselves being buffeted by giant seas off Vermilion Point, still twenty miles west of Whitefish. The stout towlines connecting the two schooner consorts of the *Dix* were under great stress, first slacking, then snapping taut as the ships rose and fell in the high seas. At about 5:30 P.M. the *Jupiter*'s towline snapped, and an hour later the towline to the *Saturn* also gave way. In the stormy seas, there was no way the lines could be reconnected, so the barges drifted away.

While he was greatly concerned for the safety of the two schooner-barges, the worsening weather forced Captain Waltman to concentrate his complete attention on the welfare of the *Dix*. The captains and small crews on the two schooners would have to fend for themselves. Temperatures had plummeted to below zero, and as the towering seas swept across the deck of the steamer it was rapidly being encased in a heavy shroud of ice. In places the ice was already a foot thick, and if the *Dix* didn't find shelter soon the heavy load of ice could sink her. Without hesitation, Waltman pointed the bow of the steamer in the direction of Whitefish Point and they eventually reached the protected waters of Whitefish Bay.

With waves rolling over the decks of the *Jupiter* and *Saturn,* their crews were unable to set storm sails that might have allowed them to work their way along the shore to the shelter of Whitefish. They were adrift, and at the mercy of the wind and waves. In the terrifying blackness of that November night, the little schooners were eventually driven ashore. In the pounding surf, both broke apart. All seven crewmembers on the *Jupiter* and the eight on the *Saturn* died in the frenzied waters of Lake Superior. There was no way the fourteen men and one woman could have launched a lifeboat. Even if they had, it would surely have been capsized or wrecked in the pounding surf along the shore.

The two hapless schooners weren't the only vessels lost that night on the raging waters of Lake Superior. At Marquette, the schooner *Libby* was driven onto the rocky shore; the schooner *Griswold,* loaded with grain, managed to stagger into Whitefish Bay, but sank off Gros Cap, her eight crewmembers perishing in the normally friendly waters at the entrance to the St. Marys. The schooner *W. O. Brown* was driven ashore at Point Maimanse on the rocky Canadian shore, north of the entrance to Whitefish Bay. The vessel's captain and four crewmembers were washed overboard, never to be seen again, and the second mate drowned in his bunk as the ship sank. The three surviving seamen from the *Brown* miraculously managed to make it ashore. In a remarkable tale of wilderness survival under the most difficult of circumstances, the three lived in the inhospitable Canadian wilderness for ten days, eventually making their way along the shore to a logging camp at Batchawana Bay.[31]

The *Jupiter* and *Saturn* had belonged to Captain Eber Ward, a highly respected shipowner from Detroit. After the brutal storm, Captain Ward expressed the opinion that the crewmembers of his two schooners might have been saved if there had been trained teams of rescue personnel stationed along the Lake Superior shore that night.[32] There were many such lifesaving stations along the Atlantic Coast, dating back to the formation of the Massachusetts Humane Society in 1785. Since 1847, Congress had been appropriating money annually to build and staff lifesaving stations up and down the East Coast. It was a good investment. The professional lifesaving crews had saved the lives of thousands of crewmembers and passengers from vessels that wrecked along the coast, and were often able to salvage the wrecked ships and their cargoes. While no lifesaving stations had been established on the Great Lakes, $12,500 was appropriated in 1854 to purchase lifeboats for twenty-five locations along Lake Michigan. Local volunteers manned those boats. The fledgling U.S. Life-Saving Service operated then as part of the Treasury Department.[33]

At Captain Ward's prompting, the Board of Lake Underwriters, made up of the insurance companies that insured most of the ships operating on the Great Lakes, immediately began to pressure Secretary of the Treasury Benjamin Bristow to allocate funds to build and man lifesaving stations on the lakes. Less than four months after the tragic storm of November 27, 1872, a board was established to conduct a survey of possible sites for lifesaving stations on America's inland seas. Their report was issued on January 21, 1874, and on June 20 of that year Congress authorized the construction of four lifesaving stations on Lake Superior.[34]

The first stations of the U.S. Life-Saving Service on the Great Lakes became operational in 1876 along the southeast shore of Lake Superior, between Whitefish Point and Marquette. Two were located at Vermilion Point and Crisp Point, near where the *Jupiter* and *Saturn* had been wrecked. The others were farther west, at the mouth of the Two-Hearted River and at Muskallonge Lake, which is often referred to as Deer Park. By 1896 there were sixteen stations on Lake Superior, sixteen on Lake Huron, twenty-six on Lake Michigan, eleven on Lake Erie, and eleven on Lake Ontario. During that year, they responded to 248 shipwrecks. Eleven of the ships involved were total losses. A total of 2,093 people were involved in the casualties, but through the efforts of the dedicated and highly trained lifesavers, only one life was lost. At the same time, vessels and cargo valued at more than $3 million were saved.[35] It's no wonder that newspapers were by then referring to the crews at the lifesaving stations as "storm warriors" and "heroes of the surf."[36]

The lifesaving stations were equipped with Lyle guns or eprouvette mortars, small cannons capable of firing a line attached to a heavy ball to ships as much as six hundred yards offshore. The line was then used to set up a breeches buoy that could shuttle crewmembers and passengers ashore. The stations also had cedar surfboats and lifeboats that were capable of being launched through a crashing surf to row out to a ship that was in trouble. Around 1908, the stations began to be equipped with motorized boats. The boats were often hauled overland on special beach carts, or even by train, so that they could be launched near a foundering vessel.

Stations were under the charge of a "keeper," with the rank of captain. His crew normally consisted of eight "surfmen." Personnel at the stations drilled relentlessly with their cannon, breeches buoy, and boats, and competitions were often held between the crews of various stations. At night the stations posted a lookout in a tower to scan the lake for any vessels that might be experiencing difficulty and to keep a record of any ships passing the station. Patrols also walked the beaches between the stations from sunset to sunrise, and they were often the first to pass word of a vessel in distress.[37]

Even before the *Jupiter* and *Saturn* were driven aground, ships had long followed the practice of ringing a bell at regular intervals during periods of fog and reduced visibility as a warning to approaching vessels. Some of the early lighthouses and lightships adopted the practice, though it was of questionable value. The ringing of a bell just wasn't loud enough or directional enough to be of much value. If the ringing could be heard by those aboard a ship, it was often impossible for them to tell what direction the sound was coming from.[38]

In 1875 the first steam-powered fog whistle was installed at the South Manitou Island Lighthouse on northern Lake Michigan. The deep roar of the powerful directional whistle carried for long distances across the water, and it became a vital aid to mariners when visibility was restricted. Soon fog whistles were in place at all lighthouses and at the entrances to many harbors.[39]

Robert Wallace and *David Wallace,* 1886

An exceptionally violent storm tore its way across Lake Michigan and Lake Superior during the third week of November 1886. On the morning of November 18, Marquette residents awakened to find that two ships had been driven ashore just west of town. The steamer *Robert Wallace,* towing the schooner-barge *David Wallace,* had set out from Duluth with a cargo of wheat on November 15. They encountered the storm in the middle of Lake Superior, between the tip of the Keweenaw Peninsula and Whitefish Point. After plowing into the growing seas for several hours,

Frank Brown, captain of the steamer, decided it would be more prudent for the two ships to turn and run with the seas.

At midnight, Captain Brown realized that they must be nearing the south shore of the lake and he reduced speed. Despite that, the two ships ran out of lake about 1 A.M. on November 18 and grounded in the shallow waters of Chocolay Reef, just east of Marquette, foundering in the heavy seas about a quarter-mile off the beach.

Throughout the day, Marquette residents tried to rescue the crewmen trapped aboard the two ships. The tug *Jay C. Morse* tried valiantly to reach the wrecks, but was forced to turn back. Local residents hauled a small yawl down the beach and made several attempts to row out to the ships, but the rolling breakers along the beach kept tossing the little boat back ashore. In the late afternoon, they even tried to fire a line out to the ships using an old mortar. Packed with too large a charge, the mortar exploded. As darkness began to settle over the raging lake, the captain of the tug *Gillette* finally sent a telegram requesting assistance from the lifesaving station at Portage Entry, located near Houghton, about 110 miles from Marquette.

In a truly epic odyssey, Captain Albert Ocha and his crew from the Portage Life-Saving Station traveled through the stormy night, first by tug to Houghton, then by special train from Houghton to Marquette. It was normally almost a ten-hour trip from Houghton to Marquette, but knowing that lives were at stake, Engineer Henry Jackson drove his train at breakneck speed through blizzard conditions to arrive at Marquette in just over three hours. By 2 A.M. on November 19, the lifesavers and their equipment were on the beach abreast of the two wrecks.

In the blackness of the night, the lifesaving crew first tried to rig a breeches buoy, but they were unable to fire a line to the ships. Despite the violent waves breaking along the shore, Captain Ocha and his men tried to row their surfboat out to the wrecks, but they were forced to turn back when the boat swamped and its rudder broke. After daybreak, they made a second effort to row through the surf. Despite the fact that their boat had no rudder, and several of the men in the boat had to constantly bail water out of it, the lifesaving team managed to make it out to the steamer. Ten of the stranded crew were taken off on that first trip. The remaining six crewmen on the *Robert Wallace* were taken off on the second trip. On their third trip out through the brutal surf, the lifesavers rescued all nine of those aboard the *David Wallace*. By 9:30 A.M. the rescued sailors and the exhausted lifesavers were being warmed around bonfires on the shore.

10. The schooner *Florida* was driven ashore and wrecked just east of the ore dock at Marquette during a severe storm that ravaged Lake Superior on November 17, 1886. The following morning, Marquette residents discovered that the steamer *Robert Wallace* and the schooner-barge *David Wallace* had been driven ashore just east of Marquette. After a record-breaking overnight train ride from Houghton to Marquette, Captain Albert Ocha and his crew from the Portage Life-Saving Station were able to rescue all those aboard the two ships on November 19. (Author's Collection)

The big November storm of 1886 scoured the lakes for the better part of three days before it finally blew itself out. While winds seldom exceeded forty-five miles an hour, the combination of prolonged winds and blinding snow accounted for thirty shipwrecks on Lake Superior and Lake Michigan.[40]

The year after the groundings of the *Robert Wallace* and *David Wallace*, the barge *Fame* was reported ashore and completely wrecked at Presque Isle on Lake Huron, a narrow spit of sand that juts out into the lake just north of Thunder Bay Island. Over the years, the sands of Presque Isle had snagged many passing ships, and few people in the industry took much note of the loss of the aging barge. She is mentioned here only because the history of the *Fame* bears mute testimony to the inherently hazardous nature of shipping in the middle of the nineteenth century.

The grounding that claimed the 132-foot *Fame* was actually the fifth of her career. Earlier, when she had still been rigged as a bark, she had gone ashore off Goderich, Ontario, in 1854. In May 1856 she ran onto Thunder Bay Island in northern Lake Huron, just south of Presque Isle. A week later, possibly on the same trip, she was again aground, this time on South Manitou Island in northern Lake Michigan. In August 1863 the bark was reported to have been sitting on a reef off Eagle Harbor, near the tip of the Keweenaw Peninsula on Lake Superior.[41] Until sophisticated navigational equipment was finally developed in the twentieth century, there was nothing out of the ordinary in a ship going aground five times during its career.

The first major improvements in the navigational equipment carried by ships actually came about as a result of technology developed for the military in World War I. In 1922 the 601-foot freighter *Daniel J. Morrell* became the first Great Lakes ship to be equipped with a gyrocompass.[42] Because they are not affected by deviations in the earth's magnetism or ferrous metals in the vicinity of the compass, gyrocompasses are much more accurate than traditional magnetic compasses, which often give erroneous readings because of the rich iron deposits around the Great Lakes. When visibility was limited, even a minor compass error could easily cause a ship to go aground.

Being able to steer an accurate course is only one of the two elements necessary for navigation, however. The navigator must also know how far the ship has traveled from the last known point. When the gyrocompasses began to be installed as standard equipment aboard ships on the lakes, navigators were still computing distances traveled by use of the taffrail log, technology from an earlier era in maritime history. Readings from the taffrail logs were often in error, though, and if you were steering the long courses across the Great Lakes, the continual compounding of even a small error could easily put you aground. At the same time, neither the gyrocompass nor the taffrail log could tell a navigator how far off his intended courseline the ship might have drifted due to the action of wind, currents, or high seas. When the captain of a Great Lakes ship needed navigational assistance the most, during storms accompanied by blinding rain or snowstorms, his compass and taffrail log were likely to be of little use.

An effective solution finally appeared on the horizon when the Navy began constructing radio beacons on the lakes in 1924. The beacons were radio transmitters for use as part of a radio direction-finding (RDF) system. With an RDF receiver, a captain or mate could use the sensitive directional antenna to "home in" on the signal broadcast from one of the stations. Each station operated on a unique frequency, and its location and frequency were shown on the navigational charts. From a compass scale on the control for the antenna, the operator could then read a heading that represented a line bearing from the ship to the broadcasting station. Plots of line bearings to two or three different stations would provide the navigational officer with a "fix," which would show on his chart as the spot where the line bearings intersected.

Of course, the line bearings seldom intersected at exactly the same point. There was plenty of room for error—both equipment error and human error—so the fixes obtained from the RDF equipment weren't always precise. It wouldn't allow you to plot your ship's position with complete accuracy, but it was certainly more accurate than anything available previously. In fact, one Great Lakes sailor grandly proclaimed at the time that "modern science and technics have given the lakes masters a goal they can steer for in complete confidence, an immovable guide across waters shrouded in fog, clogged with snow, or hidden in the blackness of the night." When they saw the magic of RDF, many people in the industry no doubt thought that groundings due to limited visibility would soon be a thing of the past.

The RDF system became operational in 1925. Within two years, there were nineteen beacons operating on the lakes and 262 ships equipped with the necessary receivers. There were at that time forty-two U.S. shipping companies, operating 411 ships. With another 446 vessels operated by Canadian companies, the ships with RDF represented just over 30 percent of the Great Lakes fleet. By 1942 the RDF network included fifty-seven stations on the U.S. side of the lakes and seven along the Canadian shore.[43]

11. The 580-foot *William C. Moreland* had a short career on the lakes. Put into service in September 1910, the steel bulk freighter ran onto Sawtooth Reef, near the tip of the Keweenaw Peninsula, on October 10 of that same year and broke in half. Reid Wrecking Company raised the bow, but it sank in deep water. The salvaged stern of the *Moreland* was mated to a new bow section in 1916, and the resulting vessel was rechristened as the *Sir Trevor Dawson*. While it went through a number of name changes over the years, the ship with the *Moreland*'s stern was a fixture on the lakes until it was finally scrapped in 1970. (A. F. Glaza Photo, Ralph Roberts Collection)

Despite the improved navigation afforded by RDF, however, groundings continued to be common occurrences.

On April 23, 1925, the year the RDF system became operational, the 532-foot *J. J. Turner* ripped her bottom out off Michigan Island in the Apostle chain at the west end of Lake Superior. That summer the 380-foot *Monroe C. Smith* hit bottom off Gros Cap in Whitefish Bay. In October the 580-foot *Charles L. Hutchinson* struck a reef off Manitou Island at the tip of the Keweenaw Peninsula. The carnage continued in 1926. In May of that year the little Canadian steamer *Beaverton* ran aground in Black Bay, near the Canadian lakehead. In early September the 456-foot *Charles C. West*, only a year old, was badly damaged when she wrecked on Gull Rock Reef off the northeast tip of Isle Royale. The underpowered 286-foot *Thomas Maytham* ran aground at Knife River on Lake Superior during a gale and snowstorm on Halloween night. On November 15, another storm drove the 253-foot steamer *Cottonwood*

12. The *City of Bangor* was launched in 1896 as a bulk freighter, but it was converted to haul automobiles in 1925. On November 30, 1926, the 445-foot steamer lost her steering while battling a violent Lake Superior storm, and she was driven ashore near Copper Harbor, Michigan, at the tip of the Keweenaw Peninsula. While the ship was a total loss, salvers were able to remove 202 of the 220 new Chrysler and Whippet automobiles she was carrying, including those seen here being dug out after a winter snowstorm. The cars were driven across the ice to Copper Harbor. (Charles Davis Photo, Ralph Roberts Collection)

ashore at Coppermine Point, north of Whitefish Bay. Strong winds on November 23 contributed to the grounding of the 210-foot lumber steamer *Herman H. Hettler* at Grand Island in the Apostles. Battered incessantly by the powerful seas, she broke up and was a total loss. During another storm at the end of November, the 446-foot steamer *City of Bangor,* carrying a load of 220 Chrysler and Whippet automobiles, lost her steam steering gear off the tip of the Keweenaw Peninsula and was driven on the rocky beach near Copper Harbor. She was a total loss, but salvers were able to retrieve 202 of the automobiles. The same storm also claimed the 286-foot *Thomas Maytham,* the same underpowered little ship that had been on the beach at Knife River the previous season. She had sought shelter from the storm in the lee of the Keweenaw Peninsula, but got too close to the reefs off Point Isabelle and went on the rocks. Once again, the *Maytham* was salvaged in the aftermath of the storm.[44]

Lambton, 1927

On the afternoon of Tuesday, December 6, 1927, the Canadian canaller *Lambton* left the dock at Fort William, Ontario, on Thunder Bay, heading out across Lake Superior with her holds full of wheat from the western prairies. Before dawn Wednesday morning, the 252-foot freighter was engulfed in a fierce snowstorm that cut visibility to zero and spawned huge seas.

For the next thirty-six agonizing hours, the *Lambton* plodded on across the angry lake in whiteout conditions. The waves breaking over her deck soon turned to ice that eventually grew to a thickness of as much as two feet. As the ship labored along under the added weight of the tons of ice and snow that coated it like a white cocoon, Captain Andrew Livingstone knew they had to be nearing land at the east end of the lake. There's no record, but it's likely that someone in the crew made note of the fact that if the shipping company that owned the *Lambton* had shelled out a few dollars to buy an RDF, they would have been able to get a fix on their position.

Normally, Captain Livingstone would have been worried about running out of water and grounding. Under better circumstances he would have turned around and run back up the lake or gone to anchor until the weather cleared and he could get his bearings. That day, however, neither was an option. Livingstone knew that if the *Lambton* didn't get off the lake and out of the storm soon, his ship was probably going to roll over or founder from the added weight of the ice and snow and the beating it was taking from the powerful waves. Chief Engineer J. F. Duncan later summed up their situation when he said, "I wouldn't have given twenty-five cents for our chances of coming through."

At 4 P.M. on Thursday, December 8, the *Lambton* ran hard aground on Isle Parisienne, just inside the mouth of Whitefish Bay. The ship fetched up on the shore of the island so hard that two crewmembers who were walking forward across the ice-covered deck at the time were almost carried overboard.

The heavy seas were still assaulting the *Lambton* as it sat perched on the shore of Isle Parisienne. Before long the engine room had flooded, and the deck heaved and the sides of the hull bulged from the tons of water that had mixed with the cargo of grain. The crew expected the ship to break in two at any moment.

An attempt was made to launch a lifeboat. The boat was lowered to the level of the main deck, and it was being stocked with provisions when a giant wave snatched the boat away, breaking the inch-thick ropes from which it hung as if they were made of cheap cotton thread.

The crew thought briefly of trying to launch their second lifeboat, but fearing they would lose it, too, they abandoned that plan and settled in for what they knew would be a long, cold night on their ship. Most of the crewmembers doubted they would survive, yet morale aboard the broken little ship remained remarkably high. Many of the freighter's crew were from the neighboring communities of Owen Sound, Wiarton, and Colpoy's Bay at the south end of Georgian Bay. Some had been friends long before they ended up as shipmates on the *Lambton*. That night they worked together to make the most of the desperate situation they found themselves in, each trying to keep the spirits of the others up.

Sometime in the evening, the snow let up just enough that they got a glimpse of the lighthouse beacon at the end of Whitefish Point. Finally, for the first time since they had left the Canadian lakehead, they knew exactly where they were. It was cause for a glimmer of hope, since they were right alongside the channel that all ships took when entering or leaving Whitefish Bay.

Throughout that long and lonely night, the sailors burned flares made from black paint and oakum on top of the *Lambton*'s after cabin, hoping a passing ship would see them. But no ships passed—or if any had, they apparently didn't see the makeshift flares.

Just after noon on Friday, two of the younger crewmen climbed up to the ship's coal bunker to get some fuel for the stove in the galley, the only source of heat on the ship. While they were on top of the stern deckhouse, they thought they could see a mill on the Canadian shore opposite the island. It looked to them like it wasn't very far away, and they decided that they would try to swim across and get help.

Elmer Baird of Colpoy's Bay, who worked as an oiler on the *Lambton*, and his friend Ivan Moon, a wheelsman from Owen Sound, dressed for what they knew would be a cold swim. They put their dress clothes on over the top of their work clothes, then each struggled to squeeze into one of the lifesuits carried on the ship. The lifesuits, sometimes referred to as "patent suits," had never really received much testing, but the rubberized coveralls were supposed to contain everything necessary for a person to survive in case of shipwreck. Once dressed, Baird and Moon tied themselves together with a piece of rope, leaving about ten feet of slack between them. Captain Livingstone and the other crewmen tried to talk them out of it, but they were confident that they could easily make the short swim to the mainland.

With a simple farewell of "Well, goodbye gang," the two vigorous and optimistic young men leaped into the bitterly cold water and struck out in the direction of the Canadian shore. For awhile, those huddled together on the deck of the *Lambton* could see the two swimmers each time a whitecap lifted them high in the water, but eventually Baird and Moon faded into a curtain of snow. Neither man was ever seen again. Later, it was determined that the mainland was actually nine or ten miles across the water, not the short distance the two thought it was. It's possible they hadn't seen the mainland at all, just some illusion created by the snowstorm and their own yearning to find a way out of their dangerous predicament, for there was no mill or other manmade structure anywhere near Isle Parisienne in those days.

For the remainder of the day, the men still aboard the *Lambton* kept a sharp lookout in case Baird and Moon were successful in bringing help. That night, they again burned their homemade flares on top of the aft cabin.

When no rescuers arrived by Saturday morning, the shipwrecked sailors began to fear that Baird and Moon hadn't made it to the mainland, and they decided to attempt to launch their other boat. The storm had moderated a little by noon, and the eighteen men managed to get the boat safely into the water. Rowing in the same direction that the strong sea was running, and forced to bail constantly, they came ashore at dusk just above Goulais Point on the Ontario shore of Whitefish Bay.

The tired troop of sailors set off along the shore in a generally south-easterly direction. Along the way, they came upon the lifeboat they had tried to launch the day they went aground, and from it they salvaged the supplies that had been put aboard. After a trek of about fifteen miles, they finally came upon an empty house at about 1 A.M. There they built a fire and camped for the night, dining on a supper of frozen bread, butter, and head cheese that they'd recovered from the lifeboat.

Sunday morning, Captain Livingstone and his men ate a solid breakfast of sardines and bread, then set off again along the shore. After six or seven miles they came to the little fishing village of Goulais Mission. That night, the survivors of the *Lambton* stayed in the homes of Alex Robinson and Alex McCoy, eating real meals and, reportedly, sleeping in real beds, though it would have been a miracle, indeed, if the Robinsons and McCoys had enough beds to accommodate all eighteen sailors. Nonetheless, on Monday morning McCoy used his team of horses to break trail and guide the men of the *Lambton* toward Sault Ste. Marie.

At 5 P.M. on Monday, the party reached the Soo and Captain Livingstone and his men took rooms in local hotels. Many of them suffered from minor cases of frostbite, but they were in high spirits and eager to partake of local hospitality. The early-December storm actually proved to be a boon for local hotel, restaurant, and bar owners, as the crew of

13. The *Lambton* was one of at least six ships that were wrecked during an intense storm that swept across the northern lakes December 6–9, 1927. The little freighter ran onto Isle Parisienne at the entrance to Whitefish Bay after running before the storm for thirty-six hours. Eighteen of the twenty men in the *Lambton*'s crew were later able to row ashore in a lifeboat, and from there they struggled along the rocky, snow-covered shore until they arrived safely at Sault Ste. Marie, Ontario. Their ship was pulled free the following spring, and it is shown here being towed through the Portage Ship Canal on its way to a shipyard to be converted into a barge. Alongside the *Lambton* is the wrecking tug *Manistique*. (Ralph Roberts Collection)

the steamer *Agawa* had also been brought into town after their ship went aground on Manitoulin Island in northern Lake Huron.

Captain Livingstone, at thirty-four, was one of the youngest captains then sailing on the lakes, and his crew roundly praised him for his "gameness and cheerfulness." Chief Duncan was similarly praised, but then he was an old hand at shipwrecks—the *Lambton* was his fourth! He had previously survived the wrecks of the *Huronton*, *Oatland*, and *Kolfage*. Even in the 1920s, there was nothing unusual about a sailor being involved in a shipwreck.[45]

The storm of December 6–9 was limited largely to Lake Superior and the northern reaches of Lake Huron and Lake Michigan. In addition to the *Lambton* and *Agawa*, the steamers *Altadoc*, *E. W. Oglebay*, *Kamloops*, and *Martian* all fell victim to "the curse of December" on Lake Superior.

On the night of December 7, the Canadian freighter *Altadoc* was bound for Thunder Bay when the onslaught of massive waves carried away her rudder and she settled helplessly into the trough of the seas. Captain R. D. Simpson immediately broadcast an SOS, but before he got any response the radio antenna was torn away.

14. A. F. "Tony" Glaza from the Eagle Harbor, Michigan, Life-Saving Station took this photo of the steamer *Altadoc* after it wrecked on Keweenaw Point during the same storm that claimed the *Lambton* in December 1927. The 356-foot freighter lost its rudder on the night of December 7 and was carried ashore by high seas the following morning. Four crewmembers trudged six miles through deep snow in brutal subzero temperatures to summon help, and their shipmates were soon rescued by lifesavers from Eagle Harbor and the crew of the Coast Guard cutter *Crawford*. (A. F. Glaza Photo, Ralph Roberts Collection)

Just after dawn the following morning, the *Altadoc* was washed ashore near the tip of the Keweenaw Peninsula. Four crewmen scrambled ashore and trudged six miles through the deep snow in temperatures of nineteen degrees below zero to reach the settlement of Copper Harbor. Residents there immediately phoned the Coast Guard station at nearby Eagle Harbor to report the *Altadoc*'s grounding. Later that day, a motor lifeboat from the Eagle Harbor station, assisted by the Coast Guard cutter *Crawford*, rescued the remaining men aboard the stranded ship. The *Crawford* had been dispatched from the Coast Guard station at Two Harbors, Minnesota, across Lake Superior, after a radio operator there heard Captain Simpson's distress call.

The following day, the *Oglebay* was also on its way to Fort William, Ontario, in ballast when her captain decided it would be prudent to alter course and seek shelter at Marquette in the face of the worsening storm. When about ten miles east of her destination, the 376-foot freighter was driven ashore. Crewmembers said the aging freighter's 1,285-horsepower triple-expansion engine just wasn't a match for the fierce wind and seas she encountered. Local residents reported the *Oglebay*'s grounding to the Coast Guard station in Marquette, and a motor lifeboat took the freighter's crew off later that day.[46]

In a few of the cases, such as when equipment failure caused a grounding, RDF wouldn't have helped to prevent the casualties. In most cases, however, direction-finding equipment might have made a difference . . . if they'd had it. Even though RDF receivers were a relatively minor investment when compared to the value of a ship and its crew, many shipowners were slow to have them installed on their vessels. The smaller and older the ship, the less likely her owners were to invest in direction-finding equipment. In those first years after the radio beacon system became operational on the lakes, you can almost excuse the shipowners for not laying out money for direction-finding receivers, though. Because there were so few transmitters around the lakes, it was extremely difficult to get an accurate fix. In those early days, shipowners often found their crews using the high-priced direction-finding radios to listen to the growing number of commercial radio stations along the shores.

Interestingly, some of the best-known groundings of the twentieth century occurred after the combination of commercial broadcast stations and government-maintained radio beacons made direction-finding reasonably accurate in the 1930s. In the spring of 1933, for example, the *Cox* went on the reefs off the Rock of Ages at Isle Royale while running in a thick fog.[47] There's no record as to whether the *Cox* was equipped with RDF equipment, though it's unlikely. The accident should have been relatively easy to avoid if officers aboard the ship had been able to plot even a moderately accurate position. A single line bearing from a station in Port Arthur or Fort William could have been enough to keep her off the rocks.

While the RDF system on the Great Lakes improved significantly during the 1930s, the slowness of many shipowners to install the equipment aboard their valuable ships can no doubt be attributed to the fact that the industry had been decimated by the Great Depression. All of the shipping companies suffered during the depression years, and many failed to survive. It wasn't until World War II broke out in Europe in 1939 that the industry finally began to get back onto a solid economic footing.

The end of World War II brought technology that was even more effective than RDF in reducing the number of groundings—radar. The new equipment had an even greater impact on reducing the number of vessel collisions. Developed and perfected during the war for the military, radar consisted of a transmitting unit that emitted a continuous radio beam. The characteristics of the radio beam made it particularly susceptible to bouncing off objects in its path—other ships, landmasses, and navigational aids—and being reflected back to its point of origin. Ships equipped with radar had a special dish-shaped antenna to receive the returning signal. The signal was then processed by sophisticated equipment and displayed on a cathode ray tube, the radarscope. Whenever the sweeping beam of the radar comes in contact with an object, what users called a "target," an amber dot of light—a "pip" or "blip"—appears on the screen. Landmasses appear as a jagged line of dots that fairly accurately represents the shoreline. A ship or navigational aid out in the water usually appears as a single blip.

The first shipboard radar on the Great Lakes was installed aboard the Coast Guard icebreaker *Mackinaw* in 1945. In 1946, the *John T. Hutchinson* and five other freighters participated in a test of radar equipment sponsored by the Lake Carriers' Association.[48] Radar soon became standard equipment on most ships on the lakes. As in the case of RDF, however, there were still companies that were slow to install the expensive new equipment, despite its obvious safety value. Many ships, particularly older and smaller vessels, ran well into the 1950s without radar.

Emperor, 1947

One of them was the 525-foot *Emperor,* owned by Canada Steamship Lines, the largest of the Canadian shipping companies. Early on the morning of June 4, 1947, the thirty-six-year-old ship was on its way from Port Arthur to Ashtabula with a load of iron ore when it ran on Canoe Rocks, a reef off the northeastern tip of Isle Royale. The *Emperor* hit with such force that she immediately broke in two. Rushing up to the pilothouse, Captain Eldon Walkinshaw knew instinctively that his ship had been mortally wounded, and without hesitating he broadcast an SOS. The *Emperor* sank within minutes, taking Captain Walkinshaw and eleven others down with it. Twenty-one other crewmembers managed to get off the sinking ship. Fourteen were picked up about half an hour later by a U.S. Coast Guard buoy tender that was in the area and heard the distress call. The survivors were in the *Emperor*'s two lifeboats, both of which had been damaged in launching and were in the process of sinking. Seven other crewmen swam to Canoe Rocks and were rescued from there by the Coast Guard.

A subsequent Coast Guard investigation into the sinking concluded that the first mate, who was navigating the ship at the time of the grounding, had probably dozed off briefly and was late in making a necessary course change. He and the wheelsman on watch at the time of the accident had gone down with the *Emperor,* so it was difficult for investigators to piece together the events leading to the casualty. Their report did note, however, that the first mate had gotten off watch just before the ship had docked at Port Arthur. It's standard practice on the lakes for the first mate to supervise loading the boat, so he hadn't been able to get any sleep while the ship was in port. When the *Emperor* finished loading and left Port Arthur, it was again time for the first mate to go on watch. It's understandable that he would have been exhausted from his long hours without sleep. Even today, sleep deprivation is a common problem for captains and mates, and it has undoubtedly been a factor in many accidents over the years.[49]

A number of other questions about the events aboard the *Emperor* have also gone unanswered. The freighter ran in and out of Thunder Bay regularly, and an experienced wheelsman would normally have noticed that the mate had failed to make a required course change. In that situation, you would expect the wheelsman to immediately call it to the mate's attention, rousing him from his nap if necessary. Since the ship reportedly steamed along for an hour or more before the mate woke up and finally ordered the course change, it's obvious that either the wheelsman was not aware that the turn had been missed, or he didn't call it to the mate's attention for some reason. Maybe he, too, had dozed off.

Regardless, when the mate did finally make the course change, it should have been obvious that he needed to replot the *Emperor*'s course to pass safely between Isle Royale and Passage Island. For some reason, he didn't do that. As the ship approached the narrow passage, it would have also been standard operating practice to post the watchman as a lookout at the bow. That was also not done. A lookout would surely have seen the navigational light that is located near Canoe Rocks and warned the mate. Of course, it's hard to imagine that neither the mate nor the wheelsman saw the red light and realized that their ship was bearing down on the reef. The actions of the mate and wheelsman in the pilothouse of the *Emperor* that night are hard to fathom. Something was drastically wrong . . . and their actions or inaction cost the lives of twelve of their shipmates, and left their ship wrecked on a clearly marked reef. Whether a radar would have allowed them to avoid the accident is highly doubtful.

Even ships equipped with radar frequently run aground. On Lake Superior alone, at least ten ships with radar were involved in ground-ings between 1960 and 1969, representing a virtual *Who's Who* of the

15. Despite being equipped with modern navigational equipment, the German-owned *Nordmeer* and its cargo of coiled steel ran onto a submerged, rocky shoal on northern Lake Huron on November 19, 1966. The 470-foot ship cracked in half a week later, during the storm that claimed the *Daniel C. Morrell*. The *Nordmeer* is one of five saltwater ships that ended their careers on North America's freshwater seas. (Author's Collection)

Great Lakes shipping industry. Those that ran aground included the *Robert C. Stanley, Richard A. Lindabury, John Sherwin, Calcite II, Walter A. Sterling, Frankcliffe Hall,* and *Meteor.* The Greek-owned *Anvarkikos* and the British-flag *Crystal Jewel,* both under the control of Great Lakes pilots, joined them when they went aground. None of the ships were seriously damaged and all were subsequently released, repaired, and returned to service.[50]

Frontenac, 1979

One of the most serious groundings involving a radar-equipped ship occurred on November 22, 1979, when Cleveland-Cliffs's 604-foot *Frontenac* ran on the rocks at the entrance to the port of Silver Bay, Minnesota, during a storm. As the *Frontenac* approached the harbor at Silver Bay that evening, the wind was blowing out of the northeast at twenty-five to thirty miles an hour and seas ran between six and twelve feet. Captain Clyde Trueax knew that getting safely into the harbor would be a tricky operation under those conditions. Based on a suggestion from the captain of a ship that had gone into Silver Bay a short time earlier, Trueax steamed the *Frontenac* about three miles past the entrance to the harbor, then made a hard turn to starboard. The ship was then steering directly into the wind and on a course to clear the entrance to the harbor. Trueax hoped the move would minimize the amount of rolling his ship would do on the open approach to Silver Bay.

As the *Frontenac* made its slow approach to the narrow opening between the breakwaters, it was engulfed by a blinding snow squall that reduced visibility to only a few hundred feet. Despite the squall, Captain Trueax and the two mates and a watchman he had posted as lookouts on the bow could still see the flashing green navigational light that was on a buoy off the westerly end of the entrance.

Minutes later, the *Frontenac* came to a grinding halt as its port side slammed into a reef that extends out from little Pellet Island at the end of the harbor's westerly breakwater. The stranded ship was unable to work her way off the reef, and the seas began to batter her against the rocky bottom. Soon the *Frontenac*'s bottom plates buckled and her number 3 cargo hold flooded.

The Coast Guard cutter *Mesquite* arrived at the scene early the following morning. As the Coast Guard personnel put pumps aboard the

Frontenac to help pump her out, they noticed that the beating she had taken during the night had buckled her hull amidships in two places, and cracks had also appeared on her deck. While she was being pumped out, a small tanker was brought alongside to take off most of the *Frontenac*'s bunker fuel. When about two-thirds of the fuel had been removed, the big freighter finally came off the reef. She was then moved to the Silver Bay dock so temporary repairs could be made to the hull before the ship went on to the shipyard at nearby Superior, Wisconsin. Almost her entire bottom and much of her framing needed to be replaced, but repairs were never completed.

The bow of the *Frontenac* was snugged into the muddy bottom of a slip near the shipyard in mid-December. There she sat, with a noticeable port list, until being scrapped in 1985. She went into the record books as the last total loss on the Great Lakes as the result of a grounding. In the aftermath of the grounding, a Coast Guard board of investigation found that Captain Trueax's actions had been negligent, and his license was temporarily suspended.[51]

By the time the *Frontenac* went on the reef off Silver Bay in 1979, all of the ships on the Great Lakes were required to have radar. In fact, most had two, one primarily for use on the open lakes, and a second for use when in the rivers. During the 1980 season, the Great Lakes LORAN system also went into operation. LORAN, an acronym for "long-range navigation" is somewhat similar to RDF. Radio transmitters at sites around the lakes broadcast a continuous signal that is picked up by a special shipboard receiver. The computerized brain of the receiver uses the signals to determine the precise location of the ship, and its accuracy is much better than that of RDF. Shortly after the debut of LORAN, a few ships on the lakes were also equipped with satellite navigation, or SATNAV, systems. They operate in a manner somewhat similar to LORAN, except that the radio signals used to calculate the ship's position are bounced off satellites in orbit around the earth. The systems are much more expensive than LORAN, however, and the accuracy of the resulting fixes is not that much better.

The latest development in navigation is the use of the global positioning system, or GPS, developed by the military and used extensively during the brief Gulf War in 1991. The GPS equipment is more compact and less expensive than SATNAV, and it's likely to eventually replace even the popular LORAN system.

Radar and navigational systems like LORAN have made lighthouses and foghorns virtually obsolete. In fact, in 1995 the Canadian Coast

Guard was midway through a program of decommissioning foghorns at most Canadian lighthouses around the lakes. A total of forty-nine of the sixty-three foghorns on the Canadian side of the lakes were slated to be deactivated. The U.S. Coast Guard continues to operate about eighty foghorns on the Great Lakes, although commercial vessels seldom rely on lighthouses and foghorns anymore.[52]

While the *Frontenac* was the last ship lost on the lakes as the result of running aground, groundings continue to be the most common type of casualty experienced on the Great Lakes, despite the universal use of radar and LORAN. During the 1994 shipping season, for example, at least twelve U.S. and Canadian ships were involved in groundings.[53] Most of today's groundings occur when ships are maneuvering in the narrow confines of the rivers and harbors around the lakes. In such instances they can often get off without any assistance, and damage is seldom significant.

Despite the vast array of sophisticated equipment carried aboard today's ships, many accidents continue to occur as a result of human error. In studying recent groundings, it seems that in some respects we haven't progressed very far since those days so long ago when ships like the *Siskawit, Monarch, Centurion,* and *Cox* went aground at Isle Royale.

Kinsman Independent, 1990

In the fall of 1990, for example, the *Kinsman Independent* ran aground at the entrance to Siskiwit Bay on Isle Royale, near where the *Siskawit* and *Centurion* had wrecked during the previous century. Unlike those ships, however, the 642-foot *Independent* wasn't driven ashore in a storm or accidentally grounded while running in fog. It was, as one reporter called it, a "what-can-be-stranger-than-truth" accident.[54]

The *Kinsman Independent* was one of two freighters operated by Kinsman Lines in the grain trade between the ports of Duluth, Superior, and Thunder Bay on Lake Superior and Buffalo on Lake Erie. One of the oldest fleets on the lakes, Kinsman is owned by George Steinbrenner, the colorful and often controversial owner of the New York Yankees.

At 11 A.M. on November 24, 1990, the *Kinsman Independent* was on its way to Thunder Bay, Ontario, to pick up a load of Manitoba wheat when it ran aground off Isle Royale's Siskiwit Bay, about midway down the south shore of the island. The *Independent* was supposed to be heading for the channel between Passage Island and the eastern tip of Isle Royale at the time, but somehow managed to get *twenty-four miles off course!* If it hadn't been for the reef, the *Independent* would probably have run ashore on Isle Royale itself. The ship was being navigated—or was supposedly being navigated—by the third mate at the time, and the 8-to-12 wheelsman was on watch with him in the pilothouse when the ship ran on a reef with only six feet of water over it. The *Independent* hit so hard that it drove 150 feet onto the reef before finally grinding to a stop.

What exactly went on the pilothouse during the almost two hours that the *Independent* had to have been headed straight for the middle of Isle Royale has never been satisfactorily explained by either the mate or the wheelsman, but it's obvious that they weren't standing "watch." As one crewmember later put it, "A blind person with a white cane could have done a better job of navigating the ship."[55]

The collision with the reef ripped the *Independent*'s hull open on both the port and starboard sides for a distance of 120–150 feet back from the bow. Fortunately, with the ship's cargo holds empty and intact, crewmembers were able to make temporary repairs. The following day, tugs pulled the *Independent* off the reef and towed it to a shipyard in nearby Thunder Bay. The total repair bill was in excess of $1 million, many times more than Kinsman had paid for the freighter when they bought it in 1988. Built in 1952, the ship had previously operated as part of Ford Motor Company's fleet.[56]

Needless to say, the mate who had been on watch when the grounding occurred is no longer sailing, and it's not likely he'll be back on the lakes anytime soon. Many people in the industry are still scratching their heads and trying to figure out exactly how he managed to run into Isle Royale. It wasn't the industry's last unexplainable accident, however. Another occurred in 1993 and involved a 1,000-foot-freighter and a sixty-nine-foot-tall lighthouse.

Indiana Harbor, 1993

American Steamship's 1,000-foot freighter *Indiana Harbor* departed Bay Shipbuilding at Sturgeon Bay, Wisconsin, late on the afternoon of September 8, 1993, after being dry-docked for repairs and its five-year Coast Guard inspection. Steaming out of Green Bay in ballast, the giant freighter set a course for Lake Superior, where it was scheduled to load coal at a terminal in Superior, Wisconsin.

At about 3:30 the following morning, with excellent visibility and moderate winds, the *Indiana Harbor* drove onto Lansing Shoal in northern Lake Michigan at full speed, even though the thirteen-foot-deep shoal

16. Early on the morning of September 9, 1993, the 1,000-foot *Indiana Harbor* ran onto Lansing Shoal on northern Lake Michigan and struck a lighthouse. Weather conditions were clear at the time, and the freighter was equipped with sophisticated navigational equipment, including radar and LORAN. The casualty was blamed on inattentiveness by the mate and wheelsman who were on watch in the big freighter's pilothouse. Seen here moored at the mouth of the Cuyahoga River at Cleveland during the 1996 shipping season, the *Indiana Harbor* required more than $1.9 million in repairs after striking Lansing Shoal Light. (Author's Collection)

was clearly marked by a lighthouse. At the time, the *Indiana Harbor* had a draft at her bow of twenty-three feet. Incredible as it may seem, the freighter's bow actually struck and damaged the sixty-nine-foot-tall concrete lighthouse!

The third mate was navigating the *Indiana Harbor* when she grounded. The captain, who was asleep in his room one deck below the pilothouse at the time of the collision, immediately raced up the stairs and took control. Quickly assessing the situation, the captain backed his badly damaged ship off the rocky shoal and into deeper water, then he and his crew assessed the extent of the damage. If there had been more damage below the waterline, the captain's hasty decision to back off into deep water could well have resulted in the ship's sinking to the bottom.

Fortunately for the captain and his crew, most of the damage was above the waterline, but plating lower on her hull was ripped open enough that the forepeak of the ship began to flood immediately. The tremendous force of the ship's impact with the decidedly immovable object while traveling at more than thirteen miles an hour tore a fifty-foot-square hole in her bow and damaged plating extended back three hundred feet from the bow.

As soon as the captain was certain that the *Indiana Harbor* wasn't going to sink, he turned the ship and headed back to Sturgeon Bay. Less than twenty-four hours after the freighter had left the shipyard, workers at Bay Shipbuilding were surprised to see the vessel returning. The reason for the return visit was pretty obvious.

The ensuing Coast Guard investigation revealed that the mate on watch had failed to make a ten-degree turn to the right as the *Indiana Harbor* neared the lighthouse. As a result, the ship ran out of the 1.5-mile-wide channel and struck the clearly marked shoal area. Neither the mate nor the wheelsman who was in the pilothouse with him at the time of the collision could give a satisfactory explanation for how they managed to drive their ship into a towering lighthouse in clear weather. The mate's license was subsequently suspended.

According to Gavin Sproul, a vice president of American Steamship, the repairs to the *Indiana Harbor* cost $1.9 million. The ship had also done more than $100,000 in damage to the lighthouse, but Coast Guard officials were quick to point out that the light itself never stopped working.

One international maritime publication termed the *Indiana Harbor*'s collision with the lighthouse "one of the most incredible maritime accidents to occur in the past year or so." A spokesperson for the Coast Guard said, "It's quite normal to have groundings here in the Great Lakes, but we rarely get anything as dramatic as this."[57]

Groundings like those of the *Indiana Harbor* and *Kinsman Independent* should never have happened. Both were the result of gross negligence on the part of the personnel on watch in the pilothouse at the time the accidents occurred. They are certainly not typical of the vast majority of groundings that occur around the lakes. Human error often plays a role in groundings, but not to the extent it did in the wrecks of the *Indiana Harbor* and *Kinsman Independent*.

The 1,000-foot *Indiana Harbor* that collided with the lighthouse on Lansing Shoal in 1993 was involved in a second major grounding just over two years later. The accident occurred on the night of January 3, 1996, while the big American Steamship freighter was downbound in the St. Marys River on its final trip of the season. Brutally cold temperatures had settled over the lakes the previous month, combined with record-breaking snowfalls, and there were several feet of hard ice covering most of the river. On its slow trip down through the ice, the heavily laden *Indiana Harbor* was being assisted by the Coast Guard icebreaker *Mackinaw*. Air temperatures were well below zero at the time.

When the *Indiana Harbor* was on the course that would take it down to Rock Cut, the man-made channel around the west side of Neebish Island, things started to go wrong. The *Indiana Harbor*'s captain turned on the powerful searchlight mounted on top of the pilothouse so that he could use it to light up the pier at the entrance to the cut. The searchlight is controlled by moving a handle inside the pilothouse that is attached to the light by a mechanical linkage. Ice had apparently coated the linkage or electrical conduit to the searchlight, however, and it was impossible for the captain to move the light. He then asked the watchman and cadet to go up on the roof and free up the light.

Since the searchlight was located right next to the ship's radar antennas and the powerful radar beams can be harmful to humans, the captain put both radars on standby so they wouldn't be transmitting while the two were on top of the pilothouse. Until then, visibility had been good, but at about the same time as the watchman and cadet went up on the roof of the pilothouse the frigid air passing over the track of relatively warm water that had just been opened by the *Mackinaw* formed a dense blanket of sea smoke fog that swirled up around the *Indiana Harbor*. Just as the ship was at the point where it needed to make the difficult left turn to enter the narrow cut, it became almost impossible for those in the pilothouse of the freighter to make out the buoys and lights they relied on to make the turn. What had been a tense situation became a confusing one.

Those in the pilothouse could see some flashing lights they knew were navigational aids along the channel, but neither the captain nor the mate on watch could tell exactly which lights they were seeing. One of the lights was definitely the turning mark they used to begin the turn into Rock Cut, but because of the fog they couldn't tell which it was. Unable to turn the radar on, the best they could do was make an educated guess. When the *Indiana Harbor* was abreast of the light the captain thought was their turning mark, he told the wheelsman to start the ship into its turn. Those in the pilothouse collectively held their breaths.

About a minute later, it became all too obvious that they had used the wrong turning mark. The *Indiana Harbor* slammed into submerged rocks around the base of a crib light on the left-hand side of the channel, then bounced off and back into the channel. They had started the turn too soon, cut the corner short, and hit the left side of the channel.

While the captain sent the mate forward to check for damage, the thick ice on the side of the channel slowed the *Indiana Harbor* to a crawl. Visibility improved somewhat, and the captain was able to get his bearings and continue on through the cut, which is only about twenty feet wider than the ship. At the same time, the captain called down to the engine room and told them to check their ballast tank gauges to see if the ship was taking on any water. The engineer replied that it looked as though the number 1 ballast tank on the port side was flooding, so the captain told them to turn on the ballast pump to that tank.

When the *Indiana Harbor*'s captain reported that his ship had struck the side of the channel, the Coast Guard asked that he anchor the ship until the extent of the damage could be determined. Divers later found an eight-foot gash in the port bow. "The rip looked like someone had dug their fingers through peanut butter," a Coast Guard investigator reported. "It looked like 'Old Faithful' with the water coming through the hull at the base of the collision bulkhead." The bottom of the watertight bulkhead between the forepeak and the number 1 ballast tank on the port side had also been buckled by the collision, allowing water to leak from the forepeak into the tank.

Before the *Indiana Harbor* was allowed to resume its voyage, about 7,000 tons of taconite pellets had to be offloaded into the steamer *Buckeye*. Lightened up, she then continued on to Ashtabula, Ohio, to unload. Once empty, the *Indiana Harbor* headed for the shipyard at Sturgeon Bay for another round of repairs.

Coast Guard investigators ruled that the unexpected fog produced when the *Mackinaw* opened the track through the ice was the primary cause of the accident, and no action was taken against the captain of the *Indiana Harbor*.[58] It should be noted, however, that when the captain put the ship's two radar sets on standby only minutes before having to make what is almost unanimously considered to be the most difficult and dangerous turn in the Great Lakes system, he robbed himself of the most valuable equipment he had. If the radars had been in operation, there is no doubt that the grounding could have been avoided. Under any circumstances, the radars were more valuable than the searchlight.

Looking Back

Groundings have always been the most common type of casualty on the lakes. Precisely because they have been so common, and because most ships that go aground manage to free themselves or be freed without doing any serious damage, we don't have good records on how many occurred in any given year. During the 1871 shipping season, however, a marine reporter at Detroit made a record of every casualty he heard about. His list indicates that there were 280 groundings that year, representing an average of one grounding a day during the entire shipping season. A one-a-day average probably wasn't at all unusual during that era, given that there were 2,475 steamers, sailing vessels, and barges operating on the Great Lakes.[59]

At the same time, the most comprehensive list we have of *serious* casualties indicates that there were only eleven groundings in 1871 that resulted in extensive damage to the vessels or the loss of life.[60] In that year, then, only about 4 percent of the total groundings were serious, and 96 percent of the incidents were minor.

If that ratio—4 serious groundings for every 96 minor ones—held in most other years, and it seems entirely reasonable that it would, we can make some estimates of the total number of groundings that might have occurred over the long span of shipping on the lakes. We know that between 1679 and 1990 there were at least 962 serious groundings.[61] If there were 96 minor groundings for every 4 of those serious ones, that would indicate that there might have been more than 24,000 total groundings between 1679 and 1990. That's a staggering total, to be sure, but certainly not out of the question given the nature of shipping on the lakes.

Prior to the availability of reasonably detailed navigational charts in the 1850s, it was commonplace for ships to wander into shoal waters and run aground. Groundings that resulted from the lack of accurate navigational charts undoubtedly represent only a very small percentage of the total that have occurred over the years, however. Most other groundings fall into two categories: ships that were accidentally *run aground* by those responsible for their navigation, or ships that were helplessly *driven aground* during storms or as the result of equipment failures.

Most groundings have resulted from errors in piloting or maneuvering ships in the confined waters of rivers or harbors. The least serious groundings fall into this category, and damage is often minimal.

Because they're generally operating at higher speeds, ships that run aground while out on the lakes are often more seriously damaged. Limited visibility—fog, snow, rain, or even smoke—is a contributing factor in the overwhelming majority of those cases, like the groundings of the *Centurion, Harlem, Monarch, Congdon, Cox,* and *Emperor* in the shallow waters around Isle Royale. In fact, there's probably a tendency to cite "limited visibility" as the cause of such accidents.

Nonetheless, a review of the circumstances of each of those casualties shows that they were all the result of human error to some extent. For example, Art Kronk, the first mate on the *Cox,* had the wheelsman steering the wrong course. Captain Ed Robertson of the *Monarch,* like many of those who drove their ships onto Isle Royale during periods of restricted visibility, made an error in dead reckoning. His taffrail log had iced up, so he had no way to tell exactly how far his ship had traveled on the course it was on, and he ran the ship aground trying to sneak past Passage Island. Jim Morey, the first mate on the *Emperor,* obviously suffering from sleep deprivation, dozed off in the pilothouse and missed a turn. In thick fog, he couldn't get back on the correct course, and his ship drove hard onto a reef off Isle Royale. In the days before RDF, radar, and LORAN, it's easy to understand how such an accident happened.

At the same time, all those captains and mates who ran their ships aground near Isle Royale chose to continue steaming along despite the fog, snow, or rain. That was their first error. Their dead-reckoning navigation was also off. That was their second error. All could have stayed in port, or gone to anchor at any time right up to the point when they drove their ships on the rocks. That's particularly true in Captain Robertson's case. When he discovered that his log had iced up, making it almost impossible for him to dead reckon his ship's position, he could easily have justified going to anchor. But he continued on . . . and he wrecked his ship . . . and one member of his crew died as a result. Similarly, Jim Morey compounded the mistake of falling asleep by continuing to steam along toward Passage Island even though he surely knew his ship was well off course. It cost the lives of twelve of his crewmembers. Yes, there were contributing factors in many of the instances where ships were run aground, but they were all a direct result of human error, nonetheless. After all, a captain's or mate's first responsibility has always been to the safety of the passengers, crew, and ship—*not* to staying on schedule.

The most blatant cases of human error, of course, are those that led to the 1990 grounding of the *Kinsman Independent* at Isle Royale and the 1993 grounding of the *Indiana Harbor* on Lansing Shoal. Visibility wasn't a factor, since both ships were equipped with the most modern navigational equipment, yet they were run aground and seriously damaged. The accidents are almost impossible to explain, except that they were the result of human error that bordered on criminal negligence.

Human error is less likely to have been a factor in cases where ships were driven aground as the result of storms or equipment failures. It's hard to fault Captain John Angus, for example, when the schooner *Siskawit* began dragging her anchor and got driven on a reef off Isle Royale when he tried to sail her out into open water. Similarly, it's hard to find much fault with the captains of the *Superior* or *Altadoc* when their ships lost their rudders and were driven aground in storms.

It's also hard to blame the captains of the *Jupiter* or *Saturn*, schooner-barges that were driven ashore in storms after they broke loose from the freighter that was towing them. Those aboard freighters like the *Robert Wallace* and *E. W. Oglebay* weren't much better off than their counterparts on the unpowered barges, even though their ships had steam engines. Seriously underpowered, there was simply no way their captains could keep the ships off the beach when caught out in severe storms.

The captains of the schooner *Conductor* and the steamer *Lambton* found themselves in a similar situation. Being driven ahead of violent storms with visibility near zero and their ships on the verge of foundering, there was no way they could risk trying to bring their ships about when they neared land. In all likelihood, the ships would have stalled in the troughs, broadside to the punishing seas, and been torn to pieces. Running aground was clearly the lesser of two evils for them.

If there was culpable human error in the wrecks of many of the ships that were driven ashore in storms, it was not necessarily the crews who were to blame, but the shipowners and government regulators. Over many decades, storms wreaked havoc on underpowered ships and manned barges. From their debut in the late 1860s until they faded from the scene around 1930, at least 192 schooner-barges were wrecked on the lakes, almost all as a result of breaking loose or being cut loose from the tow steamers in storms.[62] They carried sails, but it was usually impossible for the crews to hoist the sails while being buffeted about by high seas and strong winds. Driven into the shallows, most broke up in the surf, often with a heavy death toll. If storms were a threat to sailors, they were virtually a death warrant for those on the unpowered barges.

Many of the steamers of that period weren't much better off. With engines too small for the size of the ship, they simply didn't have the power to stay out in deep water in severe storms. As with the case of the barges, the problem of underpowered ships actually got worse over time. While the size of ships grew dramatically after the 1880s, their engines remained about the same size. "Ships built in 1888 carrying 3,000 tons have the same machinery as the *Gary*, built in 1905, carrying 10,000 tons of ore," William Livingstone, president of the Lake Carriers' Association, explained in 1911. Noting that "in comparison to their size, these freighters are obviously of very low power," Livingstone concluded

17. The schooner-barges *Moonlight* (*left*) and *Henry A. Kent* were driven ashore near Marquette during a storm that ravaged Lake Superior on September 28–29, 1895. The *Charles J. Kershaw* was towing the two schooner-barges when a steam pipe burst in the engine room and it lost power. While the *Moonlight* and *Kent* were driven onto the sandy beach, the *Kershaw* wrecked on rocky Chocolay Reef. Men from the Marquette Life-Saving Station, aided by a number of local residents, rescued the thirteen crewmen from the steamer. (Author's Collection)

they were "nonetheless sufficient for the purpose."[63] The captains of the *Robert Wallace* or *E. W. Oglebay* would probably have questioned just how "sufficient" they were.

It wasn't that more powerful steam engines weren't available, either. They were, but more powerful engines cost more money. Enough said.

Unless they had their heads buried in the sand on some Great Lakes beach, several generations of elected government officials and bureaucrats from the Revenue Cutter Service, Steamboat Inspection Service, Life-Saving Service, Bureau of Navigation, and Coast Guard must have been aware of the many shipwrecks and deaths resulting from underpowered ships and manned barges. They could have solved the ongoing problems by requiring more powerful engines and prohibiting barges from carrying crews, at least during those periods of the sailing season when storms were most likely to be encountered.

Instead, they set up lifesaving stations around the lakes in an effort to save those aboard ships that were run ashore or driven ashore. From 1876 until 1914, the crews of the Life-Saving Service stations around the Great Lakes aided 9,763 ships, carrying 55,639 passengers and crew. On those vessels that wrecked within their areas of operation, only 275 persons died during that thirty-nine-year period, amounting to less than 0.5 percent of those who had been aboard.[64] The lifesavers were incredibly effective, to be sure, but their role was primarily to reduce deaths and economic losses from shipwrecks rather than to prevent wrecks from occurring.

The government programs aimed at preventing groundings included the construction of lighthouses, lightships, and fog signals along the shorelines of the lakes, and buoys and range lights in the rivers. Most of those programs were well established by the end of the Civil War, yet the number of serious groundings continued to increase each decade until after 1910. There were only 9 serious grounding casualties during the 1830s, but that rose to 28 during the 1840s. There were 60 serious groundings during the 1850s, and again during the 1860s. After that, the number rose almost geometrically. During the 1870s there were 124, double that of the previous two decades. There were 170 during the 1880s, 131 during the 1890s, and 195 from 1900 to 1909.[65] It should have been obvious that the lights, fog signals, and buoys were not adequate to deal with the growing problem of groundings on the lakes.

After reaching a peak during the first decade of the twentieth century, the number of serious groundings began to decline. There were only 85 recorded between 1910 and 1919, 50 during the 1920s, and only 15 during the 1930s.[66]

There seems to have been a strong correlation between the number of serious groundings on the lakes and the number of ships operating in the system. Between 1830 and 1909, when the number of serious groundings increased by 2,400 percent, the number of ships on the lakes went up at almost the same rate, about 2,800 percent. Similarly, the number of ships declined by 76 percent from 1900 to 1939, while the number of groundings fell by 74 percent.[67] The extremely strong correlation between the number of ships on the lakes and the number of groundings suggests that the various government programs had little overall impact. That's entirely likely, given the fact that most groundings have been the result of problems that don't seem to have been addressed by any government or industry programs: operating when visibility was extremely limited, equipment failures, underpowered ships and barges that were driven aground in storms, and errors in navigating, piloting, and maneuvering ships.

>>2<<
THE CAULDRONS OF HADES:
Fires and Boiler Explosions

HE EARLY 1840s WAS A TIME OF GREAT EXCITEMENT in the United States. The country's population had grown by almost a third during the prior decade, bolstered by the steadily increasing flood of immigrants who had been arriving from Europe almost daily since the end of the War of 1812. Many of the new immigrants were bound for the expansive frontiers opening up west of the Appalachians, especially the territories around the Great Lakes. Buffalo, Cleveland, Toledo, Detroit, Chicago, and Milwaukee were among the fastest-growing cities in the country, and they aggressively competed with each other to attract new settlers from the East Coast and Europe.

Nothing had a greater impact on development of the Great Lakes region than completion of the Erie Canal in 1825. The canal provided an efficient water route between New York's Hudson River and the port of Buffalo at the eastern end of Lake Erie, which immediately became the gateway for travel to and from the cities along the shores of the Great Lakes. Where it had cost $120 a ton to laboriously move freight overland by wagon from the East Coast to the Great Lakes, cargo could be shipped through the Erie Canal for only $4 a ton.[1]

The opening of the canal also led to significant reductions in the cost of traveling to the Great Lakes region. Perhaps even more importantly, it was finally possible to travel from the East Coast to any location on the Great Lakes in the relative comfort of a boat, instead of making the arduous overland journey. Almost immediately, the region also became a popular tourist destination for affluent travelers who wanted to experience life on the American frontier.

One of the region's early tourists was famed British author Charles Dickens. In the early 1840s, Dickens's *Pickwick Papers, Oliver Twist,* and

Nicholas Nickleby had established him as one of the world's preeminent contemporary authors and brought him fame and wealth. He made the first of several visits to the United States in 1842, at the age of thirty, arriving in New York City in January. Dickens was an instant hit, not just with the city's *literati*, but with liberals from all social classes who applauded him because his books had been catalysts for a crusade to eliminate slum conditions in London. As much a social reformer as he was a writer, Dickens had barely settled into his New York hotel when he began speaking out against slavery in the United States, which he regarded as a great evil.

After spending the winter months on the East Coast, Dickens left New York in April for a tour of the Great Lakes. He traveled from Sandusky, Ohio, to Buffalo and Cleveland aboard the passenger steamer *Constellation*. When he arrived in Cleveland on April 25, 1842, Dickens was still suffering the effects of a serious bout of seasickness he had experienced during the brief but stormy passage from Sandusky. A large and enthusiastic crowd greeted his arrival at the dock in Cleveland, and despite being under the weather, Dickens paused briefly to share with them some of his initial impressions of the region and travel on the Great Lakes.[2]

The *Constellation* was then one of the finest ships operating on the lakes, and residents of Cleveland were proud that it regularly called at their waterfront. Their pride was no doubt buoyed when Dickens acknowledged that the steamer was "handsomely fitted up." On the other hand, they were undoubtedly taken aback a bit when the influential author expressed some misgivings about the *Constellation*'s high-pressure engines. The engines, he said, "conveyed that kind of feeling to me, which I should likely experience, I think, if I had lodgings on the first floor of a powder mill."[3]

If any owners of steamboats were present in the crowd that day, it's likely they paled noticeably at Dickens's graphic comment. The last thing they needed was an influential, internationally acclaimed author publicly suggesting that their ships might be unsafe. The steamboat fleets were already under enough pressure due to the number of fires and explosions aboard their ships.

The first steamboats on the Great Lakes, the Canadian *Frontenac* and the American-flag *Ontario*, went into operation during the 1817 season, a decade after Robert Fulton's pioneering *Clermont* first chugged its way across the waters of the Hudson River. The fleet of steamboats grew slowly but steadily during the ensuing years. There were ten on the lakes by 1832, sharing the shipping lanes with over ninety sailing ships.[4] By then, the steamboats had already carved out a niche for themselves in the growing passenger trade.

The safety of passengers on steamboats was not a major issue until 1830. Some of the early steamboats grounded or sank, to be sure, but sailing vessels also had a long history of such casualties—they were accepted hazards for anyone traveling by ship.[5] All that changed in June 1830, however, when the steamer *Adelaide*'s boiler exploded on a run across Lake Erie, killing three of those aboard. An even more serious accident occurred the following September when the boiler on the steamer *William Peacock* exploded shortly after she left the dock at Buffalo. The explosion killed fifteen persons aboard the ship, mainly immigrants.[6]

Great Lakes steamers weren't the only ones having boiler problems. In 1832, boiler explosions destroyed 14 percent of all steamboats operating in the United States.[7] Public reaction to the continuing carnage caused by boiler explosions on steamboats was reaching a fever pitch. Much of the indignation was focused on lawmakers in Washington who had failed to respond to the dangerous situation with legislation to improve the safety of steamboats. No doubt, steamboat owners, many of whom were prominent, powerful, and wealthy members of their communities, were also lobbying those in Washington during that period.

As early as 1824, Congress had directed Secretary of the Treasury William Crawford to investigate the causes of the mounting number of steamboat accidents. When Crawford reported on his findings, he said "it seems as though more steam boilers blew than ran." He recommended against any congressional action, however, arguing that any legislation was more apt to "do mischief" than prevent disasters.[8]

In the face of escalating carnage, the Congress finally acted in 1838, passing legislation that required steamboats to have their boilers inspected every six months and their hulls every twelve months. The new law also included a requirement for passenger ships to carry lifeboats, fire pumps, fire hoses, signal lights, and other safety equipment. For the first time, steamers were also required to carry an adequate number of experienced engineers, though the law didn't define "experienced." Ships that met the requirements of the new law would be issued a license, and no steamboat could carry passengers without being licensed. While it looked good on paper, the act would prove to be toothless, since it didn't provide any trained marine inspectors to enforce it.

Judges of the U.S. district courts, who were not necessarily qualified to appoint competent hull and boiler inspectors, appointed marine inspectors. Some judges simply used their new power to appoint friends, relatives, and political supporters to the positions. Some of the inspectors appointed were even close friends of local shipowners, making them less than impartial in the discharge of their duties. As a result, enforcement of the new provisions varied significantly from port to port. Many would describe enforcement of the statute as "unenthusiastic." At the same time, the 1838 legislation was the beginning, in all but name, of what would eventually become the Steamboat Inspection Service, a predecessor to today's Coast Guard.[9]

Erie, 1841

One of the steamers to come under the inspection and licensing provisions of the new law was the side-wheel steamer *Erie*. Built in 1837, the 176-foot ship was considered one of the finest passenger ships plying the waters of the Great Lakes.

On the morning of August 9, 1841, the *Erie* looked particularly striking to those who had gathered at the riverfront docks in Buffalo to say their good-byes to friends and family members. And rightly so, for the four-year-old *Erie* had just undergone a complete refinishing. In fact, the team of painters who had so carefully applied the new coats of paint and varnish during the preceding days had just finished their work the prior evening. The six painters were still aboard the ship when it set out from Buffalo. They were riding over to Erie, Pennsylvania, where the ship would stop briefly before going on to Chicago. Awaiting the painters at Erie was the steamer *Madison,* the next ship they were to work on.[10]

About 9:00 that evening, the pristine *Erie* was churning through the warm waters of Lake Erie, forty miles out of Buffalo and about six miles off the little ports of Silver Creek and Dunkirk, New York. Although many of the 250 passengers had already gone to their staterooms, some still strolled the freshly varnished decks, enjoying the cool lake breeze on what had been an otherwise stifling hot day. Captain T. J. Titus was pacing back and forth in the pilothouse near the bow, though he, too, planned to turn in shortly, since he would have to be up early the following morning to take the ship into Erie.

A loud explosion interrupted Captain Titus's pacing, and the deck shook violently under his feet. The sound had come from behind the pilothouse, and Titus hurriedly stepped out on deck and looked aft. Flames were shooting up around the twin smokestacks just behind the

18. More than two hundred passengers and crewmembers died when the passenger steamer *Erie* caught fire and burned on August 9, 1841, while the ship was off Dunkirk, New York, on Lake Erie. With only rudimentary fire-fighting equipment aboard, and with only enough lifeboats to handle a small percentage of those aboard, Captain T. J. Titus unsuccessfully tried to beach his flaming ship. It sank well offshore, in about sixty feet of water. A passing ship rescued the twenty-seven survivors, most of who were clinging to floating wreckage. The burning of the *Erie* is portrayed in this Currier and Ives print. (Ralph Roberts Collection)

pilothouse, and the deck around the stacks was burning furiously. Before he could signal the engine room to stop the engines, the breeze caused by the ship's moving forward fanned the flames into a conflagration that quickly burned its way toward the stern.

Captain Titus hurried down to the ladies' cabin on the main deck where about a hundred life preservers were stored, but the heat there was already too intense for him to enter. The main deck was the scene of mass confusion, with scores of passengers and crewmembers crowded into the narrow space between the cabins and the rail, many running about and screaming, some on fire, some jumping overboard. Captain Titus rushed back to the wheelhouse, which was already burning, and ordered Luther Fuller, the wheelsman on watch, to steer for shore, about eight miles away.

Leaving the wheelhouse, Titus hurriedly tried to coordinate the launching of the ship's lifeboats. Someone had managed to launch one of the yawls the *Erie* carried as lifeboats, and it floated along the hull just as

Captain Titus's clothes began to smolder from the heat of the fire. He knew that if he didn't get off the deck he would be a ball of flame in a matter of seconds. At the same time, he railed at the prospect of abandoning his ship. Just then, the engineer who had been on watch in the engine room, and who had stayed at his post as long as he could, came staggering onto the deck. He was a human torch, burned so badly that he was charred black from head to foot. In seconds, the engineer disappeared in the flames that consumed most of the deck. Without further thought, Captain Titus leaped over the side into the yawl. The scene before him was nightmarish. The *Erie* was a ball of fire, and all those still aboard were being consumed by the flames. Titus would carry those images with him to his grave.

"The air was filled with shrieks of agony and despair," a survivor later recounted. "I shall never forget the wail of terror that went up from the poor German emigrants who were huddled together on the forward deck. Wives clung to their husbands, mothers frantically pressed their babes to their bosoms, and lovers clung madly to each other." The situation on the *Erie*'s stern was even worse. "There the flames were raging in their greatest fury," the survivor remembered. "Some madly rushed into the flames; others, with a yell like a demon, maddened with the flames, which were all around them, sprang headlong into the waves."[11]

Two hours after the fire began, the schooner *DeWitt Clinton,* outbound from Dunkirk, saw the flaming ship and immediately raced to her aid. Only twenty-seven persons were still alive to be rescued. Some, like Captain Titus, were in the yawl, others were clinging to floating wreckage, and a few were hanging into the water from the *Erie*'s paddle boxes. The rest were dead, smoldering clumps lying on the charred decks, or gone below the surface of the lake. Luther Fuller, the wheelsman, had stayed at his post too long. His charred remains were found in the rubble of the wheelhouse.[12]

Shortly after those aboard the *Clinton* finished their futile search for survivors, two other ships arrived at the scene. While the *Clinton* departed to return to Dunkirk with the small band of survivors, the other ships got lines aboard and began towing the still-burning hulk of the *Erie* toward shore, hoping to beach her in shallow water. While they were still well offshore, however, the burnt bones of the passenger steamer suddenly plunged toward the bottom in sixty feet of water. The water hissed and boiled where the *Erie* had disappeared, and a cloud of dirty steam hovered above the water. As the gentle lake breeze dissipated the cloud of steam, the last fragile trace of the *Erie* vanished from the lake.

The exact cause of the fire aboard the *Erie* has never been determined.

Some said that her boiler had exploded, blowing a hole in the side of the hull and setting fire to the engine room and cargo hold. Others blamed the fire on cans of paint, varnish, and turpentine the team of painters had stowed next to the two smokestacks on the upper deck. Heat from the stacks, they said, had caused the highly flammable contents of the cans to explode and burst into flames.[13]

Once the fire began, its rapid spread can no doubt be attributed in part to all the fresh paint and varnish that had been applied to the ship in the few days just before the fire. Of course, the flames were immediately fanned and spread by the breeze as the ship kept moving westward across the lake. If Captain Titus had been able to get the ship stopped, or even turned around, the spread of the fire might have been slowed.

There is no indication that anyone in the crew made any effort to battle the flames with whatever fire-fighting equipment was aboard. In those days, however, the fire-fighting equipment and lifesaving equipment required by the 1838 law was minimal. There weren't enough lifeboats to handle all those aboard the ship, and lifeboat drills and fire drills weren't required. As one observer noted, "What seem to be outrageous safety hazards were accepted as normal."[14]

Fourteen years after the destruction of the *Erie*, the sunken hull was raised and towed to shore. Salvers reportedly recovered a fortune—some say as much as $200,000—most of it in sovereigns, rubles, marks and kroner, no doubt representing the life savings of the many immigrants who died on the *Erie* that summer night in 1841, nest eggs for the hopeful lives that awaited them in their new country.[15] They were not the last immigrants whose dreams would end in the flames of a passenger steamer on the Great Lakes.

Phoenix, 1847

When the steamer *Phoenix* departed Buffalo on November 11, 1847, most of the 275 passengers aboard were Dutch immigrants. The *Phoenix* was bound for Chicago and many ports in between on what was scheduled to be its last trip of the season. While some of the passengers occupied cabins on the ship's main deck, most of the immigrants were traveling in the inexpensive steerage berths that were below the main deck. The *Phoenix* also carried freight, and the cargo deck of the 155-foot ship was loaded down with coffee, sugar, molasses, and hardware. Captain G. B. Sweet was in command, heading a crew of twenty-five.

After a long season afloat, sailors always look forward with great anticipation to the last trip of the year. At the same time, they know those last trips can be a nightmare. Late-season trips are often marked by high winds, snowstorms, bitterly cold temperatures, and even ice. It soon became obvious that the last trip of the 1847 season was going to fall into that "nightmare" category.

Not long after they had left Buffalo, things started to go wrong for the crew of the *Phoenix*. While still on Lake Erie, Captain Sweet fell down and injured his knee. He chose to remain aboard for the balance of the trip, but was in excruciating pain and confined to his bed. Then, shortly after passing through the Straits of Mackinac and onto the waters of northern Lake Michigan on November 20, the *Phoenix* encountered a fierce fall storm. The run down the west shore of the storm-tossed lake was miserable for all aboard.

To everyone's relief, the *Phoenix* finally steamed into the sheltered waters of the Manitowac River at the little port of Manitowac, Wisconsin, on November 21. While the crew set to work unloading some cargo destined for businesses in the Manitowac area, many of the passengers went uptown. After being confined in the crowded quarters on the *Phoenix* during the storm, they welcomed the opportunity to stretch their legs on dry land and get something to eat and drink. After finishing unloading, the crew filled the ship's bunkers with cordwood, fuel for the boiler fires. When that task was completed, crew and passengers alike were delighted to hear that Captain Sweet had decided to stay at the dock for several hours to let the winds and seas die down before they resumed their voyage. They finally got under way during the evening.

When the *Phoenix* was about two hours out of Manitowac, the fireman tending the boiler fires told the engineer on watch that the circulating pumps didn't seem to be supplying enough water to the boilers. Second Engineer Bill Owen ignored the fireman.

A little later, the fireman warned Owen that the water in the boilers was getting dangerously low, and he suggested they call the chief engineer. Owen said he didn't want to bother the chief.

Just before 4 A.M. on November 22, steerage passengers discovered smoke coming from the firehold, where the boilers were being stoked. Short on water, the boilers had apparently overheated to the point that woodwork nearby had burst into flames. The passengers immediately panicked, attracting the attention of the engineer and fireman then on watch. When they saw the fire, they tried to put it out, but it was spreading too fast and they were soon driven from the engine room by the smoke

19. An inattentive engineer was probably responsible for the fire that burned the passenger steamer *Phoenix* to the waterline during the early-morning hours of November 22, 1847, depicted here in a painting by William J. Koelpin. Overheated boilers apparently set fire to nearby woodwork, resulting in the conflagration that killed 258 of approximately 300 passengers and crewmembers aboard. Despite the losses resulting from the fire aboard the *Erie* six years earlier, the *Phoenix* carried only two small lifeboats. It wasn't until after the loss of the *Titanic* on the North Atlantic in 1912 that U.S. law was finally changed to require passenger ships to carry enough lifeboats and life rafts to accommodate all those aboard. (Wisconsin Maritime Museum at Manitowac)

and flames. As the untended fires died in the boilers, the *Phoenix* lost power and began to drift before the swells. The ship was then about four miles off the Wisconsin shore, between Manitowac and Sheboygan.

The first mate had been alerted, and he quickly organized the crew and passengers into a bucket brigade to battle the blaze. As flames rapidly spread throughout the ship, terrifying shouts of "Fire!" roused the passengers from their sleep and they began spilling out onto the deck. Many of them were in their underwear or sleeping clothes. In minutes, the crowded decks were the scene of mass hysteria and confusion, compounded by the babble of foreign tongues.

When the first mate reported to Captain Sweet that the fire was out of control, Sweet ordered the crew to launch the two small lifeboats carried aboard the *Phoenix*. Each boat could only carry about twenty persons, so it was going to be necessary to ferry back and forth between the burning ship and the beach. In minutes, the first boat was filled with twenty persons and it headed for the distant shore with Captain Sweet personally in charge. The second boat, with nineteen aboard, followed almost immediately, under the command of the first mate.

With flames beginning to lap up the sides of the *Phoenix*'s hull, those in the two lifeboats pulled hard for the beach, but it was slow going. The lake was still covered by big swells left over from the storm, and it was hard to keep the heavily laden boats from broaching in the seas. Further compounding the problem, few of those manning the oars were expert rowers. Before long, all those aboard were soaking wet and painfully cold.

By the time the two boats finally struggled ashore about ten miles above Sheboygan, an immediate return trip was out of the question. The sailors manning the oars were just too exhausted. Captain Sweet ordered his men to build several large bonfires on the beach so everyone could get warmed up.

Long before the lifeboats made it to the shore, the wallowing *Phoenix* was a blazing inferno, and many of those left aboard leaped into the rolling waters of Lake Michigan. Others climbed up to the hurricane deck to get above the fire, but the flames soon followed them. Some even shinnied up the ship's tall wooden masts, but the fire turned the masts into torches as the flames relentlessly climbed skyward.

Several other ships out on the lake that night saw the fire on the *Phoenix*, and they hurried to the scene. By the time they arrived, they found only three persons still alive—three crewmen who were clinging to the rudder chains of the charred hull. The lake was littered with dead bodies, and the sickeningly sweet smell of burnt flesh hung heavy in the cold air.

The steamer *Delaware* picked up the three crewmen, then took the smoldering hull in tow and headed for nearby Sheboygan. There, the *Phoenix* was beached near the north pier.

Around 258 of the estimated 300 persons aboard the *Phoenix* died in the fire or drowned in the waters of the lake. Included among the dead were most of the Dutch immigrants. The *Phoenix*, named for the mythical winged creature of ancient Egypt that was said to have risen reborn out of its own ashes, would never sail again. Too far gone to be rebuilt, she was eventually abandoned by her owners.

Some in Sheboygan would argue that the burnt steamer did have a rebirth of sorts, though. After all the burned bodies had been removed from the hull of the *Phoenix*, a local resident by the name of Jimmie Berry dug around in the charred wreckage with a hoe and shovel. Deep down in the debris near the ship's keel, Berry uncovered globs of molten gold. The gold was what was left of the money and jewelry being carried by the unlucky passengers on the *Phoenix*. It had melted in the intense heat of the fire and dripped down into the rubble.

The industrious and entrepreneurial Berry used the money to buy two dairy cows from a farmer in Ohio. It is said that they were the first cows in the village of Sheboygan.[16]

While the exact cause of the fire on the *Erie* is still the subject of debate, there is no question in the case of the *Phoenix*. The fire started because Second Engineer Bill Owen allowed the boilers to overheat. What prompted his negligence is still a mystery, though. Perhaps he went "up the street" while the boat was delayed at Manitowac and spent some of his hard-earned money in a local tavern. Any sober engineer would surely have tended to the boilers when it was discovered they were getting low on water.

While Bill Owen was clearly responsible for the fire starting, the tragic loss of life on the *Phoenix* was largely due to the lack of an adequate number of lifeboats to accommodate all those aboard. While there were about three hundred passengers and crewmembers aboard the steamer, the two lifeboats had a combined capacity of only forty. That was not unusual, however. As dangerous as the practice was, U.S. passenger ships would not be required to carry enough lifeboats and life rafts to handle all those aboard until well after the *Titanic* sank in the North Atlantic in 1912. In the more than sixty years that would pass between the burning of the *Phoenix* and the loss of the *Titanic*, it's likely that thousands of people died in shipping accidents because the vessels they were on didn't carry enough lifeboats. Even after more than fifteen hundred died on the

Titanic, operators of U.S. shipping companies had the audacity to argue against being required to add more lifeboats and life rafts.

Among those opposing the proposed legislation, known as the Seamen's Act of 1915, was the Lake Carriers' Association, the trade organization representing most of the major fleets on the Great Lakes. In his report to the membership at the end of the 1914 shipping season, William Livingstone, president of the association, expressed his hope that the proposed legislation would be permanently shelved, "as no real reason ever existed for drafting it at all."[17]

As the number of steamboats in operation continued to increase on the lakes, so did the number of boiler explosions and fires. On March 23, 1850, for example, the steamer *Troy* burst her boilers while off Bird Island in the Niagara River. Twenty-nine passengers and crewmembers were killed.[18] An even more serious boiler accident occurred less than a month later aboard the passenger and freight steamer *Anthony Wayne*.

Anthony Wayne, 1850

The chief engineer on the *Anthony Wayne* was Edward "Eureka" Elmore, described as "a gentleman of choleric disposition."[19] It is said that he had complained "long, loud, and frequently" to the ship's captain about the condition of the steamer's aging boilers. Captain Gore would like to have done something about the boilers, if for no other reason than to get Eureka off his back, but he didn't have the authority. He did regularly express the chief's concerns to Charles Howard, the Detroit businessman who owned three-quarters of the boat, but to no avail. The wooden steamer had been built in 1837 and was getting a little long in the tooth. Howard thought it was quite likely that the steamer only had a season or two left in her. Why waste any money on major repairs to the boilers?

The issue resolved itself late on the evening of April 27, 1850. Howard's steamer had left Toledo early that morning. The *Wayne* steamed east along the south shore of Lake Erie and arrived in the early afternoon at Sandusky, where she took on a cargo of three hundred barrels of wine and whiskey. Forty passengers also joined the ship, adding to the twenty-five that had boarded at Toledo. Departing Sandusky that evening, the little steamer continued her journey eastward. It was a cool night on the lake, and most passengers went to their rooms shortly after leaving the dock at Sandusky.

About three hours later, when the ship was abreast of Vermilion, Ohio, and about eight miles offshore, the *Anthony Wayne*'s starboard

20. Just over a month before the *Anthony Wayne* was destroyed by a boiler explosion, the boilers on the steamer *Troy* had exploded near Buffalo. Twenty-nine aboard the *Troy* were either killed by the explosion or died when the mortally wounded ship quickly plunged to the bottom. (Louden G. Wilson Drawing, Ralph Roberts Collection)

boiler exploded. The blast literally blew Captain Gore out of his bed. Fortunately, he was shaken, but not injured. Eureka Elmore hadn't been so lucky. On duty in the engine room when the boiler let go, the irascible engineer had been "catapulted into eternity" by the explosion. Many wondered whether the last words to cross his lips were, "I told you so!"

The explosion ripped open the *Anthony Wayne*'s hull, and she plunged to the bottom in a matter of minutes. Captain Gore and the ship's clerk managed to launch a lifeboat, and they and a handful of the passengers and crewmembers eventually drifted safely ashore near Vermilion. Sixty-four others aboard the *Anthony Wayne* weren't so lucky. Like Edward Elmore, they went down with the ship.[20]

G. P. Griffith, 1850

Less than two months later, during the night of June 16–17, 1850, the packet steamer *G. P. Griffith* made a brief stop at Fairport, Ohio, just east of Cleveland, to take on passengers. The three-year-old wooden steamboat had left Buffalo the previous morning, under the command of Captain Charles Roby of Perrysburg, Ohio. Roby had brought the ship out of the yard in 1847, and he owned a small interest in it, as did Chief Engineer Dave Stebbins. Aboard with Captain Roby for a summer vacation were his mother, wife, thirteen-year-old daughter, and infant son. There were also 256 passengers aboard, mainly German, Irish, French, and English immigrants, most of whom had boarded at Buffalo when the *Griffith* docked there on the afternoon of Saturday, June 15. After leaving Buffalo, the steamer called first at Erie, Pennsylvania, where half a dozen passengers and some cargo had been taken aboard. The ship then left for other scheduled stops at Fairport and Cleveland.

During the nighttime stop at Fairport, only two passengers were waiting for the *Griffith*. One was Stephen Woodin of the nearby village of Hambden, Ohio. Shortly after he got aboard, Hambden told William Evans, one of the *Griffith's* mates, that he thought he smelled smoke. Evans reportedly swore at Hambden and told him to mind his own business. Hambden thought the mate was drunk, but he did as he was told and went off to find his stateroom. Henry Wilkinson, the ship's sleepy-eyed clerk, recorded the boarding of the two passengers, noting that there were then 326 people aboard the vessel. It would be a profitable trip.

When the *Griffith* was only two miles out of Fairport harbor, wheelsman Dick Mann excitedly told Sam McCoit, the mate of the watch, that there were sparks coming up through the narrow gap between the smokestack and the roof of the cabins. McCoit dashed aft to the smokestack and began to pour buckets of water into the opening, but he couldn't extinguish the growing flames. Realizing that his efforts were futile, McCoit yelled for Mann to steer for shore while he rousted the crew.

After being awakened by McCoit, Captain Roby and Chief Stebbins hurried to the scene of the fire. It appeared to them that it had started in the cargo hold or at the wooden bulkhead that separated the engine room from the hold. The fire must have had a good start before it was spotted by the wheelsman, and it was spreading rapidly. As the chief engineer raced to the engine room, Captain Roby shouted for the crew to awaken everyone aboard the *Griffith*. He immediately headed for the pilothouse at the bow of the ship. When he reached the main deck, Roby was startled to see that the flames had already spread to the paddle boxes that jutted out on each side of the hull. The *Griffith's* two lifeboats hung from davits just aft of the side wheels, and the ropes from which they were suspended had already burned through and both boats had dropped into the lake.

Roby knew that the only hope then was to try to beach the boat in shallow water, standard procedure in those days.

When Chief Engineer Stebbins got down to the engine room, he found that it was rapidly being consumed by flames and was filled with heavy, black smoke. Without hesitating, he jammed the throttles into the "full ahead" position, then yelled for the watch engineer and fireman to abandon their stations and head for the deck. Stebbins followed them up and out of the fiery engine room.

When they reached the main deck, they found that it was crowded with passengers, many of whom were hysterical. Some leaped overboard, only to be swept into the thrashing paddle wheels and crushed. Others were throwing their trunks and luggage overboard in an effort to save their only worldly possessions. All the while, the big steamer churned through the calm waters of Lake Erie, closing the distance to the shore. The strong breeze caused by the movement of the ship fanned the flames, and by the time the *Griffith* ground to a jolting halt on a sandbar the fire had spread throughout the ship.

Those who had not already been killed by the flames and dense smoke began to leap overboard. Captain Roby gathered his family around him and one by one helped them climb over the gunwale and jump into the blackness of the lake. Holding his infant son in his arms, he followed them into the water.

The shoreline between Fairport and Cleveland was a sparsely populated farming area in those days, but local residents had spotted the flames of the *Griffith*. As the first soft light of dawn began to break over the lake, people began to arrive on the beach in horse-drawn wagons. The scene they found was almost beyond belief. A few survivors huddled on the sandy beach, while scores of lifeless bodies washed about in the gentle surf. More than 240 bodies would eventually be pulled from the water. Those that could be identified, including the entire Roby family, were taken to Cleveland aboard the steamer *Diamond*. The rest, including most of the immigrants, were buried in two long mass graves dug along the shore.

Bodies continued to wash ashore well into July. Many were immigrant men who had been weighted down by their "prosperity anchors," heavy money belts full of gold coins that had been intended to get them started on their new lives along the shores of the Great Lakes.[21]

In Cleveland and other communities around the lakes, the tragic loss of the *Griffith* led to a another public outcry about the dangerous conditions on passenger steamers. Resolutions were drafted and sent to Congress calling for the establishment of construction standards, better inspections of boilers and furnaces, and exams for engineers. Fuel was added to the protests at the end of July when the poorly maintained boilers on the steamer *America* exploded off New York, killing eleven. It was reported that engineers on the *America* had been operating the boilers at pressures well above safe levels when the explosion occurred.

Between December 1851 and July 1852, seven disastrous steamboat accidents in the United States had resulted in nearly seven hundred deaths. Congress was finally forced to enact stricter measures.[22] Despite strong opposition from the owners of the steamship lines and officers serving aboard the ships, the Steamboat Inspection Service was created in 1852. The new agency was headed by nine "supervising inspectors" who were appointed by the president with approval of the Congress. They supervised the local steamboat inspectors and met once a year to establish rules for the inspection and operation of steam-powered vessels.

With its cadre of salaried inspectors, the new agency took over all responsibilities for the inspection of steamboats. Prior to 1852, the inspectors performing hull and boiler inspections were actually paid directly by the shipowners, in that the fees the owners paid for inspections of their vessels were kept as compensation by the inspectors. As a result, inspectors who had a reputation for being "easy" or "cooperative" got more inspection business, and thereby made more money. On the other hand, any inspector with a reputation for being demanding or difficult found little business coming his way.

The Steamboat Inspection Service was also charged to license engineers and pilots on steam-powered passenger vessels to ensure that they were technically competent to perform their duties. The new legislation took some of the heat off, but those advocating strict controls on steamboats would soon find that the Steamboat Inspection Service was riddled by indecision, incompetence, and corruption. At the same time, boilers continued to explode with frightening regularity.[23]

Independence, 1853

The first boiler explosion on Lake Superior occurred on November 22, 1853, and involved the first steamboat to operate north of the Soo. The unlucky ship was the *Independence*, which had been laboriously hauled overland around the rapids at Sault Ste. Marie in 1845.[24] The 118-foot steamer had been built at Chicago and was originally intended to haul wheat between Chicago and Europe. After launching, it was found that she could only make four to eight miles an hour, and her fuel consumption was considerably higher than had been expected. Both factors ruled the *Independence* out of the transatlantic trade. S. McKnight & Co. then purchased the ship for service on Lake Superior.

Accounts of her sinking vary significantly, but we do know that the *Independence* left the Soo on the night of November 22 under the command of Captain John McKay. She was making what her owners expected would be a lucrative late-season run to Ontonagon, Michigan, and La Pointe, Wisconsin, carrying a heavy load of cargo and passengers. Only a mile out of the Soo, however, the steamer's boiler exploded, reportedly destroying three-quarters of the ship and sinking her almost immediately in eighteen feet of water.

Amazingly, only three crewmembers and one passenger were killed by the blast and subsequent sinking of the *Independence*. Chief Engineer George Sisson was one of those who died. In all likelihood, he had been in the engine room when the ship left the dock. Many passengers and crewmembers survived by clinging to floating wreckage, including bales of hay that had been destined to feed the horses at mining camps on the Keweenaw Peninsula. The ship was a total loss.[25]

Traveller, 1865

On August 17, 1865, the Lake Superior steamer *Traveller* was totally destroyed by fire while docked at Eagle Harbor on Michigan's Keweenaw Peninsula. The fire supposedly started from some hot coals in the engine room and spread rapidly. Passengers barely had time to escape with a portion of their baggage. Crewmembers managed to save some of the vessel's furnishings, and even a little of her cargo, but the ship burned to the waterline.[26]

The *Traveller* was one of a growing fleet of passenger and cargo steamers that began operating on Lake Superior after the original Soo Locks were opened to vessel traffic in 1855. Others included the sister ships *Meteor*, *Pewabic*, and *Lac La Belle* of the Lake Superior Line, the Goodrich steamer *Planet*, and the *Ontonagon*. It was an exciting time along the shores of Lake Superior. Many of those traveling aboard the steamers were prospectors and miners on their way to and from the rich copper mines in the Keweenaw Peninsula and the iron ore range at Marquette. Other travelers were a new breed on the upper lakes—

tourists. "Our large and justly popular propellers are gathering a fine harvest in the throngs of pleasure seekers who are fleeing from the torrid heat of down below to cool and healthful air of Lake Superior," a local newspaper observed in early August 1865.[27]

Meteor, 1865

On the same day the *Traveller* burned at Eagle Harbor, residents of the Keweenaw Peninsula were shocked to read in the Ontonagon newspaper that both the *Meteor* and the *Pewabic* had been involved in accidents. In fact, on August 9 the popular sister ships had collided with each other off Thunder Bay on northern Lake Huron. The *Pewabic* had sunk, with heavy loss of life (see Chapter 3). The *Meteor* had also sustained damage, but stayed afloat and managed to limp into Sault Ste. Marie for repairs. While she was tied up at the Soo, a fire was discovered in the hold.

The ship's fire pumps wouldn't work for some reason, and for awhile it looked as though the *Meteor*, too, would be lost. Passengers and crewmembers frantically began to try to salvage what they could from the spreading fire, throwing baggage and furniture out onto the riverbank.

The captain on the steamer *Ontonagon*, which was waiting to pass downbound through the locks, spotted the fire on the *Meteor*. The quick-thinking captain ran his ship alongside the *Meteor*, and his crewmen began pumping water into its burning cargo hold. On the *Meteor*, Captain Thomas Wilson ordered everyone off the ship and told the engineers to open the sea cocks before they left. In seconds, the *Meteor* was flooded with thousands of gallons of water that rushed in through the sea cocks. Before long, the combination of water coming in through the sea cocks and water being pumped into the cargo hold by the crew of the *Ontonagon* swamped the *Meteor* and it settled gently onto the river bottom, extinguishing the flames.

The fire was believed to have started in the cargo hold, which was filled with lime. Water that got into the hold after the *Meteor*'s collision with the *Pewabic* soaked the lime and caused it to heat up enough to set the wooden bulkheads on fire. "The fire on the *Meteor* is beyond doubt the result of carelessness of the officers," the Ontonagon newspaper reported, "and though there is only loss to the owners, they are none the less censurable." The article went on to point out that if the fire had started after the *Meteor* had left the dock at the Soo and headed out onto Lake Superior, the outcome might have been far more disastrous.[28] While no one on the *Meteor* died in the fire, those on the steamer *Seabird* weren't so lucky.

Seabird, 1868

The Goodrich Line steamer *Seabird* left Milwaukee on the evening of April 8, 1868, loaded with freight and passengers for an early-season run to Chicago. Somewhere off Waukegan, Illinois, a fire of undetermined origin broke out on the *Seabird.* It spread so fast that the lifeboats couldn't be lowered and all but three persons aboard perished, including Captain Nels Nelson. Reports on the number killed vary dramatically, from thirty-five to more than one hundred.[29]

In February 1871, Congress expanded the coverage of the Steamboat Act of 1852 to include all steamboats, not just those carrying passengers. For the first time, the change in the law required deck officers and engineers on steam-powered cargo ships to be licensed. Before the 1871 legislation, there were no minimum qualifications for officers on cargo ships, and many were undoubtedly less than completely competent.[30]

The carnage resulting from shipping accidents continued during the 1871 season despite the strengthening of the steamboat inspection laws. On the Great Lakes, thirty-one ships burned during the season, while ten were damaged or destroyed by boiler explosions.[31]

Alaska, 1879

On September 5, 1879, two engineers and a fireman were killed, and two other crewmembers suffered severe scalding that later proved fatal, when the steam dome on the boiler of the side-wheel steamer *Alaska* blew up near the mouth of the Detroit River. Eight other crewmembers were also scalded. Miraculously, only two passengers were injured—one was scalded, and a female passenger cut her hands while trying to crawl out the window of her cabin. Most of the passengers and crew jumped overboard into the Detroit River and were pulled from the water by the crew of the passing steamer *City of Detroit.* The *Alaska* remained afloat, and after being towed to Detroit by the U.S. revenue cutter *Fessenden,* it was repaired and returned to service.

Prior to the disaster, the *Alaska* had stopped at Amherstburg, Ontario, just above the mouth of the Detroit River, to take on fuel at a coal dock

21. The 191-foot wooden passenger and freight steamer *Seabird,* shown in this drawing, was destroyed by fire on the evening of April 8, 1868, while the ship was off Waukegan, Illinois. It was reported that the fire started when a new porter threw a bucket of hot ashes into the wind and they blew back onto the ship. The fire spread so fast that the *Seabird*'s lifeboats couldn't be launched, and all but three of those aboard died in the fire or drowned in the cold waters of Lake Michigan. Reports on the number who died in the tragedy vary dramatically, from 35 to 102. (Ralph Roberts Collection)

before heading across Lake Erie to its destination at Put-in-Bay, Ohio. Just before the *Alaska* finished fueling, the passenger steamer *City of Detroit* churned past, also heading across Lake Erie. When the *Alaska*'s deckhands were throwing off her lines, Captain Goldsmith asked his engineers, two brothers named Stevens, to put on a full head of steam as soon as they got under way.

Many people would later claim that Captain Goldsmith was intent on racing Captain Bill McKay and his *City of Detroit* across the lake. Word was that the two captains raced whenever they got the chance, although both later denied the claim. Despite that, many concluded that the Stevens brothers, who died in the explosion, had been so eager to please their captain that they had put on a little too much steam.[32]

The speed of ships was important in the passenger trade. Travel time was often a factor for merchants and government officials, while many other travelers were simply eager to keep the amount of time they had to be aboard the cramped and often storm-tossed ships to the absolute minimum. Travelers sought out ships that had reputations for making fast passages, and shipping companies often promoted the speed of their vessels in advertising.

After steamboats entered the ocean and Great Lakes freight and passenger trades during the first half of the nineteenth century, speed was a major factor in their rapidly growing popularity. Fast boats could make more trips and carry more passengers in a season, yielding higher profits for their owners. It's no surprise, then, that speed became a major factor in the competition between different steamboat companies. Given the importance of speed in the shipping industry, it's also no surprise that boats like the *Alaska* and *City of Detroit* would race each other. Unfortunately, those races occasionally resulted in boiler explosions.

On the Great Lakes, the most famous steamboat race was between White Star Line's *Tashmoo* and Cleveland and Buffalo Transit's *City of Erie*. The race was run over a ninety-four-mile course between Cleveland and Erie, Pennsylvania, on June 4, 1901. Thousands of spectators lined the shore of Lake Erie to watch, and the *Cleveland Plain Dealer*'s marine columnist reported that over $1 million had been wagered on the widely hyped race.

Some of the newspaper articles written prior to the race noted that boiler inspectors from the Steamboat Inspection Service would be carried aboard both the *Tashmoo* and *City of Erie,* but went into no detail regarding their roles. The inspectors were undoubtedly there to ensure that the engineers on the two ships, in their exuberance to get every last horsepower out of their engines, didn't do anything that would create a safety problem. The potential for a boiler explosion was a serious concern, and for good reason.

One of the easiest ways to make a steam engine run faster was to increase the steam pressure in the boiler and cylinders. In fact, accounts of the race reported that Chief Engineer Winfield Dubois and his crew on the *Tashmoo* had installed an extra six-inch steam line into the engine's low-pressure cylinder. If they felt it was necessary, they could force more steam into the cylinder by merely opening a valve. There were limits, of course. The boilers and engine cylinders were equipped with safety valves that would automatically vent excess steam if pressures exceeded the limits deemed to be safe. The easiest way to make the engine produce more horsepower was to tighten up the safety valves so that higher steam pressures could be achieved. The fact that boiler inspectors were present on both boats may hint at how common that practice was. A major part of their job was undoubtedly to ensure that nobody tampered with the safety valves.

The *City of Erie* won the race by forty-five seconds.[33] We don't know if Chief Dubois ever got to use the extra steam line he had installed on the *Tashmoo,* or whether the presence of the government boiler inspector made that course of action impossible. Regardless, steamboat races were common in those days . . . and boiler inspectors were seldom present to ensure that pressure limits weren't exceeded. How many boiler explosions were the result of steamboat races will never be known. Of course, we don't really have good explanations for most boiler explosions. Those who could have given us the answers—those on duty in the engine rooms—seldom survived.

Arizona, 1887

When a fire started aboard a ship that was in port, it was often a threat to the community around the docks. Such was the case with a fire aboard the Anchor Line freighter *Arizona* on November 17, 1887. The little steamer was on its last trip of the season when it departed Marquette for Portage Lake on the Keweenaw Peninsula early that morning. From there she was scheduled to go on to Superior, Wisconsin, then load for her return trip down the lake. In her hold were 1,100 barrels of cement, 900 barrels of oil, 1,100 boxes of candles, rolls of tar paper, some iron-working equipment for Captain Alexander McDougall's new shipyard at Duluth, and a number of glass containers filled with acid.

When the *Arizona* cleared Big Bay Point, northwest of Marquette, Captain George Graser found that there were heavy seas out on the lake and his ship began to pound. November is no month to be out on Lake Superior in a storm, so Captain Graser ordered the wheelsman to put the helm hard over. They would return to the dock at Marquette until the weather moderated a little. As the *Arizona* came around into the trough of the sea, it rolled badly. Even though the carboys of acid were carefully padded, one or more of the glass containers broke from the jostling they got when the ship began to roll. In minutes, a fire broke out in the hold. It quickly spread to the highly flammable oil, candles, and tar paper, and the hold was soon engulfed in roaring flames. The heavy black smoke and deadly fumes in the cargo hold made it impossible for the crew to fight the fire.

Captain Graser aimed his flaming ship at the end of the breakwall guarding the entrance to the harbor at Marquette, and passed the word

22. A tug sprays water on the flaming hull of the steamer *Arizona* at Marquette on November 17, 1887. The wooden steamer caught fire when a glass container filled with acid came loose and broke when the ship rolled in heavy seas. Captain George Graser managed to maneuver his flaming ship back to the breakwater at Marquette, then he and his crew leapt ashore. The ship continued on until it grounded alongside a dock. The *Arizona* burned for twenty-four hours, until a fireman scuttled it by chopping a hole through the hull. (Ralph Roberts Collection)

for the crew to leap onto the breakwater as soon as the *Arizona* came alongside. Graser lashed the wheel hard over as soon as the ship banged against the breakwall, and he and the wheelsman followed the rest of the crew over the side. The *Arizona*'s engine was still running "full ahead," however, and the ship continued to race along the breakwater until its bow grounded at the end of a slip. Marquette firemen rushed to the waterfront and began fighting the fire, fearing that it would spread to the adjacent lumber docks. It burned out of control for twenty-four hours, until a fireman finally chopped a hole through the planking near the *Arizona*'s waterline and the ship filled and settled to the bottom alongside the dock.[34]

About the time of the *Arizona* fire, a law was finally passed requiring steamboats to have spark catchers on their smokestacks, similar to those developed for locomotives operating in wooded areas. At Saginaw, Michigan, a ship without a spark catcher, with the appropriate name of *Odd Fellow*, was later seized and sold at auction, attesting to the importance placed on spark arrestors by the residents of port communities on the lakes. And for good reason. On five separate occasions over a ten-year period, fires spreading from the area of the docks had destroyed large sections of the lumber town of Alpena, Michigan. One fire destroyed all of the town north of the Thunder Bay River.

A ship also caused one of the worst fires in the history of East Tawas, Michigan. At about midnight on July 5, 1890, a fire was discovered aboard the *Sea Gull*. The ship had taken on a load of ice for Cleveland earlier that day, but its departure had been delayed because of bad weather.

The *Sea Gull* was tied up at the dock of the Sibley and Bearinger Lumber Company when the fire was discovered. The flames spread so fast that the crew barely made it off the ship. In fact, one crewmember, a female cook named Maggie Comett, was trapped in her room and died in the blaze.

As the fire grew in intensity, the lines mooring the *Sea Gull* to the dock either burned through or were cut, and the winds pushed the ship out into the harbor. There it bumped into the anchored steamer *Calvin*, setting it on fire. Pushed along by the wind, the flaming *Sea Gull* was then blown into docks on the other side of the harbor, setting fire to stacks of lumber. "No fireworks of human design could equal the display produced by the roaring mass of lumber," the local newspaper later reported. Before it was brought under control, the fire had spread for a mile along the shore of the harbor and set fire to an estimated sixteen million board feet of pine and hardwood lumber. Four lumber companies were burned, including their docks and lumber stacks. The lumber alone was valued at more than $300,000, a fortune at that time.[35]

Manhattan, 1903

On October 25, 1903, the wooden freighter *Manhattan* was downbound on Lake Superior with her cargo holds full of wheat when the 252-foot ship encountered a typical fall storm after passing east of the Keweenaw Peninsula. The captain took the conservative approach and altered course to seek shelter behind Grand Island, off Munising, Michigan. As the ship rode gently at anchor, the storm seemed to moderate late in the evening and the captain decided to get under way. Around midnight, while the *Manhattan* was steaming slowly out the east channel, between the island and the mainland of Michigan's Upper Peninsula, one of the steering chains broke. The little ship veered out of the channel and struck a reef.

As if the captain and crew didn't have enough problems, the impact of the collision knocked a kerosene lantern over and a fire broke out. The beleaguered crew launched the *Manhattan*'s two lifeboats and abandoned ship. They were later picked up by the steam tug *Ward.* Their ship burned to the waterline, then floated free of the reef, only to be driven on nearby Sand Point by the strong winds. Part of the J. C. Gilchrist fleet that was headquartered in Cleveland, the *Manhattan* was the seventh wooden ship the fleet had lost during the 1903 season.[36] It wasn't the last casualty that would be experienced by the Gilchrist fleet, however.

W. S. Crosthwaite, 1904

On the afternoon of November 13, 1904, the Gilchrist steamer *E. N. Saunders* and its tow, the schooner-barge *W. S. Crosthwaite,* were lying at anchor under the lee of Whitefish Point, waiting for a break in the weather. The two vessels were from different eras and presented a stark contrast. The 380-foot *Saunders* was a steel-hulled steamer, built only two years earlier at American Ship Building's yard in Lorain, Ohio. It was a relatively small freighter by the standards of the day, more than a hundred feet shorter than the latest generation of goliaths being turned out for the ore trade on the lakes. In every other way, however, it was a completely modern ship.

The *Saunders*'s consort was a different story. The thirty-one-year-old wood-hulled *Crosthwaite* had been built in Saginaw, Michigan, in 1873. It predated by almost a decade the launching of the first iron-hulled ship on the lakes, and had been in service for thirteen seasons before the first steel freighter was even launched. At just 198 feet in length and rated at only 683 gross tons, the *Crosthwaite* could have been carried in the cargo hold of one of the big new freighters . . . with room to spare. She still sported her original schooner rigging, but the sails were seldom set anymore. Well past her prime, the aging *Crosthwaite* spent most of her days dangling ignominiously at the end of a towline behind the steam-powered *Saunders.*

On that afternoon in the late fall of 1904, several of the crewmembers on the old schooner were taking advantage of the weather delay to do their laundry in the forecastle. It was a typically blustery November day, and they started a fire in a small stove to take the chill off and speed the drying of their clothes. In the middle of doing their laundry the crewmen heard the dinner bell ring, so they stopped what they were doing and went aft to eat. The cook wasn't running a diner, and you either showed up on time for meals or you didn't eat.

While the crewmen were eating, a fire broke out in the forecastle. The little stove had overheated and set fire to the tinder-dry timbers of the

Crosthwaite's hull. By the time the fire was discovered, it was too late to do anything about it. The combination of the old, dry timbers and the liberal coat of tar that had been applied to the deck in an effort to keep water out of the cargo hold and living quarters provided ample kindling for the flames. In minutes, the little *Crosthwaite* was a roaring bonfire. The small crew hurriedly launched the yawl that was carried as a lifeboat and rowed over to the *Saunders*. From there, they watched in stunned silence as their familiar old ship lit the black November sky. By morning, the only thing left of the little schooner was a disturbingly small field of charred debris floating gently on the undulating waters of Whitefish Bay.[37]

One of the worst fires in the history of the U.S. shipping industry had occurred just a month before the loss of the old *Crosthwaite* when the passenger steamer *General Slocum* burned on Long Island Sound on October 8, 1904. A total of 957 died in the blaze. Almost all of the dead were passengers. Most of the crew, including the captain, had leaped overboard before the ship was consumed by fire.

President Theodore Roosevelt ordered an investigation into the *Slocum* fire, and the resulting report placed much of the blame on the inspectors from the Steamboat Inspection Service who had been responsible for inspecting the ship and its crew. All of the inspectors who had been involved in the inspections of the *Slocum* were subsequently dismissed, and Roosevelt called for the Steamboat Act to be strengthened.

In early 1905, sections of the law related to fire protection and fire-fighting were amended. Provisions were added that specified exactly what equipment a ship had to carry. Before that, such details had been left to the discretion of the local inspectors. As a result, the inspectors and the shipowners and operators often ended up negotiating how many lifeboats or fire stations a ship had to have. By strengthening the powers of the Steamboat Inspection Service, the changes to the law in 1905 made it possible for the inspectors to firmly dictate what fire and safety equipment a ship had to carry.[38] While many steamboat inspectors began to vigorously enforce the new safety requirements, it didn't put an end to fires and boiler explosions.

E. M. Peck, 1913

One of the most spectacular boiler explosions in the history of shipping on the lakes occurred on June 11, 1913, when the boilers on the freighter *E. M. Peck* blew up while the ship was docked at Racine, Wisconsin. The powerful blast rocked the entire downtown area of the port. One of

23. The *E. M. Peck* was demolished when its boiler blew up while the ship was unloading at a dock in Racine, Wisconsin. Parts of the freighter, including one of its huge Scotch boilers, rained down on the surrounding area. Steamboat inspectors later claimed that the ship had faulty boilers, even though they had inspected the ship just prior to the explosion. (Ralph Roberts Collection)

the vessel's huge Scotch boilers was blown completely out of the hull. It ripped through the aft cabin over the engine room, hurtled the length of the deck, ricocheted off the pilothouse, and ended up in a field several hundred feet away. Seven of the *Peck*'s crew were killed instantly, including all those in the engine room. Eleven crewmembers survived. Two were ashore at the time, while the rest of the survivors were either at the bow or stern of the ship. Personnel from the nearby U.S. Life-Saving Service station quickly rescued one crewman who was blown into the water by the explosion, and they also took the other survivors off. The keeper of the lifesaving station had been standing in the window at the station and actually saw the *Peck* explode. He quickly gathered a crew and hurried to the scene in their motorized surfboat.[39] Despite the fact that the *Peck* had been gone over by steamboat inspectors, reports later claimed that the aging ship had faulty boilers.[40]

Omar D. Conger, 1922

Four crewmen also died in a boiler explosion on the ferry *Omar D. Conger* on the afternoon of March 26, 1922, while the diminutive ship

24. Firemen are seen here spraying water into the burning hull of the steamer *Nyack*. The 220-foot ship caught fire while it was being laid up for the winter at its dock in Muskegon, Michigan, on December 30, 1915. Built in 1878 and well past her prime, the thirty-seven-year-old *Nyack* was damaged beyond repair. Its hull was later cut down for use as a barge. (Ralph Roberts Collection)

was docked in the Black River at Port Huron. The blast shattered windows and knocked pedestrians to the ground for a considerable distance from the riverfront docks. Pieces of debris from the ship's engine and deck were hurtled through the air like mortar rounds. A 200-pound radiator crashed through the roof of the Falk Undertaking Parlors, where mourners had gathered for a funeral. A nearby house was demolished by a piece of the boiler. A 125-pound valve from the engine room crashed through the roof of a store. A curved piece of steel lifeboat davit was driven through the corner of a building like it was a giant sailmaker's needle. It was a miracle that the explosion and flying debris didn't injure more people.

The *Conger* was literally blown to pieces, and what remained of the demolished hull sank immediately. The subsequent investigation determined that it was likely the boiler had either run out of water or at least run dangerously low on water while crewmembers were getting the ferry ready for its next trip across the St. Clair River to Sarnia, Ontario. Apparently, someone in the engine room then opened a valve and let a stream of cold water from the river into the overheated boiler, causing the explosion. The chief engineer and fireman who were in the engine room at the time were among the dead, so there was no way to determine exactly what happened in the minutes before the explosion.[41]

25. The *Omar D. Conger* was demolished when its boiler blew up on March 26, 1922. The 93-foot ferry operated between Port Huron, Michigan, and neighboring Sarnia, Ontario, and was at its dock on the Black River in Port Huron at the time of the explosion. It was later reported that an engineer let cold river water into the *Conger*'s overheated boiler, causing it to explode. Four crewmembers were killed in the violent explosion. (Ralph Roberts Collection)

By the time the *Conger* blew up in 1922, both the number of ships operating on the Great Lakes and the number of vessel casualties were rapidly declining. A total of seventy-two ships were recorded as total losses during the 1920s, forty-two during the 1930s, and only seventeen in the 1940s. Of those, twenty-nine ships were destroyed by fires or boiler explosions, representing 22 percent of the total. With few exceptions, the ships were old wood-hulled freighters, schooners, or barges that were operating on borrowed time anyway.[42]

The worst accident during the period was the September 17, 1949, fire on Canada Steamship Lines' passenger steamer *Noronic*. The fire broke out in a linen closet just after 1 A.M. while the ship was docked overnight along the Toronto waterfront. Crewmembers tried to put the fire out, but there wasn't enough water pressure on the lines to the fire hydrants and the flames raced through the wooden interior of the ship like it was a tinderbox. Most passengers were asleep when the fire broke out and were trapped in their cabins. A total of 139 persons died in the fire, all passengers. The entire crew of 170 somehow managed to get off the ship safely.

Captain William Taylor's license was subsequently revoked for one year, and a special government court of inquiry harshly criticized him and his crew. The investigation revealed that the crew hadn't received any training in what to do in case of fire. The Canadian Coast Guard was also severely chastised for allowing the ship to operate without fireproof bulkheads or an automatic fire alarm system. The ship was a total loss, and Canada Steamship Lines eventually paid out more than $2 million to survivors and their heirs. The *Noronic* was one of three Canada Steamship Lines passenger steamers that burned between 1945 and 1950. While dockside at Sarnia, Ontario, the *Hamonic* was ignited by a fire that started in a cargo shed on July 16, 1945, and the *Quebec* caught fire on the St. Lawrence River on August 14, 1950. Amazingly, nobody died when the *Hamonic* burned, and there were only three deaths in the fire on the *Quebec*.[43] Serious fires continued to plague the Canadian fleet through the 1970s.

Imperial Hamilton, 1961

The 250-foot tanker *Imperial Hamilton* arrived at the Imperial Oil Company terminal on the St. Clair River at Sarnia, Ontario, on Sunday, September 3, 1961, to load gasoline. At 8:00 the following morning, an explosion that shattered hundreds of windows in the riverfront area and tore out a 150-foot section of the Imperial Oil dock rocked the city of Sarnia. The *Imperial Hamilton* had blown up!

When firefighters and curious residents rushed to the riverfront, they found that the stern half of the tanker had turned into a ball of fire, the flames being fed by four thousand barrels of gasoline that had already been loaded into the after holds of the tanker. It was late afternoon before the raging fire could be brought under control, and by then the *Imperial Hamilton* was nothing more than a burned-out hulk. Most of the thousands of spectators who watched the fire from the Sarnia waterfront or from across the river in Port Huron, Michigan, were amazed when they learned that none of the crew aboard the tanker had been killed by the explosion and fire. In fact, only five crewmen had been injured, and two of those didn't even require hospitalization.

The destruction to the Imperial tanker was so complete that it was impossible for investigators to determine exactly what had caused the

26. A Coast Guard boat surveys the still-burning hulk of Canada Steamship Lines' passenger steamer *Hamonic*, four years before the *Noronic* burned at Toronto. The ship had been loading cargo at Canadian National Railway's freight sheds on the St. Clair River at Sarnia, Ontario, on July 17, 1945, when a forklift backfired and set fire to the sheds. The blaze quickly spread to the *Hamonic*. Miraculously, the 230 passengers and crewmembers aboard the steamer all managed to get off the burning ship, though many were seriously burned. Those aboard CSL's *Noronic* weren't so lucky. One hundred and thirty-nine passengers died in that blaze on September 17, 1949. (Ralph Roberts Collection)

explosion. Imperial Oil officials speculated that the hot, humid weather of the early September day had prevented the gasoline vapors from escaping into the atmosphere. Instead, the highly flammable fumes collected in the empty cargo holds and possibly even found their way into work spaces and living quarters. Gradually, the tanker had become a gaseous bomb. All it would have taken to set it off was a tiny spark.[44]

Cartiercliffe Hall, 1979

At 3:53 A.M. on June 5, 1979, Albert Normand was on his way to work as the 4-to-8 wheelsman aboard the diesel-powered freighter *Cartiercliffe Hall.* It wasn't a long trip for Normand. His room was on the main deck level of the ship's cabin—properly referred to as the "spar deck"—while his duty station was in the pilothouse, just two decks up.

Normand's ship was a 730-foot Canadian bulk freighter owned by the Hall Corporation of Montreal. It had been built in Hamburg, Germany, in 1960 for an offshore subsidiary of U.S. Steel. They had operated it in the ocean trades as the *Ruhr Ore* until it was purchased in 1977 by the Hall fleet. Hall had the ship converted for service in the iron ore and grain trades on the Great Lakes, including having it lengthened and widened to the maximum dimensions that could be accommodated by the locks of the Welland Canal and St. Lawrence Seaway. During conversion, a two-story cabin structure that had been located amidships was moved to the poop deck at the stern of the ship. That consolidated all accommodations, galley facilities, and the pilothouse over the engine room in a configuration that was gaining in popularity on the lakes.

The main deck level of the resulting three-story deckhouse contained the galley, messrooms, recreation room, laundry room, a workshop for the deck department, and rooms for unlicensed crewmembers. One deck up, on the poop deck level, were accommodations for the deck and engine officers, including the captain and chief engineer. The top deck of the cabin structure was the ship's pilothouse.

Normand's ship had loaded 24,830 long tons of yellow corn at Superior, Wisconsin, the previous day. It departed the dock at 2:45 in the afternoon for the long trip down the lakes and out the St. Lawrence Seaway to Port Cartier, Quebec. As Normand prepared to go on watch the morning of July 5, his ship was about midway across Lake Superior, eleven miles off the tip of Michigan's Keweenaw Peninsula.

In the predawn darkness of that calm, quiet June morning, Normand was heading for the spar deck stairwell that would take him up to the pilothouse when he encountered Colin Springer, the 4-to-8 mechanical assistant.[45] They often passed each other when they were going on watch—Normand on his way to the pilothouse, Springer on his way down to the engine room. This morning Springer appeared visibly shaken. "There's a fire in my room!" Springer exclaimed.

Normand grabbed a fire extinguisher off the bulkhead in the passageway and hurried toward Springer's room, located off the portside passageway, near the front of the deckhouse. Heavy, black smoke was already billowing out of the room and rapidly filling the corridor. Choking on the smoke, Normand retreated to the messroom near the rear of the deckhouse. There he found Roger and Raymond Dufour having coffee. Roger Dufour, the 12-to-4 watchman, was just coming off watch, and Raymond was his relief. Normand told them about the fire.

The two Dufours immediately left the messroom, with Normand close behind. They noticed that the port and athwartship passageways were already filled with smoke, which was even then spilling over into the starboard passageway. The three quickly made their way down the starboard corridor and out the door leading to the deck. There was an intercom station located at the winch controls just outside the cabin, and Roger Dufour pressed the "talk" button on the intercom and shouted, "Fire, fire, fire!"

In the pilothouse, two decks above, Second Mate James Hancock and Wheelsman Jean Marc Pruneau were just settling into what they fully expected to be an uneventful midlake watch when they heard Roger Dufour shouting over the intercom. Without hesitation, Hancock feathered the ship's variable-pitch propeller to take the way off the vessel. That would minimize the chance that the breeze created by the ship's movement would fan the fire. As Hancock reached for the telephone to call the captain's room, Pruneau began pushing the button to sound the general alarm. In the few seconds it took them to accomplish those actions, the pilothouse was already rapidly filling with dense smoke that was billowing up the open stairwell. After Pruneau had pushed the general alarm button a half dozen times, he and Hancock were forced to evacuate the smoke-filled pilothouse.

In the engine room, Jean Claude Langlois, the mechanical assistant on the 12-to-4 watch, was waiting to be relieved by Colin Springer. Fifteen minutes earlier, Langlois had gone up to Springer's room to make sure his relief was awake. As Langlois killed time waiting to be relieved, he suddenly smelled smoke and immediately alerted Be Van Trang, the engineer on watch. Together, they made a quick check of the engine spaces, but found nothing. Trang then called the pilothouse, but got no answer. Instantly, Trang knew there was a problem aboard the ship, and he started up the fire pump that supplied high-pressure water to the numerous fire hydrants located throughout the vessel.

While Trang started the fire pump, Langlois went up the ladder that led to main deck. When he opened the door to the athwartship passageway, searing flames shot through the door, setting his clothes on fire. Slamming the door, Langlois turned to retreat down the ladder, but he slipped and fell to the lower deck, breaking his ankle.

Fearing that they would be trapped in the engine room, Trang helped the hobbling Langlois up a second ladder leading to the main deck. Again, they found their escape blocked by fire. With the engine room rapidly filling with smoke, the now-desperate Trang and Langlois struggled up the ladder inside the casing of the smokestack until they were at the level of the top of the poop deck. Exiting through a security door on the starboard side of the stack, the two finally found themselves out in the cool, clean air. Nearby, Jim Hancock was struggling to free a life raft from its mountings. Quickly, they leaped to assist him, and together the three managed to dump the raft over the side. Trang and Langlois jumped into the water and climbed aboard the raft, while Hancock went forward and down the ladder to the spar deck at the front of the deckhouse.

On the deck forward of the deckhouse, Hancock found sixteen other crewmembers who had escaped from the deckhouse. Most had found it impossible to exit their rooms through the system of interior passageways and had been forced to climb out their portholes. All were looking up in amazement at the cabin structure, which was totally engulfed in flames.

Captain Raymond Boudreault, who had escaped his room wrapped in a blanket, took charge of the assembled group, instructing Jim Hancock and two other crewmembers to launch the portside lifeboat and life raft. Once in the water, they were towed up the side of the ship and tied off near the bow, as far from the fire as possible.

Captain Boudreault ordered the rest of the crew to break out three fire hoses and begin putting water on the fire. For the next forty-five minutes, the crew directed strong streams of water at the flames that raged throughout the cabin structure. By then, it was obvious to all that their efforts were totally futile. At about 5 A.M., Captain Boudreault ordered his crew to abandon ship.

One by one, the crewmembers climbed down into the waiting lifeboat. Captain Boudreault was the last to leave the deck of the *Cartiercliffe Hall*. Once he was in the lifeboat, they rowed slowly away from their burning ship. Only nineteen of the crew of twenty-five were accounted for—seventeen in the lifeboat and Trang and Langlois in the raft that had been launched previously. Six of their shipmates were missing, including Colin Springer.

Unknown to the crew, rescuers were already on their way to the *Cartiercliffe Hall*'s location. Even though Jim Hancock and Jean Pruneau had fled the pilothouse without broadcasting a distress call, crewmen aboard an upbound freighter had seen the burning ship. At 4:50 A.M., just minutes before Captain Boudreault ordered his men to abandon ship, the first mate on the *Thomas W. Lamont* had made a radio call to the U.S. Coast Guard station in Hancock, Michigan, to report that a ship was on fire off the Keweenaw. The *Lamont* immediately altered course to head for the stricken vessel. Other freighters in the vicinity—the American *Arthur B. Homer, P. D. Block,* and *A. H. Ferbert* and the Canadian *Louis R. Desmarais*—also headed for the burning ship.

The Coast Guard quickly launched rescue efforts. The cutter *Mesquite* was dispatched from its station in Duluth, Minnesota, a twenty-one-foot rescue boat got under way from the station in Hancock, and a helicopter left for the scene from the Coast Guard air station in Traverse City, Michigan.

The *Lamont*, the first ship to reach the scene, arrived at 5:40 A.M. They picked up the seventeen survivors aboard the lifeboat and notified the Coast Guard of the name of the vessel. The two men aboard the life raft were picked up a few minutes later by the crew of the *Desmarais*. As the other vessels arrived, they began to search the water for survivors who might have jumped into the water from the burning ship. None were found.

The first Coast Guard helicopter from Traverse City was on the scene at 8:28 A.M. It evacuated three injured crewmen who had been taken aboard the *Lamont*, including Captain Boudreault, who had been burned over 30–39 percent of his body. A short while later, a second helicopter arrived and took Be Van Trang and Jean Langlois off the *Desmarais*. Langlois had the broken ankle, and both men had extensive burns. The remaining fourteen survivors aboard the *Lamont* were ferried to the village of Copper Harbor, at the tip of the Keweenaw Peninsula, by a Coast Guard Auxiliary vessel.

That evening, a U.S. Coast Guard fire-fighting team went aboard the *Cartiercliffe Hall*. They were assisted by crewmen from two U.S. Coast Guard vessels and the *Griffon*, a Canadian Coast Guard icebreaker that had rushed to the scene from Thunder Bay, Ontario. The fire was at that time burning itself out, but Coast Guard personnel wanted to cool the deckhouse down so they could search for the crewmen who were still missing.

Shortly after midnight on June 5, the smoldering hulk of the *Cartier-cliffe Hall* was lashed alongside the *Doan Transport*, a Hall tanker, and with the assistance of the tug *Peninsula*, the crippled ship was towed to Thunder Bay, Ontario. It arrived there at 11 A.M. on June 6, and both U.S. and Canadian officials conducted an exhaustive inspection the following day.

The bodies of the six missing crewmen were found and removed. Four of them had died in their cabins of a combination of carbon monoxide poisoning and burns. A fifth crewmember was found in the ship's laundry room, where he had apparently been trapped by the flames. The body of Colin Springer, in whose room the fire may have started, was found in a room at the aft end of the deckhouse that housed the anchor windlass.

27. The superstructure of the Canadian freighter *Cartiercliffe Hall*, seen here tied up in Thunder Bay, Ontario, was totally destroyed by fire on June 5, 1979. Seven of the ship's twenty-five crewmembers died as a result of the blaze that started in the crew quarters on the main deck and quickly engulfed the entire cabin. Even though the ship was built in 1960, much flammable wood had been used in its construction. Hall Corporation of Canada had acquired the boat in 1977, and though they had extensively remodeled it for service on the lakes, they didn't bother to remove the flammable wood in the cabin area. (Ralph Roberts Collection)

The inspection team found that fire damage had been confined to the deckhouse, from the spar deck up to the pilothouse. Everything within the deckhouse was consumed, except for the steel decks and steel exterior bulkheads. Virtually everything else within the deckhouse had been constructed of pressed wood panels. That included walls, dropped ceiling, doorways, and stair treads leading from deck to deck.

Because the damage was so extensive, investigators were unable to determine where or how the fire started. Colin Springer was a heavy smoker and may have accidentally started the fire as he was getting ready to go on watch. The crewman in the room adjoining Springer's was also a heavy smoker, however, and the fire could have started in his room and spread to Springer's. It was found that open cans of paint had been left in the deck department's workshop, adjacent to Springer's room. Once the fire spread that far, the highly flammable paint undoubtedly ignited and greatly accelerated the blaze.

The fire burned rapidly through the dry wooden walls and ceilings on the spar deck level, then spread to the two upper decks through the stairwells. Surviving crewmembers told investigators that the wooden doors at the tops and bottoms of the stairwells leading from deck to deck were generally left open, so there was nothing to impede the progress of the fire. Not that the wooden doors on the stairwells would have slowed the fire much.

There were no smoke detectors in the cabin area of the *Cartiercliffe Hall,* and it didn't have any sort of sprinkler system. The Canadian Coast Guard then required neither, even though the ship's cabins were mainly flammable wood.

Third Mate Paul Boisvert became the seventh victim of the fire aboard the *Cartiercliffe Hall.* Badly burned in the fire, Boisvert was evacuated by helicopter to the burn center at the University of Michigan Hospital in Ann Arbor, Michigan. He died there on June 14 of massive infections resulting from his burns.[46]

A fire like the one that gutted the cabin area of the *Cartiercliffe Hall* would be virtually impossible on a ship built since the 1960s. The use of highly flammable building materials, like wood, is no longer allowed in ship construction, even as trim or accents.

Unfortunately, many of the ships operating on the lakes were built prior to the imposition of the rigid fire safety standards. Like the *Cartiercliffe Hall,* they often have wooden walls, fixtures, and doors in their cabin areas that would provide an ample supply of fuel if a fire started. When the stricter fire standards went into effect, the Coast Guard didn't force owners of older ships to retrofit them, or even to equip them with sprinkler systems. So far—knock on wood—none have had a major fire.

One modern freighter did have a serious fire, but it was limited to the ship's engine room. On October 27, 1986, a fuel line to one of diesel engines on the 1,000-foot *James R. Barker* broke and diesel fuel spewing out of the broken pipe caught fire. Before engineering personnel discovered the fire, the port engine room was fully engulfed in flames and the fire had spread to electrical panels on the deck above.

Once the fire was discovered, a quick-thinking crewmember used an emergency fuel shutoff to stop the flow of diesel fuel that was feeding the fire, and it was quickly brought under control. One massive 8,000-horsepower engine and much auxiliary machinery had to be replaced, however, and the multimillion-dollar repair job kept the *Barker* out of service for a considerable time.

The constant vibration of the powerful diesel engines caused the broken fuel line.[47] Most diesel-powered ships experience similar problems, to one degree or another. Leaks in fuel lines are common, but the *Barker* is so far the only ship that has had a major fire as a result. A leak in a fuel line of another sort was responsible, however, for one of the most dramatic fires ever on the American side of the lakes.

Jupiter, 1990

On Sunday morning, September 16, 1990, the tanker *Jupiter* was moored at the Total Petroleum dock on the Saginaw River at Bay City, Michigan, with its bow facing downstream. The ship, operated by the Cleveland Tankers subsidiary of Ashland Oil, was in the process of unloading 2.3 million gallons of gasoline it had taken on the previous day at a Sunoco refinery in Sarnia, Ontario. First Mate Pete Walton was on watch and supervising the unloading operations on deck. Chief Engineer Charlie Prescott was in the engine room, just beginning his day's work. A number of crewmembers who had gotten off watch at 8 A.M. were in the messroom eating breakfast. Others in the seventeen-person crew were asleep in their quarters on the stern of the 392-foot ship.

At about 8:30 A.M., Pete Walton noticed the self-unloader *Buffalo* approaching around a bend in the river, and he instructed his men in the deck gang to shut down pumping operations until it passed. There were only about 50,000 gallons of gasoline left in the ship's tanks at the time.

Loaded with 17,000 tons of coal, the 635-foot *Buffalo* was on its way to a dock farther up the busy commercial waterway. In the pilothouse high atop the freighter's stern cabin, Captain John MacFalda had seen the *Jupiter* and slowed his ship to only two to three miles an hour so it wouldn't suck the tanker away from the dock when they passed. The wind was setting the *Buffalo* over toward the riverbank opposite the *Jupiter*, so MacFalda held a course just to the left of the center of the river, about sixty feet off the tanker.

Walton and the crewmen working on the deck of the tanker were still scrambling to close all the valves on the pipes leading to the massive liquid cargo tanks within the *Jupiter*'s hull when the *Buffalo* inched past. None of the crewmembers on the *Jupiter* were manning the winches that controlled the heavy steel mooring cables that ran from the bow and stern of the ship to the rather dilapidated Total dock. Apparently, none of them noticed that there was about fifteen feet of slack in the mooring wire at the bow. Because of that, the *Jupiter* was largely being held in place by its stern mooring cable and the large-diameter, heavy rubber hose that ran between the piping on the tanker's deck and the pipeline ashore. Both mooring cables were fastened around large wooden pilings at the ends of the dock. Since the dock was shorter than the *Jupiter*, it was impossible to stretch the cables out very far, and both ran only a short distance from the hull to the nearby pilings.

The slow-moving *Buffalo* was making barely more than a ripple on the surface of the river as it passed, but the ship displaced many thousands of tons of water that were forced out toward the tanker. When the water pushed out by the *Buffalo* hit the hull of the *Jupiter*, the force drove the tanker backward about fifteen feet, putting a tremendous strain on the stern wire and the piping that ran between the ship and the fuel storage tanks on the shore. The strain of trying to hold back the tremendous weight of the *Jupiter* was too much for the rotting piling the stern wire was attached to, and the piling snapped in half. As the stern mooring cable dropped into the river, most of the force of the surging ship was transferred to the piping that connected the *Jupiter* to the shoreside terminal.[48]

The piping was dragged several feet along the dock, and Pete Walton noticed gas leaking out of the shoreside pipeline, just back from the shutoff valve at its end. In no more than the time it takes to gasp a deep breath, Walton saw an electrical spark at the base of the valve. Almost immediately there was the bluish flash of a second spark, and the gasoline leaking from the pipeline ignited. Like a flame racing along a fuse in a stick of dynamite, the fire instantly spread to the *Jupiter*'s rubber unloading pipe . . . then to the piping on the deck of the ship . . . then to the voluminous tanks inside the hull, filled then mainly with highly explosive gasoline vapors.[49]

Inside the Elbow Lounge, a quarter of a mile from the *Jupiter*, owner Bob Cnudde heard what he thought sounded like three loud claps of thunder: "Boom! Boom! Boom!"[50] In the bridgetender's office on the nearby Independence Bridge, Gary Keipert heard what he thought were three immense sonic booms and threw himself to the floor.[51] The deck of the *Jupiter* burst into flames that soared as much as one hundred feet into the air.

In the pilothouse of the *Jupiter*, Captain David Beckwith activated the general alarm bells, then hurriedly radioed the Coast Guard station that was located about two miles away at the mouth of the river. "The *Buffalo* pulled us off the dock," he said, "and we're engulfed in flames."[52] In minutes, a Coast Guard boat was racing to the scene, along with a number of private yachts owned by members of the Coast Guard Auxiliary. Local fire departments were also alerted, and trucks were quickly dispatched to the scene.

28. A Coast Guard helicopter circles overhead as flames and dense black smoke billow out of the hull of the tanker *Jupiter* after it blew up while unloading gasoline at a dock on the Saginaw River on September 16, 1990. A spark ignited gasoline vapors in the tanker's cargo hold after a passing freighter pulled it away from the dock and damaged the piping connecting the *Jupiter* to a pipeline on the shore. One crewmember drowned after leaping overboard to escape the rapidly spreading fire. By the time the fire was finally extinguished three days later, the 392-foot tanker was a total loss. (Bernie Eng, *Saginaw News*)

The crew of the *Jupiter* mustered on the stern. Chief Engineer Prescott and the men in the engine room climbed up a ladder that led to an escape hatch on the main deck. "When I first climbed out, I looked toward shore and the pilings the boat was moored to were on fire," Prescott said. "There was so much smoke that you couldn't see hardly anything. The fire was almost instantly out of control."[53]

Captain Beckwith calmed his men and carefully surveyed the situation. With the minimal fire-fighting equipment they had aboard, it was obvious that it would be futile to attempt to extinguish the fire. With the fire spreading rapidly across the deck of the tanker, Beckwith made the decision to abandon ship when he heard the sound of the siren on an approaching Coast Guard rescue boat. One crewman went aft to the flagpole on the *Jupiter*'s stern and lowered the American flag, then everyone jumped over the side of the ship and into the water. Some of the men didn't have lifejackets on.

As the men leaped into the water, the people on several pleasure boats circling near the *Jupiter* heard yells of "I can't swim, I can't swim!" Quickly, those aboard the Coast Guard and Coast Guard Auxiliary craft began pulling the tanker's crew from the water. Sixteen were rescued. One crewmember, forty-six-year-old Tom Sexton, drowned while trying to swim ashore. His body was recovered three days later.

Dozens of fire-fighting units were soon on the scene, some called in from as far away as Detroit, trying to keep the blaze from spreading to the thirty fuel storage tanks located near the burning *Jupiter*. As soon as Ashland Oil was alerted to the situation in Bay City, they arranged for one of the famous "Boots and Coots" oilfield fire-fighting teams to be flown in from Texas to help extinguish the fire. Even with their assistance, it took three days to put the fire out, at a cost of about $6.1 million. The fourteen-year-old *Jupiter*, totally destroyed by the fire, was valued at around $5 million.[54]

Even after the fire had been put out, the Coast Guard issued a ban on vessel traffic in the area of the *Jupiter*, fearing that the thousands of gallons of gasoline still aboard the burnt-out hulk could ignite or explode. The *Buffalo* and many pleasure boats that were above the fire site were trapped, prevented from traveling down the river. When American Steamship Company, owners of the *Buffalo*, were informed that their ship wouldn't be able to go down the river to Saginaw Bay until all the remaining fuel had been removed from the *Jupiter*, they ordered Captain MacFalda and his crew to lay the ship up. Those aboard were either reassigned to other ships in the American Steamship fleet or laid off.

A Florida salvage firm was hired by Ashland Oil to pump out the gasoline still in the *Jupiter*'s holds and remove the warped and mangled hull, which had settled to the bottom of the river. That operation took more than a month, and the river wasn't opened to vessel traffic again until October 20. The hull of the *Jupiter*, partially dismantled in the salvage process, was later cut up for scrap.[55]

Long before the blackened hull of the tanker had been removed from its resting place alongside the Total Petroleum dock, charges and countercharges had begun to fly. Only three days after the explosion and fire, attorneys for Ashland Oil informed officials at American Steamship that the *Buffalo* was being held responsible for the damage to the *Jupiter*. An official of the Michigan Department of Natural Resources charged that the mooring posts at the Total dock were rotten and "had the consistency of balsa wood."[56] An attorney representing crewmembers on the *Jupiter* also blamed the disaster on the American Steamship freighter, charging that the *Buffalo* "had a cowboy at the wheel."

The outspoken attorney also stated that Chief Engineer Charlie Prescott had written the management at Cleveland Tankers in 1984 to complain that the fire-fighting equipment on the *Jupiter* was so obsolete that the ship would never survive a major cargo fire. Prescott had pointed out that the tanker didn't have equipment that would fill empty areas of the cargo holds with an inert gas as the ship was unloaded, to prevent the buildup of explosive vapors. "It confirms the wanton recklessness that Cleveland Tankers engaged in, allowing these men to sail on a floating time bomb," concluded the attorney for the crew. A spokesperson for Cleveland Tankers responded by noting that all of the equipment aboard the *Jupiter* met or exceeded Coast Guard requirements.[57]

Coast Guard hearings into the sinking stretched on for seven days. As one observer put it, "The witnesses spent 7 days describing a fire and explosion that happened in a minute and a half."[58]

The report of the Coast Guard investigation wasn't released until more than a year later. "The inadequacy of the mooring facilities was the main cause of the accident," the investigators concluded. The dock was too small to allow ships like the *Jupiter* to moor securely, and it had not been properly maintained.

The *Jupiter*'s crew and the captain of the *Buffalo* also shared in the blame. The crew of the tanker had used poor procedures to hold their ship in place when the *Buffalo* passed, although that was partially understandable since they had no advance notice of the approach of the freighter. Captain MacFalda of the *Buffalo* had to share in the blame for passing so close, yet the Coast Guard investigators said it was "difficult to question his judgment in hindsight," given the fact that the wind was setting his slow-moving ship across the river as he passed the *Jupiter.*

Another contributing factor in the explosion and fire was the fact that the flame screens over the *Jupiter*'s cargo tanks were ineffective. The screens are designed to prevent sparks or flames from entering the cargo holds. Gaps had been left in those on the *Jupiter* so that crewmembers could drop a tape down into the tanks to measure how much they held, and those gaps made the flame screens virtually useless. The problem with the screens should have been caught, either by employees of Cleveland Tankers or by the Coast Guard personnel who had inspected the tanker.[59]

The Coast Guard said the explosion and fire on the *Jupiter* were "unprecedented on the Great Lakes," particularly during the modern era of shipping.[60] Tankships and tank barges have been operating on the lakes since the early part of the century. While their crews, owners, and government maritime agencies have all been well aware of the inherent threat of fire and explosions on tankers carrying highly flammable cargoes, there have still been a surprisingly high number of casualties—and when there's a fire or explosion on a tanker, it tends to be extremely destructive. In addition to the *Jupiter* and *Imperial Hamilton,* seven other tankers either blew up or burned between the 1930s and 1990.[61]

Tankers aren't the only ships on the Great Lakes that have to be concerned about the potential for explosions. In 1936 the Canadian canaller *Calgadoc* disappeared without a trace somewhere near where the St. Lawrence River and Atlantic Ocean merge. The little freighter, designed to be small enough to fit through the locks of the Welland Canal, was carrying a load of coal from Sydney, Nova Scotia, to Montreal at the time of her disappearance. The coal loaded in Nova Scotia had a bad reputation with crewmen on the ships that hauled it. It was a low-grade product known as "Sydney slack" that was infamous for giving off highly explosive methane gas. A number of canallers had apparently experienced cargo hold explosions when carrying Sydney coal. As a result, some of the ships that regularly hauled the stuff were eventually fitted with special ventilators on their decks to allow the methane to escape, instead of building up to dangerous levels in their cargo holds.[62]

In 1944, Pittsburgh Steamship's 611-foot *John Hulst* experienced a methane explosion while passing through the Straits of Mackinac with a load of coal. The blast, which was heard twelve miles away, blew off a number of hatch covers. The *Hulst* went into Mackinac City for an inspection and the installation of temporary hatch covers. She then went on to unload at Lorain, Ohio, before a visit to the Great Lakes Engineering Works shipyard on the Detroit River for permanent repairs. Shipyard officials later said that if all of the hatch clamps had been tightly secured, the explosion may well have blown out the sides of the ship.[63] To prevent explosive gases from building up in the cargo holds of their ships, Pittsburgh Steamship officials had small round vents installed on the single-piece hatch covers on many of their ships. The vent lids could be opened to vent the cargo holds during summer months when hot weather was likely to cause dangerous quantities of methane to escape from coal. Ships with telescoping hatch covers apparently didn't have problems with gas buildup, since the gaps between the leaves of the hatch covers allowed the gases to escape.[64] While the hatch cover vents apparently worked effectively, not every shipping company bothered to install them.

On September 15, 1986, Columbia Transportation's steamer *Middletown* experienced a methane explosion while it was downbound on Lake Michigan, off Port Washington, Wisconsin. The flash explosion occurred in a storeroom just aft of the cargo hold where Chief Engineer Stanley Chapin and Assistant Engineer Jack Morrill were working. Both of the engineers were seriously injured and subsequently died.

The *Middletown* had taken on the load of Appalachian bituminous coal two days earlier at Conrail's loading dock at Ashtabula, Ohio. Not long after the ship cleared Ashtabula there was an explosion and fire in the loading elevator at the dock, and two dockworkers were burned to death. It was suspected that the explosion had been caused by a buildup of methane gas. Unfortunately, no one thought to warn ships that had recently loaded at Ashtabula that the coal they were carrying contained potentially dangerous levels of the highly explosive gas.

Coast Guard personnel boarded the *Middletown* before it unloaded at Port Washington to conduct an investigation into the cause of the explosion. They found that dangerous concentrations of methane gas were still present in the ship's cargo hold. Almost immediately, the Coast

Guard issued a safety advisory to vessel owners, shipboard personnel, and terminal operators, warning them about the gas hazard.[65]

Methane is perhaps even a more serious threat to modern self-unloaders like the *Middletown* than it was to straight-deck bulk freighters like the *Calgadoc* and *Hulst*. On a self-unloader there's no way to prevent gas from seeping out of the cargo hold through the unloading gates that run along the bottom of the hold. Once the gas has leaked into the unloading tunnel under the cargo hold, it can easily filter into the engine room area at the stern or the forepeak areas at the bow—areas where crewmembers are not expecting dangerous concentrations of explosive gases. Unfortunately, the Coast Guard doesn't require coal-carrying ships like the *Middletown* to be equipped with gas sensors in locations that are likely to fill with explosive gases if they get a bad load of coal. Methane gas is apparently not seen as a serious enough problem at this point.

Looking Back

The age of steam propulsion began in 1807 with the first voyage of Robert Fulton's *Clermont*. The first passenger steamers on the Great Lakes, the *Frontenac* and *Ontario,* went into service in 1817, and by 1824 the problem of boiler explosions on early steamboats had already attracted the attention of members of Congress. That was six years before the *Peacock* became the first ship on the Great Lakes to experience a boiler explosion.

By 1838 the carnage resulting from boiler explosions led to the passage of the country's first marine safety legislation. That statute required passenger-carrying steamers to employ licensed engineers, have their boilers inspected every six months, and be equipped with lifeboats, fire pumps, and fire hoses.

When the number of boiler explosions and devastating fires on steamboats continued to increase, Congress enacted the Steamboat Act in 1852, establishing the Steamboat Inspection Service and strengthening marine safety requirements. Fire safety provisions of the Act were further strengthened in 1905. In 1915, the Seamen's Act expanded marine safety coverage to include all steam-powered vessels, not just those carrying passengers, and began to move the country toward a "boats for all" policy which would ensure that passenger ships carried enough lifeboats and life rafts to accommodate all those aboard. While laws and regulations dealing with boiler explosions and fires on ships were continually strengthened over the years, the most sweeping changes in fire safety requirements were implemented after the devastating *Morro Castle* fire off the East Coast in 1934.

The continuing government attention to the problems of boiler explosions and fires in the maritime industry undoubtedly had some impact. Without the forced improvements in boiler construction, better safety equipment, licensing requirements for marine engineers, and shipboard inspections, there would surely have been additional boiler explosions and fires. At the same time, despite the intense government action, boiler explosions and fires continued to be serious problems for the industry.

Boiler explosions resulted either from faulty boilers or from the faulty operation of the boilers. Inspections were intended to eliminate the first problem, while licensing requirements for marine engineers were supposed to deal with the second. We know, however, that while requirements for boiler inspections were enacted in 1838, inspection efforts were often seriously lacking and many ships were allowed to operate with defective boilers. As late as 1913, for example, there's strong evidence that the explosion on the *E. M. Peck* was the result of faulty boilers.

Licensing requirements for marine engineers also proved to be largely unsuccessful in eliminating human error or negligence in the operation of boilers. That was just as clear in the deadly boiler explosion on the *Omar D. Conger* in 1922 as it had been in the case of the devastating fire on the *Phoenix* in 1847. Licensing may eliminate some people who don't have the knowledge necessary to serve as marine engineers, but it does little to affect human behavior.

In order to have a fire, you need only two things: fuel—something that will burn—and a source of ignition. On ships built before the 1960s there was an abundance of both. As a result, shipboard fires have been a serious problem throughout most of the industry's history, despite the many fire safety programs imposed by the government.

Fires were a *fait accompli* as long as wood was used extensively in the construction of ships. Fires could be ignited by overheated boilers, hot ashes or sparks from the boilers, overturned kerosene lamps, galley stoves fueled by wood or coal, carelessly discarded cigars or cigarettes, or even arson.

As iron and steel began to replace wood in the construction of ships, the incidence of fires began to decline. The Union Dry Dock Company of Buffalo, New York, and Frank Wheeler and Company of West Bay City, Michigan, were both major builders of wood, iron, and steel ships between

Fires and Boiler Explosions *139*

1871 and 1907. The two shipyards built a total of ninety-six wooden ships and seventy-six iron and steel ships. Nineteen of the wooden ships, 20 percent, were eventually destroyed by fire. Only groundings claimed a larger percentage of the wooden ships built at the two yards. None of the iron and steel ships succumbed to fire.[66]

While iron and steel began to replace wood in the construction of ships in the 1880s, wood-hulled ships could be found on the lakes right up until World War II. Even after that time, there were still many steel-hulled ships on the lakes that had enough wood in their cabins to create an obvious fire hazard, like the *Hamonic, Noronic,* and *Cartiercliffe Hall.*

Interestingly, as early as 1906—well before the *Hamonic, Noronic,* and *Cartiercliffe Hall* were built—shipbuilders knew what they had to do in order to reduce the potential for ships to burn. When the Potomac River excursion steamer *Jamestown* was built at Newport News, Virginia, in 1905, for example, her owners and builders went to extraordinary lengths to make her fireproof. After inspecting the 262-foot ship, one naval architect wrote that "the amount of combustible material has been limited to an extent . . . that the chances of a fire are greatly reduced."[67] Most shipowners and shipbuilders were slow to embrace that knowledge, however. It was a simple matter of economics: even though wood was highly flammable, it was cheaper than more fire-resistant building materials.

From 1920 to 1949, sixty-nine ships were destroyed by fire on the lakes. At least forty-five of those—64 percent—had wooden hulls. They were also old boats, averaging just over forty-one years of age. That's *ancient* for a wooden ship. They were old, dried-up relics, and many of them had no business being out on the lakes. They were there only because of the greed of their owners . . . and the willingness of government agencies to allow them to continue operating.

Misfeasance, malfeasance, and nonfeasance by government officials have also been major contributing factors in the staggering loss of lives that has resulted from shipboard fires on the lakes. Most deaths resulting from shipboard fires have occurred only because the ships weren't equipped with enough lifeboats to evacuate those aboard and because officers and crewmembers were unprepared to deal with the fires. One or both of those facts are clearly obvious in the shipboard fires detailed in this chapter, from the 1841 fire on the *Erie* right up to and including the *Cartiercliffe Hall* in 1979.

The response by government regulatory agencies is unexplainable, almost criminal. "Boats for all" wasn't required until sometime after 1915, and crews are still—*today*—not prepared to deal with shipboard fires. Officers are required to participate in a rigorous fire-fighting school only when they get their original licenses, and the only fire-fighting training most unlicensed personnel get is in the mandatory fire drills held aboard their ships. Those drills are, and apparently have always been, largely a farce. Inspections, fire-fighting equipment, and personnel training aboard tankers like the *Imperial Hamilton* and *Jupiter* seem to have been sorely lacking, even though the threat of explosions and fires is extremely high on those types of ships . . . and the consequences can be catastrophic.

>>3<<
FATAL ENCOUNTERS:
Collisions

THE MIDDLE OF THE NINETEENTH CENTURY WAS an era of palatial steamboats on the Great Lakes. The "palace steamers," as they were often called, were combination passenger and freight carriers, but they were primarily designed for the highly lucrative passenger trade between Buffalo and the rapidly growing urban centers rising up around the lakes at places like Cleveland, Detroit, Chicago, and Milwaukee.

Following the War of 1812, a combination of cheap land and plentiful jobs attracted a flood of immigrants to the Great Lakes region. Most funneled into the lakes through the burgeoning port of Buffalo, which was then the western terminus of the Erie Canal and the railroads serving the East Coast. At Buffalo, immigrants boarded passenger steamers to continue their westward voyages.

Most of the steamers carrying passengers and freight to and from Buffalo were owned by the eastern railroads, including the New York Central, Pennsylvania Railroad, and Erie Railroad, or by the Michigan Central Railroad, which had tracks running west out of Detroit. Competition was fierce, and fleet managers soon found that the best way to attract passengers was to offer modestly priced fares on ships that were new, fast, large, and luxuriously outfitted.

The steamers that were built as a result of this competition are often described as "ostentatious." They usually had paneling of exotic woods, exquisite statuary, and hand-carved and richly upholstered furniture that would have been appropriate in a European palace or the finest American hotel.

Most of the passengers, on the other hand, were poor farmers or tradesmen fleeing the poverty and oppression of northern Europe. Many had traveled from Europe to the United States in steerage, the crudest of shipboard accommodations. When the immigrants arrived at Buffalo, however, they found themselves being sought out by representatives of the competing shipping companies, each of whom promised them grand accommodations on their fleet's luxurious ships. As the immigrants boarded the extravagantly appointed steamers for the trip west, it must have seemed as though their dreams of a better life in this new world were coming true.

In 1852, one of the most regal of the palace steamers was the *Atlantic.* The 266-foot ship, operated by the Michigan Central Railroad, was also trumpeted as one of the fastest on the lakes. Driven by two mammoth midship paddle wheels, it was capable of making the 261-mile passage from Buffalo to Detroit in less than seventeen hours, a time that couldn't be matched by today's modern freighters.[1]

Atlantic, 1852

During the night of August 19–20, 1852, the *Atlantic* was churning its way west on Lake Erie, bound for Detroit. There were between five and six hundred passengers aboard, mostly immigrants. A haze hung low over the lake, and the ship encountered occasional patches of fog as it steamed westward.[2] Shortly after 2 A.M. the *Atlantic* met the eastbound passenger and freight steamer *Ogdensburgh* off Long Point, the long peninsula that juts down into the middle of Lake Erie from the Canadian shore. The *Ogdensburgh,* owned by the Northern Transportation Company, was bound from Cleveland to Ogdensburg, New York, with a cargo of wheat, and was steering a course for the Welland Canal. The *Ogdensburgh*'s course lay across that of the westbound *Atlantic.*

Under the informal rules of the road by which most vessel masters operated in those days, the *Ogdensburgh* was the "burdened vessel" and had to give way to the *Atlantic.* A familiar ditty helped sailors remember the navigational rule: "If to starboard red appear, 'tis your duty to keep clear."[3] Those on the *Ogdensburgh* would have been able to see the *Atlantic*'s red, or portside, running light off their starboard bow, so it was their responsibility to keep clear of the approaching steamer.

Degrass McNell, first mate on the *Ogdensburgh,* kept his ship steaming ahead, however, sure that his ship would pass a good half-mile ahead of the oncoming vessel. As they drew nearer to each other, McNell was startled when the approaching *Atlantic* suddenly changed course, turning to the north as if trying to pass in front of, rather than behind, the *Ogdensburgh.*

29. Seen here in a drawing by marine artist Samuel Ward Stanton, the passenger steamer *Atlantic* collided with the combination passenger and package steamer *Ogdensburgh* during the early-morning hours of August 20, 1852, on Lake Erie. Badly holed, the *Atlantic* sank quickly, taking 130 to 250 of those aboard to the bottom with her, although most of the people aboard the steamer were rescued by the *Ogdensburgh* and other ships in the area. While there were an estimated 500 to 600 people aboard the *Atlantic,* the ship carried only two small lifeboats and a workboat. (Author's Collection)

Seeing that, McNell immediately signaled the engine room to reverse the engine and shouted for the wheelsman to turn the ship hard to port. As the two ships rapidly closed on each other, the *Ogdensburgh*'s mate could feel the stern of his ship squat as the engine went from "full ahead" to "full astern," and the rate at which the two ships were closing seemed to slow. The *Ogdensburgh*'s steam whistle wasn't working at the time, so McNell ran out onto the hurricane deck and shouted as loud as he could for the other ship to turn to starboard. Despite his efforts, the bow of the *Ogdensburgh* rammed the *Atlantic* on its port side, between the passenger steamer's bow and its paddle box, which was amidships.

The two ships were locked together momentarily, but the *Atlantic* was still making full headway and its momentum quickly carried it on past the freighter. To McNell, the *Atlantic* seemed to be steaming away. His immediate impression was that the collision had been just another of the minor "fender benders" that were then so common on the congested waters of the lakes.

Captain Robert Richardson had come running up from his cabin as soon as he felt the *Ogdensburgh* backing hard, and he quickly surveyed the damage to the bow of his ship as McNell filled him in on what had happened. Richardson knew instinctively that the other ship had to have been badly holed, so as soon as he made sure that his own ship wasn't going to sink, he gave orders to get under way and follow after the *Atlantic.*

As Captain Richardson had surmised, the *Atlantic* had been fatally holed below its waterline, and a torrent of water was flooding into the lower decks of the passenger steamer. As soon as he surveyed the damage, Jim Carney, the *Atlantic*'s second mate, ordered his wheelsman to steer for shore, which was about four miles off.[4]

Many of the passengers on the *Atlantic* had been awakened by the jolt of the collision and the sound of splintering timbers, and the cry soon went up that the ship was flooding. Someone began frantically ringing the ship's bell to signal the *Ogdensburgh,* or any other ships that happened to be in the area, that they needed assistance. Crewmembers on the *Atlantic* made no effort to ensure that all of their passengers were awakened, however. Many of those on the lower decks, mostly Norwegian and Irish immigrants, slept through the collision and the ensuing commotion.

Soon, the passenger steamer noticeably settled in the water, taking on a port list. In panic, many passengers and crewmembers jumped into the lake to escape the foundering vessel. Others began throwing overboard anything that would float—benches, chairs, tables, cargo—before they, too, leaped into the inky waters of Lake Erie.

As the *Atlantic* progressively flooded, the rising water soon extinguished the boiler fires and the steamer drifted to a stop, still well off the beach. Captain Pittes gave the order to launch the two lifeboats and one workboat carried on the ship's hurricane deck. He climbed into the first boat that was lowered, along with several crewmembers and passengers who had congregated on the hurricane deck. In the confusion, the boat capsized when it hit the water, and everyone except Captain Pittes and one crewmember was spilled into the water. The other two boats, crowded mainly with crewmembers, managed to get launched safely and then pulled away from the *Atlantic,* fearing that it would sink and capsize them.

By then the *Ogdensburgh* was nearby, and Captain Richardson and his crew could hear cries of terror coming across the still waters. Almost immediately, they began coming upon survivors struggling in the water. Captain Richardson expertly maneuvered his ship alongside the *Atlantic*, and his crewmen began helping passengers climb aboard the *Ogdensburgh* while others pulled survivors from the water. In no time, two hundred survivors crowded the freighter's deck and cabins.

By the time all those still alive aboard the *Atlantic* had been safely removed to the freighter, other passing ships began arriving on the scene. As their crews launched boats and began searching among the flotsam and jetsam that was spread for miles over the surface of the lake, the *Atlantic* settled beneath the calm waters of Lake Erie. Loaded with survivors, the *Ogdensburgh* left the scene and steamed south to Erie, Pennsylvania, the closest port on the U.S. side of the lake. Many of the survivors got off there, but most stayed aboard while the *Ogdensburgh* made an unplanned trip to Buffalo. The remaining survivors from the *Atlantic* disembarked at Buffalo, the same port where they had boarded the *Atlantic* earlier that day. Before they left the ship, the survivors joined together in drafting a resolution of appreciation to Captain Richardson and his "gallant officers and crew."[5]

The reports on the number of dead from the *Atlantic* varied dramatically, from a low of 130[6] to a high of 250.[7] In their haste to board passengers, the shipping companies didn't always keep accurate passenger manifests in those days. Regardless of which figure you settle on, the sinking of the *Atlantic* ranks yet today as one of the worst maritime tragedies on the Great Lakes.

At Erie, the survivors of the *Atlantic*'s sinking issued a resolution. While praising the actions of the clerk on the passenger steamer, who stayed "cool and collected" and was the last man to leave the boat, the survivors were harshly critical of Captain Pittes and the rest of his crew: "The total incapacity displayed by the officers of the steamer to direct any method for the preservation of lives of those placed under their care shows too clearly their unfitness for the positions they occupied."

The resolution went on to charge that the ship's owners and managers had been negligent in providing for the passengers' safety. The "so-called life preservers," as they put it, "were useless." The life preservers were, in fact, stools that were located in the various common rooms on the steamer. Under the seat of each stool there was a "tin pan" that was supposed to make it buoyant. Apparently, the life preserver stools didn't work all that well, although a few passengers were quoted as having said that they were "quite efficient." The passengers also complained that the captain and his crew had made off with the lifeboats, and that the *Atlantic*'s engine should have been stopped immediately after the collision, rather than trying to run to the beach.[8]

The holing of the *Atlantic* by the *Ogdensburgh* is one of the earliest recorded incidents of a collision caused by navigational error, a problem that would plague the industry throughout its history. Perhaps as a result of the haze that hung over the lake, the mate navigating the *Atlantic* had misjudged the distance between his ship and the *Ogdensburgh* and turned directly in front of it.

Two factors accounted for the high loss of life in the sinking of the *Atlantic*. First, Captain Pittes and his crew failed to maintain order aboard the crippled ship. Instead, most of them quickly and cowardly abandoned ship in the only three boats available, without even making sure that all those aboard had been awakened. Had the passengers been encouraged to stay aboard the *Atlantic*, it's likely that all of them could have been taken off safely by the *Ogdensburgh* and the other ships that came to the scene before the *Atlantic* finally sank. Similarly, if the *Atlantic* had carried a sufficient number of lifeboats, there's no reason that all those aboard couldn't have safely abandoned the sinking ship. Tragically, the lack of adequate lifesaving equipment was another problem that would plague the industry for many years to come.

Lady Elgin, 1860

During the *Atlantic*'s last year on the run from Buffalo to Detroit, it no doubt came across one of the newest additions to the passenger fleet on the Great Lakes—the *Lady Elgin*. The 252-foot paddle-wheel steamer had been launched at Buffalo in November 1851 for the Grand Trunk Railway, a Canadian-owned company. While she operated under the American ensign, the steamer was named for the wife of Lord Elgin, a former governor-general of Canada. The *Lady Elgin* was designed to operate on the route between Buffalo and Chicago. In 1856 a change in her ownership led to the steamer's being placed on the run from Chicago up to Lake Superior, with many intermediate stops. The *Lady Elgin* was both fast and well outfitted. She proved to be highly popular with residents of the ports she served, and many expressed their pride in the able ship by referring to her as the "Queen of the Lakes."[9]

In early September 1860, the *Lady Elgin* was on the last leg of a return trip from Lake Superior. She departed the dock at Milwaukee for Chicago shortly after midnight on September 7 with a most unusual contingent of passengers aboard.

Slavery was a divisive issue in the country in September 1860. Two months later, Abraham Lincoln would be elected president after running on a platform advocating the abolition of slavery. Before the gangly lawyer from Springfield, Illinois, could even take office, however, the southern slaveholding states began to secede from the Union, leading to the long and bloody Civil War.

Governor Alexander Randall of Wisconsin was both a vehement opponent of slavery and a strong defender of states' rights. Randall let it be known that he intended to take Wisconsin out of the Union if the federal government didn't abolish slavery.

The adjutant general of the Wisconsin Militia sent representatives out to all of the state's militia companies to determine if they would support Randall if he decided to take Wisconsin out of the Union. The commanding officer of the "Union Guard" in Milwaukee, Captain Garrett Barry, a West Point graduate with a distinguished record in the Mexican War, said that even though he was strongly opposed to slavery, his allegiance had to be to the federal government. Any other stand, he reasoned, would be treason. When that information was relayed to the state's adjutant general, he revoked Barry's commission and ordered troops in the Union Guard to turn their weapons over to a militia unit that had pledged to support the governor.

Despite the governor's actions, the seventy members of Barry's militia company took great pride in their unit and its commander, and they were committed to keeping the Union Guard together. To raise money to buy new weapons, they decided to sponsor a steamboat excursion to Chicago on the *Lady Elgin*. When the ship left the dock at Milwaukee in the predawn hours of September 7, about three hundred members and supporters of the Union Guard were aboard for the trip to Chicago. There the Union Guard was scheduled to hold a parade, after which the entire contingent would go on a sightseeing tour of the city. The *Lady Elgin* would leave in the evening to return to Milwaukee, and on the return trip the Union Guard group was going to hold a banquet and dance that would go on until the ship reached the dock.

When the Union Guard contingent returned to the *Lady Elgin* after their day of sightseeing, they were distressed to hear that their departure for Milwaukee would be delayed because the captain was expecting bad weather. In fact, with the barometer dropping rapidly, Captain Jack Wilson was considering spending the night safely moored at the dock in Chicago.

The Union Guard group still went ahead with their banquet and dance. The weather seemed fine to them, however, and various passengers repeatedly urged Captain Wilson to get his ship under way. At about 11:30 P.M., the harried captain finally relented. With the sound of boisterous dance music in the background, the mooring lines were cast off and the *Lady Elgin* departed Chicago for the short run up the lake to Milwaukee. About 385 passengers and crewmembers were aboard the ship then, though nobody in the crew had bothered to make a careful count.

The *Lady Elgin* had barely cleared the harbor at Chicago before the weather began to deteriorate rapidly. By 2 A.M. the winds had increased to gale strength and visibility had dropped to near zero as heavy rain began to fall, punctuated by intermittent flashes of lightning. Captain Wilson, regretting that he had allowed himself to be cajoled into leaving port, remained in the pilothouse as his ship plowed on through the growing seas. One deck below the wheelhouse, most of those in the Union Guard party were still carrying on their merrymaking, and Wilson could hear an occasional strain of music over the steady roar of the wind.[10]

The *Lady Elgin* wasn't the only ship caught out in the gale that black night on Lake Michigan. Beating on toward Chicago was the 128-foot schooner *Augusta*, under the command of Captain Darius Nelson Malott. She was a typical lumber carrier of that era, and both her cargo hold and deck were stacked high with lumber that had been loaded at Port Huron, Michigan.

The winds were noticeably freshening when Captain Malott went to bed around midnight, and he had told Second Mate George Budge to awaken him if there was any significant change in the weather. The little ship was racing along with full sails set, and they would have to take in some of the canvas if the winds started to blow much harder.

The *Augusta* ran headlong into the fury of the thunderstorm at about 2 A.M. Within minutes, it became obvious to George Budge that they were going to have to drop some of the sails or else risk being dismasted by the squalls. He called out several deckhands to help take in the heavy, wet canvas. As they scampered about dropping and furling sails, Budge caught a glimpse of the masthead light of another ship off the *Augusta*'s starboard bow. With the little schooner hobby-horsing in the seas and his view obscured by the stacks of lumber on the deck, Budge couldn't tell what direction the other ship was headed in. Right at that moment, though, he was more concerned with getting the sails in before they were shredded by the gusts of wind . . . and he had to awaken the captain.

Aboard the *Lady Elgin*, the second mate on watch in the pilothouse strained his eyes to see through the driving rain. The only time he could see clearly was when there was a flash of lightning, and then it was only for

30. An etching of the elegant *Lady Elgin*, which sank after colliding with the schooner *Augusta* during a September storm on Lake Michigan in 1860. The passenger and freight steamer was equipped with only four lifeboats, even though it was carrying nearly 400 passengers and crewmembers when it was lost. Only 98 to 155 of those managed to make it safely ashore. (Ralph Roberts Collection)

a second. Once he saw the masthead light of a ship off the port bow, but he couldn't see clearly enough to accurately gauge the distance between the two ships. He did call the light to the attention of Captain Wilson, who was sitting in his chair on the other side of the little wheelhouse. Both the captain and the mate were certain they were going to clear the other vessel, but just to be safe the captain ordered the wheelsman to come over several degrees to starboard.

When George Budge awakened him with news of the worsening storm, Captain Malott pulled on his oilskins and headed for the deck. On the way up, he broke into a broad grin when he realized that it was a new day—September 8, 1860—his birthday! Today, he turned twenty-seven years old.

As the young captain came out onto the deck into the driving rain, the deckhands were going forward to drop the foresail, and he moved after them to lend a hand. As he carefully picked his way down the edge of the deck, steadying himself against the tall stacks of lumber that extended to within a couple feet of the edge, Captain Malott glanced forward. There, directly ahead of the *Augusta*, were the lights of another ship. Barely visible through the downpour he could see a white and a red light.

Turning quickly, Malott screamed at the top of his lungs for the wheelsman to put the wheel over hard to starboard, and then he began scrambling back toward the stern. The wheelsman responded to the order without hesitation, spinning the big wooden wheel to bring the schooner around into the wind. The heavily loaded *Augusta* turned, but too slowly—at about 2:30 on the morning of Captain Malott's birthday, his little ship drove hard into the port side of the *Lady Elgin*.

The force of the collision heeled the *Lady Elgin* hard over to port. Everything that wasn't tied down was thrown toward the port side of the ship, passengers included. In an instant, pandemonium broke out on the crowded steamer.

The *Augusta* had struck and holed the *Lady Elgin* just forward of the passenger steamer's port paddle box. The schooner's jib and foresail rigging hung up in the broken timbers momentarily, holding the *Augusta* in the hole she had made in the *Lady Elgin*'s hull. Because of the forward motion of the passenger ship, the *Augusta* finally slid backward out of the hole and spun around until she was running side-by-side with the *Lady Elgin*. For a few moments the *Augusta* was dragged along by the bigger ship, her forward rigging still fouled in the broken timbers. Then the headsail and stay ripped loose, and the two ships separated in the blackness of the stormy night.

As Captain Malott and his crew recovered from the shock of the collision, they were all certain that their ship was mortally wounded. At the same time, they doubted they had done much damage to the larger passenger steamer. Their tapered bow had seemed to hit high on the hull of the *Lady Elgin*, so if there was any damage it was probably above the steamer's waterline. That reasoning seemed to be confirmed by the fact that the *Lady Elgin* had kept steaming along. Huddled together in the driving rain, Captain Malott and his crew were angry that the passenger steamer didn't stop to see if they needed assistance.

The *Augusta*'s cook dashed forward to check the damage at the bow. In minutes, he was back with an astonishing report: there was a little water leaking into the hull from cracked timbers and loosened seams, but nothing serious—they weren't sinking. With that, Captain Malott and his men set about getting in the damaged jib and making temporary repairs so that they could get under way again. As they worked, the weather cleared enough that they could occasionally catch a glimpse of the *Lady Elgin* as it steamed away from them. As he watched, Malott saw the steamer make a sudden hard turn to the left, putting it on a direct line to the nearby shore.

Aboard the *Lady Elgin,* Captain Wilson had quickly taken stock of the extensive damage caused by the collision. With a gaping hole in the hull that extended below the waterline, water was cascading into the lower decks and it was obvious that his ship had been mortally wounded. Wilson immediately turned the *Lady Elgin* toward the closest shore, hoping that they could beach the boat before it sank. At the time, the steamer was nine miles out in the lake, between Winnetka and Evanston, Illinois. Wilson ordered the mate to ring the ship's bell and blow the steam whistle, to let those on board and any passing ships know that they were in a life-or-death situation.

Down on the freight deck, crewmembers began trying to lighten the ship to compensate for the tons of water that were pouring in through the hole in the hull. They threw cargo overboard, and even tried to drive the sixty cattle they were carrying over the side. The cattle wanted no part of a swim in Lake Michigan that night, though, and the crew managed to get only one to go overboard. In fact, as the *Lady Elgin* began to progressively list to port, the panicked cattle herded together on the port side, further aggravating the list.

Captain Wilson ordered First Mate George Davis and a group of crewmembers to put one of the ship's four lifeboats over the side and see if they could stop the leak by stuffing canvas or mattresses into the hole in the hull. In the storm-tossed seas, the lifeboat swamped almost immediately after it was launched. As Davis and his crew bailed frantically to keep their little boat afloat, the *Lady Elgin* steamed away from them.

A second boat was immediately launched, and eleven men jumped in as it was lowered into the water. Several of the men were passengers who thought the crewmembers were abandoning ship without them. Once in the water, those in the lifeboat were shocked to find that there weren't any oars in the boat.[11] They, too, were left behind as the *Lady Elgin* continued on toward the beach.

There were still two lifeboats aboard the steamer, but none of the reports indicate that any attempt was made to launch them. Perhaps the crew saw it as a futile gesture. One boat could hold twenty passengers, the other twelve, and there were nearly four hundred people aboard the *Lady Elgin.* On the other hand, crewmembers may just not have had time to launch the remaining lifeboats.

Shortly after the second boat was launched, the *Lady Elgin* crossed that fine line between positive and negative buoyancy, and with no discernible warning she plummeted to the bottom of the lake. Those who were not trapped inside the ship found themselves thrown into the frenzied waters of Lake Michigan. There was a great mass of debris floating on the lake over the spot where the *Lady Elgin* had made her final plunge—timbers, crates, chairs, cattle pens, a snare drum, the steward's chopping block, barrels . . . and the ship's entire hurricane deck.

The hurricane deck had torn free from the rest of the hull as the ship sank, and about forty survivors had managed to climb onto it, including Captain Wilson. Those on the hurricane deck quickly began pulling other survivors from the water and onto their makeshift raft.[12] Driven by the wind and seas, the amorphous mass of wreckage and survivors began drifting toward the shore.

Battered by waves, the hurricane deck undulated through the water like an immense sea snake and soon began to break up. With the passing of each torturous hour, the deck broke into smaller and smaller pieces. One piece held eight survivors, another twelve. Captain Wilson and about forty survivors were aboard one of the largest intact pieces, though much of it had been pressed below the water by the heavy load it bore, and some of those on it were standing in water up to their waists. Around daylight, the remains of the hurricane deck neared the shore at Evanston. The spirits of those still alive must have been buoyed by the first faint light of day and the nearness of the shore. Surely, their ordeal was almost over.

It's unlikely that more than a few of those clinging to life on the pieces of the hurricane deck realized that the worst part of their trip was still ahead of them. When the huge seas that carried them shoreward reached the shallow waters adjacent to the beach, the waves tumbled and crashed with great ferocity. The last several hundred feet to the shore was a violently churning maelstrom. In it, the remaining section of the hurricane deck was smashed into its smallest constituent parts, and those aboard were thrown into the frenzied surf to struggle the last measure to the shore.

The shore itself was little more than a narrow shelf of sand and rock below forty-foot cliffs, and the entire width of the beach regularly disappeared beneath the massive waves that rolled ashore. Many of those who had survived the long hours it took to drift ashore were hurled against the face of the cliff and battered by debris floating on the water. Others who somehow managed to claw their way onto the narrow strip of beach were sucked off and back into the boiling surf by the crashing waves and the powerful undertow. "It is estimated that more than half of the people floating on or hanging onto wreckage lost their lives in the surf a scant hundred feet from shore."[13]

Among the first to successfully make it to shore was First Mate George Davis and the other men in the first lifeboat that had been launched. They had managed to bail the water out of the boat, and had rowed after the *Lady Elgin* as it steamed on toward the beach. When they came ashore, they scaled the cliff and fanned out in search of help. Soon, local residents began arriving at the top of the bluff with dry clothes, blankets, and ropes with which to help people climb the cliff. The steepness of the bluff and the raging waters below kept most from doing more than standing idly by in horror as the human flotsam from the *Lady Elgin* drowned below them.

A few of the local residents did make heroic attempts to save those from the sunken steamer. Among the heroes of the day was Edward Spencer, a young student who belonged to the volunteer lifesaving crew at the nearby Methodist college that later became Northwestern University. With a rope tied around his waist and tethered by some of his classmates, Spencer is reported to have made sixteen trips into the surf, saving seventeen persons.

Some of those who made their way down the cliff that morning were not as laudable as Spencer, however. It was later found that the wallets and pockets of many of the dead that washed ashore had been emptied of their valuables.

Among those who didn't make it ashore was Captain Wilson. As the hurricane deck began to break apart, he reportedly dove into the water in an effort to rescue a woman who had fallen in. Both drowned. Many of those who survived credited Captain Wilson with having saved numerous lives through the long and tortured night, as he continually encouraged the survivors not to lose faith. Other survivors labeled Captain Garrett Barry of the Union Guard as another hero of the shipwreck, though he, too, failed to make it to the beach alive.

Reports on the number of survivors who made it ashore that morning vary from a low of 98[14] to a high of 155.[15] The number killed in the tragic accident was somewhere between 279 and 350, even more than had died in the sinking of the *Atlantic* eight years earlier.[16]

While the final scenes of the drama were being played out along the beach at Evanston, Captain Malott and his crew brought their weather-beaten schooner safely into Chicago, only to be hauled before a hastily convened Cook County Coroner's Jury. The jury's swift verdict was released the following day.

Both vessels were judged to have been at fault in the collision. The *Lady Elgin*'s officers and owners were cited for overloading their ship and criticized for not having more lifeboats. Captain Malott and his crew on the *Augusta* were virtually exonerated of blame in the collision, although the schooner's second mate was chastised for not informing his captain when he saw the light of the approaching ship.

Under the generally accepted rules of the road that most ships operated by in those days, Captain Malott's sailboat technically had the right-of-way over the steamer. It was the more maneuverable steamer, not the sailing ship, that was required to give way.[17]

The twelve jury members also made note of the fact that the *Lady Elgin* had been built without any watertight bulkheads to subdivide the hull. If watertight bulkheads had existed, the flooding that resulted from the collision could have been confined to a limited area of the ship, and it may well have had sufficient reserve buoyancy to stay afloat.

The jurors felt that the primary cause of the tragic accident did not lie in the actions of any of those aboard either the *Lady Elgin* or the *Augusta*. Instead, it occurred because the existing navigation laws were woefully inadequate.

Captain Malott continued sailing for Bissel & Davidson, the company that had owned the *Augusta*. He commanded several of their sailing ships in the years immediately following the *Lady Elgin* affair, and is reported to have made several crossings of the North Atlantic during that period. On September 8, 1864, Captain Malott was downbound on Lake Michigan in command of Bissel & Davidson's flagship, a new bark named *Mojave*. It was the fourth anniversary of the sinking of the *Lady Elgin*, and Malott's thirty-first birthday.

During the day, the captain on the schooner *J. S. Miner* hailed Malott as their two ships passed in mid-lake under ideal weather conditions. That was the last that anyone saw of the *Mojave*, Captain Malott, or his crew of ten. What happened to the *Mojave* and its crew remains a mystery.[18]

The number of ships on the lakes increased dramatically during the first half of the nineteenth century, and that resulted in an appalling number of collisions, often with heavy loss of life, such as occurred in the sinkings of the *Atlantic* and *Lady Elgin*. It was a phenomenon that was common to most maritime nations. By the 1830s both England and France had enacted formal rules of the road, or traffic laws for boats, that were aimed at reducing the number of collisions. There were regular calls for the enactment of a similar law to apply in U.S. waters, but all such proposals met with vehement opposition from vessel masters and shipowners, who preferred a *laissez faire* approach.

In 1864, however, the unabated carnage resulting from ship collisions finally led Congress to enact the first U.S. navigational law. It prescribed the actions that had to be taken by each ship in a meeting, passing, or crossing situation and established a simple rule to define which ship had the right-of-way and which was the burdened vessel, or the one required to give way. The law also required ships to post a lookout to keep watch for any approaching vessels and alert the master or mate who was handling navigation. A "rule of prudent seamanship" was also included. If an officer was in doubt as to the intentions of another ship, the officer was required to take whatever action was appropriate to avoid a collision, including slowing down, stopping, or even backing up.

The first rules of the road enacted into law remained in effect, virtually unchanged, until 1897. At that time, the international maritime community developed a set of rules of the road that would apply internationally, and Congress subsequently enacted those rules into law. U.S. navigational laws have been updated and expanded several times since then, but those versions generally just added to the basic rules that were enacted in 1864.[19]

When the first U.S. rules of the road were enacted, there were probably some members of Congress who felt that the simple, straightforward rules would eliminate most collisions between ships. That was not to be the case. The worst collision in the history of the lakes actually occurred the following summer.

Pewabic, 1865

If ever there was a "Man of the Lakes," it would have to have been George McKay. McKay was born aboard the *Commodore Perry* while the little steamer was laid up in Swan Creek at Toledo, Ohio, in 1838. The newborn's father, Captain John McKay, was master of the *Perry*, and he and his wife were shipkeeping while the vessel was in winter layup. Captain and Mrs. McKay gave their son the middle name "Perry" as an enduring reminder of the circumstances of his birth. George Perry McKay had quite literally been born a sailor.[20]

Details of George McKay's childhood are sketchy, but we do know that he and his younger brother John spent a great deal of time aboard ships commanded by their father, and they both eventually followed in his footsteps and became merchant seamen. The family originally made its home in Buffalo, but they moved to Sault Ste. Marie in 1845. George McKay reportedly began his sailing career aboard the *Algonquin*, a small schooner commanded by his father that was the only ship on Lake Superior at the time.[21] There's also a report that George spent most of the summer of 1853 helping his father repair the steamer *Independence* after it was damaged in a grounding near Bad River at the west end of Lake Superior.[22]

The *Independence* was the first steamboat to operate on Lake Superior. In 1845 the propeller-driven ship was brought up to Lake Superior from the lower lakes. It had to be portaged around the rapids of the St. Marys River at Sault Ste. Marie, a tricky operation that reportedly took seven weeks to accomplish.[23] When the *Independence* went back into service in the fall of 1853, both George and his brother John were serving as full-fledged crewmen on their father's ship.[24]

On the night of November 22, 1853, the *Independence* left the Soo with a load of freight for Ontonagon and La Pointe. When she was no more than a mile from the dock, the steamer's boiler exploded, "blowing three-fourths of the ship to pieces and sinking her in 18 feet of water." Three crewmembers and one passenger were killed, while the rest of those aboard survived by clinging to floating wreckage.[25] It would not be the last shipwreck for the McKay boys.

In the spring of 1856, George was serving as second mate on the passenger and freight steamer *Northerner* when it collided with the steamer *Forest Queen* just above Port Huron.[26] The *Northerner* came out second best in the collision, and she sank to the bottom. There were about 142 passengers and crewmembers aboard at the time, but all except 12 managed to get off safely.[27]

In 1861, twenty-three-year-old George McKay became a captain in his own right when he was given command of the steamer *General Taylor*, owned by J. T. Whiting & Company of Detroit. Then, when the brand-new steamer *Pewabic* was launched for the Whiting fleet in 1864, George McKay was named captain of the 200-foot ship. The Whiting line then consisted of seven steamers—*Illinois, Meteor, Detroit, Mineral Rock, General Taylor, Skylark,* and *Pewabic*—all of which operated in the growing trade between Detroit and the small communities that had sprung up along the shore of Lake Superior. The opening of the first locks at the Soo in 1855, combined with expansion of copper- and iron-mining operations during the Civil War, had set off a boom in the Lake Superior region, and Whiting & Company had laid claim to a large chunk of the resulting vessel trade. By the time the *Pewabic* departed Detroit for its first trip north in 1864, Whiting controlled about two-thirds of the highly lucrative vessel trade to Lake Superior.[28]

The *Pewabic* added to Whiting & Company's reputation as a highly successful shipping company. The Peck & Masters–built combination passenger and freight steamer was a big twin-screw ship with two steam engines, reportedly valued at $100,000. Up to four hundred passengers could be accommodated in cabins, dining rooms, and sitting rooms that were as fine as any on the lakes at that time. There was even a barbershop on board. One passenger described the ship as "beautifully ornamented inside and painted black outside. There is a deer's head, neck, and horns on the top of the pilothouse that is a fine piece of workmanship." Passengers were also quick to note that Whiting & Company had not skimped on safety when they had the ship built. It was reported that the *Pewabic* was "well provided with lifeboats, life preservers, and fire engines and hose." "The living is very fine," noted one passenger. "I should prefer to go on the *Pewabic* to any other boat on the lakes."[29]

Captain McKay was described as "a fine sailor and a gentleman." He had a shock of red hair, and in 1864 it was reported that he sported long red whiskers. The whiskers were possibly an effort by McKay to partially masquerade his youthfulness. The captain of the *Pewabic* was only twenty-six years old. As young as he was, however, it appears that he was able to run a tight ship. One passenger wrote that "the officers are all very pleasant, and I heard no rough language while on board."[30]

The Civil War ended in April 1865, at the beginning of McKay's second year in command of the popular *Pewabic*. With the end of the war came an increase in the tourist trade to Lake Superior. During the summer months, many people traveled north to escape the heat and humidity of urban areas like Detroit and Chicago. The recuperative benefits of the cool, clean air of Lake Superior had long been widely touted, especially for persons convalescing from an illness or those with respiratory problems. The region had also gained a reputation for its rugged scenic beauty, especially places like Pictured Rocks, the Keweenaw Peninsula, and the Apostle Islands. Others made the trip north to catch a glimpse of what was then truly an American frontier. In 1865 there were still more American Indians around Lake Superior than there were settlers of European ethnicity.

The few communities that had been established—places like Marquette, Houghton, Ontonagon, and Copper Harbor, Michigan, and La Pointe and Bayfield, Wisconsin—were rough-hewn out of the wilderness. They were frontier settlements, with few niceties. To visitors from Detroit, Cleveland, or Chicago, the villages were undoubtedly reminiscent of what their communities had been like "back in the old days," at least several decades earlier.

It was mostly tourists who occupied the cabins on the *Pewabic* when the ship departed Houghton, Michigan, on August 7, 1865, for the trip down the lakes to Detroit. About two hundred passengers were aboard, and the freight deck below the cabins was heavily loaded. At Houghton the ship had taken on 265 tons of copper and copper ore from the mines of the Keweenaw Peninsula. The *Pewabic* was also carrying 175 tons of high-quality iron ore that had been loaded at Marquette, 200 ship's knees, 250 half-barrels of salted fish, 27 rolls of tanned leather, and about 10 tons of miscellaneous freight.[31]

Early on the morning of August 9, the *Pewabic* passed through the locks at Sault Ste. Marie. By shortly after noon, she had made her way down the St. Marys River and entered Lake Huron on the last leg of the voyage. At 7:45 that evening, the steamer was abreast Thunder Bay Island, near Alpena, Michigan. A light mist was falling, and the sea was running in big swells that rocked the boat and made some of the passengers seasick. It wasn't a pleasant evening to be out on deck, and most of the passengers had already retired to their cabins or the ship's sitting rooms.

Shortly after passing Thunder Bay Island, Captain McKay left the pilothouse to go down to the engine room and have a smoke with the engineer. Having come on watch at 6:30 P.M., First Mate George Cleveland was then left to navigate the *Pewabic*. With the mist and overcast skies, it was already starting to get dark out, so the mate had posted a lookout. His lookout that evening was John McKay, the captain's brother. About the only passengers on deck were Professor S. H. Douglass of the University of Michigan, his daughter Kate, his son Sam, and his sister, Mrs. William Welles.

Sam Douglass later recalled that he and his family saw the lights of an approaching upbound ship shortly after passing Thunder Bay Island. John McKay, who was pacing the deck near the Douglass family, told them that the ship was very likely the *Meteor*, a sister ship and near-twin to the *Pewabic*. The talkative lookout told them that the ships often passed close enough that the upbound ship could pass the latest Detroit newspapers to the downbound vessel. Ships traveling on the northern lakes were largely out of touch with what was going on "in the world," and crew and passengers alike appreciated getting the latest newspapers from the city.[32]

George Cleveland wanted to pass the oncoming ship off the *Pewabic*'s port side, as was the standard practice, and he told his wheelsman to steer to starboard until the oncoming ship was a point or two—between eleven and twenty-two degrees—off the port bow. The wheelsman put a little left wheel on, and the ship went into a long, slow turn to the right.[33]

In the engine room, the engineer on watch happened to walk over to the open gangway door on the port side to look out over the lake. Seeing the lights of the approaching steamer, he motioned for Captain McKay to come and have a look. The captain saw the upbound vessel well off the port bow. "I then walked aft and went up through the cabin, passed out of there into the smoking room, and then passed out of there and on deck on the port side," Captain McKay recounted later. "I then saw the propeller's bright [white] and green lights."[34]

A green running light is on the starboard side of a ship, while the port side has a red running light. The lights are shielded so that if you are on an approaching vessel, you will only see both lights if you are dead ahead of the other vessel. If you are to the left of the approaching vessel's midline—off its starboard side—you will only see the green light, and vice versa.

Since the approaching ship was off the *Pewabic*'s port side, if the ships were on parallel, or passing, courses, Captain McKay would only have been able to see the other vessel's red running light. The fact that he could only see its green light indicated that it was angling toward the *Pewabic*. In simple terms, the two ships were on a collision course.

Captain McKay then joined his first mate at the forward end of the hurricane deck, just outside the wheelhouse. McKay took the glasses from Cleveland and looked again at the oncoming steamer. Again he saw her white light and her green running light. It was all too apparent to McKay that the ships were going to collide. "I then went into the pilothouse and checked her down, stopped the starboard engine, and gave orders to heave the wheel hard-o-starboard," McKay recalled. At the same time he heard the other ship blow "one whistle," the signal for a port-to-port passage. McKay's last-ditch effort to avoid slamming into the side of the other ship had put the *Pewabic* into a hard right turn, directly across the bow of the upbound vessel. Within seconds, the oncoming ship struck the *Pewabic* about twenty-five to thirty feet back from its port bow. The bow of the other ship sliced eight to ten feet into the hull of the *Pewabic*. By then McKay realized that the other ship was the *Meteor*, sister ship to the *Pewabic*.

As the *Meteor* backed away from the *Pewabic*, McKay dashed down the stairs to the main deck to survey the damage to his ship. On his way, he discovered that the impact of the collision had tipped over an ashtray or lamp in the smoking room, causing a fire. "I ran to the bucket rack and got some water and helped put the fire out," McKay later remembered. "I then hailed the *Meteor* to come alongside, as we were sinking. She came up on our port again and I commenced helping passengers on board of her."[35]

31. A navigational error was probably the cause of the collision that resulted in the sinking of the steamer *Pewabic* on northern Lake Huron on the evening of August 9, 1865. In attempting to make a standard port-to-port passage with the steamer *Meteor*, the mate on watch aboard the *Pewabic* turned his ship right in front of the other vessel. The *Pewabic*, just over a year old, sank rapidly, taking about 125 passengers and crewmembers down with her. Seen here in a historically accurate painting, the *Pewabic* ran between Detroit and Lake Superior. (Artist Robert McGreevy)

According to O. C. Wood, the *Pewabic*'s African-American barber, passengers aboard the ship were panic-stricken and the scene was one of indescribable confusion. "Many escaped by jumping on board the *Meteor*, while the balance went down with the wreck, which sunk in less than five minutes after the collision," said Wood. "Then the *Pewabic* made a fearful lunge forward and sank."[36] As it made its plunge, the stern of the big steamer kicked high in the air, towering high above those aboard the *Meteor*. After hesitating for no more than the blink of an eye, the *Pewabic* dove straight for the bottom, leaving only a swirling vortex to mark where it had been. One instant it was there, the next it was gone.

Captain McKay helped many of his passengers climb aboard the *Meteor* when it came back alongside the *Pewabic,* then he followed them over. Almost as soon as he stepped foot on the other ship, McKay got into an argument with Captain Thomas Wilson of the *Meteor* over who was in charge. McKay reportedly even went so far as to accuse Wilson of wanting to drown them all, "in order that there might be no one to testify at an investigation."[37]

By the time McKay crossed over to the *Meteor,* Captain Wilson had already ordered his men to launch the ship's lifeboats to aid those in the water. When the men went to the boats, however, they found that a number of the ship's waiters had cut through the falls and were sitting in the boats on the deck, expecting the *Meteor* to sink out from under them. With the falls cut, the sailors could only chase the waiters out of the boats, then laboriously hand them down to the main deck and slide them over the side into the water.[38]

Captain McKay, along with a mix of crewmen from both ships, climbed into the first lifeboat that went into the water and began rowing around through the mass of debris that cluttered the surface of the lake to pick up survivors. Charles Mack, the *Pewabic*'s clerk, did the same.

As in the cases of the *Atlantic* and *Lady Elgin,* there was no accurate record of those who died in the dark waters of Lake Huron that night— the *Pewabic*'s passenger manifest went down with the ship. The rescue efforts, which went on through the night, resulted in 75 of the *Pewabic*'s passengers and 28 crewmembers being taken aboard the *Meteor.* Based on the best recollections of those who had been aboard the *Pewabic,* it appeared that about 125 persons died with the ship.

While rescue efforts were still under way, the passengers who had survived the sinking held a meeting aboard the *Meteor.* Professor Douglass, who had lost his sister in the accident, served as chairman of the assembly. In short order, the survivors drafted and heartily approved a resolution honoring Captain McKay and his crew for their "faithful and meritorious efforts" and extending to them "best wishes and respect."[39]

Interestingly, most of the survivors at that time thought that the *Meteor* had turned in front of the *Pewabic* in the confusing seconds before the collision, thereby causing the accident. It would later be shown, however, that it was actually the last-minute maneuvering of the *Pewabic* that had caused the tragic accident. Had the survivors known that, they might have been less effusive in their praise of the officers and crew of the *Pewabic.*

At dawn the next morning, the steamer *Mohawk* was sighted coming down the lake. It was hailed down, and the survivors from the *Pewabic* were put aboard to continue their trip to Detroit. The *Meteor,* only slightly damaged in the collision, made temporary repairs, then continued on toward Lake Superior. Two days later, water that had seeped into her hull reacted with the cargo of lime she was carrying and caused a serious fire aboard the ship while she was tied up at Sault Ste. Marie. While all the passengers and crew managed to get off, the ship's cargo was a total loss and the *Meteor* had to be scuttled in the St. Marys River to keep it from being totally destroyed by fire (see Chapter 2).[40]

News of the sinking of the *Pewabic* quickly spread to ports around the lakes. The public was outraged. "The frequency of collisions of late is really startling, and there is no doubt that more lives are lost and property damaged on the lakes through collisions between vessels than from all other causes combined," reported one Detroit newspaper. "This must be the result of gross and inexcusable carelessness." The article went on to brand the sinking of the *Pewabic* as "entirely unnecessary" and "the result of the most criminal carelessness on the part of somebody."[41] A similar article in the *Erie Dispatch* said the sinking of the *Pewabic* "was not an accident, and should not be termed such. It was an atrocious crime, and somebody should hang—hang as high as the bodies of their poor victims sank into a watery grave."[42]

At Houghton on the Keweenaw Peninsula, the August 19 issue of the local newspaper carried accounts of three vessel casualties under a single headline: "Chapter of Marine Disasters: Three Steamboats Lost." The related articles detailed the sinking of the *Pewabic*, the fire on the *Meteor*, and another fire aboard a passenger and freight steamer named the *Traveller*, which had burned at the dock at Eagle Harbor, Michigan, on August 17 (see Chapter 2). "With the exception of the burning of the *Traveller*, of which we know but little now," said one article, "it is very evident that these disasters are the result of gross carelessness on the part of the officers of the boats, and possibly the owners."[43]

Amid the public outcry, the Board of Steamboat Inspectors launched an investigation into the sinking of the *Pewabic*. The federal government in 1852 had established the Board of Steamboat Inspectors. They inspected the hulls and machinery aboard passenger-carrying steamships, and were also charged to conduct investigations into accidents involving passenger vessels. The three-member investigating panel that met at Detroit on August 18 was made up of the board's supervising inspector from Chicago, a hull inspector, and a boiler inspector.

After listening to the sometimes conflicting testimony offered by the officers and crewmembers of the two ships, the board concluded that the *Pewabic* had caused the collision. George Cleveland, the mate who had

32. In addition to passengers, the *Pewabic* was carrying 265 tons of copper and copper ore, 175 tons of iron ore, 200 ship's knees, 250 half-barrels of salted fish, 27 rolls of tanned leather, and about 10 tons of miscellaneous freight when it sank on August 9, 1865. Since sinking, the *Pewabic* has been the target of three major salvage operations. Shown here is a portion of the cargo recovered by salvers in 1917. Among the clutter on the deck of the salvage barge are stacks of copper ingots and barrels loaded with chunks of high-quality native copper mined in the Keweenaw Peninsula of Michigan's Upper Peninsula. (Jesse Besser Museum, Alpena, Michigan)

been on watch, was found guilty of manslaughter in the deaths of those aboard his ship, and he was sentenced to prison. Captain McKay was also found at fault, and his master's license was revoked. Later, both men appealed their convictions and were exonerated. Both continued with their careers as merchant marine officers.[44]

One might have assumed that the tragic events of August 9, 1865, would have adversely affected the career of Captain George McKay of the *Pewabic*, and possibly even that of Captain Thomas Wilson, the twenty-seven-year-old master of the *Meteor*. Not only was that not the case, but McKay and Wilson both had long and highly successful careers in the maritime industry on the Great Lakes.

George McKay continued as a respected captain for another seventeen years. During that time he was involved in a third marine casualty. On October 23, 1873, McKay was downbound from Duluth in command of the freighter *Geneva*, towing the barge *Genoa*. The steam-powered freighter was owned by the Hanna Company of Cleveland and had been launched just over a year earlier. Both vessels were loaded with grain. Off Caribou Island, a coupling broke on the *Geneva*'s propeller shaft, allowing the propeller to smash against the hull and rip a hole through the planking. Although they fought for twenty hours to save their ship, McKay and his crew were eventually forced to give up. They abandoned the *Geneva* and went aboard the *Genoa* shortly before the freighter sank, and they were later towed to the Soo by the freighter *Nahant*.[45] George McKay had survived his fourth shipwreck.

In 1882, Captain McKay gave up sailing to become manager of Cleveland Transportation's fleet. He later became manager of the large Hanna fleet, and remained in that position until 1901. McKay also served as the first treasurer of the Cleveland Vessel Owners' Association and, later, the Lake Carriers' Association. He served in those positions for thirty-six years, until his death in 1918 at the age of seventy-nine. During that time he is credited with having been a strong advocate of school training for seamen, financial aid programs, and improved ship safety. In 1985, Captain McKay was posthumously inducted into the U.S. Merchant Marine Hall of Fame as that year's representative from the Great Lakes shipping industry.[46]

Captain Thomas Wilson, who came to the United States from his native Scotland when he was a teenager, started his own fleet in 1872 by building the steamer *D. M. Wilson*. In a few years, he found himself at the helm of one of the larger fleets on the Great Lakes. Wilson, like McKay, was a highly respected member of the Great Lakes shipping community.

He was active in the Cleveland Ship Owners' Association and later served as a vice president of the Lake Carriers' Association. He died in Jerusalem in 1900 while on a tour of the Holy Land with his family. The fleet that he founded continued to operate on the lakes into the 1970s.[47]

The rules of the road enacted by Congress in 1864 hadn't been able to prevent the collision between the *Pewabic* and the *Meteor.* While trying to follow the navigational rules, Captain McKay and First Mate George Cleveland both made mistakes that ultimately led to the collision. A year later, an even less complicated scenario—an unexpected encounter—resulted in the loss of the *Morning Star* and *Courtlandt* in a collision.

Morning Star and *Courtlandt,* 1868

The *Morning Star* was a five-year-old passenger and freight steamer that was operated by the Detroit & Cleveland Navigation Company—the famous D&C line. D&C began operations in 1850 with two wooden steamers. The steamers operated on regular schedules between Detroit and Cleveland, hence the company's name.

D&C's *Morning Star* had departed Cleveland at 10:30 P.M. on June 19, bound for Detroit with fifty-one passengers, under the command of Captain E. R. Viger. The *Morning Star*'s freight deck held a jumble of cargo, including "100 tons of bar iron, several hundred kegs of nails, 45 boxes of glass, 25 boxes of cheese, 65 tons of chill metal, 33 mowing machines, 7 barrels of oil, 4 tons of stone, and 137 boxes of other package freight."[48] Between Cleveland harbor and the mouth of the nearby Black River, where Lorain, Ohio, is now located, the *Morning Star* met and passed several sailing ships.

As the *Morning Star* steamed west, the bark *Courtlandt,* under the command of Captain G. W. Lawton, was heading east toward Cleveland. The *Courtlandt* was nearing the end of the long voyage down from Lake Superior, where the ship had taken on a load of iron ore for the mills at Cleveland.

The wind had been blowing steadily out of the north all day, and the waters of Lake Erie rose and fell in huge swells. There was a chill in the air that night, and an entry made in the pilothouse log of the *Morning Star* at midnight noted that it was also overcast and dark out on the lake. Captain Viger was in the pilothouse of the D&C steamer at the time. With the stout wind on the *Courtlandt*'s stern quarter she was fast approaching Cleveland, and Captain Lawton had also taken up a position on the afterdeck of his ship.

Shortly after midnight, the lookout on the *Courtlandt* complained to the mate on watch that their starboard running light was burning very dimly. The mate reportedly removed the light from its mounting, cleaned the soot off the red lens, and trimmed the wick. He then relit it and, confident he had solved the problem, set about reattaching the light to its mount.

At that very moment, Captain Lawton saw the bow of the *Morning Star* emerge from the darkness. Lawton quickly reached up and rang the *Courtlandt*'s bell three times, then spun the wheel hard over. On the *Morning Star*, Captain Viger and those with him in the pilothouse heard the ringing of the bell, but too late. Running at full speed, the bow of the steamer sliced into the *Courtlandt* at the very spot where the mate was stooped over reattaching the running light. The mate was instantly crushed as the bow of the *Morning Star* cut deep into the hull of the smaller bark.

The *Morning Star* hit the *Courtlandt* with such force that the steamer's two bow anchors were ripped loose from their mounts. One anchor skidded clear across the deck of the bark and fell into the water on the far side, chaining the two ships together. As the two wooden ships began riding up and down on the passing swells, their crews could clearly hear the hulls grinding together—grinding to pieces.

The crew of the *Courtlandt* worked frantically to free themselves from the *Morning Star*. Through an almost superhuman effort they were finally able to slip loose of the steamer's anchor chain, and their badly damaged ship began to drift away toward the south shore of the lake. After drifting about half a mile, taking on water all the time, the *Courtlandt* quietly settled beneath the waves. Most of her crewmembers kept from drowning by hanging onto floating debris.

On the *Morning Star*, Captain Viger had the lifeboats swung out ready for launching. Many of those aboard scrambled into the boats, although it was later reported that crewmembers outnumbered passengers. It made little difference at that point. Before the lifeboats could be launched, the *Morning Star* plummeted toward the bottom. As it sank, the hurricane deck was torn loose and fourteen of those who had been thrown into the water when the D&C steamer went down managed to scramble aboard, including Captain Viger.

At about 3 A.M., the D&C steamer *R. N. Rice*, bound from Detroit to Cleveland, came upon the wreck site. Captain Bill McKay and his crew took aboard the survivors from both ships and transported them to Cleveland. Two seamen were lost on the *Courtlandt*, while between twenty-one and thirty of those who had been aboard the *Morning Star* went down with the ship. The bloated bodies of many of the dead were later found afloat on the lake.[49]

By 1898 more than 150 ships had been sunk as a result of vessel collisions on the Great Lakes, causing the deaths of hundreds of crewmembers and passengers. In the thirty years following the 1868 loss of the *Courtlandt* and *Morning Star,* the number of serious collisions seemed to increase annually. Good records aren't available on the total number of collisions each year, but we do know that there were at least 225 during the 1871 shipping season.[50]

In 1898, in an effort to reverse the alarming trend in collisions, Captain James Dunham of Chicago, the just-elected president the Lake Carriers' Association, proposed that the shipping companies establish separate up-bound and downbound courses on the lakes.[51] By separating the upbound and downbound tracks by a couple of miles, vessel masters would be less likely to encounter head-on traffic that posed a collision threat. To Captain Dunham's thinking, that would greatly improve the situation for vessel masters, particularly during periods when rain, snow, or fog obscured visibility.

While his proposal had some backing within the association's ranks, it was nonetheless voted down. Most of those who opposed the seemingly logical plan argued that ships would lose too much time by having to stay out in the lake on the downbound track.[52] The shortest distance between two points is a straight line, and that's where the fleets wanted their captains to run. After all, time is money in the shipping business. Besides, they argued, there wouldn't be any collisions if captains and mates would just follow the rules of the road.

Supporters of Dunham's plan thought that argument didn't carry water, and they suspected that many owners preferred not to have *any* restrictions placed on the way their ships operated. The rules of the road were helpful, to be sure, but the collision between the *Morning Star* and *Courtlandt* showed that the rules weren't very helpful when a captain simply didn't know there was a ship bearing down on him. The crews of many ships learned that lesson in subsequent years. Among them were Captain Wally Rogers and the sailors on the *John B. Cowle.*

John B. Cowle, 1909

Frank Brown's career as a Great Lakes sailor was a short one. The eighteen-year-old Brown was a farm boy from Brantford Township,

Ontario. In early July 1909, he got into an argument with his father over farm chores and left home. Brown traveled to Buffalo, where he signed on as a deckhand aboard the *John B. Cowle*, which was taking on a load of coal bound for Lake Superior. He was one of four new deckhands hired at Buffalo.

Captains of lake freighters liked to hire farm boys in those days. While the work on a freighter was often arduous, it didn't begin to compare to farm labor . . . and the pay was much better. As a result, the farm boys were generally good, hard-working crewmen who seldom complained about the work.

Whether out of love for his son or merely because he couldn't run the farm without him, Frank Brown's father chased after him. When he discovered that his son had joined the crew of the *Cowle*, which had left for Lake Superior, the elder Brown hopped on a train headed for Detroit. When he arrived in Detroit, Mr. Brown told his story to Detroit police. They took him to see Captain J. W. Westcott, who ran the mail boat and vessel reporting service on the Detroit River. When the *Cowle* came steaming up the river, farmer Brown was taken out to it in one of Captain Westcott's small boats that were used to deliver mail to the passing ships. While the mail was being handled, Mr. Brown climbed aboard the big steamer and coaxed his son into returning to their farm in Ontario. Frank Brown hurriedly packed his few belongings, said his good-byes to his shipmates, and left with his father in Captain Westcott's skiff.

The other three deckhands hired at Buffalo didn't stick around long either. They quit when the *Cowle* reached the iron ore dock at Two Harbors, Minnesota, several days later. We don't know why. It could have been that the work was too hard . . . or maybe the deckhands found the accommodations aboard the ship to be lacking . . . or they might have gotten tired of the boatswain, mates, and captain hollering at them all the time. Then, as now, there are many reasons why people decide they don't want to work on a ship, but in the case of the *Cowle*, some would later say the deckhands must have had premonitions.

There was no way that Frank Brown and the other three deckhands could have known it then, but quitting saved their lives. The four deckhands who were hired to replace them before the big freighter cleared the dock at Two Harbors were all killed less than two days later. They were among fourteen crewmembers who were lost when their ship sank following a collision.[53]

When the downbound *Cowle* neared Whitefish Bay early on the morning of July 12, 1909, Lake Superior was in the grip of thick fog.

At about 5:40 A.M., the *Cowle*, loaded with 7,000 tons of iron ore, was struck and nearly cut in two by the upbound *Isaac M. Scott* while the two steamers were about a mile north of Whitefish Point. The bow of the *Scott* penetrated twenty feet into the side of the 436-foot *Cowle*. The 504-foot *Scott* was on her maiden voyage at the time.

The badly holed *Cowle* sank in about three minutes. Before she went down, crewmen on the *Scott* threw a line to the *Cowle*, and three of the *Cowle*'s crew managed to scramble hand-over-hand across the line before their ship went down. The crew on the *Frank H. Goodyear*, a passing steamer that had been following the *Scott*, and persons aboard several small boats in the vicinity eventually pulled seven other survivors from the water, but fourteen of those who had been aboard the *Cowle* went down with the ship.

The *Cowle*, owned by the Cowle Transit Company but operated by the United States Transportation Company, was valued at more than $275,000 when she sank. The brand-new *Scott*, owned by the Virginia Steamship Company and operated as part of the large Hanna Steamship fleet, was able to limp back to the Soo for repairs. She had a gaping gash in her bow that was more than twenty feet long and eight feet high in some places, and her forepeak had flooded. The *Scott* was carrying many of the survivors from the *Cowle*.[54]

At the Soo, a lawyer representing the *Cowle*'s owners reportedly kept the survivors "in hiding" and prevented them from talking with reporters so that they couldn't inadvertently say something that might suggest the shipowners had been somehow negligent. In the corporate atmosphere of the twentieth century, this was a fairly common practice. Claims were even occasionally heard that shipwreck survivors were "coached" by company lawyers on what they should say to the steamboat inspectors. After keeping them incommunicado, the company lawyer bustled the survivors from the *Cowle* aboard the first passenger boat headed in the general direction of Cleveland.[55]

Steamboat inspectors later held a hearing at Marquette. They suspended the license of Captain Rogers and Mate Ed Carlton of the *Cowle* for thirty days, after concluding that their ship was traveling too fast for conditions when the accident happened. Mate F. W. Wertheimer of the *Scott* lost his license for one year for traveling too fast and not signaling.

As one Great Lakes historian put it, "For the *Scott*, this fatal collision on her maiden trip had sinister forebodings."[56] She vanished with all hands just four years later in the Great Storm of 1913. The *Goodyear*, which had helped rescue survivors from the *Cowle*, wouldn't even last that long.

Overall, the 1880s were a boom period for shipping on the lakes. At the same time, many shipowners saw themselves under attack from all quarters. The continuing expansion of the railroads had crippled the passenger trade on the lakes, and there was a threat that they would do the same to cargo shipments. Government regulation was continually increasing, yet government agencies were often slow in responding to the industry's needs. Too many ships were being lost or damaged—collisions and groundings were virtually a daily occurrence. Then, too, it was becoming increasingly difficult to find good crews to operate the modern steamers, in part because of the competition between the shipping companies.

In the mid-1880s, shipowners and operators formed two trade associations—the Lake Carriers' Association and the Cleveland Vessel Owners Association—intended to allow their respective members to work together to solve problems that affected the industry as a whole. Both groups took aggressive stands against a bill introduced in Washington that would have established load lines for ships on the Great Lakes, and they managed to defeat the proposed legislation.

The member companies of the Cleveland Vessel Owners Association also set up a system to keep track of any obstructions on the waterways that might damage their ships, such as snags, sunken hulks, and shoaling. The association also worked with officials of the Bureau of Navigation, which was established in 1884, to improve aids to navigation around the lakes, such as lighthouses and buoys.

Some of the activities of the trade associations were, perhaps, less laudatory, however. In those days before antitrust legislation, for example, an early goal of the companies belonging to the Cleveland Vessel Owners Association was to set seamen's pay each season. Many sailors bounced from ship to ship and from company to company so much that they seldom bothered to completely unpack their seabags. Feeling no particular allegiance to any company, the sailors were often attracted to whatever company was offering the highest wages at the time. By setting a pay rate that would apply on all ships operated by its member companies, the association hoped to reduce the number of sailors jumping from one company to another and, simultaneously, hold down labor costs by keeping seamen's pay at the lowest possible level.

In 1892 the two trade associations merged to form the Lake Carriers' Association (LCA), which still represents Great Lakes shipowners today. One of the LCA's first major projects was to lobby Congress to enact legislation regulating vessel traffic on the hazardous St. Marys River. With traffic to and from Lake Superior increasing each year because of growing iron ore shipments, collisions in the narrow and winding stretches of the St. Marys were taking a heavy toll on shipping.

Congress wasn't then very used to having industries actually ask to be regulated, and they were more than happy to go along with the LCA's proposal. The necessary legislation was promptly enacted, authorizing the Treasury Department and its Bureau of Navigation to implement the necessary rules. The LCA drafted a set of rules for consideration, and those rules were approved and implemented, as written, by Secretary of the Treasury Charles Foster. The new navigation rules for the St. Marys included a nine-mile-an-hour speed limit on narrow stretches of the river.[57]

The navigation rules looked good on paper, but since no system had been established to enforce them, the captains of many ships transiting the St. Marys ignored them. That reality was pointed out in a resolution passed at the 1896 meeting of the Ship Masters Association, held in Washington. The resolution noted that a "great danger of collisions" still existed in the St. Marys.[58]

At the urging of the LCA, the Revenue Cutter Service established a river patrol in the St. Marys River in 1897 to enforce the navigation rules. The Revenue Cutter Service would eventually operate three patrol boats on the river, augmented by six lookout stations built at strategic locations.[59] They enforced the new speed limit in the river, issuing tickets to the masters of ships that were speeding. River patrol personnel also advised captains of other traffic in the St. Marys and made sure that ships checked down and sounded fog signals when visibility was limited.

The LCA's leadership in trying to reduce the number of collisions and groundings in the St. Marys may seem exceptionally enlightened and altruistic. It's quite possible, however, that the LCA's efforts were motivated largely by economics.

One of the greatest fears of the shipping companies in the iron ore and grain trades was that the vital St. Marys waterway would be blocked by a sunken or stranded ship, as it had been on a number of occasions. A wreck in any of the numerous narrow channels of the river threatened to bring shipping to a halt until the vessel could be removed. Such blockades had serious economic consequences for the shipping companies that belonged to the LCA.

Despite the navigation rules and the vigilance of the river patrol service, collisions and groundings were never eliminated in the St. Marys, and traffic in the river ground to a halt on a number of occasions. The worst blockade of the river, in fact, took place several years after the accident prevention programs went into effect.

33. The salvage barge *Monterey* works alongside the hull of the steamer *Douglass Houghton*, which was rammed and sunk in a narrow channel of the St. Marys River in the fall of 1899. The big steel steamer blocked the vital artery between the iron ore ranges of Lake Superior and the industrial centers on the lower lakes for six days before it could be raised and removed. More than two hundred ships were idled by the *Houghton* blockade. (Author's Collection)

Douglass Houghton, 1899

On September 5, 1899, the brand-new freighter *Douglass Houghton* was downbound on the river, towing its steel-hulled barge consort, the *John Fritz*. Both vessels were heavily laden with iron ore. As the *Houghton* approached the difficult turn at Johnson's Point, on the east side of Neebish Island, one of the chains connecting the ship's wheel to the rudder broke. Those aboard quickly reduced speed and dropped the anchor, but the unsteerable ship drove bow-first into the riverbank alongside the narrow channel. The strong current then caught the *Houghton*'s stern and swung it across the St. Marys until it grounded on the opposite bank.

The small crew aboard the unpowered *Fritz* tried to stop their vessel by dropping its anchors, but momentum carried it downstream and it rammed the *Houghton*'s midsection, "cutting through [her] steel plates like a tin can." The freighter's cargo hold quickly flooded, and the *Houghton* sank to the bottom, totally blocking the river channel.

The "*Houghton* blockade" closed down the St. Marys for six days, cutting off Lake Superior from the lower lakes. For most of the companies belonging to the LCA, it was "the most appalling situation in lake freight traffic that has been experienced in a quarter of a century." Before the crippled hull of the *Houghton* could be patched and raised, more than two hundred ships were idled by the blockade.

Even before the *Houghton*'s sunken hull was cleared out of the river channel, shipping companies began to call for construction of another channel around Neebish Island. In 1908 a manmade channel was completed through the solid rock along the west side of the island. The "Rock Cut," as it came to be known, was used by downbound freighters, while upbound ships continued to use the channel on the east side of the island at Johnsons Point.[60]

Although the LCA had played a leadership role in implementing navigational rules for the St. Marys River and setting up the river patrol, member companies were still opposed to separating the upbound and downbound courses on the lakes. Course separation seemed to crop up year after year from 1898 on, usually after yet another ship had been lost in a collision on the open lake . . . and there were plenty of ships sunk in midlake collisions. In 1899 the schooner *Typo* and four of her crew were lost in a collision off Rogers City on Lake Huron. In 1902 the steamer *City of Venice* collided with the steamer *Seguin* and went down on Lake Erie, taking three crewmembers along to the bottom. In 1905 the freighter *Thomas Palmer* was rammed and sunk by the big steamer *Harvard* off Stannard Rock on Lake Superior.

The following year, the wood-hulled steamer *New Orleans* came out second best in a collision with the steel-hulled freighter *William R. Linn*. The *New Orleans* went down off Thunder Bay Island on northern Lake Huron. On June 22, 1909, the little wooden steamer *W. P. Thew* also joined the list of collision casualties. The 132-foot *Thew* was the victim of a "hit and run" accident. She was run down off Thunder Bay Island by the 545-foot *William Livingstone*, a modern steel freighter named, interestingly enough, for the longtime president of the Lake Carriers' Association. The *Livingstone* didn't stop after the collision.[61]

Henry Steinbrenner, 1909

Another in the ongoing string of collisions occurred late on the afternoon of December 6, 1909, when the freighters *Henry Steinbrenner* and *Harry*

A. Berwind collided on the Round Island turn in the lower St. Marys during a blinding snowstorm. The 420-foot *Steinbrenner* was downbound carrying 7,000 tons of iron ore in her hold. In her pilothouse were Captain Loher, Second Mate Inches, and Wheelsman Isaacs. As their ship began the long, slow turn at Round Island, an upbound freighter emerged out of the snow and dwindling light. While the navigational rules required ships to pass port-to-port if at all possible, those in the pilothouse of the *Steinbrenner* heard the approaching ship blow two blasts on her whistle, the signal for a starboard-to-starboard passing. Inches agreed to the passing arrangement by replying with two whistle blasts.

With the ships rapidly closing on each other, the three men in the *Steinbrenner*'s pilothouse were startled to hear a single long whistle blast from the *Berwind*, the signal for a port-to-port passage. It was immediately obvious to everyone in the pilothouse of the *Steinbrenner* that the two ships were going to collide. Captain Loher leapt from his chair and threw the indicator on the engine order telegraph to the "stop" position, while Inches blew a series of short blasts on the whistle, the danger signal.

As everyone in the *Steinbrenner*'s pilothouse braced themselves, the bow of the *Berwind* smashed into the starboard side of their ship, about even with the number 3 hatch. The *Berwind*'s engine had been thrown into full reverse just before the collision, and seconds after the impact she backed away from the *Steinbrenner* and was rapidly obscured by the snow and fading light.

When Captain Loher ran out on the bridge wing and looked down the side of his ship, he could see that the bow of the *Berwind* had torn a twenty-five-foot-wide hole in the hull. Since the hole extended well below the waterline, the *Steinbrenner*'s cargo hold was rapidly filling with water and the ship began to settle to the bottom. Loher shouted for Inches to sound the "abandon ship" signal. By then, deck personnel could already be seen racing aft along the deck from their rooms in the forward end of the vessel.

Down in the engine room, the chief engineer instructed his men to hurriedly put out the fires so the boilers wouldn't blow up when the engine room flooded. Working frantically, they began pulling the burning coals out of the fireboxes, dumping them in flaming piles on the steel deck. When the engine room staff was laboring knee-deep in the rapidly rising water, the chief ordered them to drop their tools and head for the lifeboats.

The main deck was awash and the lifeboats were already being lowered by the time the chief and his men had climbed the ladder out of the engine room. Minutes later, all of the *Steinbrenner*'s crew except Captain Loher,

Mate Inches, and Wheelsman Isaacs boarded the boats and rowed away from their sinking ship. As they pulled away, a dull heavy explosion was heard and there was a shower of sparks from the *Steinbrenner*'s smokestack as the icy river water came in contact with one of the red-hot boilers and triggered an explosion.

The three men in the pilothouse had dallied too long, and before they could head aft to the lifeboats, the deck was already awash. Fortunately for them, the ship was in a shallow stretch of the river, and when it settled upright on the bottom the pilothouse and the top half of the forward cabins were still above water.[62]

While the men marooned in the pilothouse weren't going to drown, they were in danger of being run down by another ship. With the steam engine and generators out of commission, there was no electricity to power the ship's running lights. There they sat, smack in the middle of the shipping channel, without a light to warn approaching ships. "Several vessels downbound were headed straight for us," Inches later recounted. "At times I thought they would run us down. I shouted until I got hoarse. They heard and moved out a little, although one big fellow came within 20 feet of us."

The three men left aboard the sunken *Steinbrenner* eventually found a kerosene lamp that they lit and hung from the mast as a beacon to warn off other ships. Shortly afterward, a lifeboat that had been launched from the *Berwind*, anchored nearby, took off Loher, Inches, and Isaacs. By then, the rest of the *Steinbrenner*'s crew was safely ashore on nearby Round Island after a harrowing trip through the blowing snow.

The following morning, the crew of the *Steinbrenner* was carried up to Sault Ste. Marie aboard the steamer *Sonoma*. There they passed the day at the Sherman House hotel while waiting for their fleet's *Philip Minch* to carry them down the lakes.

The *Berwind* had also been seriously damaged in the collision. She had a hole in her bow "large enough to drive a load of hay into," and her cargo hold was partially flooded. Had she been loaded at the time of the collision, it's likely that she, too, would have gone to the bottom. Once temporary repairs had been made and the ship was pumped out, she headed for the nearest shipyard.[63]

During the winter of 1909–10, salver Tom Reid of Port Huron raised the *Steinbrenner*, and the ship was subsequently repaired and returned to service.[64] It wasn't the vessel's last accident, however—not even her last collision. The *Steinbrenner* was one of those ships that always seemed to be in harm's way. The *Frank H. Goodyear*, on the other hand, led a

34. The bow and stern cabins of the *Henry Steinbrenner* were still above water after the freighter was rammed and sunk while negotiating the lower St. Marys River during a blinding snowstorm on December 6, 1909. The 420-foot *Steinbrenner* was raised during the following winter, and subsequently returned to service in the ore trade between Lake Superior and the lower lakes. On May 11, 1953, the aging steamer lost some of her hatch covers and foundered on Lake Superior during a spring storm. (Ralph Roberts Collection)

comparatively charmed life after she was launched in 1902. Right up until the spring of 1910, that is.

Frank H. Goodyear, 1910

Early on the morning of May 22, 1910, the steamer *Frank H. Goodyear* was headed down Lake Huron in one of the pea-soup fogs that were so common during the spring sailing season. Owned by Mitchell and Company, the freighter was on her way to Lake Erie with a load of iron ore.

Captain Russell Heminger was on watch in the *Goodyear*'s pilothouse, having relieved Archie Fulton so the second mate could go aft for breakfast. It was chilly in the pilothouse, because Captain Heminger had the front window open so that he could hear the fog whistle of any upbound ships. His wasn't the only set of ears that scanned the gray mist for that first faint sound of a steamboat's whistle that would alert them to an approaching ship. Down below Captain Heminger, standing in the very bow of the boat, was Watchman William Pitt. Bundled up in his heaviest clothes to help ward off the damp chill of the spring air, Pitt leaned on the *Goodyear*'s gunwale and listened carefully for oncoming ships. Every minute, the eerie silence of the foggy morning was pierced by the deep-throated roar of the *Goodyear*'s own steam whistle as Captain Heminger blew the fog signal to warn other ships that they were on their way down the lake.

Many people have difficulty seeing any beauty in a lake freighter. For the most part, they're designed to haul iron ore, coal, stone, and grain efficiently, with little attention paid to appearances. Captain Heminger often referred to his ship as "a beauty," however, and he never tired of contemplating her fine lines. She was never considered a big freighter, not even when she was first launched eight years earlier. In 1902, the biggest ships, like American Steamship's *John W. Gates*, were 497 feet long, while the *Goodyear* was only 436. Now, in 1910, even the *Gates* seemed small when compared to the giant freighters like the 606-foot *Shenango* that had come out of the shipyards in the past few years. The 600-footers were the standard for the industry those days, but there weren't enough of them to haul all the cargo that needed to move on the lakes. There was still plenty of room in the industry for a fine ship like the *Goodyear*.

Besides, thought Captain Heminger, ships like the *Shenango* were decidedly ugly. Washington I. Babcock had designed it without a stern deckhouse. That was supposed to reduce the likelihood that the ship would foul itself at the loading and unloading docks, but the "submarine sterns," as they were called, left them with an unfinished look. "Submarine" was a good word for them, Heminger thought to himself. The galley and all the living quarters on boats like the *Shenango* were down below their spar decks, almost underwater. For the galley and engine room crews who quartered at the stern, it was like living in a cave. And if there was a sea running, it was like living in an underwater cave! No thanks, Russell Heminger thought to himself, big isn't always better.

Nope, the *Goodyear* had it all over on the big boats when it came to looks. To Heminger's eye, she was perfection personified. God bless old Frank Goodyear, Heminger said to himself. The late president of the Buffalo and Susquehanna Railroad had been an original owner of the *Goodyear*, and he'd seen to it that the shipyard didn't skimp on the ship that was going to bear his name. It even bore a personal touch of its namesake. Goodyear had been a regular passenger aboard the ship when he was alive, and he's had his luxurious private railroad coach installed on deck for his use.

Heminger stared ahead into the gray nothingness, trying to focus his ears and brain on the crucial task of listening for the fog signal of an approaching ship. The longer you stood watch in the fog, the more tense you got. He didn't like to run in the fog, no captain did, but there really wasn't any alternative. In the spring and fall, fog was as common on the northern lakes as seagulls. If you didn't run in the fog, you wouldn't be in business very long. Nonetheless, it was a risky business. A slight mistake in navigation, and you were aground; a simple lapse in attention, and you could find yourself in a collision.

Heminger instinctively thought back to the July day of the previous year when he and the *Goodyear* had followed the *Isaac M. Scott* out of the Soo and onto Lake Superior in a thick fog. Shortly after the *Goodyear* had rounded Whitefish Point at about 5:30 in the morning, he heard what sounded like a muffled explosion. Minutes later, Heminger and his crew had come upon sailors thrashing about desperately in the cold water. The sailors were survivors from the *John B. Cowle*, which had accidentally been rammed and sunk by the *Scott*. That memory, still sharply etched in Captain Heminger's mind, made it easier for him to concentrate on listening for the sound of an approaching ship.

At the stern of the *Goodyear*, most of the crewmembers were eating breakfast in the galley of Steward Frank Bassett. Bassett's galley was a family operation. His wife and mother served as his second cook and porter, and his three-year-old son John sat in his highchair in the corner and "supervised" the operation. In the days before labor unions and shipboard assignments based on seniority, it was quite common for galleys to be run by husband-and-wife teams. The cook's wife gave the galley a feminine touch that was valued by most of the sailors. In many ways, it was like going into your mother's kitchen at home. And having Bassett's son and mother aboard gave the galley of the *Goodyear* even more of a homey touch.

The *Goodyear*'s galley was an oasis of warmth and hospitality that chilly May morning. The air was heavy with the aromas of fried eggs, potatoes, and bacon wafting into the messroom and officer's dining room from Bassett's stove, and the hearty smell of freshly brewed coffee coming from the big urn in the corner of the galley. With breakfast just about over, Bassett's mother had set to work scrubbing the deck in the galley.

Those who were just preparing to go to work tended to eat quietly, most not quite fully awake yet, nor particularly happy to be up. On the other hand, those who had just gotten off watch were more boisterous and, with no place to go but to bed, tended to linger a little longer in the galley, often chatting with the Bassetts while the cook and his family sat down to eat their own breakfast after the crew had been fed.

That morning in May of 1910, the conversations in the galley were interrupted by a series of sharp blasts on the *Goodyear*'s steam whistle. It was the danger signal, and several of the crewmen started to get up from the tables to go out on deck to see what was happening when all of the sudden there was a loud crash and the *Goodyear* heeled over. Several of those in the galley were thrown to the deck by the impact, and they were instantly showered with an assortment of silverware, plates, pitchers of milk, and pots and pans that became airborne when the ship listed.

Hurrying out onto deck, the Bassetts and their breakfast customers saw the bow of another freighter just a few yards away from the *Goodyear*'s hull. The ship—the *James B. Wood*—was almost perpendicular to the hull of the *Goodyear,* and she appeared to be dead in the water. Leaning over the gunwale that ran alongside the galley, they looked down the side of their hull. Nearly amidships, a swirl of water disappeared into a massive void in the side of the *Goodyear*'s hull that had apparently been created by the bow of the *Wood.* Tons of water were cascading into the freighter's cargo hold, and they could almost feel her settling into the water.

The crewmen who had been forward at the time of the collision were already rushing aft along the starboard side of the *Goodyear*'s deck. While some dashed for their rooms to get their lifejackets, others raced up the stairs leading to the boat deck in a desperate effort to launch the two lifeboats. Some of the crew looked at how fast the *Goodyear* was sinking and merely jumped overboard and began swimming toward the *Wood,* not wanting to get trapped in the suction when their ship went down. Before those at the lifeboat stations could even get the canvas covers off the boats, the mortally wounded *Goodyear* noisily dove for the bottom, pulling those on deck beneath the cold water.

The few crewmembers who were able to fight their way back to the surface found themselves amidst a cluttered mass of debris that had floated loose from their ship. Those who had the strength grabbed onto whatever happened to be floating nearby. There was a lot of confused shouting, crewmembers calling out the names of friends, or yelling for help from those on the *Wood.* Frank Bassett and his mother floated near each other, both holding onto pieces of wreckage.

"Emma, Emma? John?" Frank hollered as loud as he could. Tightly gripping the hatch plank that supported him, Frank pulled himself up until his head and shoulders were partially out of the water and scanned the debris-strewn surface of the lake for any sign of his missing family members. He could make out the heads of a few crewmembers sticking out of the water amongst the flotsam, but there was no sign of his wife or son.[65]

The crewmembers on the *Wood* immediately launched their own lifeboats and began pulling the *Goodyear*'s survivors from the water. There weren't many. The ship had simply gone down too fast—"like a stone," one of the *Wood*'s crewmembers said. In addition to Frank Bassett and his mother, only Captain Heminger, Engineer George Grant, and Fireman Frank Mallick were plucked from the water. The cook's wife and son and seventeen crewmembers had gone to the bottom with their ship. Most were trapped in their cabins when the *Goodyear* sank, while others were sucked under in the whirling vortex of water created when the ship dove to the bottom. That was probably the fate of Emma Bassett and her baby son. In the moments before the ship had gone down, Frank had tied life preservers around both of them, yet they were never seen again.[66]

The crewmen from the *Wood* continued to search for survivors at the scene until early afternoon. By then, the sun had burnt off the layer of fog and it was painfully obvious to all that there were but five survivors from the *Goodyear*. Finally, with Captain Heminger's blessing, the master of the *Wood* recalled his crew and set a course for Port Huron. With its bow crushed and the forepeak taking on water, the *Wood* limped on down the lake at an excruciatingly slow four miles an hour. The 120-mile run, which would normally have taken them nine or ten hours, consumed the better part of a day and a half, fully thirty hours from the time they left the scene of the collision. To go faster would have risked damaging the watertight bulkhead between the forepeak and the cargo hold, and that was the only thing keeping the *Wood* afloat.[67]

When the *Wood* arrived at Port Huron, newspaper reporters hounded Captain Heminger and the four other survivors, but they were very tight-lipped about the details of the accident. Their standard reply when questioned was that they were "under orders from our owners."[68]

The loss of the *Goodyear* was a major financial blow to Captain John Mitchell's shipping company. The ship had been insured for $255,000, a fair representation of her value, right up until the policy expired on May 19. Business wasn't great, though, so to save a little money, Captain Mitchell carried only a $30,000 policy on the boat after that date.[69]

As a result of the continuing carnage resulting from midlake collisions each year, the shipping companies that belonged to the Lake Carriers'

Association finally agreed to establish separate upbound and downbound courses on Lake Huron and Lake Superior in 1911, thirteen years—and many collisions—after they had first been proposed by Captain J. S. Dunham. The upbound courses were set up closest to shore, with the downbound courses about two miles farther out into the lake. The scheme put the big ships coming down the lakes loaded with iron ore out into deeper water.

In 1914, members of the LCA had a change of heart about the nine-mile-an-hour speed limit they had helped to establish on the St. Marys River. Many of their ships were being ticketed by the river patrol, and shipping executives were concerned that their liability might be increased if their vessels were involved in an accident while they were speeding. Those concerns prompted the LCA to lobby for an increase in the speed limit on the St. Marys to eleven miles an hour. "The great majority of ships on the lakes could not exceed that speed," they argued, "and it would do away with the checking of the ship and watching the time limits on the various runs."[70] In other words, they wanted the speed limit high enough that their ships *couldn't* exceed it! It was a novel solution to the problem of ships speeding in the river. Interestingly, the Bureau of Navigation that administered federal navigational laws and regulations adopted the proposal.

From 1915 on, the new speed limits on the St. Marys were enforced by the Coast Guard, which was created that year by merging the Revenue Cutter Service and Life-Saving Service. Secretary of the Treasury William McAdoo had recommended the move as a way of increasing efficiency and cutting costs. Both agencies, he argued, were involved in preventing shipwrecks and deaths in U.S. waters.[71]

In 1915, the members of the Canadian Lake Carriers' finally agreed to abide by the separate courses that had been established by the LCA for Lake Huron and Lake Superior. Separate courses weren't set up for Lake Michigan until 1926, while those on Lake Erie and Lake Ontario weren't established until after World War II.[72]

Course separation didn't end collisions on the lakes, unfortunately. Many of the smaller ships, like the dozens of lumber hookers that operated on the lakes, weren't registered with the LCA, and their owners or masters didn't necessarily feel obligated to abide by the separated courses. Besides, compliance with the separate courses was purely voluntary anyway. Other ships merely got off course and accidentally wandered into the track of oncoming traffic. In other instances, captains cut corners to save a little time and crossed over into the other shipping lane. Regardless, the system definitely eliminated some collisions that would otherwise have occurred, saving some ships and the lives of some sailors. Not those on the *Superior City*, however.

Superior City, 1920

On the evening of August 20, 1920, the ore freighter *Willis L. King* made the big sweeping turn around Whitefish Point and set a course across Lake Superior. Visibility wasn't very good. The last rays of sunlight were just disappearing over the western horizon, and a haze and occasional patches of heavy fog covered the lake. Shortly after leaving Whitefish Bay, the master of the *King* made out the silhouette of an approaching ship. It appeared that the oncoming vessel would pass to port of the *King*, and the captain sounded the required passing signal, one long blast on the ship's whistle. Leaning out the front window of the pilothouse, he heard the downbound vessel answer with one long blast.

What occurred during the next several minutes is still the subject of debate. What we do know is that at about 9:30 that evening, the *King* and the downbound vessel—Pittsburgh Steamship's *Superior City*—collided. In the last moments before the crash, it must have been obvious that the two ships weren't going to clear each other, because the captain of the *Superior City* sounded the general alarm to alert his crew even before the collision. As crewmembers on the Pittsburgh freighter scrambled for the ship's two lifeboats, the sturdy bow of the *King* punched through the hull of the heavily laden *Superior City* on its port side, near the ship's stern. A gaping hole was ripped in the hull at the forward end of the engine room. As the momentum of the two ships pulled them apart, water began cascading into the *Superior City*'s engine room and the ship's stern settled in the water. By then, many of the crew were gathered on the stern, working frantically to launch the two lifeboats. Among them was Walter Richter, the boatswain. Richter had been off watch and in his room at the bow of the ship when the general alarm sounded. He had dashed out of his room and down the *Superior City*'s deck clad only in his underwear.

According to Richter, only minutes after the collision the cold water flooding the engine room must have come in contact with the superheated boilers, and the boilers blew up, taking much of the stern of the ship with them. Almost immediately, the heavily laden *Superior City* plunged to the bottom in two hundred feet of water.

"I would not be surprised if most of the boys were blown to pieces from their places over the boiler house where they had lined up in order to get into the lifeboats," said Richter. The force of the blast blew Richter's underwear off and hurled him into the water. "I sank deep into the icy water, which evidently brought me to my senses," he said. "I thought I would never reach the surface. I swam for about 4 minutes and up from the depths came a steamer's hatch cover upon which I climbed and hung for a half hour until the *Turner* showed up."[73]

Richter was pulled aboard the *Turner,* a small yawl that was in the area. Also pulled from the water were the *Superior City*'s captain, second mate, and wheelsman, all of whom had been on duty in the vessel's midship pilothouse when the collision and subsequent explosion occurred. Twenty-eight of the *Superior City*'s crewmembers and the wife of the second assistant engineer went down with the ship. No bodies were ever recovered, even though many of the dead had been on the boat deck at the stern when the boiler blew up and the ship sank. Their bodies were either blown to bits by the explosion, or the ship sucked them under as it plummeted to the bottom.

The *King,* with a gaping hole in her bow, was able to reverse course and return to Sault Ste. Marie for repairs. When the *King* was inspected at the Soo, it was found that her stem had been set back ten feet and seventeen of her shell plates had been buckled. In no danger of sinking, she was allowed to leave for a shipyard at Superior, Wisconsin, for repairs.[74]

Both masters were later found guilty of "not satisfying themselves as to the intent of the other," as required by the rules of the road. There was obvious confusion over the passing signals given, but neither ship slowed down or made an effort to stop, as required by the "rule of prudent seamanship."[75]

Three years after the loss of the *Superior City,* forest fires ravaged Michigan's Upper Peninsula. If the wind happened to be blowing in the wrong direction, smoke from such fires would occasionally cause problems for ships. That was the case around Sault Ste. Marie in mid-October 1923. Smoke from numerous forest fires west of the Soo was causing serious visibility problems for ships on the St. Marys River and around Whitefish Bay at the entrance to Lake Superior. Upbound vessels were reporting delays of as much as thirty-six hours due to heavy smoke, which often combined with fog during the morning and evening hours to cut visibility to zero.

That was the situation on Whitefish Bay the afternoon of October 11, 1923, but the fog and smoke didn't stop two steamers, although their captains probably later wished they had gone to anchor. Off Parisienne

Island at the headwaters of the St. Marys River, the steamer *John McCart-ney Kennedy* collided with the ill-starred *Henry Steinbrenner*, the same ship that had sunk in the lower St. Marys after a collision with the *Harry A. Berwind* in 1909.

The *Kennedy's* anchor ripped a four-foot hole in the *Steinbrenner's* bow, but it was above the waterline and the freighter was able to make its way to the Soo for repairs. While the damage sustained by the *Steinbrenner* was relatively minor, costing only $5,000 to repair, many superstitious sailors took note of the fact that the ship then had two strikes against it.[76]

Huronton, 1923

Even though visibility was still obscured the next day, the Canadian freighter *Huronton* steamed around Whitefish Point and headed out across Lake Superior. Coming down the lake, Interlake Steamship's *Cetus* also pushed on through the fog and smoke toward Whitefish Bay. Lake Superior proved to be too small for the two ships that day.

About twenty-three miles north of Whitefish, the two ships collided, the bow of the *Cetus* driving deep into the hull of the *Huronton*. Looking out the pilothouse window at the bow of his ship sticking into the side of the *Huronton*, the master of the *Cetus* had the good sense to keeping his engine turning ahead, thereby holding his ship into the badly holed Canadian, temporarily slowing the flow of water into its hull.

Quickly taking stock of the damage to their ship, those on the *Huronton* concluded that she was going to sink and began climbing over onto the *Cetus*. When all of the crewmembers were safely aboard his ship, the master of the *Cetus* backed his vessel out of the *Huronton*. As soon as the gaping hole in the side of the *Huronton* was opened up, tons of water began to pour into its cargo hold and the ship settled deeply in the water. It soon took on a heavy list, then plunged to the bottom.[77]

The combination of fog and smoke from forest fires impeded shipping for a total of four days in that instance. Many ships merely tied up at docks in the river or went to anchor in Whitefish Bay until visibility improved. At one time, sixty-six ships were stalled in the river.[78] Other ships, like the *Steinbrenner*, *Kennedy*, *Cetus*, and *Huronton*, gambled and tried to sail blind. Many captains had a deep-seated disdain about going to anchor, and they would keep on sailing whether they could see anything or not.

The decline in the number of ships that operated on the lakes, which had begun at the turn of the century, was accelerated by the Great

Depression that began in the fall of 1929. There were 2,872 ships on the lakes in 1900, but only about 839 when the depression started. By 1940 the size of the fleet had dropped to 817 ships, of which 524 were operated by U.S. companies and 293 by Canadian firms.[79] As the number of ships in service on the lakes declined, so did the number of casualties of all sorts, including collisions. Nonetheless, ships still occasionally managed to ram into each other.

George M. Humphrey, 1943

During the early-morning hours of June 15, 1943, a pea-soup fog hung over the Straits of Mackinac at the junction of Lake Huron and Lake Michigan. Shortly after 3 A.M., two big freighters were steaming along through the fog. Traveling west on the Lake Huron side of the Straits was the *George M. Humphrey,* the 605-foot flagship of the Kinsman Transit Company, on its way to Chicago with 13,992 tons of iron ore. Eastbound, in ballast, was the *D. M. Clemson,* a 580-foot freighter owned by U.S. Steel's Pittsburgh Steamship.

Even under the best of conditions, going through the Straits is a bit tricky. All the shipping lanes used by the freighters on northern Lake Huron and northern Lake Michigan converge there in waters that are dotted with islands. In addition to freighter traffic, car ferries running between Michigan's two peninsulas cut across the shipping lanes on the Lake Huron side of the Straits, as do smaller passenger ferries that run to Mackinac Island from docks in St. Ignace and Mackinaw City. Add to that a nighttime passage in heavy fog, and you've got a situation that will fray the nerves of even the most experienced lakes pilot.

Aware of the heavy traffic they would likely encounter, Captain Arlie Dennis was in the pilothouse of the *Humphrey,* along with the mate and wheelsman who stood the 12-to-4 watch. An extra pair of eyes and ears were always helpful on a foggy night in the Straits, especially when they were the eyes and ears of an experienced master like Arlie Dennis. The cautious Dennis also had his ship running at reduced speed, just as the rules of the road called for him to do during fog.

Captain Chris Johnson was also on the bridge of the *Clemson.* Johnson didn't like to be slowed down by fog, though, and he had his ship plowing along at full lake speed.

Both ships were blowing fog signals. Both captains had their pilothouse windows open so they could hear the fog whistle of any approaching steamer.

Despite all that, the two ships collided at about 3:15 A.M., just under two miles off Old Point Mackinac Light, with the bow of the *Clemson* driving hard into the side of the *Humphrey*. Carried on by its momentum, the *Humphrey* then slid away from the *Clemson* and disappeared in the fog.

When Captain Dennis surveyed the damage to the *Humphrey*, he knew that the ship was mortally wounded. His first thought was to make a run for the beach and ground the boat before it had a chance to sink. With the ship settling rapidly in the water, however, his instincts told him that there wasn't time. Without hesitation, he turned on the general alarm bells. Waiting just a second or two for the loud ringing to rouse any crewmembers who might not have been awakened by the jolt of the collision, he then blew the "abandon ship" signal on the ship's steam whistle.

Within seconds of Captain Dennis's sounding the general alarm, the crew of the *Humphrey* was gathered at the two lifeboats on the stern. The boats were quickly cranked out and lowered, and the crewmembers scrambled down the Jacob's ladder into the boats. No sooner had the lifeboats rowed away from the hull of the *Humphrey* than it disappeared beneath the calm waters of the Straits, only about twenty minutes after the collision. A short time later, the thirty-nine survivors were picked up by the *Clemson*, which had stopped nearby.

Later that morning, Captain Dennis and his crew were taken to Mackinaw City aboard the tug *Oscar Laitenin*. The *Clemson* remained at anchor in the Straits for several hours, waiting for the fog to lift a little. It then went on to Rogers City, Michigan, about fifty miles south of the Straits on Lake Huron, for temporary repairs.

When the fog lifted, the tips of the *Humphrey*'s two masts could just be seen sticking out of the water amidst a field of floating debris. The hull rested upright on the bottom in about eighty feet of water.[80] At that time, the *Humphrey* was the longest ship ever lost on the Great Lakes. Only sixteen years old, she was valued at $1.6 million by her owners.

There was some consideration given to attempting to salvage the big freighter. Under normal circumstances no thought would have been given to trying to raise a ship in that depth of water, but circumstances were far from normal in 1943. The United States was then embroiled in World War II, and even though America and her allies had defeated Rommel in North Africa and seemed to have turned the tide of war in the Pacific, the outcome was still far from certain.

On the lakes, shipments of raw materials to support the gigantic war effort were at record levels. Every available ship had been pressed into service, and shipyards were turning out sixteen new Maritime-class freighters to increase the tonnages the industry could move. The loss of a ship the size of the *Humphrey* had to be viewed as a major setback for the industry and the nation.

When the *Humphrey* went down, ownership of the vessel reverted from Kinsman Transit to the underwriters who had insured the ship. Representatives of the underwriters met immediately with a number of marine salvage experts to determine whether the vessel could be raised. The answer from the salvers was a unanimous "No!" She was just too deep. Given that verdict, the underwriters formally abandoned the hull.

Since the sunken hulk of the *Humphrey* was a hazard to navigation in the Straits, the Coast Guard promptly sought bids to cut down the superstructures on the wreck. Only one contractor submitted a bid, and that bid was an unusual one.

Captain John Roen of Sturgeon Bay, Wisconsin, said he would clear the shipping channel, not by cutting down the superstructures on the *Humphrey*, but by raising the ship! The only condition was that if he succeeded, the *Humphrey* would be *his* ship. If he couldn't raise it, he would then remove the superstructures, and the government would only pay for that part of the undertaking.[81]

Captain Roen was highly motivated. In addition to his salvage business, he ran a small shipping company. On September 21 of the previous year, Roen's *City of St. Joseph* and *Transport* had broken loose from the tow of the tug *John Roen* during a storm on Lake Superior. The holds and decks of the two barges were stacked high with pulpwood that had been loaded at Grand Marais, Minnesota, for delivery to Port Huron, Michigan. Pulpwood, used in the manufacture of paper, was the standard cargo for the barges.

The high seas eventually carried the barges ashore on the rocky coastline near the tip of the Keweenaw Peninsula. Badly battered by the crashing waves, both were declared total losses. Even the highly resourceful Captain Roen couldn't patch them up enough to put them back in service again.[82] The loss of the two barges had put a serious dent in the carrying capacity of Roen's fleet, which would be more than made up for if he could acquire the *Humphrey*.

Roen soon had a contract in his hand, and by late October his crews arrived in the Straits to begin the task of removing the almost 14,000 tons of iron ore in the hold of the *Humphrey*. A barge was moored over the wreck, then hard-hat divers set about clearing the deck of the sunken hulk and removing any hatch covers that had not been blown off when the ship sank. Once the hatches were open, a steam-powered crane equipped with a clamshell bucket began the slow process of removing iron ore from the hold of the *Humphrey*.[83] Divers marked the corners of the holds with small buoys to serve as a guide for crane operators.[84] By December 6, work was progressing well and nearly 9,000 tons of ore had been scooped out of the *Humphrey*. Most of the remaining ore was expected to be removed before the end of December, but adverse weather conditions forced Roen to delay raising the sunken hull until the following spring.[85]

In May 1944, Roen returned to the waters off Mackinaw City with two barges, the *Industry* and the *Maitland*. They removed as much of the remaining ore as they could, and then teams of divers went to work to make the *Humphrey*'s ballast tanks airtight. The tanks had been ruptured by water pressure when the ship sank. The divers used quick-setting cement to put temporary patches on all the holes in the ballast tanks.

Roen's plan was to eventually fill those tanks with air so that the *Humphrey* could help to lift itself off the bottom. The primary lifting force to raise the sunken freighter would be provided by partially submerging the *Maitland* and attaching it to the *Humphrey* by an elaborate system of heavy steel cables. Fifteen thousand feet of seven-eighths-inch steel cable would be needed, attached to the *Humphrey* and *Maitland* at a hundred different points. The water in the barge would then be pumped out, providing a powerful lift. Roen knew that that lift, combined with the lift provided by the air in the *Humphrey*'s own ballast tanks, would be sufficient to raise the sunken hull clear of the bottom by about eight feet. The *Maitland*, with the *Humphrey* suspended below it, could then be towed into shallower water. By repeating the process several times, Roen planned to progressively move the *Humphrey* into shallower and shallower water.

Eventually, the hull would have been raised so much that it would be impossible to make additional lifts using only the *Maitland*, because there wouldn't be enough clearance between the barge and the *Humphrey*. The plan was then to attach the *Maitland* to one side of the *Humphrey*, and the barge *Hilda* to the other side, like pontoons. Together, the two barges would make the additional lifts necessary to raise the 6,000-ton freighter until its deck was clear of the water. The fifteen- by twenty-two-foot hole in the hull could then be patched and pumps could then be taken aboard to remove the water in the *Humphrey*'s cargo hold and refloat the ship.

It was a complicated system, and the risks were formidable for Roen. The salvage plan looked good on paper, and a similar system had been used previously. Famed salvager Tom Reid of Port Huron had actually developed the system to raise the freighter *Philip D. Armour* after it sank in 1915. That fact was probably of little reassurance to Roen, however. The *Armour* was a 264-foot wooden freighter, almost miniature in comparison to the 605-foot *Humphrey*. The *Armour* had also gone down in much shallower water, and in a protected area. In the Straits of Mackinac, Captain Roen and his crew could expect to occasionally experience both strong winds and high seas that could jeopardize their operations. Roen undoubtedly also knew that Reid's comparatively small salvage operation had taken two years to complete and, at best, Reid's company had broken even on the project.[86]

Despite all the obstacles, the *Maitland* had made five lifts by August 23, raising the *Humphrey* six to eight feet with each lift. The wrecked freighter had also been moved more than a mile south of its original location, well out of the shipping lanes. At that point, Roen expected that it would take another three or four lifts, using both the *Maitland* and *Hilda* to complete the monumental salvage venture.[87]

After the first combined lift, the *Humphrey*, suspended between the two makeshift pontoons, began to take on a list while it was being towed into shallower water. Something had gone wrong with the system that regulated the amount of air in the *Humphrey*'s ballast tanks. The air compressors were putting too much air into the tanks on one side of the hull, threatening to roll the ship over. A quick-thinking crewmember saved the day when he grabbed a gun and fired several shots into the air hose running from the compressor to the ballast tank. Almost instantly, the excess air vented from the ballast tank and the *Humphrey* settled back onto an even keel.[88]

The final lift of the *Humphrey* was made on August 29. The hull was then in thirty feet of water, and the freighter's deck was above water. Divers immediately set to work to plug the gaping hole in the hull with timbers and tarpaulins. Once the hole was patched, pumps were set to work to remove the water from the freighter's cavernous cargo hold.[89] On September 10, 1944, fourteen months after she sank to the bottom of the Straits, the *Humphrey* was again able to float on her own.[90]

The raising of the *Humphrey* was hailed as "a feat unparalleled in American marine history," and Captain Roen received widespread accolades. Roen was a businessman, however, and while he enjoyed the attention he was receiving, he had taken on the salvage project in hopes of economic gain. And gain he did. Roen estimated the salvage job had cost him $200,000–$300,000. Even in its damaged condition, the *Humphrey* was valued in excess of $1 million.[91]

35. The wrecked hull of the steamer *George M. Humphrey* cradled on cables strung between two salvage ships owned by Captain John Roen of Sturgeon Bay, Wisconsin. The 605-foot *Humphrey* sank on June 15, 1943, after colliding with another ship in the foggy Straits of Mackinac. It was raised just over a year later, after a salvage effort that was hailed as "a feat unparalleled in American maritime history." After the extensive damage to the ship was repaired, Roen put it into service as flagship of his Roen Steamship Company. (Ralph Roberts Collection)

As the *Humphrey* bobbed at anchor in the Straits, most observers agreed that she wasn't much to look at. The sinking had taken a toll on the once-beautiful ship. In addition to the big hole in her hull, the *Humphrey*'s cabins had been seriously damaged, and her tall smokestack had been crushed.[92]

Roen, on the other hand, thought the *Humphrey* was beautiful. He knew that most of the damage was largely cosmetic. There was work to be done, to be sure, but the engine and most of the machinery were in surprisingly good shape given the fact they had spent more than a year underwater.

Early on the morning of September 16, 1944, the *Humphrey* was taken in tow, riding easily behind the tug *John Roen III*. Car ferries crossing the Straits of Mackinac and the railroad ferry *Chief Wawatam* blew whistle salutes to the ship as it headed west on its way to Roen's yard in Sturgeon Bay for refitting.[93]

The *Humphrey* returned to service on the lakes in 1945. Rechristened as the *Captain John Roen*, it was flagship of the Roen Steamship Company. Its reappearance on the shipping lanes of the Great Lakes was greeted enthusiastically by all those in the industry, and she was accorded whistle salutes by most ships she passed. The *Roen*'s most enthusiastic salute undoubtedly came when it passed one particular Pittsburgh Steamship vessel—the *D. M. Clemson*, the ship that had sunk the *Humphrey* that foggy June night in 1943.

The dispute over which ship had been at fault in the sinking of the *Humphrey* waged on long after Captain Roen had raised the ship. In 1955 a federal admiralty judge finally ruled that the *Clemson* had been more at fault than the *Humphrey*, and U.S. Steel was ordered to pay Kinsman $495,084 in damages.[94] Many people in the industry were pleased to hear of the award. Ships in the Pittsburgh fleet were notorious around the lakes for running at full speed in fog. There were even rumors that captains of the Pittsburgh steamers were under orders from their company's office not to slow down, fog or no fog. That rumor resurfaced again in 1965, after the company's steamer *Cedarville* was involved in a tragic collision near where the *Humphrey* had gone down.

Cedarville, 1965

Running in fog as thick as pea soup is never a pleasant experience for sailors, but it was far less nerve-racking in 1965 than it had been in the days before freighters on the Great Lakes were equipped with radar. As U.S. Steel's freighter *Cedarville* steamed north toward the Straits of Mackinac on the morning of May 7, 1965, Third Mate Charlie Cook had an almost crystal-clear view of the shipping channel, even though a heavy morning fog limited visibility to only about a quarter of a mile. No, Cook didn't have X-ray vision. He could see because he kept his eyes glued to the *Cedarville*'s radar set as the ship sailed up the narrow South Channel approach to the busy strait that separates Michigan's two peninsulas.

With each sweep of the amber beam, a detailed picture of the waters around the *Cedarville* was drawn on the radar's cathode ray tube. On the left of the scope was a continuous jagged line that represented the Michigan shore of Lake Huron. To the lower right was the arcing line that showed the northwest end of Bois Blanc Island, which they had just passed. At the top right were several converging arcs that Cook knew were Round Island and Mackinac Island. Running across the top of the scope was another jagged line where the radar's signal was bouncing off the southern shore of the Upper Peninsula. Other smaller targets on the

36. The bow and cabin of the 601-foot *J. P. Morgan, Jr.* were badly mangled in a collision with the steamer *Crete* on June 23, 1948, on Lake Superior. Both ships were operating in heavy fog when the accident occurred. Two crewmembers on the *Morgan* were killed and three were injured when the cabin area was driven inward by the bow of the *Crete*. Despite their extensive damage, both ships were quickly repaired and returned to service. (Ralph Roberts Collection)

radar screen represented mostly navigational aids, such as buoys and crib lights, except for a target almost dead ahead of the *Cedarville* that was a downbound ship.

Captain Martin Joppich, who was in the pilothouse with Cook and Wheelsman Leonard Gabrysiak, had already contacted the downbound ship on the radio. It was the steamer *Benson Ford*, and Captain Joppich had checked to make sure that they were planning to make a standard port-to-port passage. Even though the passing arrangement had already been verbally agreed to, no sooner had Joppich gotten off the radio than the men in the pilothouse of the *Cedarville* could hear a slightly muffled roar from the *Ford*'s whistle. It was the whistle signal for a port-to-port passing agreement that was required by the nautical rules of the road that governed navigation on the lakes.

From his position on the bridge wing just outside the *Cedarville*'s pilothouse, Watchman Ivan Trafelet called out, "One whistle, cap." Captain Joppich sounded one long blast on the steam whistle mounted on the *Cedarville*'s stern smokestack, thereby formally agreeing to the passing arrangement signaled for by the *Ford.* Having done that, he flipped the switch that activated the ship's automatic fog signal. It would sound one blast every minute to alert other ship's to their position, even though any other ships in the area that morning would undoubtedly also be using radar. Even with the coming of radar, the fog signals were still required under the rules of the road.

On the radarscope, Charlie Cook could see the target representing the *Benson Ford* on a parallel downbound course, gradually passing about half a mile off the *Cedarville*'s port side. Because of the thickening fog, those in the *Cedarville*'s pilothouse never actually saw the other freighter.

When the *Cedarville* was still three or four miles south of the Mackinac Bridge, which spans the Straits, Captain Joppich received a radio call from the captain of the German freighter *Weissenberg.* Captain Werner May told Joppich that his ship was just then approaching the Mackinac Bridge from the Lake Michigan side, and he intended to proceed down the South Channel. Joppich and the German captain agreed that their ships would pass port-to-port. When Joppich ended his radio conversation, Ivan Trafelet shouted from the bridge wing that he could hear fog signals from ships ahead of them.

A few minutes later, at 9:38 A.M., Captain May called the *Cedarville* again, telling Captain Joppich that there was a downbound Norwegian ship ahead of the *Weissenberg.* Captain Joppich tried to call the Norwegian ship on the radio, but got no answer. By then, Charlie Cook could see the approaching ship in the radar, about one and a half miles off. At the speed the two ships were closing, they would be on top of each other in just five minutes. Joppich told the wheelsman to put the wheel hard over to the right, trying to keep the oncoming ship on the *Cedarville*'s port side. At the same time, he signaled the engine room to cut the engine back from full to half speed.

Cook alerted Joppich that the approaching ship was closing in on the *Cedarville,* and its bearing wasn't changing. Captain Joppich then blew one very long blast on the ship's whistle in between the fog signals, but got no reply. While the men in the pilothouse were still listening intently for a reply to their passing signal, Trafelet shouted, "There she is. I see the ship coming on!"

Out of the fog, no more than two hundred feet away, was another ship, heading for the *Cedarville* at almost a right angle. Joppich quickly rang up "slow ahead" on the engine order telegraph, cutting the *Cedarville*'s speed even more. The bow of the *Cedarville* passed the bow of the other ship, and Joppich shouted for Wheelsman Gabrysiak to put the wheel "hard left." At the same time, the captain threw the engine order telegraph to the "full ahead" position, hoping to kick the stern of his ship around to the right enough to clear the oncoming salty.

Despite Joppich's evasive action, at about 9:45 A.M. the tall, sharply pointed and ice-reinforced bow of the saltwater ship struck the *Cedarville* about halfway down its port side, slicing through the outer hull and into the cargo hold like a knife through warm butter. Because the *Cedarville* still had considerable way on, Captain Joppich's ship pulled itself clear of the bow of the salty and disappeared into the dense cover of fog.

Joppich hurriedly signaled the engine room to stop the engine, then switched on the general alarm. Throughout the ship, the nerve-shattering clanging of the loud bells alerted crewmembers to get their lifejackets on and go immediately to their lifeboat stations. As the ship drifted slowly in the fog, Joppich broadcast a "Mayday" message on the radio, giving the *Cedarville*'s position and the basic details of the collision. With the ship almost stopped at that point, Joppich ordered Ivan Trafelet to drop the port anchor.

First Mate Harry Piechan had run up to the pilothouse from his cabin right after the general alarm had been turned on, and while Captain Joppich was getting the ship anchored, he went aft to assess the damage. A few minutes later, Piechan called the pilothouse and informed Captain Joppich that a tremendous amount of water was flooding into the cargo hold. Crewmen had tried to close off the gaping wound by lowering a heavy canvas collision mat over the side, but the rushing water had carried it right into the hole and the vessel was taking on a pronounced port list.

All the crewmen not on duty had hurried to the stern when the general alarm went off. The lifeboats, located on each side of the roof of the after cabin, were swung out and lowered to the level of the spar deck, ready to be boarded. There was no panic among the crew. In fact, the mood was surprisingly jovial. "We didn't think we were in any danger of sinking," one crewman said later. "In fact, we joked about it, recalling that we spent a few weeks last summer in the shipyard and it looked like we would be doing the same thing again."[95] With the boats ready to be launched, the crewmen stood around waiting for an order to abandon ship.

In the pilothouse, meanwhile, someone brought in three lifejackets for the watchstanders. Leonard Gabrysiak put one on, but Captain Joppich and Charlie Cook didn't. Joppich radioed the *Weissenberg,* trying, without luck, to get the name of the ship that had hit them. He then made the snap decision to try to beach his ship to keep it from sinking in the deep waters of the Straits. Joppich ordered the anchor to be raised, and he made a security call on the radio, alerting ships in the area that he was going to attempt to beach the *Cedarville.*

At 10:10 A.M., about twenty-four minutes after the collision took place, Joppich signaled "full speed ahead" on the engine order telegraph and had Gabrysiak put the wheel over into a hard left turn to head toward the shore. Using the radar to navigate with, Charlie Cook recommended they steer a course of 140 degrees, and Gabrysiak steadied the ship on that heading. While the *Cedarville* steamed toward shore, Joppich broadcast several more "Mayday" messages and called the *Weissenberg* to instruct them to keep out of his way.

In the engine room, Chief Engineer Don Lamp and his men were doing their best to control the flooding. They were using the main ballast pump to pump water out of the ballast tank that had been holed, when the telephone rang and someone from the pilothouse ordered them to put ballast water into the tanks on the starboard side in an effort to counter the effects of the portside flooding and get rid of the port list. Two other pumps were put to work removing water from the tunnel beneath the hopper-shaped cargo hold. Joppich called the engine room a few minutes later to report that the list was gone and to instruct the chief engineer to turn off the ballast pump putting water into the starboard tanks.

Already loaded with 14,411 tons of limestone, the cargo hold was rapidly flooding as the *Cedarville* steamed toward the beach. Joppich commented to Cook and Gabrysiak that he didn't think the ship was going to make it. Those on the stern could see that the bow had settled noticeably, and the forward end of the deck was awash. They, too, doubted their ship was going to make it into shallow water in time, and began to launch the two lifeboats without being instructed to do so. At that very moment, 10:25 A.M., the *Cedarville* lurched to starboard, rolled onto her side, and slipped beneath the water.

Most of the men on the stern either jumped or were thrown into the thirty-six-degree water, although several who were in the number 2 lifeboat managed to release it as their ship went down. The other lifeboat, as well as the rafts carried on both the bow and stern of the *Cedarville,* floated clear as the ship plummeted.

In the pilothouse, Charlie Cook struggled to slip into his lifejacket as the ship rolled over. He was never seen again, and his body was never recovered. Captain Joppich was plunged into the water with his lifejacket still over his arm. When he was picked up later, he was still clinging to it.

Most of the crewmembers who ended up in the icy water were able to quickly swim to one of the boats or rafts floating over the spot where the *Cedarville* went down, and they immediately began to row around and search for survivors. Others who went into the water were picked up by lifeboats launched from the *Weissenberg,* which had followed along behind the *Cedarville* on its desperate run for the beach. As soon as Captain May realized that the stricken ship had gone down, he ordered his men to launch their lifeboats and search the area for survivors.

The crewmen from the German freighter pulled five survivors from the water. Captain Joppich was among them. The lifeless body of a sixth *Cedarville* crewman was also recovered. Twenty-one crewmembers from the *Cedarville* were aboard a lifeboat and raft from their ship, and they were towed to the *Weissenberg* and taken aboard.[96]

Despite the quick action by Captain May and his crew, one of the *Cedarville* crewmen died about an hour later. The cause of his death was later listed as "shock and exposure."

Eight other crewmembers from the *Cedarville* could not be found. Among them were Charlie Cook, Chief Engineer Don Lamp, and the engineer, oiler, and stokerman who had been on watch in the engine room when the ship went down. Both of the dead seamen and seven of the eight missing sailors were from Rogers City, the small community on the north shore of Lake Huron that was home port for the *Cedarville* and the other ships in U.S. Steel's fleet of self-unloaders. The *Cedarville* was the second Rogers City ship to be lost in less than seven years. In the fall of 1958, the steamer *Carl D. Bradley* had gone down in a fierce Lake Michigan storm (see Chapter 4).

As the fog lifted a little in the early afternoon, the *Cedarville* survivors could make out the hull of the Norwegian freighter *Topdalsfjord,* anchored nearby. It was obviously the ship that had rammed theirs, as the lower portion of the gracefully tapered bow was deeply stove in.

Captain Joppich and many of the surviving *Cedarville* crewmembers, along with Captain Rasmus Haaland and various members of the crew of the *Topdalsfjord,* testified at the quickly convened Coast Guard inquiry that got under way the day following the collision at Sault Ste. Marie. The board's findings were released nine months later.

The three Coast Guard officers who served on the board concluded that Captain Joppich was primarily responsible for the collision. Even though Joppich claimed that he had slowed the *Cedarville* to "slow ahead" after his initial conversation with the captain of the *Weissenberg,* that testimony was contradicted by Wheelsman Leonard Gabrysiak, as well as by time and distance calculations made by the Coast Guard. "The version as related by Gabrysiak is considered correct, and that as related by Captain Joppich is considered self-serving and false and is accordingly rejected," the board concluded. Joppich was faulted for operating the *Cedarville* too fast in the fog, running at full speed until just minutes before the collision. That violated the long-standing navigation rule that requires ships to slow down in the fog, and even come to a stop if in an ambiguous "close quarters" situation.

Joppich was also criticized for trying to beach his boat while the full crew was still aboard. "The master judged poorly the peril to his crew and vessel and the time remaining for him to beach his ship," wrote the board. Most tragically, the Coast Guard had found, the beaching course given to Captain Joppich and the wheelsman was not the course to the nearest shallow water. The *Cedarville* traveled 2.3 miles from the point of collision to where she sank, which was still 2 miles short of the beach. On the other hand, the shallow water of Graham Shoal was only 1 mile from the point of collision, and it was just 2.2 miles to the beach at Old Mackinac Point. The crippled ship could have made it to either spot before sinking. While the third mate had provided the erroneous beaching course, the Coast Guard felt that a captain with Joppich's long experience "should have immediately realized this."

Once Joppich was told the extent of the damage to his ship, he should have known that sinking was inevitable, particularly since the *Cedarville* had no watertight bulkheads to subdivide its cargo hold. Given that, the appropriate action would have been to first ensure the safety of his crew, then worry about the ship.

Because of the risk involved, the attempt to beach the ship should have been made with only an absolute minimum crew aboard. One person to steer the boat and two crewmen to tend the engine were really all that was needed. Joppich himself could have done the steering. Instead, Joppich's hasty decision put thirty-five lives in jeopardy, and ultimately cost the lives of ten of his crew.

Based on the recommendation of the three members of the board, the Coast Guard immediately took action to suspend the license of Captain Martin Joppich. He would never sail again.[97]

Like Captain Pittes of the *Atlantic* and First Mate George Cleveland of the *Pewabic*, Captain Joppich had tried to force a port-to-port passage out of what had developed as a natural starboard-to-starboard passing situation. Confused by the fog and disconcerted because of his inability to make radio contact with the Norwegian freighter, it was the hard right turn he ordered that put the *Cedarville* directly into the path of the *Topdalsfjord* and made a collision inevitable. Had he remained on his original course, or widened out to the left, the two ships would have comfortably passed each other in the fog. In that case, fifty-four-year-old Martin Joppich would probably have sailed another eight or ten years and retired with dignity, and the *Cedarville* might well still be in operation today.

The *Cedarville* was a "self-unloader," a type of ship that had first made its debut on the Great Lakes scene in the first decade of the twentieth century. The hybrid bulk freighters were equipped so that they could unload their cargoes of bulk materials without assistance from shoreside unloading equipment.

The very first self-unloader, the *Hennepin*, came out in 1902. The *Hennepin* wasn't a new ship, however. It had been launched in 1888 as a standard "straight-deck" bulk freighter, the *George H. Dyer*. The 220-foot *Dyer* was one of the smaller freighters on the lakes when it was first launched, and by 1902 it was having difficulty competing in an industry that had seen the launching of the first 500-footers a couple of years earlier. In an effort to carve out a niche for the little freighter, it was converted to a self-unloader. That would allow the ship, renamed *Hennepin*, to serve many small ports around the lakes that did not have shoreside unloading equipment. Viewed as an oddity by most of those in the Great Lakes shipping industry, the compact self-unloader operated mainly in the stone and coal trades for the next twenty-five years.

In 1908, Wyandotte Chemical Company built the *Wyandotte*, the first ship on the lakes built from the keel up as a self-unloader. The firm had constructed a manufacturing facility at Wyandotte, Michigan, on the lower Detroit River, and needed to transport large quantities of limestone to the facility. Officials at Wyandotte Chemical weighed the various advantages and disadvantages of installing shoreside unloading equipment at their plant, or investing in self-unloading ships. The economics favored the use of self-unloading ships, and they ultimately had the *Wyandotte* built at the nearby Great Lakes Engineering Works.

By the early 1970s, most U.S. and Canadian fleets on the Great Lakes were operating self-unloaders. One of those was the Erie Sand Steamship Company of Erie, Pennsylvania, which had acquired its first self-unloader, the *Niagara*, in 1956. In 1972 the company purchased the self-unloading freighter *J. L. Reiss*, renaming it the *Sidney E. Smith, Jr.* in honor of the firm's president.

Sidney E. Smith, 1972

On June 4, 1972, the *Sidney E. Smith, Jr.* took on a partial load of 6,646 tons of coal at Toledo, Ohio, and departed for Lime Island in the St.

Marys River south of Sault Ste. Marie, Michigan. Lime Island was a fueling station for ships transiting the busy St. Marys. There, vessels could take on bunkers of either coal or oil.

By 1 A.M., the *Smith* was steaming up the St. Clair River, just south of Port Huron. Captain Arn Kristensen was in the pilothouse, along with Second Mate Henry Gaskins and Wheelsman Paul Diehl. Watchman Alfred Shanahan was stationed as a lookout on the bow. During the previous three days, Captain Kristensen had been able to get only about three hours of sleep. A combination of bad weather and long hours navigating in the congested shipping channels had kept him at his post in the *Smith*'s pilothouse. Coast Guard regulations didn't specifically require him to be there, but like most masters of Great Lakes vessels, he made it a practice to be in the wheelhouse whenever the ship was in the narrow, winding river channels, or whenever his ship was in a potentially hazardous situation. He spent most of that time sitting in his tall chair over on the starboard side of the pilothouse, where he could keep an experienced eye on happenings. As the *Smith* churned its way north toward Port Huron, Kristensen left the pilothouse to use the toilet facilities in his stateroom, one deck below.

Second Mate Henry Gaskins continued piloting the *Smith* up the river in the captain's absence. The aging freighter was steaming at full speed, but with only 1,650 horsepower, full speed on the *Smith* meant only nine miles an hour. At Port Huron, ships traverse a long bend to the right that takes them under the towering expanse of the Blue Water Bridge that connects Port Huron with Sarnia, Ontario. Just north of this bridge, ships enter the lower end of Lake Huron. The current tends to be quite strong in the area of the Blue Water Bridge, anywhere from two to six miles an hour, with the strongest currents usually encountered near the middle of the river.

Shortly after 1:30 A.M., the *Smith* was passing Port Huron and approaching the Blue Water Bridge. Gaskins and his wheelsman were alone in the pilothouse; Captain Kristensen had not yet returned from his cabin. That surprised the *Smith*'s mate a little, but it didn't concern him. Gaskins was an experienced deck officer and had made hundreds of passages under the Blue Water Bridge. He, in fact, also held a master's license, the same license held by Captain Kristensen.

At that point, a security call came over the *Smith*'s radio. The call was from the downbound Canadian freighter *Outarde*, which was several miles above the bridge. Based on their relative locations, Gaskins knew that the *Smith* would reach the bridge long before the Canadian freighter.

Gaskins then made a security call himself, notifying the *Outarde* and any other vessels in the area of his ship's location.

When the ship was abreast of the water filtration plant that sits along the riverbank in Port Huron, Gaskins told the wheelsman to begin the long, slow right turn that would take them under the bridge and out onto Lake Huron. The wheelsman swung the big wheel clockwise until the rudder angle indicator showed twenty-five degrees to the right. As the ship responded to the helm, Gaskins and his wheelsman heard a downbound ship blow one long blast on its whistle, indicating that it would pass the *Smith* on the port side. Gaskins could see the lights of the downbound ship about a mile ahead of them, around the bend of the river and just above the bridge. Gaskins agreed to the other ship's passing signal by answering with a long blast on the *Smith*'s steam whistle.

Gaskin was a little concerned that the *Smith* was too close to the riverbank on the Canadian side, and he told the wheelsman to take some of the right rudder off. Wheelsman Paul Diehl responded immediately, turning the wheel slowly to the left until the rudder angle indicator showed only twenty degrees of right rudder. The distance between the *Smith* and the riverbank widened almost immediately.

In just a minute or two, however, both Gaskins and the wheelsman noticed that the *Smith* was tending to steer a straight line, rather than following the bend of the river to the right. Gaskins ordered, and got, more right rudder. The ship still wouldn't come around. Gaskins then asked for "hard right rudder." Paul Diehl spun the wheel as far as it would go to the right, but still the *Smith* plowed on straight ahead toward the riverbank on the Port Huron side. Henry Gaskins's heart leaped into his throat when he realized that the bow of the *Smith* had gotten caught in the strong current near the middle of the river and the current was pushing the bow around downstream. Glancing at the downbound steamer, Gaskins could see both the ship's red and green running lights. The downbound ship was heading straight for the *Smith*. Gaskins knew immediately that the two ships were going to collide!

Grabbing the handle for the whistle, Gaskins blew a string of short blasts—the danger signal, followed by two blasts—the signal for a starboard-to-starboard passage. That would let the downbound ship know that the *Smith* was not going to pass it on the port side, as they had agreed upon with their previous exchange of signals. At the same time, Gaskins threw the handle on the engine order telegraph from "full ahead" to "full astern," and reached over and flipped the switch to activate the *Smith*'s general alarm. The *Smith* was no more than 2,000 feet from the downbound freighter at that time, and the two ships were closing at a rate of 1,200 to 1,400 feet per minute. Subsequent events occurred very rapidly—in the space of seconds.

Alfred Shanahan, the lookout, watched the scenario develop from his position at the bow. When it became obvious that the downbound ship was going to strike the *Smith* somewhere near its bow, Shanahan retreated to a safer position back down the deck. Gaskins called down to him on the intercom to get mooring lines ready on the port side of the ship.

The loud ringing of the general alarm bells abruptly awakened Captain Kristensen, who had fallen asleep in the easy chair in his room. As he jumped up from his chair to rush to the pilothouse, he felt the impact of the collision.

In the pilothouse of the downbound steamer, the 557-foot Canadian freighter *Parker Evans*, Captain Tom Davis had put his ship's engine on "full astern" when he heard the *Smith* blow the danger signal. Carrying more than 11,000 tons of grain, and in the strong river current, there was no way to get the ship stopped in the short distance between her and the *Smith*. All those in the pilothouse with Captain Davis grabbed onto something solid as the bow of their ship drove into the starboard bow of the *Smith,* just aft of her forward cabins. The *Evans* struck the *Smith* so hard that it rebounded from the collision, then rammed the *Smith* a second time, about twenty-five feet farther aft. Both impacts penetrated the hull of the *Smith.*

When Captain Kristensen got up to the pilothouse door, he met Henry Gaskins coming out. Gaskins raced down the stairs and around to the bow and released the brakes holding both of the *Smith*'s bow anchors. Kristensen ducked into the pilothouse and attempted to call the Port Huron Coast Guard Station on the radio to ask for assistance. When he got no answer, he moved the handle on the engine room telegraph to "half ahead," then blew seven short and one long blasts on the *Smith*'s whistle—the signal for the crew to abandon ship. The *Smith* was beginning to list badly to starboard, and Captain Kristensen was afraid it might roll over.

The crippled steamer was at that time almost all the way across the river. Its bow was only about six feet from the Peerless Cement dock on the Port Huron side. Henry Gaskins and Watchman Al Shanahan stood ready to put out a mooring cable, but there was nobody on the dock to take the line.

On the *Parker Evans,* Captain Davis, rang up "full ahead" on the engine in an effort to hold the bow of the *Smith* against the Peerless Cement dock. The strong current had caught the stern of his ship, however, and it began to swing out across the river. To prevent any more damage to the *Evans,* Captain Davis had the starboard anchor dropped and used the rudder and engine to swing the stern of his ship back into the riverbank on the U.S. side. As soon as he could, Davis had several crewmembers swung ashore on the boatswain's chair so they could handle the ship's mooring lines.

The *Smith* drifted downstream from the *Evans* and out into the main channel of the river, its list worsening. Three crewmembers threw the *Smith*'s aluminum workboat over the side and scrambled down into it. The other thirty-one crewmen were on the boat deck at the stern, preparing to launch the lifeboats and life rafts, when the pilot boat from the Port Huron pilot station maneuvered alongside the stern of the *Smith.* All thirty-one climbed down onto the pilot boat. Captain Arn Kristensen was the last to leave his ship.

Shortly after the crew got off, and about twenty minutes after the collision, the *Smith* sank on its starboard side in thirty-five to fifty feet of water, partially blocking the river channel. Since the *Smith* had a beam of fifty-two feet, a large portion of the port side of the hull remained above the water.

Damage to the *Parker Evans* was minor. Interestingly, until 1917 the *Evans* had been named the *Harry A. Berwind.* The ship that holed and sank the *Smith* in 1972 was the same one that had sunk the *Henry Steinbrenner* in a collision in the St. Marys River in 1909.

The ensuing Coast Guard investigation found no one at fault aboard either ship. Henry Gaskins had simply made a mistake—an "error in judgement," the investigating officer called it. The investigating officer's report did recommend that security calls between upbound and down-bound vessels in the vicinity of the Blue Water Bridge be made mandatory and that consideration be given to implementing a traffic control system in the same area. A traffic control system was already in operation by the Coast Guard for vessels operating in the St. Marys River. Coast Guard records showed that during the four previous years, there had been four collisions with docks, three major ship collisions, and four groundings near the Blue Water Bridge.[98]

With the sunken hull of the *Smith* partially blocking the river channel, the Coast Guard set up a temporary traffic control center to coordinate shipping activity in the vicinity of the Blue Water Bridge. Only one-way traffic was allowed, with downbound vessels using the channel during the day and upbound vessels transiting at night.

The Navy Salvage Group was called in to supervise the complicated removal of the sunken hulk of the *Smith.* A system of hydraulic pulling

37. A portion of the side and after cabin of the *Sidney E. Smith, Jr.* was all that was sticking out of the St. Clair River after the freighter was rammed and sunk on June 4, 1972. The sunken hull partially blocked the busy shipping channel just below the Bluewater Bridge at Port Huron, Michigan. The Navy Salvage Group later pulled the *Smith* out of the channel. Since the wreck, the Coast Guard has allowed only one-way vessel traffic in the stretch of river. (Ralph Roberts Collection)

machines firmly anchored to the shore adjacent to the wreck were used to pull the *Smith*'s hull up against the riverbank. Sponge plastic was also pumped into the hull to provide some buoyancy while it was being moved. The operation was completed on June 30, at which time the channel was largely clear.[99]

The Coast Guard decided to continue its policy of allowing only one-way traffic in the dangerous stretch of river running under the Blue Water Bridge. Upbound and downbound vessels were allowed to transit at any time of the day or night, but only one ship could pass through the stretch at a time, with downbound traffic given the priority. That policy continues in effect yet today.

Looking Back

There have been at least 206 major collisions between ships on the Great Lakes since 1840.[100] How many total collisions there have been, including "fender benders," we don't know. In 1871, however, there were 225 collisions,[101] but only 5—just over 2 percent of the total—were of a serious nature.[102] If that ratio was consistent throughout the history of the industry, there could have been as many as 9,090 collisions between 1840 and the present.

As in the case of groundings, the number of serious collisions increased in almost direct proportion to the increase in the number of ships on the lakes from 1840 through 1909, reaching a peak of thirty-two between 1900 and 1909. After that, as the number of ships in the Great Lakes fleet dwindled, the number of collisions also declined. There was only one major collision during the 1930s, six in the 1940s, nine in the 1950s, one in the 1960s, and one in the 1970s.[103]

Two factors account for almost all of the serious collisions on the lakes. Either the ships were operating during periods of limited visibility—fog, snow, rain, and even smoke from forest fires—or the deck officers navigating one or both of the ships made mistakes.

A number of steps were taken to reduce the number of collisions. When the Steamboat Inspection Service was created in 1852, it was charged with the responsibility of examining and licensing deck officers on steam-powered passenger ships. In subsequent years, the licensing requirements were expanded to include the officers on all steamers, including those in the bulk cargo trades.

In 1864 the United States enacted rules of the road, prescribing the actions that were to be taken by shipboard officers in meeting, crossing, or passing situations or when visibility was obscured. The Steamboat Inspection Service then began to test applicants for licenses as deck officers on their knowledge of the rules of the road, a practice that continues yet today.

When the rules of the road failed to stem the tide of collisions, the major shipping companies that belonged to the Lake Carriers' Association worked to establish navigational rules for the St. Marys River in 1892. In 1897 they lobbied to have those navigational rules enforced by a river patrol of the Revenue Cutter Service. Interestingly, while at least 79 of the 206 major collisions took place in the river channels connecting the Great Lakes, only 7 of those were on the St. Marys. This suggests that the members of the LCA might not have been as interested in eliminating collisions as they were in ensuring that the vital St. Marys River was kept open to ship traffic. If the primary goal had been to reduce the number of collisions on the rivers, it would have been more logical to set up navigational rules and river patrols on the Detroit and St. Clair Rivers, both of which experienced more collisions than the St. Marys did. Those rivers are much wider than the St. Marys, though, and much less likely to be blocked by a wrecked ship.

After a number of new steel freighters were lost as a result of midlake collisions, the LCA developed a voluntary program of course separations in 1911. Where possible, widely separated tracks were established for upbound and downbound ships to reduce the likelihood of collisions, particularly when visibility was restricted. In areas where the shipping lanes of the lakes converged at the headwaters or mouths of rivers like the St. Marys, Detroit, and St. Clair, however, it was impossible to have much separation between the upbound and downbound tracks. Unfortunately, those areas have been the sites of most of the serious collisions that have taken place on the lakes over the years.

There is no doubt that the various programs instituted by the government and the members of the LCA prevented some collisions. At the same time, the number of collisions didn't show any marked decline until the number of ships on the lakes dropped dramatically after the turn of the century. Fewer ships meant that there was less of a likelihood that two ships would have a fatal encounter.

None of the programs instituted by the shipping companies or the government dealt effectively with the two scenarios that caused almost all of the collisions on the lakes. Ships were allowed to continue to operate during periods of reduced visibility—even expected to do so—and deck officers continued to make grievous errors in dangerous meeting and crossing situations.

While the vast majority of the deaths in collisions occurred because passenger ships weren't required to carry enough lifeboats or life rafts to handle all those aboard if it became necessary to abandon ship, neither the shipping companies nor the various government maritime agencies took any action to correct that problem until after the *Titanic* sank in 1912. The horrendous loss of life in collisions like those involving the *Atlantic, Lady Elgin, Pewabic,* and *Morning Star* could probably have been avoided if those ships had been required to carry an adequate number of lifeboats or life rafts.

As in the case of ships destroyed by fire, crews on passenger ships that sank in collisions also consistently failed to assist passengers to lessen the loss of life. Virtually nothing was done to correct the problem, or hold ships' crews accountable for their actions, and thereby set a clear precedent for the industry.

In addition to the dramatic downsizing of the fleet on the lakes that has taken place since the turn of the century, there's also no doubt that the advent of radar has had a dramatic impact in cutting the number of collisions since the end of World War II. Captain Martin Joppich of the *Cedarville* proved, however, just how easy it is to be involved in a collision even when a ship has radar. With today's ships equipped with highly sophisticated radars and collision avoidance systems, we can anticipate that any collisions that occur are going to be the result of human error.

>>4<<

THE CURSE OF
THE ELEVENTH MONTH:
Founderings

T HERE ARE A LOT OF SEASONED GREAT LAKES sailors who take the month of November off every year. For most, it's not because they want to be home for Thanksgiving or deer-hunting season—they just don't want to be out on the lakes in November. They don't want to risk getting caught in a bad storm. More specifically, they don't want to risk being on a ship that sinks in a storm!

The most serious threat to ships and sailors on the inland seas of North America has always been from "heavy weather"—the incessant procession of gales and storms that assault the lakes each year. It's just as true today as it was at any time in the past. And while gales and storms can occur during any month of the sailing season, November has the reputation of being the month of the "killer storms" on the Great Lakes. And rightly so. A third of all the storm-related shipwrecks on the lakes have occurred during the eleventh month.[1] Sailors know that. For generations, they have referred to it as "the curse of the eleventh month."

Sailors also know that it's not a question of whether there will be a storm any given November. It would be more unusual—highly unusual—if the thirty days of November passed *without* a storm beating its way across the lakes. Several storms, in fact.

Storms are caused by differentials in the temperatures of air masses that come in contact with each other. Those temperature differentials are generally most extreme during the fall. Bitterly cold air rushing down from the Arctic clashes with warm, even hot, air over the western plains. The conflicting air masses trigger a counterclockwise swirling motion around a center of low pressure, and the entire weather system begins to move in a generally easterly direction. Ahead of the low is a warm front, behind it a cold front. As the system comes in contact with relatively warm, moist air, like that generally found over the Great Lakes, the low intensifies. When that happens, the distance between the two fronts is narrowed, forming what is called an occluded front. The weather system—technically an "extra-tropical cyclone"—is then approaching its peak strength. It exhibits that strength in high winds and driving rain or snow.

Out on the lakes, as the winds increase in speed, waves form. At about fifteen miles an hour, whitecaps form. Between twenty and thirty miles an hour, spray torn off the crests of the growing seas is blown horizontally across the surface, like snow blowing across a farmer's open field. The height of the waves depends not just on how hard the wind is blowing, but how long it has been blowing from the same direction. Wind shifts will tend to knock the seas down, or produce confused seas, while prolonged winds from the same direction will gradually build higher and higher waves. Gales on the Great Lakes will generally produce waves of eight to twelve feet. The highest waves encountered on the lakes, those in the twenty- to thirty-foot range, are usually formed only in hurricane-strength storms.

In the technical jargon of marine weather today, a "gale" has developed when winds are between thirty-nine and fifty-four miles an hour. If winds exceed fifty-four miles an hour, the weather forecasters upgrade it to a "storm." Many gales and storms sweep across the Great Lakes each year. In 1982, for example, there were 47 gales and 13 storms on Lake Superior, 42 gales and 10 storms on Lake Michigan, 25 gales and 6 storms on Lake Huron, and 27 gales and 5 storms on Lake Erie. Lake Ontario experienced 8 gales, but no storms.[2] While the number of gales and storms will vary from year to year, 1982 was fairly typical.

On the Great Lakes, a "storm" is the highest rating that can be attached to a low-pressure weather system. In tropical waters, however, once winds exceed 73 miles an hour, the weather system is classified as a "hurricane"—and it's given a name. Winds associated with Great Lakes storms occasionally exceed 73 miles an hour; in fact, wind speeds of as high as 103 miles an hour have been recorded. A study of weather records for the Great Lakes going back to 1835 shows that at least twenty storms that have struck the lakes over the years were actually of hurricane intensity. One of those storms took place in the month of October, while the other nineteen hit the lakes in November.[3] It's no wonder that many sailors on the Great Lakes would prefer to spend November "on the beach."

Great Lakes historians and boat buffs can recite a litany of "great storms" that have swept over the lakes, storms that took an exceptional toll on shipping. Many were of hurricane intensity. Others fell short of hurricane strength, but they swooped down on the lakes so fast, or lasted so long, that they left a trail of destruction in their wakes that equaled any hurricane. Best known are "the *Alpena* Storm" of October 1880, "the Big Storm" of November 1905—sometimes called "the *Mataafa* Storm," "the Great Storm" of November 1913, "the Black Friday Storm" of October 1916, "the Armistice Day Storm" of November 1940, "the *Bradley* Storm" of November 1958, "the *Morrell* Storm" of November 1966, and "the *Fitzgerald* Storm" of November 1975.[4] When we pool all the available information, we find that about fifty-five of these "great storms" have struck the lakes since 1835, averaging out to about one every three years.

But a storm doesn't have to fall into the "great storm" category to be a threat to ships, sailors, and people traveling on the lakes. When we review the best available information on serious storm-related shipwrecks,[5] we find that from 1846 through 1930 at least one ship was lost as the result of gales or storms *every* year. That's at least one ship a year for eighty-five consecutive years.

In most years, however, more than one ship was lost to these "killer storms." Fifty-nine ships went down in storms in 1905. Thirty-four ships were lost in 1887, 1903, and 1913. There were twenty-eight losses in 1880, and twenty-six in 1883 and 1886. Twenty-five losses were recorded in 1901, twenty-three in 1906, and twenty-two in 1902. Altogether, there were forty-two seasons when ten or more ships were lost in storms. From the loss of the *Griffon* in 1679 to the sinking of the *Edmund Fitzgerald* in 1975, a staggering 1,077 storm-related shipwrecks have been recorded on the lakes. Since early records are less than perfect, the actual number of wrecks certainly exceeds that count.

In mid-November 1835, for example, the first storm ever referred to as a "cyclone" roared across Lake Michigan and Lake Erie,[6] "announcing its approach like the sound of an immense train of cars."[7] The water rose so high at Buffalo that the steamers *Sandusky*, *Henry Clay*, and *Sheldon Thompson* were washed into the streets near the harbor. Off Point Pelee, in the middle of Lake Erie, the schooner *LaGrange* was one of several ships that were capsized and sunk. It fared better than most, as two nearly frozen survivors were taken off the wreck the following morning. All six sailors and one passenger aboard the schooner *Comet* were lost when the ship foundered off Dunkirk, New York, sinking to the bottom with only the tips of its masts visible above the water. In all, at least thirteen ships were lost or seriously damaged on Lake Erie, with another four reported lost on Lake Michigan.[8] At the time, the entire fleet on the Great Lakes amounted to only about 230 vessels, mostly sailing ships.[9]

Three years later, in November 1838, another killer storm raged across the lakes, seriously damaging twenty-five ships and claiming many lives.[10] In 1842, a mid-November storm with winds of fifty-five to seventy-two miles an hour wrecked more than fifty ships and killed more than one hundred people on Lake Ontario, Lake Erie, and Lake Michigan.

By 1860 the size of the fleet operating on the Great Lakes had grown to 1,457 vessels, a sixfold increase in just twenty-five years. Unfortunately, the number of deaths that resulted from marine casualties on the lakes kept pace with the growth in the number of ships. In 1860, 578 reportedly died in shipping accidents during the eight-month shipping season, most as the result of storm losses.[11]

During the evening hours of November 16, 1869, the wind began to blow strong out of the northwest, whipping the lakes into a tempest. When the winds finally abated four days later, 97 vessels had been wrecked, including 6 steamers, 8 barks, 4 brigs, 56 schooners, 18 scows, and 3 barges. Thirty-five were total losses.[12] In the aftermath of the storm, the shores of the lakes, from Chicago and Duluth in the west to Buffalo and Oswego in the east, were littered with broken ships and dead sailors. The 1869 storm ranks yet today as one of the worst to ever strike the lakes. In terms of the number of ships lost, it *is* the worst.

There was one positive outcome of the staggering losses experienced on the lakes during the fall of 1869. On November 1 of the following year, a marine weather service began serving a few of the major ports on the Great Lakes. President Ulysses S. Grant signed legislation into law creating the "storm signal service," as it was originally called, on February 8, 1870. As suggested by its name, agency personnel forecast the weather, and whenever a storm was predicted they alerted passing ships by flying warning flags. Shipowners from Cleveland, stung by the high number of storm losses in 1869, had played a major role in lobbying for creation of the weather service.[13]

Despite establishment of the weather service, the 1871 shipping season took a heavy toll on ships on the lakes. A total of 19 ships foundered during the year, 26 capsized, 60 sailing vessels were dismasted, 110 ships lost deck loads, 280 boats went aground, and 65 were "waterlogged." At least 214 people died as a result of shipping accidents that season.[14] Most of those casualties were storm-related.

Two severe storms struck the lakes during the fall of 1872. The first

38. Despite the availability of marine weather forecasts at ports around the lakes, the big four-masted schooner *J. H. Rutter* was caught out on Lake Michigan and driven aground off Ludington, Michigan, in a severe storm on November 1, 1878. Here, many of the ship's crew can be seen climbing into the rigging to escape the powerful waves that were crashing over the exposed deck. The U.S. flag is being flown upside down as a distress signal. Valiant local residents used a small boat to ferry the forty-four crewmembers ashore through the pounding surf. (Ralph Roberts Collection)

was a two-day blow that began on September 29. Despite the availability of weather warnings at many ports, the storm wrecked ninety-three vessels.[15] The second blow, centered mainly on Lake Superior, exhibited many of the characteristics that we now associate with hurricanes. Winds began to blow on November 23, slackened somewhat during the night of November 26–27, and then built to maximum strength by the afternoon of November 27. The temporary lessening of the winds probably occurred when the very center of the low-pressure system passed over the lakes. It's a phenomenon that has tricked many captains into leaving port over the years, thinking that a storm had blown itself out. Hours later the winds would rapidly increase, from a different direction, and the captains would find themselves sailing in harm's way.

Three of the ships lost in the violent storm at the end of November 1872 were driven ashore by the high winds and violent seas. All fourteen crewmembers aboard the schooner-barges *Jupiter* and *Saturn* died (see

Chapter 1), while six of nine crewmembers on the schooner *W. O. Brown* drowned, all within a stone's throw of the safety of the shore.

The circumstances of the tragic losses of the *Jupiter, Saturn,* and *Brown* led the Board of Lakes Underwriters, made up of the insurance companies that wrote policies on Great Lakes ships, to lobby the Treasury Department to set up lifesaving stations on the lakes similar to those in operation along the Atlantic Coast. The initial funds were appropriated in 1874, and construction began on four stations along Lake Superior's south shore the following year. All four stations were in operation by the shipping season of 1876.[16]

By 1875, weather forecasts were being telegraphed to thirty-six ports and red warning flags would be flown to alert sailors whenever a gale or storm was anticipated. Unfortunately, most captains ignored the weather warnings. Used to making their own weather forecasts based on the appearance of the sky, the rise or fall of their barometers, and even a "feeling" they got in their bones, they didn't trust the weather service's forecasts, and they didn't want anyone impinging on their historic right to make the decision about whether to sail or not. Interestingly, a later evaluation showed that during its first years of operation the marine weather service accurately predicted about 80 percent of the storms that hit the lakes.[17] It's unlikely that many captains were that accurate in their weather predictions. If they had been, there would undoubtedly have been far fewer shipwrecks than records indicate.

Manistee, 1883

In 1883, Captain John McKay was one of the most popular and highly respected officers on the Great Lakes. He was virtually an institution around Lake Superior. The son of a well-known early captain, Johnny McKay had literally grown up on the lakes. He followed in his father's footsteps, signing on as a sailor when he was just a boy. As a teenager, he had been serving under his father as a deckhand on the *Independence* when the steamer's boiler blew up and destroyed the ship shortly after setting out from a dock at Sault Ste. Marie in 1853. In 1865 he was a lookout on his brother George's ship, the *Pewabic,* when it collided with the *Meteor* and sank on northern Lake Huron.

A few years after the sinking of the *Pewabic,* Johnny McKay became a ship's master in his own right. In ensuing years he had the privilege of commanding some of the best-known steamers on the lakes, and he clearly had an affinity for ships in the Lake Superior trade. Captain McKay made his home in Buffalo, but according to an article in the *Cleveland Herald*, he was so popular around Lake Superior that a small settlement on the north shore was named "McKay's Harbor" in his honor.[18]

In the mid-1870s, Captain Johnny McKay was master of the 184-foot *Manistee*, a wood-hulled passenger and freight steamer operated by the Ward Line on the Buffalo-to-Duluth run. When the ship was sold to the Lake Superior and North Shore Line of Duluth in 1876, McKay went north with the ship. Over the next seven seasons, he and the *Manistee* operated on the west end of Lake Superior, running mainly between Duluth and Houghton, on Michigan's Keweenaw Peninsula, the northern terminus for many of the steamers that came up from the lower lakes.

The *Manistee* was then an aging ship, having been built at Cleveland in 1867. While she wasn't the equal of the newer steamers on the lakes, many of which were opulent "palace steamers," Johnny McKay made sure his boat was kept in the best possible condition. He oversaw a complete overhaul in 1879, and she eventually got all new frames and planking. At the end of the 1882 season, the *Manistee*'s boilers got a complete going over, an expensive project that cost her owners $4,000.[19]

No, the little *Manistee* was no palace steamer, but she was a pretty ship. Her hull and cabins were pure white, set off by a tall black smokestack. Even the wooden fenders that hung along the sides of her hull were painted white. At the forward end of her hurricane deck was an octagon-shaped wheelhouse, topped with a large gilded eagle. On each side of the bow, just forward of her nameboards, was a detailed carving of an angel holding an unfurled scroll. Like the eagle, the carving on the hull was covered with gold leaf. In every respect, the *Manistee* was a well-kept ship, a ship that residents of the west end of Lake Superior could be proud of, as Captain Johnny McKay was proud of it.

In 1883, travelers on western Lake Superior had their choice of numerous steamers, many of which were newer, larger, and fancier than the *Manistee*. Still, the little steamer always left the docks with its share of passengers. Most weren't drawn to the ship because it was well cared for, however. People along Superior's shores wanted to ride the *Manistee* because they preferred to travel with their old friend Johnny McKay.[20]

On November 10, 1883, Captain McKay guided the *Manistee* out of the busy harbor at Duluth and set a course for the port of Ontonagon, seventy-five miles across the lake. After unloading at Ontonagon, the steamer would go on another forty miles to Houghton on the Portage Ship Canal before returning to Duluth. There were only seven passengers aboard for the late-season run, but the freight deck of the steamer was loaded down with 10,000 bushels of oats, 90 tons of mill feed, 1,254 barrels of flour, 9 tons of general freight, and some doors and sashes.[21]

Before the steamer was clear of the Apostle Islands, it ran headlong into a driving snowstorm. Captain McKay hauled his ship around, ducked into the shelter of the Apostles, and ran for Bayfield, Wisconsin, the closest harbor of refuge. The *Manistee* would ride out this storm tied safely to the dock in Bayfield. The delay was an inconvenience for all concerned, but it was considerably better than trying to cross Lake Superior in a November blow. Besides, those aboard the *Manistee* weren't alone. Several other steamers had docked at Bayfield to wait out the storm, including the *City of Duluth*.

As the fall storm stretched into its fourth and fifth days, all of those aboard the stranded steamers began to feel restless. The captains of the ships were definitely impatient. Their passengers had begun to complain. Their crews were getting edgy, and some were spending a little too much time in the local watering holes. And it went without saying that the owners of their ships were getting edgy, too. A boat doesn't make any money when it's tied up to a dock.

After five long days of forced idleness, Captain McKay's patience had worn thin. Even though high winds were still blowing across the lake, on the morning of Friday, November 16, he decided to throw off the mooring lines and head for the Keweenaw. We don't know what motivated Johnny McKay. He might have thought the winds were going down. Maybe the mercury in his barometer rose a bit. Maybe he was just impatient. It no longer makes much difference.

The storm continued to blow for the better part of two days after the *Manistee* left the shelter of the harbor at Bayfield. When the *City of Duluth* finally got to the Keweenaw on Monday, November 19, those aboard were startled to learn that Captain McKay and his ship hadn't arrived. When the *Manistee*'s owners were notified, they immediately hired the tug *Maytham* from Houghton to search for their missing steamer.

Forty-five miles northeast of the Keweenaw Peninsula, the crew of the *Maytham* found a small field of floating debris that included some charcoal, a piece of a pilothouse, and a bucket. Stenciled on the side of the bucket was the name *Manistee*.[22] It was apparent that Captain McKay and his ship had fallen victim to the storm, but what happened aboard the *Manistee* in the hours after it left Bayfield remained a mystery.

39. The little wooden bulk freighter *H. C. Akeley* foundered in a Lake Michigan storm on November 13, 1883. She had taken the disabled tug *Protection* in tow early in the storm, but had to cut it loose after she lost her rudder. As the *Akeley* slipped into the trough of the powerful seas, her cargo of corn shifted and the 232-foot ship foundered. Six crewmembers died in the sinking, shown here in a painting. (Ralph Roberts Collection)

That mystery was cleared up when a lifeboat carrying three survivors from the *Manistee* washed up on the shore of the Keweenaw Peninsula after three days adrift on the angry seas of Lake Superior. They reported that the steamer had been overtaken by strong southwest winds and high seas shortly after leaving the sheltered waters of the Apostle Islands. Captain McKay attempted to bring the ship around to return to Bayfield, but the waves were too much for the old girl and the *Manistee* began to break up.

The ship's lifeboats were swung over on their davits, but before they could be launched all but one were swept away by the powerful seas. Nine of those aboard the *Manistee* managed to get aboard the remaining boat just minutes before the steamer plunged to the bottom. Captain Johnny McKay was not one of them. One survivor said that when the three lifeboats were swept away and it became obvious that not everyone was going to be able to get off the sinking ship, Captain McKay calmly and magnanimously said, "I am captain of this boat, and if she is a coffin for anybody, she will be my coffin." The *Manistee* proved to be a coffin, not just for Captain McKay, but for more than twenty of those aboard his ship. Six of those who escaped in the open lifeboat also perished during the three brutally cold days the little boat tossed around on the frenzied waters of Lake Superior.[23]

All around Lake Superior, residents were shocked to learn of the death of Johnny McKay. For many it was almost as though they'd lost a family member. Over the following year, there would be many reminders of the tragic plight of Captain McKay and the *Manistee*. That fall and the following spring, wreckage from the steamer washed ashore at such disparate locations as Eagle Harbor, Eagle River, Sand Bay, and Ontonagon on the Keweenaw Peninsula; at Ashland, Wisconsin, at the extreme west end of Lake Superior; at Isle Royale, along Superior's north shore; and as far away as Caribou Island and Mamainse Point at the extreme east end of the lake.[24] It was almost as though Captain Johnny McKay and the *Manistee* were making one final circuit of the lake before calling it quits.

The *Manistee* wasn't the only ship lost or damaged in the November storm of 1883. When all the insurance claims were all settled, damage totaled $1,150,000.[25]

Niagara, 1887

On September 7, 1887, the steamer *Australasia* was downbound on Lake Superior towing the schooner-barge *Niagara*. Both ships were carrying heavy loads of iron ore they had taken on at Ashland, Wisconsin. On the long leg of open water between the Keweenaw Peninsula and Whitefish Point, the two vessels were overtaken by a violent and unexpected storm that swept in from the northwest and turned the lake into a frenzied maelstrom of crashing waves. Caught in an exposed position, all the captain of the *Australasia* could do was struggle on toward Whitefish.

When the *Australasia* and its consort were only about ten miles from the sheltered waters of Whitefish Bay, those in the steamer's pilothouse were shocked to notice that the *Niagara* was no longer at the end of its towline. One minute the 205-foot schooner was struggling along in the wake of the steamer, the next minute it was gone!

When the *Australasia* reached the Soo and reported the *Niagara* missing, there was much speculation about what had happened to the schooner. Those on the *Australasia* thought that the violent tossing of the two ships had possibly wrenched the wooden bow off the schooner. Others felt that she might have broken her back as she worked in the high seas, or that she simply filled with water and sank. The only thing people knew for sure from the early, and somewhat sketchy, reports from the Soo was that Captain Clements, his wife and five children, and the nine seamen who served with him on the *Niagara* were gone.[26]

The shipping company that owned the *Niagara* couldn't even supply the newspapers with an accurate list of the crewmembers aboard the schooner. "It will be difficult to obtain the names of the drowned sailors," said a spokesperson for James Corrigan of Cleveland. "They changed around so often that we can seldom keep track of them, and the fact that the ship's papers are lost will keep the names from being known for a long time."[27]

Subsequent newspaper coverage of the sinking of the *Niagara* brought several surprises. First, it was discovered that Mrs. Clements and her children had not been aboard. They had gone to Ashtabula with the intentions of making a trip, but Mrs. Clements changed her mind and she and her children had eventually returned to their home in Cleveland and the tragic news that Captain Clements and his ship had been lost.[28]

Second, a downbound ship had reported seeing the masts of a sunken schooner two miles off the beach, near the Vermilion Point lifesaving station. When lifesavers investigated, they found what seemed to be indisputable evidence that the *Niagara* hadn't gone down as fast as those aboard the *Australasia* had reported. The schooner's sails had been set after she broke free from the *Australasia,* although it looked as though the fierce winds had quickly ripped them to shreds. Even more startling was the news that Captain Clements and his crew had managed to abandon their sinking ship. It appeared that the little yawl boat had then been capsized in the high seas and all those aboard drowned.[29] How those on the *Australasia* could have been so far wrong about the fate of their tow is unexplainable.

In the aftermath of the sinking, there were also reports from Ashland that the fourteen-year-old schooner had been loaded so heavily when she left the ore dock that her deck would have been awash in even the slightest sea. That came as a surprise to no one. With no regulations to govern how deep a ship could be loaded, it was a fairly common practice for ships to carry as much ore as could be stuffed into their holds, especially during the fall season when freight rates were at their highest.

The loss of the *Niagara* and its crew led one Detroit newspaper editor to print a scathing editorial about unsafe conditions in the shipping industry. "Many of the old schooners are 'rattletraps,' which it is almost an act of manslaughter to send crews out in," he wrote. "They are so dangerous, in fact, that the insurance companies will only take risk on them at ruinous figures," he continued. "Their value is small and the loss to their owners would be insignificant if they were wrecked; while if they pulled through—especially for several trips in the fall, when freight rates are high—they would pay their cost several times over."

The outspoken editor never made it clear whether he considered the *Niagara* to have been a "rattletrap." While the ship was fourteen years old, well along for a wood-hulled vessel, it had reportedly been rebuilt four years before it sank. How extensive that rebuilding was is not known.

In his column, the editor did make the point, though, that it wasn't just the rattletraps that were being overloaded. "The same greed causes owners to overload staunch and seaworthy craft," he noted. "But what chance has a single-decked vessel loaded to such a depth when sea after sea breaks over her, adding, before she can free herself of it, hundreds of tons of weight to the overload she is already carrying." Many of the sinkings that were a direct result of overloading were covered up, according to the editor. Many were attributed to "the heavy gale," or "the memory of some poor man who was compelled in the struggle for bread to ship as master of such an overloaded craft is vilified and the loss attributed to poor seamanship."

The union that represented some seamen on the lakes had reportedly been lobbying for several years to get Congress to enact legislation banning overloading by implementing load-line standards similar to those already in effect for British ships. The union also wanted to outlaw the use of uninsured ships, many of which were without insurance because they were in such poor condition that underwriters either wouldn't write policies on them, or the premiums they wanted to insure the "death traps" were so high that the shipowners would decide to operate the vessels without insurance.[30]

Western Reserve, 1892

When the *Western Reserve* cleared the breakwaters at Cleveland and steamed out onto Lake Erie on the evening of August 29, 1892, nobody aboard the freighter was happier to be out on the lake than Peter Minch. For the three days it would take the ship to reach the ore docks at Two Harbors, Minnesota, Minch could escape his normal day-to-day responsibilities as manager of his family's extensive shipping interests. He had business to tend to at Two Harbors, but until the ship arrived there he would be on vacation—and it was a vacation he badly needed.

It had been an oppressively hot and humid summer in Cleveland. Sitting in his often stifling office day after long day and handling the unending stream of paperwork it took to run a fleet, Peter Minch had frequently thought about the cool breezes and fresh air out on the lakes. There were many days when he would gladly have traded his managerial responsibilities for a chance to command a ship again. Although he was merely a passenger aboard the *Western Reserve* for the trip to Two Harbors, Peter Minch had himself been a highly regarded ship's captain. His father's death five years earlier had forced him to come ashore, but everyone still called him "Captain," and he was in many ways much more at ease on the deck of a ship than in the offices and boardrooms frequented by the leaders of the Great Lakes shipping industry.

It had not been a good summer for Captain Peter Minch, or for the Minch fleet. A month earlier, their schooner *Fred A. Morse* had sunk following a collision on Lake Huron. Thankfully, nobody had been lost in the sinking, but it caused many headaches for the office staff. Besides having to deal with the insurance underwriters, they had to shift cargoes around so they could meet their contractual commitments. Then, just a week earlier, engineers on the *Western Reserve* had noticed a small bulge in the wall of one of her boiler furnaces. It was a weak spot, caused either by overheating or by a weakness in the metal used in its construction. Regardless, the big freighter had to be sent to the shipyard for repairs. The work had taken most of the week, but earlier that day the boiler inspectors from the Steamboat Inspection Service had finally put their stamp of approval on the repairs, and Minch was finally able to put the big freighter back into service.

The *Western Reserve* was the pride of the Minch fleet. The 300-foot steel-hulled ship had been launched at the Cleveland Ship Building yard only two years earlier. When the modern steamer slid off the ways, only about thirty of the two thousand ships in the Great Lakes fleet were built of steel. There were some iron freighters around, like Minch's *Onoko*, but most of the cargo moved in those days was still carried on wooden ships. The *Onoko*, built in 1882, was another point of pride for the Minch family. It had been only the second iron-hulled freighter ever built on the lakes.[31]

A lot of people in the industry had criticized Peter's father when word got out that he had ordered an iron ship. At that time no one knew how well iron would hold up under the wear and tear of the ore trade. Most shipping company executives strongly believed that wood was not just the *best* material to built ships out of, but the *only* suitable material. The experience with the *Onoko* and the other iron ships that followed in its wake had proved them wrong, and established Peter Minch's father as one of the most progressive fleet owners on the lakes. By building the steel-hulled *Western Reserve*, Peter had sent a message to the industry that the Minch fleet would remain in the forefront of Great Lakes shipping while he was at the helm.

As the *Western Reserve* set out from Cleveland that warm, summer evening in 1892, though, Captain Peter Minch was glad that he could put the responsibilities of running the fleet aside for a few days and simply enjoy a trip up the lakes. In fact, he had turned the trip to Two Harbors into a summer outing for his family. His wife and two of his children were along, and he had invited his sister-in-law and her daughter to accompany them.[32]

When the *Western Reserve* reached the locks at Sault Ste. Marie early on the afternoon of August 30, the Minch family stood out on deck under an overcast sky to watch the activities involved in raising their ship to the level of Lake Superior. Captain Minch pointed out the red storm pennant flying from the flagpole next to the lock, and explained to his family that it meant that a storm warning was in effect for Lake Superior.[33] The telegraph office at the locks had begun displaying weather signals the previous September in an effort to reduce the number of ships that got caught out on the lakes in storms.[34] If the weather prediction proved to be accurate, a bumpy ride could be expected between the Soo and Two Harbors.

The *Western Reserve* had barely cleared the locks and headed up the St. Marys River before the wind kicked up. By the time the ship reached Whitefish Bay at 4 P.M., the winds had intensified and white-capped waves were rolling across Lake Superior. Captain Albert Myers, master of the *Western Reserve*, suggested going to anchor in the lee of Whitefish Point, but Peter Minch didn't think that would be necessary.[35] With winds out of the west, they would be heading almost directly into the seas and should ride quite well. After all, it was just a little summer storm.

As the *Western Reserve* steamed westward through the growing seas, the Minch family turned in for the night. The big freighter was laboring some, and occasionally she would pound very hard. Captain Myers had put ballast water in the aft tanks to make sure that the propeller was well down in the water, but the bow of the ship was riding quite high. Every so often a wave would lift the bow clear of the water, and she would pound and shake as it settled back down into the seas.[36]

At about 9 P.M., "a violent, jolting shock and jar" could be felt through-out the *Western Reserve*, "followed by the noise of a spar breaking and falling on deck." Wheelsman Harry Stewart was resting on the bunk in his room under the forward cabin, and he immediately rushed out and started up the ladder to the main deck level. Right about then, Captain Myers appeared and yelled for everyone to get out quickly, because the ship was going to sink. Stewart ran back into his room and quickly pulled on some clothes before heading for the lifeboats that were located on the stack deck at the stern.

As Stewart hurried aft along the port side of the dark deck, he saw that there was a four-foot-wide crack running across the deck just forward of the mainmast that was located amidships. The mainmast had snapped off about halfway up, and the top of the mast and a tangle of stays were lying in a heap on the deck. Stewart jumped across the crack, dodged the debris on the deck, and dashed toward the stern.

When Stewart reached the lifeboats, things seemed very orderly. "Everybody seemed very cool," he commented later. Crewmembers swung out the lifeboat davits and lowered the two boats to the level of the main deck.[37] They had some trouble lowering the boats, because neither had been in the water before.[38] The two women and the three children were helped into the starboard boat, a traditional wooden lifeboat that could be rigged as a yawl. Captain Minch, Captain Myers, Harry Stewart, and nine other crewmembers then climbed in and lowered the boat the rest of the way into the surging water. The lifeboat on the port side, a modern steel boat with nine crewmembers in it, went into the water on the other side of the *Western Reserve*.

As the boat with Harry Stewart in it began to row away from the sinking hull, they took aboard another crewmember, a wheelsman who had inadvertently been left aboard the freighter. Seconds later, they heard someone hollering in the water, and they pulled aboard one of the crewmembers who had been in the steel lifeboat. He told them that the lifeboat had capsized and sunk shortly after they had launched it. The others who had been aboard the metal lifeboat had disappeared beneath the angry black seas.

As they rowed off into the darkness, the survivors heard the roar of rushing water and a muffled explosion as their ship plummeted beneath Lake Superior. The wind, which had seemed to drop off for awhile, began to increase in intensity again, blowing from the north-northwest, and seas continued to build. All those crowded aboard the small lifeboat could do was try to keep it running with the wind and seas. Waves continually broke over the overloaded boat, and those aboard had to bail constantly to keep it from sinking.[39]

During the night, the spirits of the survivors were buoyed when they saw the lights of a passing steamer. Those in the lifeboat screamed and yelled for about a half an hour, but there was no sign that those aboard the steamer saw the little lifeboat amidst the towering waves. There were no flares in the boat, so they tried to set fire to a shawl that one of the women had brought with her. The shawl proved to be too wet to ignite, however, and the lights of the steamer gradually disappeared into the blackness of the night, leaving the dispirited survivors again alone on the storm-tossed lake.[40]

Ten hours after they abandoned their sinking ship, the sky lightened with the coming of dawn and those in the lifeboat could see that they were only about a mile off the beach. The big waves that carried their little boat along crashed and broke as they rolled into the shallow water, however, and with the safety of the beach seemingly within their grasp a succession of big waves stood the lifeboat on its end and it capsized as it dropped back into the water. The survivors of the *Western Reserve* suddenly and unexpectedly found themselves in the violently swirling waters of Lake Superior. Only the two women had lifejackets on, but one that had been thrown into the bottom of the boat popped up next to Harry Stewart and he put it on while treading water. Held up by the lifejacket, Stewart began swimming toward the shore.[41] "I saw none of the occupants after I started for the shore," Stewart later remembered, "but the cries of the children, the screams of the women, and moaning of the men were terrible for a few moments, then all was silent."[42]

Stewart struggled through the crashing surf, clawed his way onto the beach, and collapsed in exhaustion. He watched the water's edge, hoping to see other survivors emerge from the surf, but it soon became obvious that no others were coming ashore that morning.

In time, Stewart began trudging east down the shore. He walked, staggered, and even crawled along the sand until after ten agonizing and desolate miles he finally came to the Deer Park Life-Saving Station. Captain Frahm and his crew got Stewart into dry clothes and brewed a pot of hot coffee for him, then set off down the beach to search for other survivors. The lifesavers found the wooden yawl boat washed up on the beach, but Harry Stewart was to be the only survivor.[43]

The loss of the *Western Reserve* and the deaths of Captain Minch and his family stunned the Great Lakes maritime community and touched off a heated debate about the cause of the sinking. As is usually the case, a number of theories about why the big, new steel freighter went down emerged in the days following the sinking. Since the *Western Reserve*

40. There was only one survivor when the big bulk freighter *Western Reserve* foundered in an unusually powerful late-August storm on Lake Superior. Among those who died when the 300-foot steel steamer broke up and sank were Captain Peter Minch, owner of the *Western Reserve,* and his wife and two children. It was later speculated that the ship, seen here in a drawing by Samuel Ward Stanton, was built with steel that was too brittle. (Author's Collection)

was the first steel-hulled freighter to be lost in a storm, people in the shipping industry were treading in virgin territory as they tried to explain the sinking.

For some reason, insurance underwriters tended to think that the *Western Reserve*'s steam engine had broken through the bottom of her hull. That, of course, would have meant that the ship had gone down as a result of structural weaknesses tied to the way she was built. In that case, her builders might have had to assume the financial cost of the loss.

On the other hand, many experienced sailors attributed the loss to structural weakness, aggravated by the likelihood that the ship "was being rushed into head seas as big steel steamers of her kind always are." Captain Minch's presence, they speculated, probably led to the boat's being unduly pushed. That scenario would have resulted in the *Western Reserve*'s straddling a wave, like a giant teeter-totter, or having the ends of the ship lifted by waves while the center of the vessel had no support. In either case, the strain on the hull would have been immense and the ship would have started to shuck her rivets.

Some in the industry thought the hull of the *Western Reserve* had probably been damaged in loading and unloading. "Want of proper care in loading and unloading, especially by big boats, has strained many of them and done no small amount of damage," the *Detroit Free Press* reported. "Ore and coal is piled into the hatches forward and aft, and the hatches amidships are left empty. This is a great strain on the boat, and in time tells."[44]

The frequent mention of possible structural weaknesses sparked an immediate response from the Cleveland Ship Building Company, builders of the *Western Reserve*. The company president maintained that the Minch freighter was the best boat his yard had ever built. "No wind or sea could disturb her," he boldly claimed. "She must have struck a rock, or her engines gave way."[45]

The debate over why the *Western Reserve* went down took a new twist two months later when, on October 28, 1892, the freighter *W. H. Gilcher* disappeared during a storm on Lake Michigan. The *Gilcher* was virtually a twin to the *Western Reserve*, having been launched four months after the Minch boat at Cleveland Ship Building. The *Western Reserve* was the Cleveland yard's hull number 9, the *Gilcher* was hull number 10. Since there were no survivors from the loss of the *Gilcher*, her sinking was even more of a mystery than that of the *Western Reserve*. Some people even thought that since the two ships were so similar, there might be some common thread in the sinkings.

One plausible explanation was that the steel used to build the two ships was substandard. When the *Western Reserve* and *Gilcher* were built, steel was a new building material and had been used on the lakes for only four years. Before then, steel was produced only in small quantities and was too expensive to use in ship construction. Henry Bessemer's development of the patented "Bessemer process" in the late 1870s had changed all that, however. Use of the Bessemer process made it possible to produce large quantities of steel at costs that were competitive with those of iron. Since steel was both stronger and lighter than iron, it seemed to be particularly well suited for use in shipbuilding. Its strength meant that bigger ships could be built, and since steel was lighter in weight, steel ships would be able to carry more cargo than comparable ships built of iron.

After the *Western Reserve* and *Gilcher* went down, however, officials at some of the shipyards that had experience in building steel ships began to voice their concerns about the quality of steel produced through the Bessemer process. Fred Ballin, a naval architect at a Detroit shipyard, reported that his yard had "found it almost impossible to get a homo-geneous stock of steel even in the same plate. We had lab tests made," Ballin continued, "and found that the plates and angles would crack in handling, heating, or punching. We seriously considered the probability of returning to iron."

Ballin, along with many others in the shipbuilding business, had reached the conclusion that the inexpensive steel produced through the Bessemer process wasn't suited for use in building ships. It simply couldn't stand up to the many stresses found in the marine environment. In time, the classification societies that set the standards for ship construction concurred with that thinking and prohibited the use Bessemer process steel, requiring instead the more expensive open-hearth or electric furnace products.[46]

Many people in the industry quickly embraced the theory that the *Western Reserve* and *Gilcher* had been lost because the steel in their hulls was faulty. After all, it was a convenient explanation. It largely exonerated Captain Myers and Captain Minch, and all the other captains who regularly ignored gale and storm warnings to head out onto the lakes. It also exonerated shipping company executives who often encouraged their captains to keep running in the face of inclement weather. It also shifted attention away from loading and unloading practices that could potentially damage a ship's hull.

Interestingly, we know today that the vast majority of the steel ships built around the time the *Western Reserve* and *Gilcher* proved to be sturdy vessels and had long careers on the lakes, even though they had been built with steel made in the Bessemer process. Of the first thirty steel bulk freighters, only four succumbed to Great Lakes storms. In addition to the *Western Reserve* and *Gilcher*, the *Ira H. Owen* went down on Lake Superior in the Big Storm of 1905 and the *Lakeland* sank on Lake Michigan in 1924. Most of the other early steel ships operated on the lakes for forty to sixty years before ending their careers under the shipbreaker's torch, a credible showing in anyone's book.

The year following the losses of the *Western Reserve* and *Gilcher*, an estimated forty ships were sunk or seriously damaged in a severe storm that began on October 14, 1893. Among those lost was the freighter *Wocoken*.

Wocoken, 1893

The *Wocoken* had loaded 1,800 tons of coal at Ashtabula, Ohio, then coasted over to Erie, Pennsylvania, to pick up the schooner-barge *Joseph Paige*. As Captain Albert Meswald watched his men rig the towing bridle to the *Paige,* he noticed that storm warning flags were flying. Despite that, the *Wocoken* and *Paige* steamed out of the harbor at Erie and set out across Lake Erie on a course that would take them to the mouth of the Detroit River.

The predicted storm rushed down on the two vessels when they were about in midlake. Captain Meswald altered course to head for Long Point, the long peninsula that juts down into Lake Erie from the Canadian shore. If they could tuck in behind Long Point, they would be in sheltered waters and could comfortably ride out the storm. It might have been wiser if he had decided to ride out the storm at Erie.

Huge waves were soon tearing at the two ships. Before long, the *Wocoken*'s windows had been smashed and her railings were torn away. Then, looking aft, Captain Meswald could see that the waves had pried some of the wooden hatch covers loose, and with each breaking sea the cargo hold was filling with water.

Captain Meswald ordered his men to cut the *Paige* loose. Within minutes the crew on the schooner had set their storm sails and scudded off rapidly in the direction of Long Point. Freed from the burden of towing the *Paige,* the steamer at first seemed to be doing better. More hatch covers worked loose, however, and it became obvious that the ship was settling more with each wave that rolled down the deck. About 10 P.M., while the *Wocoken* was still several miles off the tip of Long Point, Captain Meswald had no choice but to give the dreaded order to abandon ship.

Those on the forward end of the freighter struggled aft over a deck that was constantly awash. Captain Meswald's wife was aboard for the trip, and he tried to reassure her as he helped her along the deck. By the time the Meswalds got aft, the fifteen members of his crew had uncovered the lifeboats and were in the process of lowering them over the side. Before the two boats could be dropped into the water, however, a massive wave rolled over the stern. Captain and Mrs. Meswald and twelve of the fifteen crewmen were overwhelmed and swept overboard by the angry sea. At the same time, the immense weight of the wave dealt the death blow to the *Wocoken* and it slipped beneath the surface.

As the ship settled toward the bottom, the three crewmen still on the *Wocoken*'s deck half-swam, half-crawled to the stern mast, the only part of the ship still sticking out of the water. Fortunately for them, the freighter came to rest in an upright position on the bottom in only forty-eight feet of water. At the surface, Second Mate J. P. Saph, Wheelsman J. H. Rice, and Deckhand Robert Crowding pulled themselves up the mast until they were clear of the waves that rolled across the lake. There they stayed, hanging in the rigging, until Canadian lifesavers from Port Rowan rescued them the next day.

The three survivors from the *Wocoken* were probably surprised to learn that the schooner-barge they had been towing had made it to the shelter of Long Point, and was even then riding comfortably at anchor in the lee of the peninsula.[47] While the *Paige* survived after being cut loose by its tow steamer, which then sank, the situation was often the reverse.

In that same 1893 storm, for example, the steamer *White and Friant* cut loose the schooner-barge *Annie Sherwood* just west of Whitefish Point on Lake Superior. Both had loaded lumber at Washburn, Wisconsin, and were downbound for Chicago when the storm overtook them. The steamer made it safely to the Soo, but there was no word on the little schooner and its seven crewmembers, although an upbound steamer reported coming across floating wreckage west of Whitefish that could have been from the *Sherwood.*

On October 16, the steamer *Sitka* found the crew of the *Sherwood* afloat in a lifeboat near Caribou Island, north of Whitefish Bay. Five of the crewmembers were still alive, but Captain Louis Guthrie and a deckhand had died of hypothermia and injuries during their long ordeal in the lifeboat. Crewmembers recounted that after the *Sherwood* was cut loose it began to take on water. Off Caribou Island it became obvious to all that the schooner was going to sink at any moment and Captain Guthrie ordered the crew into the lifeboat.

To everyone's surprise, the tenacious *Sherwood* was found washed up on the Canadian shore a week later. It had been badly damaged in the storm, but the hull was still intact. The winds and seas had driven it ashore seventy miles from where it had been abandoned by its crew.[48]

Sevona, 1905

The record for the 1905 shipping season was dismal. According to records of the Lake Carriers' Association, 79 of the 542 ships registered with them that year were totally destroyed during the season. A staggering 213 sailors died, including 116 who were lost in the three major storms that rocked the lakes that fall—one each in September, October, and November.[49]

The first of the three storms struck Lake Superior on Friday, September 1, 1905, as winds gradually built throughout the day and reached gale force just before midnight. The steadily increasing winds piled the lake into towering waves, the spray ripped from their crests mixing with the blinding sheets of rain that accompanied the gale. Even though the U.S. Weather Bureau had posted storm warnings earlier in the day, a storm of this magnitude was totally unexpected in early September. Most captains had ignored the weather warnings and, as a result, their ships were caught out on the open lake.

One of the ships caught out in Lake Superior's fury was the 373-foot steamer *Sevona*. She had finished loading at Superior, Wisconsin, Friday evening and, despite the fact that storm warnings were prominently posted, Captain Donald MacDonald headed his ship out onto the lake. By 2 A.M. Saturday the *Sevona* was steaming into huge seas that crashed into her bow and rolled the length of her deck. Just past Outer Island at the east end of the Apostle Islands, about seventy miles out of Duluth and Superior, Captain MacDonald decided to haul around and run for shelter in the islands. He knew it was a dangerous tactic.

With visibility down to nothing, there was a risk that the ship would run aground amidst the reefs and islands of the Apostles. Apparently that risk was more than offset in Captain MacDonald's mind by the danger of staying out in the open lake in a storm of that magnitude. Since MacDonald was a part-owner of the fifteen-year-old ship, you can be assured that he made what he thought was the most prudent decision.

There were two young women aboard the *Sevona* on that trip, friends of James McBrier of Erie, Pennsylvania, head of the company that owned the freighter. At 3:30 on Saturday morning, Captain McDonald went down and awakened the two and told them to get dressed. He then had four seamen help the women back to the stern cabin, nearer to where the *Sevona*'s two lifeboats were located. Waves were rolling steadily across the deck as the women were assisted aft. They and the four seamen were hooked up to the lifeline that was stretched above the deck between the forward and after cabins, but there were still times when they found themselves up to their waists in chilly water.

At 6 A.M., with the engines checked down to half speed, the *Sevona* crashed hard onto the granite ledges of the misnamed Sand Island Shoal and immediately broke in half at the number 4 hatch. With the crashing waves battering the stern, the crack quickly widened until those on the forward half of the freighter were cut off from the stern . . . and from the ship's lifeboats.

Trapped on the bow of the wrecked ship, Captain MacDonald shouted through his megaphone for those on the stern to launch the two lifeboats, but to hold off getting into them as long as possible. MacDonald knew that they were better off staying aboard the *Savona* as long as they could.

The starboard boat was partially in the lee provided by the hull of the ship, and it was quickly put into the water and tied off alongside. Because the waves were crashing into the port side of the hull, the lifeboat on that side couldn't be launched. Instead, crewmembers dragged it across the deck and put it into the water on the sheltered starboard side. Once the boats were in the water, most of those on the stern retreated to the warmth of the ship's messroom, where there was a plentiful supply of hot coffee.

At 11 A.M. the stern of the *Sevona* began to list badly, and Chief Engineer William Phillipi decided it was time to get into the boats. In the absence of the captain and mates who would normally have been in charge of the lifeboats, the chief engineer took command of one lifeboat, while Charles Scouller, a deckhand, was in charge of the second, smaller boat. Once the boats were loaded, they did their best to row up to the bow section so that Captain MacDonald and the rest of the deck crew could climb aboard. The waves kept washing the boats away from the *Sevona*, however, and those aboard feared they would soon be swamped.

Captain MacDonald and the six men on the forward end had gone into a cabin below the spar deck for shelter, and those in the lifeboats couldn't rouse them. Since the bow section seemed to be solidly grounded on the reef and in no threat of breaking up, the chief engineer decided to leave them behind and strike out for shore.

Phillipi's boat eventually reached shore outside of Bayfield, Wisconsin, near a lumber camp where the occupants of the lifeboat soon found shelter. Charles Scouller's boat went ashore on Sand Island itself, and those aboard took refuge in an abandoned cabin. Early the next morning, Phillipi borrowed a horse and wagon and drove to Bayfield to arrange for a tug to go out and rescue Captain MacDonald and the rest of the crew. By the time the tug *Harrow* arrived at Sand Island Shoal, however, there was no one left aboard the *Sevona*.

Several hours after the lifeboats had rowed away from the wreck, the bow section began to break up. Captain MacDonald and his men hastily constructed makeshift rafts from the ship's wooden hatch covers, and in the early afternoon hours the keeper of the Sand Island Lighthouse saw them set off for shore. Unfortunately, the crude rafts broke apart and capsized when they got into the boiling surf along the shore.

The bodies of Captain MacDonald and the other six deck crewmen were later found washed up on the beach at Sand Island. The $1,500 that Captain MacDonald was known to have been carrying with him to cover the ship's various expenses was missing when his body was found.

41. Twenty-seven ships were wrecked in a storm that scoured the lakes October 20–21, 1905. The passenger and freight steamer *Argo* is shown here after it was driven ashore near Holland, Michigan. Local lifesavers were able to get a line aboard the stranded ship and take the passengers and crew off with a breeches buoy before the vessel broke up in the pounding seas. (Ralph Roberts Collection)

Later, three Bayfield men were seen spending unusually large sums of money. After questioning by local law enforcement officials, the three were charged with robbing the bodies of the dead sailors when they washed ashore. Forty-three sailors died in the September storm of 1905.[50]

Thirty-six sailors died in a second 1905 storm that swept across all five of the Great Lakes on October 20–21 and left twenty-seven ships totally wrecked. The twenty-seven vessels had one thing in common: they were all built of wood. The steel and iron ships caught out in the storm—and there were many of them—managed to get through it alright, but the storm decimated the ranks of the wood-hulled boats. One historian has even gone so far as to claim that "October 20, 1905, may have done more in one day to end the era of wooden ships . . . than all other storms combined."[51]

In reality, the curtain had been drawn on both the era of wooden ships and the age of sail long before the October 20, 1905, storm. Wooden ships and sailing ships were vestiges of an earlier time. The number stricken from the rolls each year greatly outnumbered the new ones being turned out by shipyards, guaranteeing their eventual extinction.

By 1886 steamships outnumbered sailing ships for the first time on the lakes, and by 1900 there were twice as many steamships as sailing vessels.

42. The schooner *Iver Lawson* was left high and dry on a beach in Green Bay in the aftermath of the brutal storm of October 20–21, 1905. The little wooden ship was in her thirty-sixth season on the lakes, and well past her prime, when the storm ended her career. All twenty-seven of the ships claimed by the storm were of wooden construction. (Ralph Roberts Collection)

Steel was first used in ship construction on the lakes in 1886, but it proved so popular with shipowners that most major Great Lakes shipyards didn't build any wooden ships after 1895.[52]

The demise of wooden hulls and sail power was a simple matter of economics. Steel was more durable than wood and, even more importantly, the use of steel allowed shipbuilders to construct much larger ships than could be built of wood. It was, at that time at least, technically impossible to build a wooden ship longer than about 350 feet. If you went beyond that length, the wooden hulls were just too limber and they tended to hog and sag, even when braced with trusses. Steel ships, on the other hand, passed the 350-foot mark in the 1890s. By 1905, the latest generation of steel freighters, Pittsburgh Steamship's famous *Gary* class, measured an astonishing 569 feet in length. A 350-foot ship could carry about 3,500 tons of bulk cargo, compared to more than 10,000 tons for a 569-footer. Because of economies of scale in the maritime industry, the per-ton cost of transporting a product went down as you were able to haul more. That meant lower costs for shippers, and higher profits for the owners of big ships—and the death knell for wooden ships.

Similarly, steamboats were more efficient than sailing ships. Many of the early steamboats weren't any faster than sailing ships of the day, but steamers weren't dependent on the wind. Sailboats were often becalmed, or delayed by having to tack back and forth if the wind was from the wrong direction, which was often the case on the lakes. Time is money in the transportation business. Faster passages by the steamers meant that they could make more trips in a season, thereby carrying more cargo than a sailboat of similar size.

By 1905 the sailboats and wooden steamers were no longer in the mainstream of the Great Lakes shipping industry. Most were carrying lumber or pulpwood from the northern lakes to the big urban centers like Chicago, Detroit, and Cleveland. Others eked out a living carrying small loads of freight that couldn't be moved on the big freighters, mainly machinery or general cargo that was shipped in boxes or barrels. For example, fruits and vegetables were often moved from the orchards and farms around the lakes to waiting produce markets in Chicago and Detroit on sailboats or small wooden steamers. Still others were converted to sandsuckers or fueling lighters.

Some of the largest sailboats were actually engaged in the dynamic bulk cargo trades, but only as barges that were towed by steamers. Towing one or two schooner-barges was at that time an inexpensive way for an owner to increase the per-trip carrying capacity of a steamboat.

By the time the storm of October 20, 1905, struck the lakes, the bleak economic picture faced by the owners of most wooden ships was clearly having an impact on the number of shipwrecks that occurred each year. The wooden ships that were still operating were getting old, dangerously old. During earlier times they would probably have been replaced with new ships, but by 1905 their owners were trying to wring the last possible miles out of the wooden hulls. While there isn't any concrete evidence to prove it, human nature and economics being what they are, it's also likely that owners often cut back on the maintenance of their aging wooden ships.

Most wooden ships on the lakes in 1905 were well past their prime.

Because of that, they were more likely to founder in bad weather. The twenty-three wooden steamers and schooners lost in the 1905 storm, for example, had an average age of just under twenty-six years. Fourteen of them were over twenty years old, nine were more than thirty, and two of them had been around for more than forty years.[53]

While the October storm of 1905 wreaked havoc on the wooden steamers and schooners across the five inland seas, even the most modern steel ships were fair game for a storm that bludgeoned its way across Lake Superior the following month. It caught many ships out on the lakes when they should have been in port.

The shipping companies had been bogged down by the succession of storms that swept across the lakes during the fall of 1905. There was plenty of cargo to move, and at good rates, but a lot of time had been lost to the storms, and winter was fast approaching. By late November, many shipping company managers were beginning to worry that with further delays they wouldn't be able to make good on the contracts they had, or their ships could get trapped by early-winter ice. Some shipping officials had already started to bring their boats into their winter layup docks, while others were hoping to get in another trip or two.

After the devastating storms of September and October, however, a lot of captains were gun-shy, and they'd drop the hook or tie up to a dock at the slightest provocation. It's a scenario that has been repeated many times throughout the long history of shipping on the lakes: on the one hand, fleet managers urging their captains to get in as many trips as possible before the end of the season; on the other hand, captains trying their best to avoid getting caught out on the lakes in a severe storm, without unnecessarily antagonizing the bigwigs in the company office. In 1905 this "November conundrum" set the scene for disaster.

Mataafa, 1905

Storm flags were hoisted at Duluth during the morning hours of November 27, 1905. At the time, the weather at Duluth was fair and cold, with temperatures near zero. There was a breeze out of the northeast, but the lake was calm. All in all, the weather was quite good for a November day, and many captains who saw the red warning flags chose to ignore them. At least four modern steel steamers, a tug, and two barges left the harbor at Duluth and headed out onto Lake Superior after the storm warnings had been posted.

Giving a wink and a nod to the storm flags were the steamers *Mataafa, Ira H. Owen, Harold B. Nye,* and *Isaac L. Ellwood,* and the tug *F. W.*

Gillette. The *Mataafa* was towing the barge *James Nasmyth,* while the *Gillette* was towing the barge *George Herbert.* What the captains of those vessels didn't know was that weather bureau staff at Duluth had put the warnings up after they learned by telegraph that a severe snowstorm was moving east out of North Dakota.

The snowstorm hit Duluth at 6 P.M. An hour later, the winds had increased to gale strength, blowing at forty-four miles an hour. By 6 A.M. on November 28, winds reached storm levels. Gusts of seventy miles an hour had been recorded, and steady winds in excess of sixty miles an hour were recorded for the next twelve hours.[54]

As Duluth residents dug themselves out from under a deep blanket of snow on November 28, they got their first hint of how the storm was affecting shipping. It was the beginning of what would later be referred to as "the worst two hours in the history of shipping in the port of Duluth."[55]

Shortly after noon, the 363-foot *R. W. England,* less than a year old, was steaming toward the narrow canal that forms the entrance to the Duluth harbor. Unable to control his ship in the towering seas, Captain Richard England feared he wouldn't be able to make it through the canal. At the last minute he turned his ship to head back out into the lake. When the *England* got around into the trough of the sea, however, the waves held the ship as if in a vise. Minutes later, the freighter was pushed sideways into shallow water at Superior, Wisconsin, several miles south of the canal. Several huge waves then lifted the ship and literally threw it stern-first onto the snow-covered beach.

Shortly after the *England* was planted on the beach at Superior, the 478-foot *Isaac L. Ellwood* put in its appearance off the Duluth Ship Canal. Captain C. H. Cummings had steamed past the storm flags at Duluth harbor and out onto Lake Superior the previous day, bound for Two Harbors, Minnesota, just down the north shore. Unable to get into Two Harbors because of the storm, the *Ellwood* had taken a heavy pounding during the night. Waves tearing across her deck had shredded the tarpaulins that kept water out of her cargo holds and loosened some of her hatch covers. Knowing that his ship was in a dangerous situation, Captain Cummings hauled her around and headed back to Duluth.

When the *Ellwood* approached the piers at the entrance to the harbor just after 1 P.M., visibility was still poor because of the falling snow, and the heavy seas pushed the ship around as if it were a toy boat better suited to a millpond. Despite the poor visibility and difficulty controlling his ship, Captain Cummings took dead aim at the middle of the ship canal and charged ahead. At first it looked as though the *Ellwood* was going to safely negotiate the canal, but then a big wave lifted the ship and threw it against the north pier, buckling several of the steel plates on her starboard side. Bouncing off the north pier, the *Ellwood* was totally out of control. She veered across the canal and struck the south pier, smashing several plates on her port side.

Taking water in through the gashes in her hull, the battered *Ellwood* finally squeezed through into the shelter of the inner harbor. There several tugs were standing by to help the crippled freighter, and they quickly pushed her into shallow water. Almost immediately, the *Ellwood* settled to the bottom.[56]

Just after 2 P.M., Pittsburgh Steamship's *Mataafa*, towing the barge *Nasmyth*, showed up off the piers at Duluth. Two miles out, Captain R. F. Humble of the *Mataafa* dropped his tow. It was obvious that his ship would never make it through the ship canal towing the barge, so he signaled those aboard the *Nasmyth* to go to anchor off the Duluth entry and ride out the storm.

Duluth is perched on a sprawling hillside that rises up from the harbor and the shoreline of Lake Superior. From everywhere in town, residents have a view of the harbor and the west end of the lake. In the waning light of that stormy November afternoon, thousands noticed the drama that was being played out off the ship canal, and many began to make their way toward the piers.

Ships normally slow way down to pass between the two long piers that lead into the harbor at Duluth, but Captain Humble rang up "full speed ahead" on the engine order telegraph, knowing that he had to get up as much speed as possible if he was going to maintain any maneuverability in the big seas. With black smoke billowing from her stack, the *Mataafa* raced toward the long concrete piers. All twenty-four members of the crew held their breath, including Captain Humble. All he could do at that point was take dead aim at the center of the canal; the rest would depend on the wind and waves.

When the freighter was almost abreast of the piers, a huge wave lifted the stern of the *Mataafa* so high that the bow momentarily dug into the bottom. In the instant that the bow drove into the sandy bottom of the canal, the ship's momentum and the powerful waves combined to swing the stern of the ship off to the port side. A second later, the *Mataafa*'s big bronze propeller bit deeply into the water and the freighter surged ahead. It was no longer aimed straight down the center of the canal, however, but headed straight for the end of the north pier. Before the ship could be straightened up or slowed down, the bow collided hard with the pier, throwing many of those aboard to the deck.

In the same instant that the bow rebounded from the pier and the ship again picked up headway, the waves drove the stern of the *Mataafa* around to starboard until it smashed into the end of the north pier. In the engine room, the steamer's engine suddenly began to race wildly, and those on watch knew instantly that the propeller had been sheared off. The *Mataafa* and those aboard her were then totally at the mercy of the wind and waves.

The crippled ship hung for a second on the end of the pier, then a succession of vicious waves lifted the *Mataafa*, spun her around 180 degrees, and drove her into the rocky shallows north of the canal. She came to rest about six hundred feet off the beach, with her stern about one hundred feet north of the north pier and her bow pointed toward downtown Duluth.

With the *Mataafa* stranded broadside to the waves, the powerful seas began to break over the ship with explosive force. In minutes her two lifeboats and life raft were ripped loose and carried away toward the shore. Next, the gangway on the starboard side of the engine room was stove in and water began flooding into her stern.

The *Mataafa* had been built with what was commonly referred to as a "submarine stern." Unlike most ships, she had no stern deckhouse atop her spar, or main, deck. Instead, the galley and all crew quarters were located down inside the hull, below the main deck. For the twelve crewmembers who were trapped at the stern when the ship was wrecked, the design quickly lived up to its name. Between the flooding through the open gangway and the constant succession of waves breaking across the deck, the stern of the *Mataafa* was more underwater than above it. The crewmembers were driven out onto the open spar deck, where they tried to avoid the waves by hiding behind the smokestack and ventilators. It was a desperate situation.

With waves constantly breaking over the spar deck, anyone trying to go forward was in danger of being carried away by the seas. The deck and cabins forward were sitting high above the stormy surface of the lake, however, and Captain Humble and the eleven crewmen at the bow seemed to be in a safe position, certainly safer than those trapped out on the open stern. Despite the obvious hazards of trying to cross the wave-ravaged deck, the second mate and three other crewmembers trapped at the stern decided to attempt to work their way along the deck. The mate and two of the crewmen moved cautiously across, racing forward between the waves, then ducking behind the hatch coamings and holding on for dear life when a wave would crash over the ship. In that way, the three managed to make it to the shelter of the forward cabin. The fourth crewman, a

43. The 430-foot steel steamer *Mataafa* is shown here stranded and broken in half at Duluth, Minnesota, in the aftermath of a killer storm that swept across Lake Superior on November 28, 1905. Nine crewmembers trapped at the stern of the freighter froze to death before lifesavers were able to get out to the ship. The *Mataafa* was among four steamers that had left Duluth earlier in the day, despite the fact that storm flags had already been raised. Three of the ships— the *Mataafa*, *Ira H. Owen*, and *Isaac L. Ellwood*—were wrecked by the storm. (Author's Collection)

fireman who worked in the engine room, wasn't so lucky. Three times the seas knocked him down and tried to wash him overboard. Each time he managed to grab onto the cable fence that ran along the side of the deck, and when the wave would pass he would drag himself back aboard. After the third wave almost carried him away, the fireman gave up and made his way back to the shelter of the smokestack.

About 4 P.M., the crowds of Duluth residents who had gathered along the shore to watch the ongoing tragedy heard what sounded like the report of a cannon coming from the wrecked ship. The constant battering of the seas had snapped the *Mataafa* in half about midway down her deck, causing the stern to sink even lower in the water. Seconds later, those on the shore saw Captain Humble come out on deck carrying his megaphone. He put the megaphone to his mouth and shouted something, but most of the message was drowned out by the roar of the wind and seas. From the bits and pieces they heard, it was clear to all that the captain was begging for help, begging those on the shore to rescue him and his crew.

Captain Humble and those aboard the *Mataafa* were undoubtedly wondering where the crew from the Duluth lifesaving station was. Normally, you would have expected the lifesavers to be on the scene only minutes after the ship settled in the shallows, but almost two hours after the wreck occurred there was still no sign of them.

What Captain Humble and his crew didn't know was that the lifesaving crew had left their station around 1 P.M. to go to the aid those aboard the *R. W. England*. The lifesavers had gotten a line aboard the beached freighter and helped remove some of the crew. Arriving back at the Duluth by tug shortly after 5 P.M., the cold and tired lifesavers immediately set to work trying to rescue those aboard the *Mataafa*.

The lifesavers quickly concluded that it was futile to attempt to launch their lifeboat in the overpowering waves. Instead, they set up their Lyle gun to fire a line out to the *Mataafa* so they could rig a breeches buoy and take the crew off that way. In the rapidly failing light, they managed to get a total of four lines aboard the battered ship. The first couple fell on the wave-ravaged deck, where it would have been suicidal for any of the crew to attempt to retrieve them. When it was almost dark, the lifesavers finally shot a line directly over the pilothouse, but Captain Humble and his crew were too numb with cold to rig the breeches buoy. The lifesavers remained on the scene until almost midnight, firing other lines onto the *Mataafa*, but by then it had become obvious that the only way to get the crew off was by lifeboat, and that would have to wait until the seas subsided a little.

On the shore, an estimated ten thousand Duluth residents had gathered to watch the drama unfold. There they maintained their vigil throughout the long, cold Minnesota night, huddling for warmth around bonfires that had been built along the beach. Most thought the bonfires would be seen as beacons of hope by those aboard the stricken freighter. It's more likely that they merely reminded the crew of the *Mataafa* how dire their predicament was.

The fifteen men on the forward end of the *Mataafa* were crowded together in Captain Humble's cabin, the only room on the forward end that wasn't completely flooded. There was no heat coming from the steam pipes, but they had lit all the kerosene lamps they could find and that provided an eerie glow of warmth. The powerful waves had broken the glass out of all the portholes on the starboard side of the ship, so some water from each succeeding wave sprayed through the open ports, freezing wherever it hit. All of the men were soaked, and the only way they could keep from freezing stiff was to keep moving, dancing around the captain's room. One crewman later likened it to "an Indian pow-wow."

When the last of the kerosene lamps burned out at about 5 A.M., Captain Humble waded down through the flooded passageways of the forecastle and found some kerosene, rags, and dry matches that he could use in starting a fire. Brandishing a heavy fire ax, he then knocked down the walls of a bathroom and chopped them up into firewood. The windlass room, on the main deck at the very bow of the ship, was fairly dry, and it was there that Captain Humble built a fire in a bathtub. Once the fire was roaring, the captain called for his crew to come down and get warmed around the bonfire.

At 7:30 A.M. the lifesavers were finally able to row their surfboat out through the rolling seas. They got seven of those in the forward end off on their first trip, then returned for the other eight. As soon as the *Mataafa*'s survivors were unloaded on the beach, they were put into waiting carriages and rushed directly to a hotel, where they were warmed and fed. Most hadn't eaten for more than twenty-four hours.

On their third trip out to the *Mataafa*, the lifesavers swung alongside the stern of the ship to pick up the nine men they knew were stranded there. They found only four sailors left on the stern, all dead. The other five men must have been washed overboard and drowned during the night. The stern of the *Mataafa* was shrouded in a cocoon of ice that had gradually built up in the wake of each passing waves, and the four dead sailors were frozen stiff. Three were found lying on the open deck in the lee of the stack. The fourth, a deckhand, had climbed into one of the ventilators for shelter and "with a hand clutching each side, was peering out toward shore, his sightless eyes and contorted countenance presenting a ghastly sight." If it was still light out when the deckhand had climbed into the ventilator, he might well have noticed the tattered storm warning pennants still flying from the flagstaff near the canal.[57]

When the *Mataafa* had been launched in 1899, she was hailed as a completely modern ship. Around the turn of the century, though, the art and science of shipbuilding evolved so rapidly that the term "modern ship" had little meaning. In the decade after the launching of the *Mataafa*, shipbuilders made radical changes in the design and construction of freighters on the lakes. For example, the development of sidetanks greatly improved ballasting and simplified the unloading of cargo, the shift to the use of deck girders eliminated the need for cargo hold stanchions, "walking tunnels" provided a way for crewmembers to move back and forth between the bow and stern areas during inclement weather without going out on deck, and spacing hatches on twelve-foot centers, rather than the traditional twenty-four-foot centers, speeded both loading and unloading.

No innovation was greeted more warmly by the deckhands who toiled aboard the freighters on the lakes, however, than the shift to telescoping hatch covers. As up-to-date as ships like the *Mataafa* were, they still used the same sort of wooden hatch covers that had been in use on ships for centuries. Constructed of thick hardwood timbers, each rectangular hatch cover was about three feet wide and long enough to span the hatch opening, normally six to eight feet. The ends of the hatch covers rested on the hatch coaming, and they were held in place by their weight.

It took about a dozen hatch covers to close each hatch on a ship like the *Mataafa*. At each dock, the heavy wooden hatch covers had to be manually taken off and stacked along the side of the deck or between the hatches, only to be put back on after they were done loading or unloading. It was mindless, time-consuming, and backbreaking work, the scourge of generations of deckhands.

The new telescoping hatch covers were made of overlapping leaves of steel that could be pulled back to the outboard ends of the hatch opening by using the steam deck winches. As the winches took up slack on cables attached to pad eyes at the center of each hatch cover, the leaves would slide over the top of each other until they were all stacked in a neat pile at the outboard edge of the hatch. The steel hatch covers were stronger than the old wooden ones, and the power of steam had replaced the sweat-labor of deckhands in opening and closing hatches.

Cyprus, 1907

Telescoping hatch covers made their debut in 1904, and by the time the steamer *Cyprus* was launched at Lorain, Ohio, on August 17, 1907, they were standard equipment on almost all of the steel freighters being turned out by Great Lakes shipyards. The 420-foot *Cyprus* was built for Lackawanna Transportation Company, a subsidiary of Lackawanna Steel, but its operations were managed by Pickands Mather & Company, one of the largest fleet operators on the lakes and forerunner of today's Interlake Steamship Company. When fitting out was completed in mid-September, the new freighter went into service on the ore run between Lake Superior and the steel mills and railheads on Lake Erie.

On her second trip on the lakes, the *Cyprus* loaded a little more than 7,000 tons of iron ore at Superior, Wisconsin. She departed the ore docks at about 8 A.M. on October 10, 1907, and headed across Lake Superior, on her way south to Fairport, Ohio, on Lake Erie.

The following day, when she was crossing the broad expanse of open water between the tip of the Keweenaw Peninsula and Whitefish Bay, the *Cyprus* ran headlong into a storm that blew in from the north. The storm

44. The steamer *Lafayette* (*left*) and her barge consort, the *Manila*, were caught out on Lake Superior and driven ashore by the same storm that wrecked the *Mataafa* on November 27, 1905. The 454-foot freighter and her 436-foot tow barge are shown here on the beach near Two Harbors, Minnesota. The vessels were pushed so far up on the rocky shore that some crewmembers escaped the ships by climbing down trees that were next to the hulls. (Ralph Roberts Collection)

was described as being of only "moderate" strength, but it was enough for the new freighter to regularly take some of the bigger seas over her decks.

At about 7 P.M. the *Cyprus* suddenly and unexpectedly took on a severe list to port. Heeled over as she was, waves began to roll constantly over the port side of her deck and it was obvious to all aboard that the cargo hold was flooding. Captain F. B. Huyck ordered his crew to put their lifejackets on "just in case," but they were only about thirty-five miles west of Whitefish Point and he was convinced that they would easily make it into the sheltered waters of Whitefish Bay. The pumps in the engine room had been turned on and were pumping water out of the cargo hold, and besides, the weather just wasn't that bad. By 7:30 P.M., however, the ship's port rail was completely underwater, and Captain Huyck ordered his men to swing out the lifeboat on the port side of the freighter's stern, but not to launch it. The *Cyprus* actually carried two lifeboats on top of the stern cabin, but because of the list it would have been impossible to launch the boat on the starboard side.

45. Two crewmen aboard an unidentified freighter loaded with coal are shown removing one of the ship's wooden hatch covers. The clamps that can be seen around the low hatch coamings are designed to secure battens that hold tarps in place when inclement weather is expected. The hatch covers themselves are held in place only by their weight. Many ships were lost over the years when seas rolling over their decks carried their wooden hatch covers away. (Author's Collection)

All the crewmen on the forward end of the *Cyprus* made their way aft across the steeply pitched deck, except for Captain Huyck, two mates, a watchman, and a wheelsman. Captain Huyck remained in the pilothouse, still intent on getting his brand-spanking-new ship into Whitefish Bay. The others stood by the rigid life raft that was located near the freighter's bow.

At about 7:45, the *Cyprus*'s list suddenly increased and it appeared that the ship was going to "turn turtle," or roll over. The four men on the bow cut the lashings holding the life raft in place, but before they could launch it, the ship sideslipped below the surface of the lake and they were submerged in the bitterly cold water.

When the four sailors popped back up, the life raft was floating nearby and they hurriedly boarded it. By then the *Cyprus* had plummeted to the bottom. The four men could hear some shouting from the direction where the stern of the freighter had been, but in the pitch blackness they couldn't tell whether the crewmen there had been able to launch the lifeboat before the ship went down.

Through the long night, the life raft was carried by wind and seas toward the south shore of the lake. Just before 2 A.M., the men on the raft could hear the roar of the surf as it rolled onto the shore of Michigan's Upper Peninsula. Minutes later, the raft began to be tossed about in the powerful surf and it flipped over, dumping the four into the ragged seas. All four climbed back aboard. The little raft was tipped over four more times. Three times all four of the men were able to climb back aboard; the fourth time, when Second Mate Charlie Pitz struggled back to the surface, he was alone on the lake. Exhausted from his long ordeal, Pitz didn't have the energy left to climb back onto the battered raft. Instead, he merely hung onto the rope that was strung around the outside of the raft and let it tow him toward the shore. Minutes later, able to feel bottom with his feet, Pitz let go of the raft and half-crawled, half-surfed onto the sandy beach, where he collapsed in a wet heap.

In those days, the lifesavers from the U.S. Life-Saving Service stations along the shores of the Great Lakes used to patrol the beaches after dark, keeping an eye out for ships in trouble. Often, the first indication they had that a ship was in distress was when they found the body of a sailor washed up on the beach. That was the case on the morning of October 12, 1907, when a lifesaver from the Deer Park Life-Saving Station came across the crumpled heap that was Charlie Pitz.

Pitz was carried back to the Deer Park station, where he was revived enough to give the lifesavers a few details on the foundering of the *Cyprus*. Over the next few days the lifesavers recovered the bodies of twenty of the twenty-two crewmembers who had died with their ship, including that of Captain Huyck. All twenty were wearing lifejackets, but had died from "exposure," what we would today call hypothermia.

From Charlie Pitz it was learned that the weather had been nice when the *Cyprus* left the lakehead and Captain Huyck had decided that there was no need to put canvas tarpaulins over the hatches. That decision probably put a smile on the face of each and every deckhand on the freighter. Stretching the heavy tarps over the hatch covers and fastening them down with wooden battens was a tough job, and it was just as tough to take them off at the other end of the lakes, especially if there was a little wind blowing.

Without tarps on the hatches, however, there was nothing to stop water from pouring into the gaps between the leaves of the telescoping hatches once the ship began taking seas over its deck. The incoming water mixed with the red ore in the hold of the *Cyprus,* and the waterlogged mass eventually slid to the port side as the ship rolled in the seas, resulting in the port list. As more water poured in, the *Cyprus* progressively flooded, sinking deeper and deeper in the water until she totally lost buoyancy and dove sideways toward the bottom.

That scenario seemed to be confirmed several days later when Captain H. G. Harbottle of Pittsburgh Steamship's *George Stephenson* reported that his ship had passed the *Cyprus* only a few hours before it sank. The ship seemed to be handling the sea just fine at the time, but Harbottle did notice that it was leaving a trail of red in its wake. The telltale mix of water and ore dust being pumped out of the *Cyprus* was clear evidence to Harbottle that the ship was taking water into her hold.

It's questionable whether the pumping system on the *Cyprus*, or any other straight-decker for that matter, could keep up with anything more than a minor amount of water leaking into the cargo hold. While the hold of a modern freighter is hundreds of feet long, water can only be pumped out at its very aft end. If the ship is loaded, any water that gets into the hold has to migrate through the cargo all the way to the aft bulkhead before it can be pumped out.

Recessed into the bottom of the bulkhead at the aft end of the hold are two "rose boxes" from which the pumps draw water. Each rose box is about three feet wide and four feet high, and they're faced with a steel plate that has holes cut in it to let water pass through. The holes are small enough to keep ore, coal, or stone from passing through and clogging the pumps. At the same time, when the hold is full the rose box screens are covered by cargo that partially blocks the holes and impedes the flow of water.

Although the *Cyprus* was able to pump out some of the water entering her hold, the water wouldn't have been able to flow freely to the pumps. If a deluge of water was entering the cargo hold, possibly only a trickle was being pumped out.

The beautiful $250,000 *Cyprus*, in service for only twenty-one days, had been claimed by Lake Superior. Gone to the bottom with her was the stack of never-used tarps that were neatly stowed in the dunnage room at the bow. Gone, too, were the deckhands who had been so glad to hear that Captain Huyck had decided that they didn't have to put the heavy, unwieldy tarps on before the *Cyprus* left the ore dock.[58]

It was ice rather than storms that plagued sailors during the spring of 1913. On April 19 the 291-foot wooden freighter *Uganda* became trapped in thick ice floes near White Shoals, west of the Straits of Mackinac. The ice cut through the hull, below the ship's waterline, and water began to leak into the cargo hold, which was loaded with corn. When crewmembers realized what had happened, the captain ordered them to fly the ensign upside down as a distress signal. The steamer *John A. Donaldson* was

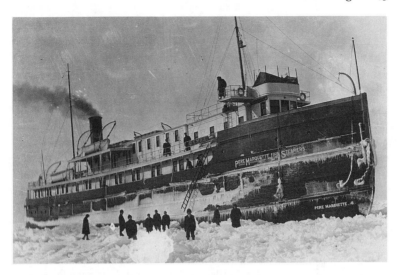

46. The cross-lake steamer *Pere Marquette 4* is shown here trapped in heavy ice in Sleeping Bear Bay on northern Lake Michigan around 1915. The ship's captain, wearing a heavy fur coat, can be seen standing on the wing adjacent to the flying bridge. While many ships have been crushed or holed by ice on the Great Lakes over the years, the *Pere Marquette 4* managed to break free. She was finally wrecked beyond repair in a collision with the *Pere Marquette 17* on May 15, 1923. (Ralph Roberts Collection)

nearby and took off the crew just before the hull of the *Uganda* plunged to the bottom. Later that same week, the 328-foot steel package freighter *Kearsarge* put into Mackinaw City after crushing her bow in the ice of the Straits of Mackinac. Further to the north, the ice was so bad on Lake Superior that the shipping season didn't get under way there until the third week of May.[59]

The problems caused by ice during the spring sailing season were nothing new in 1913. Detroit historian Silas Farmer had previously attributed much of the problem to overeager vessel owners. "Sometimes high prices for transportation tempted the owners of boats to start them on their trips earlier than prudence justified," wrote Farmer . . . about ice damage incurred, not during the 1913 season, but in the spring of 1851![60] Sixty-two years later, ships and their crews were still being put at risk by owners too eager to get the shipping season under way. While many ships encountered difficulties with ice conditions in the spring of 1913, the damage incurred seemed miniscule when compared to the toll exacted by storms that fall.

Charles S. Price, 1913

The 524-foot freighter *Charles S. Price* departed Ashtabula, Ohio, on Saturday morning, November 8, 1913, with her cavernous cargo holds filled with 9,000 tons of coal bound for Milwaukee, Wisconsin. Although storm flags were flying when Captain Bill Black nosed his ship through the breakwater at Ashtabula and headed her across Lake Erie, the weather was unusually mild at the time. We can surmise that Captain Black may well have made some derogatory comments about the U.S. Weather Bureau to the mate and wheelsman who were in the *Price*'s pilothouse with him that morning. Sailors placed little credence in the forecasts of the Weather Bureau in those days, and the agency was a common target of ridicule by many captains.

Around 6 A.M. Sunday morning, the *Price* steamed slowly up the St. Clair River, past the sleeping community of Port Huron, Michigan, and out onto Lake Huron. Captain Black again noticed that storm flags were flying at the Fort Gratiot lighthouse that sits just a few hundred feet north of where the river meets the waters of Lake Huron. The weather was still quite mild for November, although the wind had started to blow out of the northwest and the barometer was falling. It still didn't look like it was going to be much of a storm—enough to keep the little boats off the lake perhaps, but the *Price* was a big, new freighter. Besides, Captain Black was intending to set a course up the west shore of the lake where, with the wind blowing out of the northwest, his ship would be in the lee of the land.

What Captain Black didn't know was that the predicted storm had already moved onto Lake Superior and Lake Michigan. At 2:00 that Sunday morning, while the *Price* was still south of Port Huron, the storm had claimed its first victim. With its engine running full ahead, the steamer *Louisiana* had been blown backwards onto the shore of Washington Island in Green Bay. A fire started when she went aground, and in minutes it had burned the old wood-hulled ship to the waterline.

Just before noon on Sunday, the *Price* was spotted north of Harbor Beach on Michigan's thumb by Captain A. C. May of the downbound steamer *H. B. Hawgood*. By then, the long-overdue storm had clearly announced its presence on Lake Huron, and it was turning out to be a dandy. After 6 A.M. the winds steadily increased, and by 10 A.M. they were blowing a steady thirty-six miles an hour, with some gusts as high as forty-two miles an hour. The size of the waves had kept pace with the wind.[61]

Just after noon, Captain Dan McKay, downbound on one of the Detroit & Cleveland passenger steamers, also saw the *Price*. It appeared to him that the big freighter was turning around to head back toward Port Huron.

The next time the *Price* was seen was at about 8:30 A.M. on Monday, November 10. The *J. H. Sheadle*, battling its way down the lake in the teeth of seventy-mile-an-hour winds, heavy snow, and waves that were estimated to be as high as forty feet, passed what turned out to be the overturned hull of the *Price* in the middle of the steamer channel, about eight miles north of the St. Clair River. At the time, however, Captain S. A. Lyons and the crewmen aboard the *Sheadle* didn't know that the hull was that of the *Price*. Nobody would know that for more than five more days.

From the time the overturned hull was discovered on Monday until it was belatedly identified the following Saturday by a diver hired by the Lake Carriers' Association, it could have been any of a number of ships that had disappeared in what soon came to be known as "the Great Storm of 1913." On Tuesday the bodies of three crewmen from the steamer *Wexford* washed up on the Canadian shore southeast of the floating hulk, and it was immediately assumed that the unidentified ship was the little Canadian steamer. Later that same day, however, ten other bodies were found on the Canadian shore. Based on markings on the life preservers they wore, it appeared that seven of the men were from the *Charles S. Price*, while three were from the missing Canadian steamer *Regina*. The confusion over the identity of the overturned ship deepened on Wednesday when a life raft with the bodies of three crewmen from the steamer *John A. McGean* came ashore near Goderich, Ontario. Then, later on Wednesday, wreckage from the *James Carruthers* and *Argus* washed ashore. In addition, the owners of the *Turret Chief* announced that their ship was missing and they feared the overturned hull might be it.[62] The *Chief* was a sturdy little Canadian steamer that had actually been built for service on the North Atlantic. Owners of the *Isaac M. Scott*, *Hydrus*, and *Leafield* also reported their ships missing.[63]

Wexford, Price, Regina, McGean, Carruthers, Argus, Turret Chief, Scott, Hydrus, Leafield—which was it? The puzzle was driving shipping officials and the families of missing sailors virtually mad.[64] The mystery was solved when diver Charles Baker identified the overturned hull as the *Charles S. Price* on the morning of Saturday, November 15. Two days later the wreck of the *Price* finally sank.

When U.S. and Canadian shipping officials tallied their losses in the days following the 1913 storm, they found that nineteen ships had

47. The overturned hull of the 524-foot freighter *Charles S. Price* is shown floating upside down on lower Lake Huron in the aftermath of storms that pounded the lakes in early November 1913. The *Price* was one of nineteen ships destroyed during the storm, and her 28 crewmembers were among a total of 248 who died on the lakes during the three-day blow. While many within the Great Lakes shipping community blamed the losses on inadequate weather warnings from the U.S. Weather Bureau, there is irrefutable evidence that storm warnings had been posted before many of the ships, including the *Price*, went out onto the lakes. (Ralph Roberts Collection)

been totally destroyed. In addition to the *Price*, the list included the *Wexford, Regina, McGean, Carruthers, Argus, Turret Chief, Scott, Hydrus,* and *Leafield.* More than twenty other ships had been driven ashore and wrecked, while thirty others sustained serious damage from the wind and seas. The vessels and cargoes lost or damaged amounted to more than $10 million—in 1913 dollars! The toll of human life was even worse. Altogether, 248 U.S. and Canadian sailors lost their lives in the storm.[65]

Many sailors were quick to blame the Weather Bureau for the devastation that had occurred on the lakes. One of the most vocal accusers was Captain Frank Pratt of the steamer *James S. Dunham.* "The United States Weather Bureau itself is responsible for the great loss of life and property in this storm," said Pratt. "The storm signals were not only inadequate, but non-existent. No warning was given us along the lakes and we didn't know there would be a storm."[66] While many sailors echoed Captain Pratt's sentiments, and many would go to their graves still damning the Weather Bureau, there is an irrefutable record that storm warnings had been posted for all of the Great Lakes from 10 A.M. on Friday, November

48. This photo by surfman Tony Glaza of the Eagle Harbor Life-Saving Station shows the Canadian freighter *Turret Chief* aground on the Keweenaw Peninsula on Lake Superior in May 1914. During the storm of November 1913, the 253-foot ship was blown more than fifty miles off course and driven ashore by the furious seas. The *Turret Chief* had been built in England in 1896 in the standard three-island design used for most ocean ships. Its engine room and pilothouse were both located amidships. Salvaged and rebuilt in 1914, it returned to service as the *Jolly Inez*. (A. F. Glaza Photo, Ralph Roberts Collection)

7, until the winds finally blew themselves out. Storm flags had been displayed at 113 locations around the lakes.[67] Pratt and those who shared a similar view were simply wrong.

The forecasts produced by the Weather Bureau from November 7 on were far from perfect, however. They didn't, for example, clearly predict the hurricane-strength winds that were associated with the storm. In 1913 a "storm" technically existed whenever wind speeds exceeded thirty-three miles an hour. When wind speeds of thirty-four miles an hour or more were expected, the meteorologists of the Weather Bureau would issue a storm warning that was immediately telegraphed to ports all around the Great Lakes. At the various ports, signal flags indicating a storm warning would then be hoisted—two square red flags with black squares at their center. Detailed written copies of the Weather Bureau's forecasts were also made available at most ports, and they were also given out to passing ships at the marine post office at the Soo Locks and the mail boat at Detroit. Detailed weather maps were even available at some ports.

If winds were expected to exceed sixty miles an hour, the meteorologists would normally refer to the storm as a "hurricane" in their written forecasts. In the forecasts issued before and during the 1913 storm, however, Weather Bureau officials never used the term "hurricane." Instead, they merely predicted "high winds," terminology that was used whenever winds of thirty-four miles an hour or more were expected.

The storm flags flown at ports around the lakes were similarly ambiguous. On the Great Lakes, there was no special flag that could be flown to denote an anticipated hurricane-force storm. Consequently, when sailors saw the storm flags flying, all they knew was that winds of at least thirty-four miles an hour were expected. That ambiguity was compounded by the slow approach of the storm system.

The storm warnings for the Great Lakes were posted on Friday morning, November 7, when the storm was still centered over Minnesota. It wasn't until late Sunday morning, two days later, that the worst of the storm hit the lakes. Until Sunday, the winds were moderate, certainly not strong enough to interfere with most shipping traffic on the lakes. Many captains were undoubtedly lulled into thinking that the Weather Bureau's forecast was either wrong or that the storm was going to be of moderate strength, accompanied by winds just marginally over the thirty-three-mile-an-hour parameter. For two days, most of them sailed right along without any problems, probably bad-mouthing the Weather Bureau the whole time.

Regardless of whether the meteorologists were accurate or not, *many captains would still have sailed past the storm flags and out onto the lakes.* "In twenty years of conversing with men who have been sailing first-class steel ships, similar to those which were lost, no master ever paid any attention to the weather reports," said A. A. Wright, manager of the Canadian shipping company that owned the *Carruthers.* "If they had, they would never have got anywhere, and they have always guided their actions by the weather they were experiencing and what they could judge they were likely to encounter."[68] The captains and their shipping companies felt the Weather Bureau was guilty of the meteorological equivalent of "crying wolf." The bureau was too eager to post storm warnings, so the warnings weren't taken seriously by the captains.

In response to Wright's charge that ships on the lakes "would never have got anywhere" if they went to anchor whenever storm warnings were posted, the director of the Canadian weather service's response was terse: "Nonsense," he said. Storm warnings had only been posted twice that year on Lake Huron, and only five times on Lake Superior. The previous season, storm warnings were issued only six times on Lake Huron and four times on Lake Superior. The storm warnings were clearly not being overused by personnel of the weather services.[69]

One thing that Wright didn't mention was that there have always been "heavy-weather sailors" who seem to delight in taking their ships—and crews—out into storms, and there have always been over-anxious captains who will try to outrun a storm. Captain Story of the steamer *Maricopa* later admitted, for example, that the storm signals were flying when he took his ship out of Duluth harbor and headed east across Superior in the storm. "The wind was howling when I left Duluth," said Story, "but I thought I could run to the Soo and be that much ahead of the game." It was a long and harrowing trip for the crew of the *Maricopa*. "The tension was awful," Story later recalled. "Nothing can touch the bitterness of that trip." The entire ship was encased in a solid coat of ice when the steamer finally battled its way through to the Soo.[70]

While so many of the captains who were caught out on the lakes with their ships pointed their fingers accusingly at the Weather Bureau, it has to be noted that most of the ships on the lakes rode out the storm at anchor. By Sunday night, when the storm had reached hurricane proportions, there were forty ships at anchor in the St. Clair and Detroit Rivers, fifty ships anchored in Thunder Bay at Alpena, Michigan, and another fifty on the hook between the Soo and Whitefish Point.[71] Despite the ambiguities of the weather forecasts, most ships on the lakes took refuge during the early hours of the storm and their crews rode it out in relative comfort and safety. Sitting at anchor is always boring for sailors, but it's far preferable to getting caught out in a killer storm.

Some captains who took their ships out into the storm can be at least partially exonerated. With the winds predicted to stay northwest to west, they were comfortably beachcombing along a sheltered lee shore when the winds suddenly shifted to the northeast. That left them in a dangerously exposed position and forced them to battle the full force of the wind and seas. The weather forecasts hadn't predicted that wind shift, which occurred during the late-morning hours of Sunday, November 9.

The Weather Bureau didn't predict that critical wind shift simply because they didn't anticipate it. In a low-pressure storm system, the winds circulate around the center of the low in a counterclockwise pattern. As the low moves through on a course that is almost always in a generally west-to-east direction, winds would be expected to go from northeast to northwest, or southeast to southwest—depending on whether the center of the storm was north or south of your position—but *never* from northwest to northeast.

The 1913 storm didn't violate any laws of physics when its winds shifted from the northwest to the northeast, nor did it make an unexpected departure from the normal west-to-east storm track and drop straight

49. The wrecking tugs *Manistique* (*left*) and *S. M. Fischer* are shown raising the wrecked hull of *Lightship 82*. The lightship was blown off its station at Buffalo, New York, and sunk during the November storm of 1913. Its captain and five crewmembers went down with their ship. Reid Wrecking Company salvaged the eighty-foot lightship, and it eventually returned to government service as a tender. (Ralph Roberts Collection)

south down Lake Huron, as some captains later claimed it had. From Sunday morning on, the lakes were actually feeling the effects of a *second* low-pressure system that had slipped into the region, not from the west, but from the south. The second storm had formed on Saturday in northern Georgia, then began tracking up the Atlantic Coast. Influenced by an unusual dip in the jet stream, the storm slipped inland from the coast and made a beeline for the lakes, intensifying as it moved to the north and west. The fast-moving second storm system was centered near Buffalo on Sunday evening, causing the aberrant northeast winds that resulted in such destruction on Lake Huron.[72]

Many of the twenty-four ships that sank or were seriously damaged on Lake Huron during the storm were sneaking along the west shore of the lake on Sunday when the approach of the second storm caused winds to veer unexpectedly to the northeast and leave them in dangerously exposed positions. Generally speaking, crews don't like it when a captain decides to run along a lee shore in a storm. They get nervous, and the mood on the ship hangs heavy with tension. Most crewmembers would prefer to go to anchor until the storm is safely over. "To hell with those guys from the office," they say, "they're sitting safe and snug in Cleveland . . . or Duluth . . . or Buffalo . . . or . . ."

Captains often have a tendency to dismiss crewmembers offhandedly at such times. After all, few of them know anything about weather. "We'll just sneak along the shore," says the captain, usually with a smile on his face. "But what if the wind changes?" ask the anxious crewmembers. When the wind unexpectedly went to the northeast on Sunday, November 9, 1913, that question was vividly and tragically answered for many of the 248 sailors who died in the Great Storm of 1913 . . . and for hundreds more whose ships somehow struggled through, but who were forevermore scarred by the horrible experience.

While shipping executives like A. A. Wright were placing blame for the devastation of the 1913 storm at the feet of the weather services, the shipping companies were also coming in for their share of criticism. In the flood of newspaper coverage after the storm, some people claimed that the shipowners, who were often making 20–30 percent annual profits, had been "sending out unseaworthy ships and forcing their captains to ignore weather conditions."[73]

Many suggestions were offered in the hope that similar shipping disasters could be avoided in the future. Some wanted to force captains to remain in port whenever storm warnings were posted. One person even advocated leaving the decision of whether or not to sail in bad weather up to the deckhands on a ship. Wright said that "would be like putting the office boy in charge of a business ashore."[74]

Others argued for the adoption of load-line standards similar to those that had been in force for British ships for many years. To preclude ships' being sent out in an overloaded condition, each British vessel had a "Plimsoll mark" painted on both sides of its hull. The mark clearly indicated the maximum depth to which the ship could be loaded. Legislation had been introduced in Congress in the 1880s to require ships on the Great Lakes to have load lines, but the proposal had been defeated by the Lake Carriers' Association.[75]

A highly experienced naval architect, W. E. Redway of Toronto, called for ships on the lakes to be built stronger. According to Redway, their construction was too light, they had too many hatches, and their holds weren't separated by watertight bulkheads. "There are 2 screens in the main hold of the lake boat, but not watertight," he explained. "The hold is about 390 feet long, so that in case of collision and serious damage to any part of this space, the pumps cannot keep the vessel free and she must inevitably sink." Ships on the lakes were said to be only about half as strong as those built for ocean service.[76]

Captain James Watt, who had taken the *J. F. Durston* up Lake Huron during the storm, felt that many of the ships had been lost because their hatch covers came loose and their cargo holds flooded. While telescoping steel hatch covers had come out in 1904, eleven of the nineteen ships lost in the storm had been equipped with wooden hatch covers. "There is too much dependence put on the weight of the hatches, which is expected to hold them down on the coaming," Watts said. "Frequently they lift up from the coaming anyway." Even when the hatches were covered with canvas tarps, the tarps were easily torn off if the ship took waves over its deck. Without tarps, the wooden hatch covers would often simply float away if waves rolled over the deck.[77]

After the *Mataafa* storm in November 1905, a steamboat inspector at Duluth had recommended to General George Uhler, supervising general of the Steamboat Inspection Service, that ships with wooden hatch covers be required to install clamps to hold the covers in place, similar to those used on ships with steel, telescoping covers. Uhler apparently showed no interest in the inspector's suggestion. Following the 1913 storm, the inspector again approached his superiors to advocate hatch clamps for ships with wooden hatch covers. On that occasion, he was reportedly ordered to "drop it." For some reason, the top brass of the Steamboat Inspection Service had no interest in forcing the owners of ships with wooden hatch covers to make them more stormproof.[78]

The heated debates made front-page news around the lakes for many months after the 1913 storm. In the final analysis, however, no significant changes were made to the ships that sailed the lakes or to the way they operated. There was continued pressure on the U.S. and Canadian weather services to improve their marine forecasts, and they eventually made several changes.

In July 1914 the Weather Bureau began broadcasting weather forecasts over U.S. Naval Radio Service stations around the lakes at 10 P.M. each day. Any storm warnings in effect were also included in the service's daily noon broadcast.[79] Unfortunately, only passenger ships were required to be equipped with radios at that time, and few owners of freighters voluntarily installed radios. In fact, most managers of freight lines on the lakes were vehemently opposed to having radios on their ships. In 1910, the Lake Carriers' Association (LCA) had argued effectively before Congress to have their ships excluded from the Wireless-Ship Act that made radios mandatory on passenger vessels. When the Wireless-Ship

Act was amended in 1912 to also require radios on cargo ships, the LCA and representatives of several major fleets on the lakes were again successful in having their ships exempted from the federal law.[80]

Also in 1914, the Steamboat Inspection Service recommended to Congress that they be allowed to develop a "corps of experts" to approve vessel plans prior to commencement of construction. That would allow them to head off design problems that would affect the seaworthiness of ships being built around the lakes. Despite the fact that officials of the Steamboat Inspection Service could provide many examples of vessel casualties that were the result of design errors, Congress rejected the proposal.[81]

The year 1914 was a dismal one for the shipping industry. There wasn't much cargo to haul, and it looked as though many ships would spend the season laid up. The cargo that was available was moving at such low rates that even many of the ships that were operating weren't making any profits for their owners. Hundreds of sailors, including a great many experienced captains, were out of work, and prospects for the future didn't look good.

While the term wouldn't become popular for many generations, in 1914 the Great Lakes shipping industry was in the midst of a massive "downsizing." That year there were only 438 ships enrolled with the LCA, compared to 597 in 1909, a reduction of more than 25 percent in only five years.[82]

At the same time, many schooners and wood-hulled steamers whose owners didn't belong to LCA were also falling by the wayside, victims of either age or wont of cargoes. There aren't good figures available to trace the gradual demise of wooden steamers, but we do know that the number of sailing ships on the lakes—almost all of which were built of wood—plummeted from more than 1,600 in 1878 to only 960 in 1898.[83] In 1919 there were just 211 wooden steamers and sailing ships left on the lakes.[84] By 1930, they were all gone. For every wooden schooner or steamer that sat rotting in the shallows along the shores of the lakes, there was a captain out looking for a new command.

Eastland, 1915

The worst maritime casualty in the history of the Great Lakes occurred at Chicago on Saturday, July 24, 1915, when the heavily loaded passenger steamer *Eastland* rolled over at its dock. Best estimates place the resulting death toll at 836, qualifying the *Eastland* for the dubious distinction of being the worst maritime disaster in the annals of Great Lakes shipping and the third worst in U.S. maritime history.[85]

The *Eastland* was launched on May 6, 1903, at the Jenks Shipbuilding Company along the Black River in Port Huron, Michigan, the same yard that had built the freighter *Henry Steinbrenner* two years earlier. The Jenks shipyard wasn't known for building passengers steamers. In fact, the *Eastland* was the first one built at Port Huron in over twenty years, and its launching was viewed as a major cause for celebration by local residents. Schoolchildren were given part of the day off to watch the big steamer slide down the ways, an event that drew a boisterous crowd estimated at six thousand.[86] Articles in the local newspapers described the *Eastland* in graphic detail, praising its stylish dining rooms, its staterooms, and even its ballasting system.[87]

In designing the *Eastland,* Sidney Jenks had been most concerned about making it as fast a ship as possible. The preeminence of that concern had been dictated by the rather unusual contract his firm had entered into with the Michigan Transportation Company for construction of the steamer. The owners wanted the ship to be capable of making two round-trips a day between Chicago and South Haven, Michigan, a resort community and center for the region's fruit-growing industry. To do that, the vessel would have to be able to cruise along at a speed of at least twenty miles an hour for the eighty-mile run across lower Lake Michigan. To make sure the new ship would meet their needs, officials of the Michigan Steamship Company entered into an "incentive contract" with Jenks.

The contract set the purchase price for the passenger steamer at $250,000. If the ship could not run at a speed of at least nineteen miles an hour, however, Michigan Steamship would not have to accept it. In addition, if the ship couldn't cruise at the desired twenty miles an hour, $2,500 would be deducted from the purchase price for each quarter-mile-per-hour shortfall. On the other hand, if the ship ran faster than twenty miles an hour, the shipping company would pay a bonus of $2,500 to the shipyard for each additional quarter of a mile per hour it achieved.

Since failure to produce a ship that could reach a speed of at least nineteen miles an hour could have had disastrous financial consequences for his firm, Jenks did everything he could to design a fast boat. The steel-hulled ship was to be 275 feet long, but only a couple of inches over 38 feet wide. Jenks knew that by cutting a couple feet off what would have been the normal beam for a ship of that length, he could increase the vessel's speed. Pumped out, the hull would only draw about ten feet of water. That, too, would help her to race along, and a shallow draft was also necessary if the boat was going to clear the sandbar off the entrance to the riverfront docks at South Haven.

To drive the sleek hull through the water, Jenks decided to install two engines and two propellers. Each of the triple-expansion steam engines would produce a thundering 3,500 horsepower. That would make the ship get-up-and-go! Just for comparison, the freighter *Samuel F. B. Morse,* one of the largest and most powerful ships on the lakes at that time, had a single steam engine that was rated at only 2,700 horsepower—and the *Morse* was two hundred feet longer than the *Eastland*!

Despite her powerful engines, when Michigan Steamship put the sleek new steamer into service on the run from Chicago to South Haven, it could not reach the desired twenty miles an hour. In September 1903, her owners and Jenks agreed that the best the ship could do was nineteen miles an hour, and her purchase price was reduced by $10,000.[88]

Michigan Steamship officials decided to reinvest the $10,000 in the ship. During the winter of 1903–4, the *Eastland* was returned to the shipyard at Port Huron for installation of air-conditioning and induced draft machinery. Experience during the summer of 1903 had shown that even with the cool lake breezes, the *Eastland*'s parlors and dining rooms often tended to be uncomfortably warm and humid. The new cooling tower air-conditioning system installed in the cabin area recirculated air from the ship's common rooms through a cascade of cool water. The air-conditioning would definitely make passengers more comfortable during the crossing between Chicago and South Haven.

The induced draft system consisted of two heat exchangers that pre-heated air being fed to the ship's four Scotch boilers. By preheating the air going to the boilers, the output of steam could be increased, and that was expected to increase the ship's speed. The project proved to be a success, as the *Eastland* was noticeably faster during the 1904 season, achieving a top speed of just over twenty-two miles an hour.

Some other machinery in the engine room was also repositioned by workers at Jenks Shipbuilding during the winter of 1903–4 in an effort to reduce the ship's already shallow draft. Even though the *Eastland* drew only ten to sixteen feet of water, it had still experienced some problems in clearing the sandbar off the entrance to South Haven.

When the *Eastland* went into operation in the spring of 1904, it became immediately obvious that the installation of the heavy new air-conditioning and induced draft equipment, along with the repositioning of other machinery, had significantly affected the ship's stability. From then on, sailors would say that the steamer was "cranky" or "tender," while naval architects would describe her as having a low "metacentric height," resulting in poor "transverse stability." Simply put, the *Eastland* was top-heavy.

A ship in the water is somewhat analogous to a teeter-totter that is balanced vertically instead of horizontally. Think of the balance point of the teeter-totter as being equivalent to a vessel's waterline. As long as the weight at the bottom of the teeter-totter is greater than the weight at the top, the teeter-totter will be stable and remain in its upright position. On the other hand, if the weight at the bottom is shifted upward, or if the weight above the balance point is greater than the weight below it, the teeter-totter will tend to become unstable and flip completely around.

Ships are built so that their heavy machinery and cargo are largely carried below the waterline, or balance point, so that they are very stable and remain upright in the water. When the *Eastland* was built, its center of gravity was probably about eighteen inches below the waterline, fairly standard for ships of that era, although there's no evidence that tests were ever conducted to determine that precisely. When the machinery was added or moved during the winter of 1903–4, however, it raised the ship's center of gravity dangerously close to its balance point, perhaps only four inches below the waterline when the ship was loaded.[89]

The *Eastland* experienced its first major stability problem on July 17, 1904, on a run from South Haven to Chicago. Providing transportation for an outing of postal workers, the ship left South Haven with 2,142 adults and an unspecified number of children aboard. It was a beautiful summer day, and a lot of the passengers, perhaps as many as 1,200, went up to the *Eastland*'s top deck, the open-air hurricane deck, to take maximum advantage of the weather.

Just over a mile out into Lake Michigan, the *Eastland* listed twelve to fifteen degrees to port. When the chief engineer noticed the list, he instructed his men to pump ballast water into the ballast tanks on the starboard side of the ship to counter the list. The *Eastland* then righted itself, but almost immediately took on a starboard list of twenty to twenty-five degrees. When that happened, the captain slowed the ship down and asked passengers to leave the hurricane deck and go below to the main deck. Most of the passengers ignored the repeated requests to go below until aggravated crewmembers finally turned a fire hose on them.[90] By the time some of the crowd finally began to move down the stairwells, water was already pouring through two of the gangway doors on the starboard side of the boat, flooding the main deck to a depth of eighteen inches in some places. Leaving the bridge, the captain raced down to the engine room and ordered the chief to pump water into the ballast tanks on the port side. After about twenty-five minutes, the *Eastland* finally righted itself and they continued on to Chicago. By that time, however, most of the passengers were terrified that the ship was going to roll over, and many had put lifejackets on. When passengers spread the word about the frightening experience they'd had aboard the *Eastland,* it's said that the ship developed a "sinister reputation."[91]

After learning of the listing problem, the *Eastland*'s owners began to restrict the number of people that could be on the hurricane deck to a maximum of five hundred. The following year, passengers were banned altogether from the open deck. Additionally, it became company policy to always keep the number 3 port and starboard ballast tanks filled with water, adding about 165 tons of weight at the very lowest part of the ship.[92] The ballast water lowered the ship's center of gravity, making it more stable.

A second serious stability problem occurred on August 5, 1906, when the *Eastland* was again on a return voyage from South Haven with 2,530 passengers aboard. As the ship turned into the Chicago River, many of the passengers went to the starboard rails to watch the sights along the riverbank, causing a serious list to starboard. The *Eastland* managed to limp to its dock.[93]

Because of the heavy competition on the run from Chicago to South Haven, the *Eastland* had never been a moneymaker for her owners, and after the 1906 season they sold the ship to investors looking for a vessel to haul passengers between Cleveland and the amusement park at nearby Cedar Point. The *Eastland* operated on that Lake Erie run for the Eastland Navigation Company from 1907 through 1912. Either rumors that she was an unsafe ship followed her or else the *Eastland* experienced some stability problems after going to Lake Erie. On August 9, 1910, her owners ran a half-page ad in the *Cleveland Plain Dealer* offering a $5,000 reward "to any person that will bring forth a naval engineer, a marine architect, or anyone qualified to pass on the merits of a ship, who will say that the steamer *Eastland* is not a seaworthy ship, or that she would not ride out any storm or weather condition that can arise on either lake or ocean."[94] Apparently, nobody came forward to challenge the seaworthiness of the ship.

Despite that, her owners were undoubtedly shaken when the steamer suffered yet another stability problem on July 1, 1912. While leaving Cleveland, the *Eastland* began listing twenty-five degrees to port, then flopped over and took on a thirty-degree starboard list before she could be righted. When steamboat inspectors in Cleveland heard about the problem, they reduced her carrying capacity to two thousand if she was going to be operating more than five miles from shore. Since the route from Cleveland to Cedar Point was within that five-mile limit, the change in her carrying capacity wasn't a serious handicap.[95]

In the summer of 1913, the *Eastland* was purchased by the St. Joseph and Chicago Steamship Company and returned to service on lower Lake Michigan. Sometime shortly after her return, a naval architect from Chicago by the name of John Devereaux York was making a trip on the steamer when it experienced one of its episodes of listing. "She listed badly," York later recalled. "In trying to make the harbor, it was like steering a log of wood." Once he got ashore, York fired off a succinct letter to Chicago's harbormaster. "You are aware of the condition of the *S. S. Eastland*," he wrote, "and unless structural defects are remedied to prevent listing . . . there may be a serious accident."[96] The *Eastland*'s capacity was later reduced to 2,183, though there's no indication of what role York's letter might have played in that decision.

A number of changes were made to the *Eastland* during the winter of 1914–15. The wooden floor in the dining room and bar area was beginning to rot because of all the drinks that had been spilled on it, and the deck near the boarding gangways was showing a lot of wear from heavy traffic. The flooring in both areas was removed, and concrete was poured in its place. Together, the two sections of concrete added an estimated forty-four to seventy-five tons of weight to the ship on the level of the main deck, above the waterline.

Three additional lifeboats and their davits and six life rafts were also added atop the *Eastland*'s hurricane deck. Together, the additional boats and rafts added another fourteen to fifteen tons of weight at the very highest point of the ship.

The owners of the *Eastland* added the boats and rafts in an effort to avoid having their ship's carrying capacity reduced when the newly passed Seamen's Act went into effect on November 4, 1915. The Seamen's Act was largely a response to the April 14, 1912, sinking of the British liner *Titanic* after hitting an iceberg on its maiden voyage across the North Atlantic. About 1,523 of the 2,228 passengers and crewmembers aboard died in the tragedy. When it was made public that the new passenger liner had only been equipped with enough lifeboats and rafts to handle slightly more than half of those aboard, the worldwide public reaction was one of disbelief and extreme anger. The following year, an International Conference on Safety of Life at Sea was convened by the maritime nations of the world to deal with issues raised by the loss of the *Titanic*. On January 14, 1914, participants in the conference issued an "International Convention" that called for ships to be equipped with enough boats and rafts to accommodate *all* passengers and crewmembers.

Later that year, a "boats for all" provision was tacked onto a bill that was before the Congress to increase the number of seamen required on U.S. ships. During legislative hearings, operators of Great Lakes passenger ships sought to be excluded from any "boats for all" requirement. They argued that the heavy vessel traffic on the Great Lakes made lifeboats less important because there were generally other vessels in the vicinity that could come to the aid of a ship in distress. Testimony indicated that ships passed each other at intervals of fourteen minutes on Lake Huron, eleven minutes on Lake Erie, and three minutes on the Detroit River. A. A. Schantz, general manager of the Detroit & Cleveland Navigation Company, one of the largest operators of passenger ships on the lakes, also testified that because Great Lakes vessels had shallow drafts, the addition of more lifeboats would make them top-heavy. The other option, of course, was simply to reduce the number of passengers carried to conform to the boats available, but that wasn't an alternative the Great Lakes operators wanted to talk about.

When the Seamen's Act was finally signed by President Woodrow Wilson on March 4, 1915, it required that each passenger ship carry enough lifeboats to handle 75 percent of the passengers aboard, with life rafts or collapsible boats for the balance. Between May 15 and September 15, however, ships on the lakes needed to have enough lifeboats for only 40 percent of the passengers aboard.[97]

Once they reviewed the provisions of the Seamen's Act, the owners of the *Eastland* quickly calculated that if they didn't provide some additional lifeboats or rafts, the ship's carrying capacity was going to be reduced from 2,183 to somewhere between 1,000 and 1,500 after the new law went into effect. By adding three lifeboats and six rafts at the start of the 1915 season, the *Eastland*'s owners hoped that when the provisions of the Seamen's Act took effect in November they would still be able to carry about 2,000 passengers.

In the interim, hoping to maximize the value of the new boats and rafts, they immediately applied for an increase in their carrying capacity based on the new lifesaving equipment they had installed. The request was approved by Robert Reid, the steamboat inspector at Grand Haven, Michigan, who filled out the paperwork to authorize the ship to carry 2,500 passengers and 70 crewmembers.

Business wasn't that great in 1915, and the *Eastland* was never loaded anywhere near her approved capacity until July 24, when the ship was one of five chartered by the Hawthorne Club, a social organization for employees of Western Electric Company. Saturday, July 24, had been set as the date for the club's popular summer picnic and boat trip from Chicago to nearby Michigan City, Indiana. The outing would include tug-of-wars, pie-eating contests, canoe races, and baseball games. The biggest activities planned would be a parade, with floats from the company's various departments, and a pageant depicting the linking of New York and San Francisco by long-distance telephone wires. The equipment for that undertaking had been supplied by the Chicago plant of Western Electric, a point of immense pride for its 9,000 employees. When ticket sales were tabulated the night before the event, organizers found that 7,300 had been sold, the most in the event's five-year history.

The skies were a dirty gray and there was a light rain falling on the day of the outing, but that didn't discourage many of those who had purchased tickets. By 6:30 in the morning, about 5,000 had already arrived at the docks along the Chicago River, waiting to board the five ships.

The *Eastland* was scheduled to be the first of the five steamers to load, and at 6:40 passengers were allowed to begin boarding. Two customs officers were posted at one of the ship's starboard gangways with hand counters to make sure that no more than 2,500 passengers went aboard. The first passengers let onto the *Eastland* tended to congregate along her starboard rails, where they could watch the crowd remaining on the dock. As a result, the ship developed a starboard list of about ten degrees almost immediately.

In the engine room, Chief Engineer Joe Erickson noticed the list on the plumb bob that hung from one of the bulkheads, and he began pumping water into two of the ballast tanks on the port side. After pumping for only two or three minutes, the ship righted itself.

Just two minutes later, the *Eastland* began to list again, but to the port side. Erickson had the valve to one of the starboard ballast tanks opened up, and in five to ten minutes the ship again righted itself.

Passengers were boarding the *Eastland* at a rate of about fifty a minute. By a few minutes after 7:00 there were already 1,600 aboard.

At this time, Chief Erickson noticed that there was a slight port list. Assuming it was caused by passengers congregating along the port rail, he told his men to pump the water out of the number 3 ballast tank on the port side that had been partially filled earlier. He didn't have them pump out the number 2 port tank, because he didn't think there was enough in it to make much of a difference. About that time, Erickson got a call from Captain Harry Pedersen, asking him to warm up the engines so they'd be ready to leave the dock just as soon as they were loaded. On the dock, Adam Weckler, Chicago's harbormaster, noticed that the *Eastland* had taken on what he estimated was a seven-degree list to port at 7:10 A.M. By then, the *Eastland*'s full complement of 2,500 passengers had boarded and those waiting on the dock were being sent to the steamer *Theodore Roosevelt*, which was docked nearby.

Many passengers were still crowded along the *Eastland*'s port railings to watch activity on the river. Because of the light rain, most of them were on the covered main deck, and there were only about 150 people on the open-air hurricane deck. One of the *Eastland*'s mates tried to get some of the passengers to move around to the starboard side to get rid of the list, but they weren't very cooperative.

By 7:16, the steamer was listing between ten and fifteen degrees to port. Chief Erickson opened the valves to pump ballast water into two of the tanks on the starboard side, but for some reason the pumps wouldn't take a suction. Erickson thought the strainer on the water intake might have become clogged with debris, so he sent one of his men to clean it out.

At 7:18 the *Eastland* slowly righted itself. Many of those aboard had been worried by the list, and they were relieved when the ship was again upright. The harbormaster signaled to Captain Pedersen that he could leave the dock anytime he was ready. On Captain Pedersen's signal, crewmembers began taking the gangplank in.

At 7:20 the list to port resumed and Chief Erickson noticed that water was coming onto the main deck through one of the scuppers on the port side. Erickson quickly stopped the engines, thinking that they could be causing the list, but the list continued to grow worse. The door on a refrigerator behind the bar in the main deck saloon flew open, and beer bottles fell out and rolled across the sloping deck. Concerned passengers began to move from the port rail to the starboard side of the ship, alongside the dock. Despite that, the ship continued to sag toward its port side.

At 7:23, Chief Erickson was so concerned by the heavy port list that he sent his first assistant engineer on deck to see if he could get more of the passengers to move to the starboard side. The worried passengers were more than willing to comply with the engineer's request. By then, water was flooding onto the main deck through the gangway doors on the port side. When the ship was fully loaded, those doors were only a few feet above the level of the water even when the ship was upright.

At 7:24, Captain Pedersen rang "stand by" on the engine order telegraph, indicating to the men in the engine room that he intended to get under way momentarily. At the same time, he signaled for the bridgetender to open the Clark Street bridge, which was just downstream from the *Eastland.* Harbormaster Weckler quickly countermanded the signal to the bridge operator, telling Captain Pedersen to trim his ship before leaving the dock.

At that time, Assistant Harbormaster Joe Lynn estimated that the *Eastland* was listing twenty to twenty-five degrees to port. Concluding that the ship's situation was hopeless, and expecting it to roll over at any moment, Lynn hurried to the nearest telephone to call the fire department for emergency assistance.

While Lynn was scampering to find a phone, Captain Pedersen signaled the mate stationed on the *Eastland*'s stern to throw off the stern mooring line. That was done, and the stern of the ship began to swing out into the river.

At 7:25 the *Eastland* momentarily straightened up, then took on a slight starboard list. That lasted only a few seconds, however, then the cranky ship flipped back over to port again and quickly took on a list of about twenty degrees. In the engine room, Chief Erickson was frantically trying to deal with the list. He also ordered the bilge pump turned on to pump out some of the water that was coming in through the scuppers and gangways. Right about then, the stokers and oilers working in the boiler room and lower engine room decided that the ship was going to roll over or sink, and they climbed up to the level of the main deck.

The list continued to worsen, quickly reaching twenty-five to thirty degrees. There it stabilized for a few minutes before continuing to sag. When the list reached about thirty-three degrees, Second Mate Pete Fisher ordered the passengers on the hurricane deck to move to the starboard side, but the deck was too wet and too steeply pitched for them to comply, though they tried desperately.

At 7:28 A.M. the list reached forty-five degrees. Dishes flew off the shelves in the pantry and crashed to the deck in pieces. The refrigerator in the saloon tipped over and slid across the deck, pinning two women against the bulkhead on the port side. The piano on the promenade deck also rolled downhill until it smashed against the bulkhead. Water was flooding into the ship through the gangways and portholes on the port side. There were lots of shouts and screams, and many people began jumping off the starboard side of the ship, landing on the dock or in the water.

At 7:30 the *Eastland* slowly rolled over into the river on her port side, barely making a splash. With the water only about twenty feet deep, almost the entire starboard half of the steamer was sticking out of the water for its whole length.

Hundreds of people were trapped inside the hull of the *Eastland*, while many of those on deck were thrown into the water. An eighteen-year-old man who was standing with a friend on the hurricane deck later recounted that folding deck chairs began sliding to the river side as the boat went over, and they could hear people screaming on the deck below them. The man and his friend scrambled for the rail on the starboard side, and managed to crawl over it and onto the side of the hull. From their perch on the hull, the two young men could see people in the water. Some of the men, they said, were holding women by their hair, trying to keep them from drowning. "The screaming was awful," the young man reported. "People were calling out, looking for loved ones."[98]

Bystanders along the riverbank began throwing anything that would float into the water, including empty chicken coops and egg crates from a nearby poultry shop. Firefighters were on the scene within minutes, alerted by Joe Lynn even before the *Eastland* rolled over. Many boats also raced to the scene, and their crews began pulling people from the water. Divers were sent for, and rescue workers forced open the gangways and portholes on the starboard side of the *Eastland*'s hull in an effort to get at those trapped inside.[99]

As the bodies of the dead began to pile up along the riverbank, they were at first taken to a nearby warehouse. When it became obvious that the number of dead would exceed the capacity of the warehouse, the coroner took over the Second Regiment Armory on Washington Boulevard for use as a temporary morgue. As the number of bodies rose, an efficient bureaucrat in the Coroner's Office quickly had a rubber stamp made for use in imprinting the hundreds of death certificates: "Drowned, July 24, 1915, from steamer *Eastland*, Chicago River at Clark Street." At the armory, the bodies were laid out shoulder-to-shoulder in neat rows of 85 to make it easier for family members to search for their loved ones. Altogether, 812 bodies passed through the temporary morgue. Another two dozen died at local hospitals, bringing the total to 836. Among the dead were twenty-two entire families.[100] While there were about 70 crewmembers aboard the *Eastland* that fateful morning, only 2 were counted among the dead. One was an assistant purser and the other a deckhand.[101] Many in the crew apparently sensed their ship was in trouble and jumped to the dock in the minutes prior to the time it capsized, or

50. The single worst casualty in the history of the Great Lakes occurred at Chicago on July 24, 1915, when the passenger steamer *Eastland* rolled over and sank at its dock in the Chicago River. This photo was taken from another passenger steamer only ten minutes after the *Eastland* capsized. While many survivors can be seen atop the overturned hull, hundreds more were still trapped inside the ship. More than 800 of the 2,500 passengers aboard the excursion boat were killed, but all except two of the *Eastland*'s crew of seventy managed to escape. Despite many inspections by the Steamboat Inspection Service, the *Eastland* had been dangerously top-heavy throughout most of its twelve-year career. (Ralph Roberts Collection)

at least got themselves into positions where they would not be trapped when it rolled over.

While rescue workers were still frantically searching for survivors inside the hull of the *Eastland*, Chicago's deputy superintendent of police arrested Captain Pedersen and his first mate. As they were being led away, Captain Pedersen was attacked by an angry crowd, and only the presence of police officers saved him from being seriously injured.[102]

In the days immediately following the tragedy, every city, county, state, and federal official in the Chicago area with any authority whatsoever seemed to be intent on fixing blame for the disaster. By late July, six different inquiries were under way, and squabbles frequently broke out over which officials had jurisdiction.

The U.S. District Attorney ordered the arrests of twenty-seven other *Eastland* crewmembers, ranging from the chief engineer to firemen and mess boys. The Cook County Coroner ordered the arrests of all the officials of the St. Joseph and Chicago Steamship Company and the

Indiana Transportation Company, the firm that had arranged the vessel charters for the Hawthorne Club. The two steamboat inspectors from Grand Haven who had issued the *Eastland*'s most recent certificate of seaworthiness were also detained by authorities.

The owners of the *Eastland* wouldn't stand behind Captain Pedersen. Through an attorney, they issued a statement saying that Pedersen was responsible for the disaster because he didn't ensure that passengers were evenly distributed or ballast the vessel properly. Their ship was seaworthy, they argued, and they had a certificate from the Steamboat Inspection Service to prove it.

Captain Pedersen, on the other hand, pleaded complete innocence:

> The master of a ship nowadays does not possess the powers he did years ago. It formerly was the custom for the captain to be in absolute control of his boat and the business carried on by the vessel. Now, the captain has nothing to say about the freight, passengers, crew, or sailing. The only man I had power to employ was my first mate. Officials hired the engineer, and practically everything else was handled from the main office. The responsibility is not mine. I often noticed the boat list, but it was never anything serious and I believed the engineer knew his duties and business. I had certain duties to perform and my power was limited to those. I carried out those orders to the best of my ability.[103]

It was a pitiful and self-serving statement, and one that was at odds with centuries of maritime law and tradition which held that a captain was responsible for everything that went on aboard his ship.[104]

Pedersen was only one of many who blamed the capsizing on Chief Engineer Erickson, claiming he hadn't ballasted the boat properly. In reality, however, Erickson had only been following procedures that had been established for ballasting the boat long before he was appointed chief engineer. During the legal proceedings, Erickson was represented by Clarence Darrow, the famed defense attorney from Chicago.

Darrow claimed that the starboard side of the *Eastland* had been sitting on some old underwater pilings that weren't discovered until salvagers began working to raise the sunken hulk. Those pilings, Darrow argued, had prevented Erickson from being able to properly ballast the boat. The capsizing resulted, he said, when a large crowd of passengers moved quickly to the port side to watch a passing boat. Prosecutors quickly produced evidence to show that the bottom of the *Eastland* was never less than twelve inches above the pilings, however. Many of those who had been on the ship also testified that there had been no mass movement of passengers just before the ship rolled over. In fact, most said that couldn't have happened, since people were so crowded together along the port rail that it was virtually impossible for them to move.

The two inspectors from the Steamboat Inspection Service stood by their *a priori* decisions that the *Eastland* was seaworthy and capable of carrying 2,500 passengers. Many disagreed, including at least one highly regarded naval architect, yet it was virtually impossible to pinpoint who was correct. The science of naval architecture was then in its infancy, and there were no hard-and-fast rules for how to determine the number of passengers a ship could carry.

During the investigations, it was discovered that Robert Reid, one of the inspectors, was Chief Engineer Erickson's father-in-law and a friend of several officers of the St. Joseph and Chicago Steamship Company. When that juicy tidbit was made public, many immediately jumped to the conclusion that Reid was corrupt. That fire was readily fanned by officials of the seamen's union who charged that the Steamboat Inspection Service had been in the pockets of shipowners for years.

Secretary of Commerce William Redfield, who was the cabinet officer then responsible for the Steamboat Inspection Service, ordered a thorough investigation. Unfortunately, the panel he appointed to investigate the possible role of the Steamboat Inspection Service in the *Eastland* disaster was overwhelmingly made up of officers of the Steamboat Inspection Service. It came as no surprise, then, when the two inspectors and the Steamboat Inspection Service itself were found to have acted properly and professionally in the matter of the *Eastland.* The investigating panel used the opportunity to once again cite a need for the Steamboat Inspection Service to have a "corps of experts" with the power to approve vessel plans prior to construction. Once again, the Congress rejected the proposal, largely because of opposition by shipbuilders and shipping companies.

Although all those charged in the criminal case were exonerated in 1916, legal haggling in the *Eastland* cases dragged on until 1935. In the civil cases that sought damages for the families of those who died on the *Eastland,* the 1935 decision by a federal court of appeals upheld a previous federal district court opinion that the sinking was due to Chief Engineer Erickson's failure to properly fill the ship's ballast tanks. The steamship company officers, Captain Pedersen, the rest of the crew, and the steamboat inspectors were all exonerated. Since the steamship company wasn't negligent, a federal law that shipping companies had pushed through the Congress in 1851 limited their liability to the value of the ship—more specifically, the *sunken* ship.

Raised shortly after the disaster by the Great Lakes Towing Company, the *Eastland*'s hull was subsequently sold at auction for $46,000. Most of that went to pay for having the ship raised, so only about $10,000 was left to be split up among those who had lost the most when the *Eastland* capsized—the families of the 836 dead.

The complex *Eastland* case has been reviewed many times over the years. The most thorough study of the facts of the case suggests that the ship was *not* seaworthy on July 24, 1915. With lifeboats and life rafts added because of the "boats for all" legislation passed after the loss of the *Titanic*, the weight of the concrete added to the ship prior to the 1915 season, and the maximum load of passengers, the *Eastland* was fatally top-heavy. That top-heaviness was aggravated when Chief Erickson put some water into the ballast tanks. Since the tanks weren't full, it created a "free-surface effect."

The ballast tanks had no baffles in them to keep water from sloshing back and forth if the tanks weren't full. After the chief engineer pumped in some ballast water, the first time passenger movements caused the *Eastland* to list the water began to slop back and forth in the tanks, adding to the ship's instability and helping to eventually push it over.

There are probably only two things that could have prevented the *Eastland* from rolling over that morning. One would have been to reduce the passenger load, especially on the hurricane deck. Once the ship started tipping back and forth, Captain Pedersen should have immediately instructed his crew to ask passengers to get off the vessel. A captain's first responsibility is to see to the safety of the passengers and crew, but Pedersen merely stood around waiting for the chief engineer to correct the progressively worsening list.

The second thing that might have saved the *Eastland* would have been to completely fill the ship's ballast tanks, thereby eliminating the free-surface effect that occurred and simultaneously lowering the vessel's center of gravity. In 1915, however, chief engineers didn't have a thorough understanding of either stability or the effect of free-surface water, nor apparently did the steamboat inspectors who licensed the engineers.

It's clear that throughout her career it was common for the *Eastland* to experience stability problems whenever she was heavily loaded. The Steamboat Inspection Service had been made aware of that on a number of occasions. Either because of their lack of technical expertise or because of their acquiescence to the various shipping companies that owned the vessel, they took no action to determine the extent of the *Eastland*'s stability problem.

Even before the *Eastland* had been launched, naval architects had developed a test to determine a ship's stability. The "inclining test" was used to calculate a vessel's metacentric height. That figure then made it possible to determine the total weight that could be loaded aboard the ship before it would become unstable. Inclining tests were normally performed on new ships, or anytime a vessel was modified in a way that was likely to affect its center of gravity, such as the changes made to the *Eastland* after its first season of operations and prior to the start of the fateful 1915 season.

No inclining test was ever performed on the *Eastland*, however, and the stability—or instability—of the ship was never really taken into consideration by the steamboat inspectors when determining how many passengers it could carry. Instead, inspectors based their decisions on the square footage of deck space on the *Eastland* and the number of lifeboats and life rafts she carried. It wasn't until the 1920s that ships on the Great Lakes were finally required to undergo inclining tests.[105]

Instability as a result of overloading was almost certainly the cause of the *Eastland* tragedy. The needless disaster resulted in great pressure being brought to bear on government officials to do something about the grisly carnage resulting from overloading.

In the early fall of 1915, Secretary of Commerce William Redfield personally wrote to William Livingstone, president of the Lake Carriers' Association, expressing concern about the potential for shipwrecks during the remaining days of that year's shipping season. For a year and half, the shipping business on the lakes had been dismal and there were many times when there were more ships laid up than operating. Early that fall, however, business picked up dramatically and it looked as though there was going to be a rush to haul as much cargo as possible before the season ended. "Under these circumstances," Redfield wrote, "risks may be taken which would under ordinary circumstances be avoided." He was particularly concerned about the problems of overloading and improperly trimming cargo, two problems that the Steamboat Inspection Service had no legal powers to control.

Because of the seriousness of the overloading problem, however, Redfield had ordered the steamboat inspectors to begin monitoring vessel loading. Anytime they observed a ship that had been overloaded, they were to call that fact to the attention of the ship's captain. "If, however, the captain or owner chooses, the vessel may proceed and the law cannot stop her," Redfield freely admitted.[106]

Redfield's decision to heavily involve his department's steamboat inspectors in a problem over which they had no legal authority is a clear testament to the perceived severity of the overloading problem, particularly since the Steamboat Inspection Service was then chronically understaffed. For several years, agency administrators had literally been begging Congress to appropriate funds so that additional inspectors could be put out into the field. They had only 188 inspectors to handle the entire U.S. fleet. In 1915, the 188 field personnel had inspected 7,553 vessels and licensed 18,412 steamboat officers. Implementation of the Seamen's Act had also imposed fifteen new responsibilities on the inspection service, but no additional personnel had been authorized. In some districts, inspectors were being required to work from 5:00 in the morning until 10:00 or 11:00 at night.[107] Given that situation, it's hard to believe that the agency would voluntarily take on the added duty of identifying cases of overloading unless they thought improper loading posed a serious threat.

In his letter to the LCA, Redfield argued that it was in the self-interest of the vessel owners and captains to see that their ships weren't overloaded and that cargo was properly stowed and trimmed. "Many owners and many captains, doubtless the greater number by far of both, will take care in such matters," Redfield acknowledged. "Some captains, however, will hesitate to take the care they wish if they feel the owners are pressing them for time and cargoes." he added. "Some owners will take risks for a great stake that their own sober judgment would not approve were the reward for passing the risk less visible. In both cases, the responsibility that exists toward the crew of the vessel is overlooked."[108]

Livingstone wrote back to Secretary Redfield that he and the members of the LCA were in full agreement, but that the "danger of overloading our ships is eliminated" due to the shallow river channels of the Great Lakes. Until further dredging was done in the rivers, the new freighters operated by LCA companies couldn't even load to their designed drafts. Livingstone also passed along to Redfield a copy of a letter that Harry Coulby, head of the hundred-ship Pittsburgh Steamship fleet, the largest on the lakes, had sent to all his vessel masters. The letter warned the captains not to take chances during the balance of the season—to comply with navigation rules, obtain weather forecasts before leaving ports, and make sure the hatches on their ships were secured.[109]

While it was true that the shallow river channels made it virtually impossible for the newest and largest freighters on the lakes to overload, that was not true for most of the 541 ships owned by the association's member companies. In fact, exactly the reverse was true for the vast majority of the vessels enrolled with the LCA. Most of the iron and steel freighters built in the 1880s and 1890s were designed with drafts of only ten to eighteen feet, the maximum that could then be accommodated by the river channels and the locks at the Soo. By 1915, however, the new Davis lock at the Soo could handle vessels with drafts of almost twenty-three feet, and the river channels were rapidly being dredged to that same depth. When you take into consideration all of the vessels enrolled with the LCA, it was definitely easier for them to overload in 1915 than it had been in the past.

It's also important to note that only about half of the U.S. ships operating on the lakes in 1915 were owned by companies that belonged to the LCA. In fact, the companies that didn't belong generally operated smaller and older vessels that were probably much more likely to be overloaded than the big new freighters.

It's also hard to know how to evaluate Harry Coulby's letter to the captains in the Pittsburgh Steamship fleet. Did the captains take Coulby's warnings literally, or was the letter merely viewed as eyewash, while the vessel masters knew they were expected to continue operating as they always had? There's no way for us to know, but Coulby's letter certainly didn't say "Do not overload!"

One historian later discounted overloading as a major cause of sinkings. "No sailor will go to certain death on an overloaded vessel," he reasoned.[110] That's a sound statement, but it has little to do with whether a captain will take an overloaded ship out. When a ship sailed in an overloaded condition, "certain death" was not the normal outcome. Quite the contrary. Most ships that left port overloaded had safe passages, thanks in large measure to the usually calm conditions found on the lakes. That's why overloading was such a common problem.

The LCA had even acknowledged overloading as a significant problem in their *1909 Annual Report:* "A great deal of trouble was experienced during the first half of the season by vessels overloading and causing damage to the bottom of the lock and during the latter part of the season, though vessels did not appear by their marks to exceed the recommended draft, nevertheless the closing cables were frequently cut, indicating that their marks were not correct."[111]

During November, the most dangerous month of the year for violent storms, the closing cables at the bottom of the locks were cut twenty-two times in 1909.[112] Not only were ships being loaded to greater depths than could be accommodated by the locks, but the draft marks on their hulls were apparently being altered so workers at the locks wouldn't know their actual drafts.

There's also no question that there was often either overt or insidious pressure on captains to overload their ships. Once one captain carries more than the safe maximum load on a ship and it doesn't sink, all subsequent captains are going to feel pressured to follow suit.

In addition to watching ships loading in the major iron ore ports on the upper lakes, steamboat inspectors were also stationed at the Soo to watch for overloaded ships during the busy fall of 1915. We have no record of how many overloaded vessels they witnessed, but there must have been enough to justify continuing the program during the 1916 season, despite the continuing shortage of field staff.

S. R. Kirby, 1916

In spite of the pleadings of Secretary Redfield and the efforts of the steamboat inspectors, overloading was blamed for the loss of the steamer *S. R. Kirby* and twenty crewmembers on Lake Superior in 1916. The *Kirby* was a 294-foot freighter built by the Detroit Dry Dock Company in 1890 for the North Western Transportation Company. In its twenty-sixth year of operation in 1916, the *Kirby* had a reputation around the Great Lakes for being overloaded much of the time. The root of the problem is that when a ship is loaded with a heavy cargo, like iron ore, the cargo hold is only about two-thirds full when the ship is carrying the maximum safe tonnage. With lighter cargoes, like grain or coal, the hold could be filled right to the hatch coamings and the ship would still not be carrying its maximum safe tonnage.

The maximum safe tonnage leaves the ship with a reasonable amount of freeboard, the distance between the waterline and the deck of the ship—or the amount of the hull not submerged. An adequate amount of freeboard is needed to ensure that the deck of the ship is not constantly awash and the vessel has some reserve buoyancy.

A shipping company's profits depend in large part on how much cargo each of its ships carries in a year. Similarly, for much of the industry's history, a significant portion of a captain's income for the year was in the form of a bonus based on the amount of cargo his ship carried during the season, or the number of trips it made. Given those economic incentives, some shipping companies and many captains would load their ships beyond the safe limits, especially in the ore trade. In doing so, ships like the *S. R. Kirby* often left the ore docks seriously overloaded. With the lakes calm during so much of the shipping season, they generally got away with the overloading.

On the evening of May 7, 1916, Captain David Girardin pulled the *Kirby* away from the ore docks at Ashland, Wisconsin, towing the barge

George E. Hartnell. Both were heavily loaded with iron ore, loaded beyond the limits that most captains would consider safe. As the two ships headed out past the Apostle Islands, the surface of Lake Superior was like a mirror—flat calm. It was a fine spring day, and perfect sailing weather.

Captain Girardin probably noticed that his barometer had started to fall, indicating that a storm system was approaching, but it wasn't something that would have concerned him too much. Spring storms, most often thunderstorms, can be quite intense, but they're usually short-lived. Besides, Dave Girardin had a well-earned reputation as one of the foremost heavy-weather sailors on the lakes. He was a skilled navigator, and ships under his command had safely come through some of the worst fall storms that had struck the Great Lakes over the years. Crewmen who had sailed with him often joked that the owners of the *Kirby* had wasted their money when they put anchors on the ship, because Girardin never used them.

The day after the *Kirby* left Ashland, an unusual spring storm of hurricane intensity ripped across the lakes. The powerful winds soon piled the surface of the lake into towering waves. Some said the waves were as high as forty or fifty feet, though that is undoubtedly an exaggeration. Regardless, the overloaded *Kirby* and her consort were struck by the full force of the seventy-mile-an-hour winds and brutal waves when they were off the tip of the Keweenaw Peninsula, about midway across the lake.

At 10 A.M. on May 8, the steamer *E. H. Utley* was headed westbound toward Duluth when those in the pilothouse saw the *Kirby* and its tow laboring heavily in the towering waves. It was obvious to those on the *Utley* that the *Kirby* was overloaded. Captain C. C. Balfour, master of the *Utley*, blew the whistle signal for "Do you need assistance?" He got no reply from the *Kirby*.

Balfour decided to keep the *Kirby* and *Hartnell* in sight as long as he could, so he checked down his ship until it was making the bare minimum headway. Those in the *Utley*'s pilothouse were still watching when the *Kirby* was lifted high by a pair of giant waves and the struggling freighter cracked in two just aft of her forward cabin. While Captain Balfour and his crew stood transfixed, the *Kirby* sank right before their eyes.[113]

Balfour quickly brought his ship around and raced for the scene. When the *Utley* reached the spot where the *Kirby* had disappeared, all Balfour and his crew could see was a red stain on the surface caused by water mixing with the sunken ship's cargo of iron ore.

When the *Kirby* plunged to the bottom of the lake, the stout towing hawser that connected it to its consort had broken, and the *Hartnell* and its crew were drifting helplessly toward the dangerous reefs off Eagle Harbor. Seeing that, Balfour brought the *Utley* alongside the barge and rigged a towline, then pulled the *Hartnell* to the sheltered waters of Bete Grise Bay on the east side of the Keweenaw Peninsula.

While the *Utley* was rescuing the *Hartnell* and its crew, two other ships that had seen the *Kirby* go down began searching for survivors. The crew of the *Harry A. Berwind* sighted two men clinging to a piece of wreckage. A ladder was put over the side of the *Berwind*, and the first mate went down and helped one man to climb onto the deck of the freighter. While the *Berwind*'s mate was occupied, the second man slipped off the wreckage and disappeared. A short while later, another crewman from the *Kirby* was picked up by the steamer *Joseph Block*. The two, First Mate Joe Mudray and Fireman Otto Lundquist, were the only survivors. Captain Girardin and nineteen crewmembers had gone down with their ship, most trapped inside by its rapid sinking.

Otto Lundquist said that he had gotten off watch about 11:45 and stopped for a moment on deck to talk to an oiler who was just going down to work in the engine room. The two stood in the shelter of the stern cabin and talked about the huge seas, which they thought had to be thirty to forty feet high. As they watched the tortured surface of the lake, they saw several waves approaching that were noticeably larger than the rest.

The first of the massive waves passed under the hull, lifting it high in the water. When the second wave struck and lifted the bow, Lundquist said he heard "a dull, rending sound," and was startled to see the number 1 hatch crumble as the ship was literally torn apart by the power of the wave.

As the wave passed and the *Kirby* settled into the trough, the broken hull kept right on going, plummeting toward the bottom. Lundquist climbed onto the gunwale and leaped into the turbulent water. It seemed as though he was submerged for an eternity, and when he finally struggled to the surface, the ship was gone and the surface of the water was covered with floating debris.

The fireman swam to a large piece of debris that was floating nearby, which turned out to be a section of the roof of one of the ship's cabins. It wouldn't support him, though, so he let go and swam to another mass of flotsam that included several large planks that had floated free when the *Kirby* dropped to the bottom. As he swam toward the planks, Lundquist saw Captain Girardin swimming nearby, followed by his dog. As the men made eye contact, Lundquist said that the captain "threw up his arms in a sort of 'so long' way . . . and sank from sight."[114]

Two days after the *Kirby* went down, Captain Girardin's bulldog "Tige" was found on a piece of floating debris by lifesavers from the Eagle Harbor station. The dog, the *Kirby's* mascot, was eventually returned to Captain Girardin's widow in Detroit.

The subsequent investigation into the sinking by officials of the Steamboat Inspection Service revealed that while the *Kirby* had been designed to load to a depth of fourteen feet, she had a draft of nineteen feet when she left Ashland. That left the ship with only a scant two feet of freeboard. In 1916, a "safe" load for the freighter would have left her with at least seven feet of freeboard.[115]

In the aftermath of the loss of the *Kirby*, editorials in a number of influential newspapers around the lakes called for the institution of load-line regulations similar to those that had been adopted in England in 1876.[116] The British regulations had been promoted by Samuel Plimsoll, a member of the House of Commons. Appalled by the staggering loss of life as the result of an average of almost two thousand shipwrecks that occurred in British waters each year, Plimsoll published a book—*Our Seamen, An Appeal*—in which he identified nine major causes of vessel casualties. For each, Plimsoll offered suggestions for ways the government could cut the number of vessel casualties and resulting deaths.

Overloading was one of the nine causes of shipwrecks addressed by Plimsoll:

> Suppose a ship will take 900 tons of cargo with safety, leaving her side one-third as high out of the water as it is deep below it; and suppose, further, the freight of 700 tons is absorbed by expenses—wages of seamen, cost of fuel, wear and tear, interest of capital, cost of insurance, etc.—leaving the freight on the remaining 200 tons as profit to the owner, it is clear that by loading an additional 200 tons the profits are doubled, while the load is only increased by about a quarter more. And this addition will not load her so deeply as to prevent her making a good voyage, if the weather if favourable. What wonder is there, I say, that needy or unscrupulous men adopt the larger load?

Plimsoll also pointed out that the shipowners were in an advantageous position. If the overloaded vessel made it safely to her destination, they made a healthy profit. If the ship went down, insurance covered the cost of their loss—*often more than the loss*. According to Plimsoll, shipowners commonly insured vessels for more than their actual value, guaranteeing themselves a profit if it went down.

Plimsoll suggested that ships be required to maintain three inches of freeboard for every foot of depth of the cargo hold. Once a ship's necessary freeboard was calculated, a mark would then be painted on the side of the hull showing the maximum depth to which the vessel could load. Local port officials could then observe every ship leaving harbor and make a record of any that were overloaded. If an overloaded vessel subsequently sank, the record made by the port authorities could be used by the insurance underwriters to negate the owner's claim.

Plimsoll's book identified other major causes of shipwrecks as well: undermanning; bad stowage of cargo, especially deck loads; inadequate engine power; defective construction; failure to maintain ships in a sea-worthy condition; and the practice of over-insuring hulls. Plimsoll's recommendations were enacted into law by Parliament in 1876 and led to significant reductions in the numbers of shipwrecks and resulting deaths that occurred in subsequent years. In time, the maximum load-line mark painted on the hulls of ships came to be universally referred to as "the Plimsoll mark," an enduring honor to the British politician.[117]

Many of the problems cited by Plimsoll in his book were also common on the Great Lakes, including overloading. A number of Washington politicians from states bordering the lakes soon began to speak out in favor of adopting Plimsoll's load-line recommendations. In 1889, legislation was introduced in Congress to establish load lines for ships operating on the lakes. The threat of having load lines imposed on the industry had been a major factor in bringing shipowners together to form the Lake Carriers' Association in 1885 and the Cleveland Vessel Owners Association in 1886. When the load-line legislation was introduced in 1889, the two groups mounted a formidable lobbying campaign in Washington, handily defeating the bill.[118]

While overloading was often cited as a major factor in shipwrecks, shipowners were at that time a powerful political force, and they proved capable of forestalling all attempts to enact load-line legislation. It wasn't until 1936—sixty years after Plimsoll's system was put into effect in England—that load lines were finally required on Great Lakes ships. The *S. R. Kirby* was just one of countless ships lost as a result of overloading during those six decades of government inaction.

On Friday, October 20, 1916, four ships were lost on Lake Erie in what came to be known as the "Black Friday Storm of 1916." Twenty-six of twenty-seven crewmembers aboard the whaleback freighter *James B. Colgate* died when waves lifted off her wooden hatch covers and flooded the cargo hold. In addition, the lumber hooker *Marshall F. Butters* had gone down near Southeast Shoals, the seams on the schooner *D. L. Filer* had opened up and she sank near the mouth of the Detroit River, and the

Canadian steamer *Merida* simply disappeared with all twenty-three hands on board. All those aboard the *Butters* were rescued by passing ships. The captain of the *Filer* survived, while his six crewmembers were lost.[119]

Water leaking in through its exposed hatch covers was a major factor in the loss of the *Colgate,* and it was suspected to have contributed to the loss of several other ships in the Black Friday Storm. Before the start of the 1917 shipping season, the Steamboat Inspection Service strengthened its regulations regarding the use of tarps on ships with wooden or telescoping hatch covers. Tarps were required *on all trips* before March 31 and after August 31. Masters were also responsible to see that tarps were put on anytime bad weather was expected. Any captain who didn't comply with the regulations could have his license suspended on grounds of "inattention to duty."[120]

Milwaukee, 1929

The crew of the railroad car ferry *Milwaukee* breathed a collective sigh of relief on October 22, 1929, when their ship steamed through the piers and into the protected outer harbor of the Wisconsin city that was their ship's namesake. The trip across the lake from Grand Haven, Michigan, had been a rough one. A full-blown fall storm had roared in from the north, and the 383-foot car ferry had wallowed its way across the lake, spending much of the trip in the trough of the big seas. By the time the cook sounded the dinner bell for the noon meal, the crew could already see the skyline of Milwaukee rising toward the dirty gray skies ahead of their ship. But the wild ride had left many of those aboard feeling a little green around the gills, and the turnout in the messroom was sparse.

While the *Milwaukee* was still making its way to its riverfront dock, the crew went to work removing the jacks and chains that locked the railroad freight cars securely in place. Within mere minutes after the ship was securely tied up, the strings of boxcars were being pulled ashore and twenty-five cars bound for the Grand Trunk Western's railhead at Grand Haven were readied to be loaded onto the ferry. The car ferries didn't dillydally in port. They could normally unload, load, and have their lines cast off for the return trip in just three hours.

As the crew worked, most of their conversations were about the worsening weather. Many crewmembers speculated that their ship would stay at the dock until the weather broke. The Pere Marquette car ferry that had made the westbound crossing just ahead of the *Milwaukee* was loaded and ready to return to Ludington, Michigan, but she was going to stay tied up until the storm slacked off a little. Workers on the dock also reported that a second Pere Marquette ferry that had come in after the *Milwaukee* also planned to take a delay because of the weather. Three of the *Milwaukee*'s off-duty crewmen were so sure the return trip would be delayed that they hopped a streetcar and headed for downtown Milwaukee to take in a movie. Before they left the ship, some of the old-timers warned them not to count on a delay. With Captain Robert McKay in command, there was no guarantee they'd stay at the dock, regardless of how bad it was blowing. After all, people didn't refer to the captain as "Heavy Weather" McKay for no reason. Besides, the people in the Grand Trunk Western Railroad's office didn't like to see their ships tied up, fall storm or no fall storm.

The storm that rolled across Lake Michigan on October 22–23, 1929, wasn't "just another fall storm," however. It was a natural-born killer looking for victims. The storm struck with the force of an Atlantic Coast hurricane. With the howling winds blowing straight out of the north, waves built to frightening proportions as they rolled the full length of the lake. Along the shore, piers and docks were carried away and pleasure boats were swamped at their docks or blown ashore and battered to pieces. Quaint cottages and luxurious beachfront homes were washed away by the crashing seas, as were many miles of roads that ran along the lakeshore. Several sections of a new breakwater at Milwaukee were pounded to pieces by the surf, and a number of lighthouses around the lake were seriously damaged by the combination of high winds and towering seas. It would later go into the record books as one of the worst storms ever to hit Lake Michigan.

There's no record of the reactions of the crew when the eastbound railcars had been loaded aboard the *Milwaukee* and word was passed that Captain McKay intended to depart immediately on the return trip to Grand Haven. Many undoubtedly groaned at the prospect of going back out into the storm. Others probably felt an immediate queasiness in the pits of their stomachs. Some certainly cussed and swore, declaring that you had to be nuts to sail with a madman like McKay. It's likely that a few even vowed it would be their last trip on the *Milwaukee*.

The three crewmen who had gone downtown were probably still enjoying their movie when the *Milwaukee* steamed slowly out of the shelter of the river and prepared to again do battle with the storm. As the ship passed the Milwaukee Coast Guard station, the storm flags flying from the flagpole were blown taut by the strong winds. The ship started rolling even before it got out of the harbor. A short time later, the captain of the lightship that was stationed three miles off Milwaukee watched the car ferry pass. He would later report that she was "pitching and rolling heavily." She was headed due east at the time, once again wallowing in the trough of the seas. After ten minutes, the *Milwaukee*'s jet-black hull and twin black smokestacks disappeared in the rain and driven spray that obscured the line between the steel-gray lake and the dirty gray sky. The storm was then at its peak.

By the morning of October 24, the storm had finally blown off to the east and the waves subsided to nothing more than gentle swells. Stories were already circulating about ships that had run-ins with the storm. The package freighter *Delos W. Cooke* had left Chicago before the storm warnings were posted on the morning of October 22. Twenty-seven hours later, she fought her way back into Chicago after being unable to beat up the lake in the teeth of the storm. Interlake Steamship's 600-foot *Robert Hobson* struggled into South Chicago after taking a terrible beating. She, too, had been heading up the lake when the storm struck. Running light, the two-year-old ship worked so much in the giant seas that many of the rivets in her hull worked loose or sheared off, and cracks had appeared in her deck plates. Before she was fit to sail again, shipyard workers had to replace more than 25,000 rivets and several steel plates. The 590-foot *William P. Snyder, Jr.* had to have 50,000 rivets replaced. The steamers *Amasa Stone, Neptune, J. J. Block, James E. Davidson,* and *W. D. Calverly, Jr.* all reported heavy storm damage. The Grand Trunk car ferry *Grand Haven*, which had left Milwaukee at 2 A.M. on October 22, finally struggled into the dock at Grand Haven after battling the storm for fifteen hours. The crossing normally took only six hours.

Another Grand Trunk ferry, the *Grand Rapids*, left Milwaukee four hours after Captain McKay and his ship had departed. When it reached the dock in Grand Haven on the morning of October 23, the crew was mildly surprised to find that the *Milwaukee* hadn't arrived yet. Some guessed that Captain McKay had been forced to abandon the normal west-to-east courseline that would have put the *Milwaukee* in the trough of the seas. They suspected McKay had turned north, putting the bow of his ship into the sea so it would ride better. That wasn't McKay's usual approach in storms, however. Heavy Weather McKay was seldom willing to deviate one degree from the course between Milwaukee and Grand Haven, regardless of weather.

Just after dawn on the morning of October 24, the second mate on the steamer *Colonel* spotted some debris floating in the water off Racine,

Wisconsin. Upon close examination, it proved to be wreckage from a ship. The crew of the *Colonel* fished as much of the debris as they could from the lake, but there was no clue as to which ship it came from.

At Milwaukee, officials of the Grand Trunk Railway were getting anxious over the whereabouts of the *Milwaukee*, then thirty-six hours overdue. When they received word about the debris discovered by the crew of the *Colonel*, they arranged for several planes to fly over the field of floating wreckage to see if they could find anything that would link it to their missing ship. At the same time, Coast Guard stations on both the Michigan and Wisconsin shores were notified that the *Milwaukee* was overdue, and they promptly launched a systematic search.

On the morning of October 25, two bodies were found floating off Kenosha, Wisconsin, both clad in lifejackets stenciled with the name *Milwaukee*. Other bodies of crewmembers from the missing ferry were found later that day. The next morning, a Coast Guard boat found one of the *Milwaukee*'s lifeboats. In it were the bodies of four crewmen, all of whom had died of hypothermia. Another lifeboat from the *Milwaukee* was found later in the day, but it still had its canvas cover lashed in place.[121]

When it became obvious that the *Milwaukee* had been lost, the Grand Trunk office in Grand Haven was crowded with the mothers, wives, and children of crewmembers pleading for some news of their loved ones. Thirty of the ferry's crew made their homes in the little shoreside community, which was devastated to hear that the ship had been lost. It was the second marine disaster that had touched Grand Haven that fall. On September 11, the self-unloading steamer *Andaste* had gone down in a storm while on a run from Grand Haven to Chicago with a load of gravel. Thirteen of the twenty-five crewmembers who disappeared with the *Andaste* were from Grand Haven.[122]

Several days after the first solid evidence of the ship's loss was found, a surfman from the lifesaving station at South Haven discovered the *Milwaukee*'s message case floating along the shore. Inside was a note signed by the ship's purser: "*S.S. Milwaukee*, October 22, '29 8:30 P.M. This ship is making water fast. We have turned around and headed for Milwaukee. Pumps are working but sea gate is bent in and can't keep the water out. Flicker is flooded. Seas are tremendous. Things look bad. Crew roll is about the same as on the last pay day."

Much of the mystery surrounding the disappearance of the *Milwaukee* was cleared up by the note. The "sea gate" was a heavy steel gate that dropped in place to close off the end of the main deck where the railcars were loaded. If the gate was damaged, there was nothing to stop water

51. The Grand Trunk Railroad's ferry *Milwaukee* carried railroad cars and passengers between Milwaukee, Wisconsin, and Grand Haven, Michigan, from its launching in 1903 until it disappeared in an October storm in 1929. Captain Robert "Heavy Weather" McKay took his ship out of Milwaukee and sailed into the teeth of a Lake Michigan storm, never to be seen again. There is some evidence that a railroad car broke loose during the storm and wrecked the sea gate that normally kept water from coming in through the vessel's stern. McKay and fifty-one others aboard the *Milwaukee* at the time went down with the ship. (Ralph Roberts Collection)

from flooding onto the main deck. From the main deck, water coming aboard would eventually find its way down into the hull, gradually filling the ship. The "flicker," in fact, was what sailors on the car ferries called the crew quarters that were located one deck below the main deck near the stern of the ship. While some of the forty-seven crewmembers aboard the *Milwaukee* had managed to abandon ship before it went down, none had survived to explain exactly what had happened during the final minutes.

Another note was found later, sealed in a bottle. "This is the worst storm I have ever seen," it said. "Can't stay up much longer. Hole in the side of the boat." It was signed simply, "McKay." There was some uncertainty as to whether the note was genuine or not. If it was, the Scottish captain's reference to a hole in the side of the ship was most puzzling, since the purser had mentioned no such damage.

The Steamboat Inspection Service conducted a thorough investigation into the sinking. With no survivors, and the hull of the ship sunk deep below the waters of Lake Michigan, the investigation was similar to a coroner performing an autopsy without having the body. In light of the obvious limitations, the inspectors thoroughly reviewed the ship's plans and went over results of its most recent inspections. They also interviewed the captains of all the Grand Trunk car ferries, as well as those on similar Lake Michigan ferries operated by the Pere Marquette Railroad and the Ann Arbor Railroad. They also talked at length with Grand Trunk officials, including Captain Charles McLaren, the company's marine superintendent. By the time they had finished with their interviews, the inspectors felt they had a good understanding of why the ship went down, and why it was out on the lake in such a storm.

The inspectors were certain that the *Milwaukee* sank as a direct result of damage to the sea gate at her stern. They felt the sea gate was probably damaged by the high seas when Captain McKay attempted to turn his ship around.[123] Years later, evidence was discovered that seemed to suggest that railcars near the stern broke loose during the storm and crashed into the vital sea gate.[124] The damage to the sea gate allowed waves to flood the car deck, and eventually to flood the ship's hull.

The inspectors also concluded that the *Milwaukee* should never have been out on Lake Michigan on the evening of October 22, 1929. "It is evident that Captain McKay of the *Milwaukee* knew full well the weather conditions when he started out on his last trip, having just crossed the lake a few hours previously," wrote Dickerson Hoover, inspector general of the Steamboat Inspection Service.[125] "We all know that the *Milwaukee* should never have gone out, but it seems to us that from past experience, the criticism of eyewitnesses to the *Milwaukee*'s departure—all experienced sailor men—and the condition of the weather, that it was a foolhardy thing to do, and showed poor judgment on the part of Captain McKay."[126]

The inspectors had spent a considerable amount of time trying to determine just why Captain McKay had sailed out into what he knew was a severe storm while other car ferries were riding it out at their docks in Milwaukee. Some of the other Grand Trunk captains said that McKay was simply obsessed with keeping to the schedule, regardless of the weather. It was a matter of professional pride with him, they said.[127]

Dickerson Hoover and the other inspectors weren't sure that it was just McKay's "moral urge" that motivated him to regularly take his ship out into storms. There was some evidence that the captains of the four Grand Trunk car ferries were pressured by the company to keep to their schedules, but it was a hard thing for the inspectors to pin down. All the Grand Trunk captains had said they resented Captain

McLaren's frequent communiqués about weather conditions. They felt that McLaren's messages tended to downplay the severity of the weather, and, at the same time, he would always point out that other ships had ventured out.

McLaren claimed he never meant for his captains to feel pressured. "My company would not knowingly take any risks, either with the lives of its employees or with its property," he said. He merely felt responsible to provide the captains with the most up-to-date and accurate weather data and information on vessel movements. The inspectors couldn't find fault with McLaren's actions, feeling that any prudent and conscientious manager would act similarly.

At the same time, Hoover found it somewhat curious that all four of the Grand Trunk ferries had gone out into the October 22 storm, while ferries owned by other railroads stayed in port. One ferry operator had even wired its captains to "take no chances" during the storm. "Perhaps if there had been such advice extended to Captain McKay, there would be a different story to tell today," Hoover concluded.[128]

One inspector also raised the specter that the *Milwaukee* may have been overloaded when it sailed on October 22. "The car ferries . . . are probably being loaded more deeply than years ago when they first came out," he wrote, noting that the railroad cars in 1929 were much bigger and heavier than those in use when the *Milwaukee* came out in 1903. There was no evidence to suggest that the ferry lines had made any adjustments for the heavier loads, so ships like the *Milwaukee* were sailing with less freeboard than they had been intended to have. The inspector also lamented the fact that "there is no law of authority that [the Steamboat Inspection Service] possesses with reference to indicating what the freeboard shall be on the Great Lakes."[129]

"Of the lessons to be learned from this disaster, one stands out clear," Dickerson Hoover wrote in his report, "and that is the value of radio communications. We do believe that had radio communication been available from the *Milwaukee*, earlier search could have been made with the possibility of saving life." Hoover recommended that the Wireless Ship Act be changed to require vessels on the Great Lakes to be equipped with radio transmitters and receivers like ocean ships were.[130]

While most of those in the Great Lakes industry had fought tooth and nail to have their ships excluded from the Wireless Ship Act, some fleet owners had voluntarily installed radios on their vessels. In 1906 the Ann Arbor Railroad became one of the first fleets to install radios on its ships, and in 1910 the Pere Marquette Railroad followed suit. Both were competitors of the Grand Trunk Railroad in the car ferry trade across Lake Michigan.

On September 9, 1911, the Pere Marquette Railroad's *Pere Marquette 18* got caught out on the lake in a severe storm and began taking on water through a number of portholes that were smashed out by the pounding seas. When the pumps couldn't keep up with the incoming water and the stern of the ship continued to settle deeper in the water, the captain had the radio operator send out a message in Morse code asking for help.

The distress call was heard by the *Pere Marquette 17,* which arrived at the scene just as the flooded ferry sank. The ship's lifeboats were quickly lowered, and crewmembers from the *Pere Marquette 17* managed to pull thirty-two people from the stormy waters. Twenty-seven others went down with the ship or drowned before rescuers could get to them.[131] If the two car ferries hadn't been equipped with radios, all fifty-nine of those aboard the *Pere Marquette 18* may have perished. It was a clear demonstration of the practical utility of shipboard radios, but it was apparently lost on the managers of the Grand Trunk ferries.

In 1929 the U.S. Weather Bureau at Duluth began including weather observations from ships out on Lake Superior in their forecasts. Vessels with radiotelegraph equipment were encouraged to participate in the voluntary program by telegraphing in reports of wind and sea conditions they were encountering on the lake. The program was designed to reduce the variance between what the Weather Bureau was predicting in its forecasts and what was actually happening. The shipboard weather observer program was eventually extended to all the lakes, and it continues to operate today.[132]

While many observers of the shipping industry thought the needless loss of the *Milwaukee* and its crew would bring about sweeping changes in the regulation of shipping on the lakes, no major changes were made until 134 persons died in a September 8, 1934, fire aboard the cruise ship *Morro Castle* on a voyage from Havana to New York. Investigations conducted following the tragic fire, intentionally set by one of the ship's radio operators, found that both the crew and the Bureau of Navigation and Steamboat Inspection were responsible for the heavy loss of life.[133]

Under the leadership of President Franklin D. Roosevelt and Dickerson Hoover, assistant director of the Bureau of Navigation and Steamboat Inspection, the bureau was reorganized and given new powers. The Merchant Marine Act of 1936, which amended the Seamen's Act of 1915, changed the name of the bureau to the Bureau of Marine Inspection and Navigation. The reorganized agency was charged with the responsibility

52. The wrecked hull of the Canadian passenger and freight steamer *Hibou* is shown after being raised in Owen Sound of Georgian Bay in 1942. The 122-foot ship capsized and sank during a storm on November 21, 1936. Captain Norman McKay took his improperly loaded boat out into heavy seas on what was to be the little steamer's last trip of the season. Ten of the seventeen crewmembers aboard managed to escape by clinging to a life raft. After being salvaged, the ship was refitted and operated in the banana trade between Canada and South America. She was lost off Chile in 1953. (Ralph Roberts Collection)

of impaneling marine casualty investigation boards to investigate any casualties that resulted in the loss of life. A new technical division was also established within the agency with the power to approve the plans for any passenger vessels prior to the start of construction. The technical division was essentially the "corps of experts" the Steamboat Inspection Service had been wanting to establish since 1914. In fact, the language of the statute regarding the technical division was *identical* to the language the Steamboat Inspection Service had tried to get into the Seamen's Act after the *Eastland* capsized in 1915.

Despite another round of opposition from shipping companies and organizations like the Lake Carriers' Association, Roosevelt and Hoover were also able to ram through legislation in 1935 that required U.S. ships to have load lines. In 1936, each U.S. passenger and cargo vessel was required to have a Plimsoll mark on each side of its hull, showing the maximum level to which it could be loaded and ensuring that it operated with a safe amount of freeboard. Almost overnight, founderings resulting from overloading were virtually ended.

In 1942, President Roosevelt transferred the Bureau of Marine Inspection and Navigation to the Coast Guard, which had also taken over the Bureau of Lighthouses in 1939. The consolidated agency had

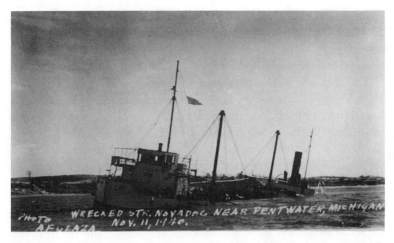

WRECKED STR. NOVADOC NEAR PENTWATER, MICHIGAN
NOV. 11, 1940.
PHOTO A.F.GLAZA

53. The 253-foot canaller *Novadoc* is shown wrecked along the beach at Pentwater, Michigan. The underpowered little Canadian freighter was driven ashore during the Armistice Day Storm of 1940. After the ship was battered by breaking seas for two days, a fishing tug managed to take seventeen survivors off the wreck. Two crewmen had been washed overboard during the storm. (A. F. Glaza Photo, Ralph Roberts Collection)

total responsibility for vessel safety in U.S. waters. Their powers ranged from approving plans for the construction of ships to inspecting and documenting vessels, testing and licensing officers, and issuing seamen's papers to unlicensed seafarers. They also maintained the system of aids to navigation and operated the lighthouses and lifesaving stations along U.S. coasts, including those on the Great Lakes. In addition, the Coast Guard had its own fleet of lifeboats, buoy tenders, and icebreakers.[134]

Henry Steinbrenner, 1953

There have always been one or two ships around the lakes that seem to be jinxed. Bad luck has a habit of following them. One such ship was the *Henry Steinbrenner*.

The *Steinbrenner*'s reputation as a hard luck boat started before she was even launched. While she was still under construction at the Jenks Shipyard in Port Huron, Michigan, in the spring of 1901, a fire totally destroyed the shipyard. The partially completed freighter was saved only because firefighters sprayed the hull with water to keep it from being warped by the intense heat.[135]

In December 1909 the *Steinbrenner* sank in shallow water in the lower St. Marys River after colliding with the steamer *Harry A. Berwind* during a snowstorm. Over the winter the damaged freighter was salvaged and repaired, and she was back in service the following season (see Chapter 3).

The ship was involved in a second collision on October 11, 1923. With Whitefish Bay socked in by a combination of heavy fog and thick smoke from nearby forest fires, the *Steinbrenner* was feeling its way along near Isle Parisienne when it collided with the steamer *John McCartney Kennedy*. One of the *Kennedy*'s bow anchors opened a four-foot hole in the *Steinbrenner*'s bow. Fortunately, the gash was just above the *Steinbrenner*'s waterline, or she might have made a second trip to the bottom.

Even then, repairs cost her owners $5,000, a sizable sum in 1923.[136] Writing that big check surely didn't make Henry Steinbrenner very happy. Steinbrenner, the ship's namesake and president of the Kinsman Transit Company, wasn't one to willingly spend money unless he knew his company was going to get a favorable return on the investment. You can be assured that the frugal Steinbrenner didn't consider patching boats to be a good investment.

Henry Steinbrenner died in 1929, but he would undoubtedly have been pleased to learn that after the 1923 collision, the ship that bore his name operated for thirty successive seasons without a major mishap. That string came to an end in the spring of 1953, however.

Just as the sky was lightening in the east on the morning of May 10, 1953, the venerable freighter departed the Great Northern Railway's docks at Superior, Wisconsin, on her way down to Lake Erie with 6,800 tons of iron ore in her holds. As Captain Albert Stiglin maneuvered his 427-foot steamer out of the busy harbor, it looked as if it was going to be an absolutely gorgeous spring day. With a strong southerly breeze blowing, the temperature already stood at sixty-five degrees.

Clad only in shirtsleeves, the boatswain and his crew of deckhands set about the task of winching shut the telescoping hatch covers on the *Steinbrenner*'s twelve hatches as the ship cleared the lighthouse at the end of the pier. If they were smiling a little more than usual as they began screwing down the 336 clamps—28 per hatch—that held the sliding hatch covers in place, it wasn't just because the weather was unseasonably warm. The captain had decided that they didn't have to put the canvas tarps over the hatches, and that saved them a lot of work.

Captain Stiglin would later recall that when the freighter sailed out of the harbor that morning, Lake Superior was "smoother than a pond."[137] He and his crew were enjoying the unusually balmy weather, especially since they knew it wasn't supposed to last. Gale flags had already been run up before the freighter cleared Superior, and temperatures were supposed to plummet to below freezing when a cold front passed through later in the day. Winds trailing the cold front were expected to blow at thirty to thirty-five miles an hour, with occasional thundersqualls. If the forecast proved to be accurate, the lake would be a little choppy by evening, but nothing the venerable old *Steinbrenner* couldn't handle.

As predicted, the winds continued to increase in strength as the *Steinbrenner* steamed eastward across the lake. By 4:30 P.M., waves were being taken over the deck and Captain Stiglin sent a couple of his men out to make sure that all the hatch clamps were tightened down. With the deck steadily awash, many of the ten men in the deck department who lived at the bow of the ship decided not to go aft for supper.

While newer ships on the lake had tunnels below the main deck that crewmembers could use to move between the ship's fore and aft cabin areas during inclement weather, they were invented many years after the *Steinbrenner* had been built. If you wanted to go aft on the old Kinsman freighter, you had to cross the long, open deck. Instead of tunnels, the *Steinbrenner* had a "lifeline," a steel cable rigged down the middle of the deck between the fore and aft cabins. A number of "traveling lines" hung down from the lifeline. The top end of each traveling line was formed into an eye around the lifeline, so the traveling lines could slide along the lifeline. If a crewman needed to cross the deck when it was icy or awash by waves, he either held onto the end of one of the dangling lines or tied it around his waist so that he wouldn't be washed overboard. You were still likely to get wet and cold, though, so many of the crewmen from the forward end simply skipped meals if the weather was too bad. Those who planned ahead usually kept a loaf of bread, or box of crackers, and some peanut butter and jelly in their rooms for just such situations.

By 6:30 P.M., winds had increased to sixty miles an hour—far in excess of the velocities predicted by the Weather Bureau—with gusts as high as eighty miles an hour. Driven by the hurricane-force winds that swung rapidly around to the east-northeast, the surface of Lake Superior was soon being raked by waves that were nineteen or twenty feet high. Thermometers dropped just about as fast as the wind speeds went up. The balmy temperatures of the morning plummeted to only nineteen degrees after the cold front passed. Rain fell in a torrential downpour, then turned to driving snow when the front passed.

At 8 P.M., a leaf in the hatch cover on the next-to-last hatch worked loose, and the third mate and three seamen grabbed onto traveling lines and went aft to secure it. In the process, a wave breaking over the deck knocked Tom Wells, a deck watch, through the opening in the hatch they were trying to secure. Fortunately, he managed to hold onto his traveling line when he fell, and he dangled in midair just below the deck level. After the wave passed, the other crewmen were able to pull Wells out of the hold. After the four had finished securing the hatch, they went aft to the galley, feeling it was too dangerous out on deck to try to go all the way forward.

What had started out as such a fine day for Captain Stiglin and his crew had turned into a nightmare. Worried about his ship, Stiglin spent the night in the pilothouse. He kept her headed into the seas, but cut back speed to reduce the strain on the hull. Many times throughout the night he asked to have the deck lights turned on so he could make sure all the hatch covers were in place. When he did, though, the sight of the high waves rolling the length of the deck almost made him sick to his stomach. He knew that some water from each wave was finding its way into the hold through the narrow gaps between the overlapping leaves of the hatch covers. Even worse, the angry waves were beating hell out of the hatch covers and the clamps that held them. Time and again he thought about the twelve hatch tarps that were folded and stowed in the crosswalk above the engine room. If wishing could have made it so, the tarps would have been battened down over the hatches . . . where they belonged.

At about 5 A.M. on May 11, the leaf on the number 11 hatch that had worked loose the previous evening came loose again. This time, however, there was no way anyone dared to go out on deck to secure it. With the hatch cover ajar and waves rolling down both sides of the *Steinbrenner*'s deck, water immediately began pouring into the cargo hold. The only thing Captain Stiglin could do was call the engine room and tell them to begin pumping the hold.

Around 6 A.M., the movement of the beleaguered ship became notice-ably sluggish as water continued to flood into the cargo hold. By 7 A.M. other hatch covers had worked loose, increasing the amount of water flooding into the hold. In a desperate act, Stiglin ordered "full speed ahead" on the engines and put his ship into a hard turn to port, hoping that by turning the stern to the sea the aft cabin would shelter the deck enough that his men could secure the hatches. When the ship finally labored around onto the reciprocal course, however, the seas breaking over the deck were even worse than before. Stiglin quickly brought the ship back around to its previous course and again reduced speed.

At that point, Captain Al Stiglin knew the situation was hopeless. Taking a deep breath to calm his nerves, he told the mate to have the crew dress warmly and put their lifejackets on. It looked like they might have to abandon ship. Stiglin then went to the radio in the corner of the pilothouse and made the radio call that no captain wants to make: "Mayday, mayday, mayday," Stiglin said over the lump in his throat. "This is the *Henry Steinbrenner.*"

Immediately, the ears of all those aboard ships or at shore stations within range of the *Steinbrenner's* radio were riveted to Captain Stiglin's transmission. Stiglin went on to announce that his ship was foundering just over fifteen miles due south of Isle Royale Light, then he repeated the entire message.

After Captain Stiglin finished his businesslike message and set the microphone down next to the radio, there was a long silence. Then the radio crackled to life again as ships that had heard the distress call responded.

"Roger, *Steinbrenner,* this is the *Joseph H. Thompson.* We're 30 miles behind you, but we'll get there as quick as we can."

"Roger, *Steinbrenner,* this is the *Wilfred H. Sykes.* We're about 35 miles ahead of you, and on our way."

"*Steinbrenner,* this is the *D. M. Clemson* . . ."

In all, six freighters heard the distress call, and all six immediately set courses for the stricken ship's location. The Coast Guard buoytender *Woodrush* was also dispatched to the scene from its station at Duluth. At Coast Guard stations at the Portage Ship Canal on the Keweenaw Peninsula, and from Grand Marais and Two Harbors along Minnesota's north shore, Coast Guard boat crews boarded their little forty-foot motor lifeboats and bravely headed them out into the towering black seas. Some would later say that it was foolish to take a forty-foot boat out into that killer storm, but the Coast Guardsmen in the lifeboat crews were sailors, and there were other sailors in peril out on Lake Superior that morning who needed their help. In addition to the various search vessels, Coast Guard helicopters and Air Force fixed-wing aircraft also headed for the *Steinbrenner's* location.

At about 7:30 A.M., the hatch covers on the three after hatches let go completely. Without hesitation, Stiglin turned on the general alarm, alerting crewmembers to go to their lifeboat stations. He then moved the indicator on the engine order telegraph to the "stop" position. The watch engineer in the engine room acknowledged the order.

With the stern of the *Steinbrenner* sinking dangerously low in the water, Captain Stiglin sounded the "abandon ship" signal on the ship's whistle at 7:36. There was no longer any question about the fate of the old freighter.

Stiglin and the nine other men in the deck department who were on the forward end of the ship clustered around the pontoon-type life raft that was located on top of the forecastle deck at the bow. At the stern, the other twenty-one crewmembers had begun to prepare the two lifeboats for launching as soon as they heard the "abandon ship" signal blown. Quite a number of the men didn't have lifejackets on, even though they had been instructed to put them on more than half an hour earlier.

The lifeboat on the starboard side was cranked out and lowered to the level of the deck. For some unknown reason, only seven men climbed aboard the boat that was designed to hold up to twenty-four persons, and the boat was lowered into the water and released from the boat hooks.

Across the boat deck, crewmen struggled to launch the port lifeboat, but they couldn't get it to swing out. With their ship sinking out from under them, they unhooked the boat from the falls, so it would at least float free when the *Steinbrenner* went down. Two men climbed in to insert the plug in the drain hole in the bottom of the boat so it wouldn't flood and sink when it went into the water.[138]

There was some shouting from the men in the starboard lifeboat, which was still alongside the hull. All of a sudden, the men on the boat deck realized that the lifeboat's painter line was still tied to the ship's railing. Third Assistant Engineer Art Morse was still on the stern of the *Steinbrenner,* and he dashed across the deck and untied the line. "You're on your own now, boys," he shouted to the men in the lifeboat, waving his arm in a seemingly casual gesture of farewell. It didn't appear that Morse had any intention of abandoning the sinking ship.

There was a momentary break in the heavy snowfall, and the men at the freighter's bow caught a glimpse of Isle Royale. It looked so close that one of the crewmen, Kenneth Kumm, climbed over the rail and prepared to dive into the water to swim to Isle Royale. One of his shipmates grabbed him and shouted that the water was too cold and that he'd never make it. As he paused to think about the warning, a wave caught Kumm and washed him down the middle of the ship, directly over the last four or five hatches, and over the side.

When Kumm finally rose to the surface, the starboard lifeboat was only about ten feet away. As he started to swim toward the lifeboat, there was a loud gurgling noise behind him. When he turned to look, he saw the mortally wounded *Henry Steinbrenner* dive for the bottom of Lake Superior.

Swimming more frantically than ever toward the lifeboat, Kumm felt the impact of a concussion as the *Steinbrenner*'s boilers exploded. The air around him was suddenly filled with flying debris, and he felt a brief wave of heat pass through the bitterly cold water of Lake Superior, the last blast of steam from the boilers of the *Henry Steinbrenner*.[139]

As the stern of his ship went under, Captain Stiglin looked aft. "I saw the 2 lifeboats clear the ship," he later recalled. "I know that all the men were clear, for I caught a brief glimpse of the 2 boats clear off the after deck." Stiglin and the men around the life raft scrambled aboard as the ship sank out from under them. With water swirling up the deck, it floated free for a moment, then a giant wave caught the six- by twelve-foot raft and flipped it over, throwing its passengers into the water. After what seemed like an eternity, Al Stiglin surfaced—directly under the raft. Ducking under a pontoon, Stiglin popped up in the swirling waters next to the raft and pulled himself aboard. Only six of the original ten passengers managed to climb back onto the raft.[140]

As the waves finally ripped the port lifeboat free of its cradle, one of the two crewmen in it was thrown overboard and the other seaman was hurled against the side of the steel boat and mortally injured. After the ship sank, Keith Kumm and another crewmember managed to pull themselves into the boat, which had a foot-long gash in its side.

For the next four and a half hours, the fourteen survivors of the *Henry Steinbrenner* were tossed around by the massive swells as though they were on a roller-coaster ride that would never end. Those who hadn't been thrown into the frigid water when the boat went down were soon soaked to the skin by the frenzy of spray that was whipped off the top of the waves by the bitter winds.

Captain Stiglin had once told some of his crewmen that the raft was their best bet if the ship ever went down. Now he was doubting those words. The raft was supposed to be able to carry fifteen men, but with just six aboard it was terribly crowded, and the men were literally lying on top of each other as they tried to keep from being washed over the short boards that enclosed the deck area. All of the men suffered horribly from the cold, and First Mate Andy Kraft soon lost consciousness.

The seven men in the starboard lifeboat huddled under the canvas sea anchor that was stowed in the bow of the boat. "That's what kept us alive," said Al Augsburger, an oiler. "Another half hour and we would have been dead." At one point a Coast Guard helicopter flew over, but there was no indication that they spotted the tiny lifeboat amidst the giant seas.

The damaged port lifeboat was almost filled with water. Ken Kumm and the other survivor in the boat were soon numbed by the piercing cold, and it was all they could do to hold on so they weren't washed away. Kumm later said that the only reason the two survived was that they were beefy fellows, carrying a lot of extra weight from eating the always-plentiful steamboat food.

The *Wilfred Sykes* and *Joseph H. Thompson* arrived off Isle Royale at about the same time, just after noon, and the steamer *D. M. Clemson* wasn't far behind. The *Thompson*, then the longest ship on the lakes, soon sighted the life raft. Captain Bob Lang carefully maneuvered the giant freighter alongside the raft, and his men took the five survivors and Kraft's body aboard. The survivors literally had to be hoisted up the side of the *Thompson*. It was obvious to all who witnessed the sight that those aboard the raft probably wouldn't have survived much longer.

Captain George Fisher of the *Wilfred Sykes*, then the second-longest ship on the Great Lakes, spotted one of the lifeboats when it was lifted by a wave, and he quickly pulled his ship as close to the boat as he could. A line was then thrown to the lifeboat, and it was pulled alongside the *Sykes*. The freighter's Jacob's ladder was lowered, and Ken Kumm grabbed onto one of the lower rungs, but he didn't have enough strength left to make the steep climb up to the deck of the *Sykes*. With Kumm holding on with what was later referred to as a "death grip," the crewmen on the *Sykes* pulled the ladder aboard with Kumm dangling from it.

Before the other *Steinbrenner* crewmen could be brought aboard, the lifeboat lifted high on a swell and the line holding it alongside the *Sykes* snapped. Before crewmen could get another line over, the lifeboat was carried past the steamer's stern. In the pilothouse, Captain Fisher quickly got his ship under way. As soon as the engine reached full power, he brought the *Sykes* about in a big sweeping turn. As the freighter churned through the angry seas, Fisher timed the turn so that at the end of the circle the *Sykes* would be close to the drifting lifeboat. The maneuver took almost ninety minutes.

Fearing that the one man still alive in the boat wouldn't be able to catch or secure a line thrown to him, and that the lifeboat would simply drift on past the *Sykes* a second time, Fisher's third mate and nine crewmembers volunteered to launch one of their own boats to retrieve the *Steinbrenner*'s lifeboat. It was a risky proposition, though. Very few Great Lakes sailors have any experience rowing a lifeboat. If they do, it was undoubtedly gained in a flat calm harbor during a Coast Guard inspection at spring fit-out, not on Lake Superior in a hurricane-strength storm.[141] If the crewmen from the *Sykes* couldn't handle their boat once they got it into the water, there was a real chance that there would be yet another lifeboat adrift on the lake.

Despite their inexperience and the potential hazards, the ten men performed their rescue mission admirably. They rowed briskly over to the *Steinbrenner*'s boat, held themselves alongside it, transferred the one survivor and the body of the dead crewmember into their boat, and then headed back to the *Sykes*. In just a few minutes, they were all back aboard the freighter.

Captain Art Everett and his crew on the U.S. Steel steamer *D. M. Clemson* rescued the seven men in the *Steinbrenner*'s starboard lifeboat. "When I saw that big tin stack coming through the water, it was beautiful," said Al Augsburger. "It was like a miracle."[142]

The *Clemson* missed the bobbing lifeboat on its first pass, and Captain Everett had to bring the steamer around for a second try. Augsburger and the other six survivors were too weak to climb the ladder lowered to them, so they had to be hoisted aboard the *Clemson* with a stout Manila line.

The *Sykes*, *Thompson*, and *Clemson* continued to crisscross the wreck scene, along with a number of other U.S. and Canadian ships that responded to the distress call. The bodies of a number of dead crewmembers were retrieved from the water. By midafternoon, Coast Guard vessels were arriving, and the three freighters carrying the survivors from the *Steinbrenner* departed for their planned destinations. The *Sykes* headed for Superior, while the *Clemson* and *Thompson*, both downbound, went on to the Soo.

While the *Thompson* was completing its run across Lake Superior, an enterprising newspaper reporter from Detroit scooped other papers by talking with Captain Stiglin by radiotelephone. Stiglin, who sounded weary and discouraged to the reporter, summed up the loss of his ship by saying, "We ran into a little more sea than she could take." He went on to praise his crew. "There was no panic," he said. "Everything was orderly."[143]

The reporters, who invariably follow in the wake of a sinking ship like a swarm of voracious sharks, weren't the only ones who wanted to talk with Captain Stiglin and the other survivors. Most of the survivors from the *Steinbrenner* arrived in Detroit by airplane on Tuesday, May 12; the following day the Coast Guard convened a board of inquiry at the federal building there.

Many of the survivors blamed the sinking on the condition of the ship. "Nothing worked as it should aboard the ship," testified Norm Bragg, a watchman. "For my money, it just wasn't seaworthy." Bragg was one of several crewmembers who said that the threads on many of the hatch clamps were stripped, including those on the troublesome number 11 hatch.[144]

Others disagreed, feeling that the *Steinbrenner* had been seaworthy. She was definitely an "old bucket," Al Augsburger testified, but he noted that they'd been through some pretty good blows in her the previous season without any difficulties.

Those who had gathered at the ship's stern in the minutes just before the *Steinbrenner* sank also told a story that was at odds with Captain Stiglin's assertion that everything had been orderly. Even though Stiglin had ordered everyone to put their lifejackets on more than an hour before the ship sank, the mate and three members of the deck gang who had been stranded overnight at the stern didn't have lifejackets, nor did several members of the engine room staff who had been on duty when the general alarm had gone off. They couldn't get to their rooms because of the seas washing over the deck, but in the turmoil none of them remembered that four spare lifejackets were stored in the engine room.

Oiler Augsburger was one who testified that there was "nothing orderly" about the actions on the stern of the *Steinbrenner* that morning. For example, he told investigators that one crewman had brought some blankets to keep them warm in the boats. Instead of throwing them into the boats, however, the crewman stuffed them down one of the engine room ventilators. Others told about the premature launching of the starboard lifeboat, and how they couldn't get the port boat swung out.

When the Coast Guard board released its findings two months later, they concluded that the sinking was "an act of God," due to the adverse weather and mountainous seas. The *Steinbrenner*, they said, was seaworthy. After all, she had just had her five-year hull and machinery inspection by the American Bureau of Shipping the previous February, and Coast Guard inspectors had gone over her at fit-out, just a few weeks before she went down, and had found her fit.

The claims that many of the hatch clamps had stripped threads was basically dismissed by the members of the board. "The harrowing experience, plus considerable newspaper attention, caused a tendency for exaggeration," they concluded. The few stripped threads that might have existed, they felt, didn't contribute to the casualty. The problem was really a "general loosening of clamps with the ship working in a heavy sea, metal to metal, metal clamps turned down on metal hatch covers, that aided the heavy seas in loosening the clamps."

The board felt that if tarpaulins had been battened down over the hatch covers, water would have been prevented from freely entering the ship's hold, but they upheld Captain Stiglin's decision not to put them on. Any "reasonably prudent master" might have done the same, given the favorable weather conditions when the ship left Superior and the erroneous weather forecast he received before departing. Based on their investigation, the Coast Guard board members concluded that "there is no evidence that any licensed or certificated personnel of the vessel committed any act of incompetence, inattention to duty, or negligence, or willful violation of any law or regulation."

The board did, however make a number of recommendations based on what they learned during the *Steinbrenner* inquiry. They suggested, for example, that extra lifejackets be carried in the pilothouse, in the engine room, and in a watertight box on the boat deck. They also felt that the use of tarps should be made mandatory on ships with telescoping hatches, except from May 15 through September 15, what's known as the midsummer sailing period.

When P. A. Ovenden, the head of the Coast Guard's merchant vessel inspection division, reviewed the board's report, however, he emphatically disagreed with the findings. The foundering of the *Steinbrenner* was no "act of God" in his book—a master is *required* to make sure that "hatches are closed and made properly tight" before he takes the ship out. As he saw it, the *Steinbrenner* sank, not through some act of God, but because Captain Stiglin hadn't had the tarps put on. Stiglin should be held responsible for the sinking and the subsequent loss of seventeen lives, he concluded.

Ovenden recommended that the Coast Guard revoke Captain Stiglin's license. Going well beyond that, he forwarded duplicates of the board's records to the U.S. Attorney's Office. "Such record contains evidence of probable criminal liability on the part of the master of the *Henry Steinbrenner*," he wrote.[145]

Many sailors, particularly captains, vehemently disagreed with the head of the vessel inspection division. His referral of the matter for possible criminal prosecution scared the hell out of them. If all Coast Guard officials were as stern as the head of the vessel inspection division, the jails and prisons around the Great Lakes would undoubtedly be housing many captains. The loss of the *Steinbrenner*, they argued, was the result of an inaccurate weather forecast. If Captain Stiglin, or any other captain, knew his ship was going out into a hurricane, the tarps would have been put on. As much as they disagreed with the head of the Coast Guard's inspection division, though, most captains started using tarps on their ships a lot more often after the sinking of the *Steinbrenner*.

Most, but not all. Not Captain A. P. Goodrow of Bethlehem Transportation's steamer *Maryland*, for example. On September 12, 1953, almost exactly four months after the loss of the *Steinbrenner*, and only two months after the controversial finding by the head of the Coast Guard's vessel inspection division, the *Maryland* was caught in a freak squall on Lake Superior. Since bad weather hadn't been forecast, her hatch covers hadn't been tarped. After battling high seas and fifty-five-mile-an-hour winds for five hours, the *Maryland* had two of her hatch covers ripped off and water began flooding into the cargo hold. Acutely aware that if the hatch covers weren't replaced the ship was going to sink, crewmembers risked their lives to go out on the storm-washed deck and wrestle them back into place. Despite that, Captain Goodrow couldn't keep the *Maryland* out of the troughs, and she went aground near Marquette a few hours later. Twenty of the crew were taken off with a breeches buoy, and eleven others were lifted off by a Coast Guard helicopter.[146] The lesson of the *Steinbrenner* had apparently been lost on Captain Goodrow.

Carl D. Bradley, 1958

There were times when Captain Roland Bryan couldn't help but feel like an outsider on his own ship, the *Carl D. Bradley*. Bryan was one of only ten men in the *Bradley*'s crew of thirty-five who weren't from the ship's home port of Rogers City, Michigan, a small community on the northwest shore of Lake Huron. Four other crewmembers, while not from Rogers City, were from the nearby communities of Onaway and Metz in Presque Isle County.

The *Bradley* was one of nine ships of the Bradley Transportation Line, a fleet that had operated out of the Port of Calcite at Rogers City since 1912. In 1952 the Bradley fleet became a subsidiary of U.S. Steel, which also owned Pittsburgh Steamship, the largest fleet on the Great Lakes. U.S. Steel was also the owner of the sprawling limestone quarry at Rogers City. It was because of the limestone quarry, in fact, that the Bradley fleet had been formed. The gray-hulled ships in the fleet, all of which were self-unloaders, transported limestone mined and processed at the quarry to customers around the lakes, including steel mills, cement manufacturers, construction firms, and chemical companies.

The Bradley boats were always crewed primarily by men from Rogers City. In fact, around the lakes it was common to hear the Bradley boats referred to derisively as "the Polack fleet" because so many of the sailors from Rogers City were of Polish descent. The fleet's personnel office almost always had a list of Rogers City men who were waiting for job openings on the boats, so it was fairly unusual for sailors who weren't from the local area to be hired. Occasionally, however, they would need someone with an oiler's ticket or a mate's license, and if none of the local men on the waiting list had the necessary rating they would have to hire an "out-of-towner."

Many of the out-of-towners didn't stick with the Bradley fleet too long. The word around the lakes was that the Rogers City sailors didn't take kindly to outsiders. If you weren't from Rogers City, you weren't always treated too well on the Bradley ships.

It's fairly easy to understand why someone who wasn't from Rogers City might feel uncomfortable in the Bradley fleet. There was an sense of community on the Rogers City boats that was quite unusual within the Great Lakes shipping industry. Most of the crewmen had known each other virtually all their lives. Hell, many were related! If you were going to talk unkindly about someone from Rogers City, maybe a crewman you'd sailed with on another Bradley boat, you had to be careful. There was a pretty good chance that the person you were talking to was a friend or relative.

After sailing on the Bradley boats for twenty-four years, fifty-two-year-old Rollie Bryan was quite comfortable with all that, even though he still called Loudonville, New York, home. When the Rogers City men talked in their particular local patois, conversations were liberally sprinkled with nicknames, smatterings of Polish, and oblique references to events of the past, Bryan generally knew what they were talking about. He was even comfortable with a menu that regularly included kielbasa—Polish sausage—purchased from a neighborhood market in the "Polish town" section of Rogers City, and raw, chopped steak liberally accented with onions that was a tradition around the holidays.

In most ways, Bryan had adapted to the peculiarities of the Bradley boats. There were, however, still plenty of days when he felt like an outsider. When the *Bradley* pulled into Calcite, for example, which it did once or twice a week, any crewmembers who weren't on watch usually headed home while the boat was being loaded. The married crewmembers went home to their wives and children. The sailors who were single, as Bryan was, generally stopped to see their parents before meeting up with girlfriends or former school chums, often congregating at local hangouts like the Cozy Corner and Greka's Tavern. Often gone from Rogers City for only a couple days at a time, the sailors stayed unusually involved in the lives of their families, friends, and community. In that way, Rollie

Bryan and the other "outsiders" on the *Carl D. Bradley* would always be different from their Rogers City shipmates.

In the 1950s, sailors on the lakes didn't get regular vacations. While most of the *Bradley* sailors saw their families and friends every few days, crewmembers who weren't from Rogers City seldom got home or saw their loved ones during the entire eight-month shipping season. Bryan's girlfriend, for example, lived in Port Huron, Michigan. About the only time he got to see her during the season was when the *Bradley* got one of its infrequent loads to a stone dock in Port Huron, or when Florence would occasionally be waiting along the riverbank when the ship passed. On those occasions, Rollie Bryan would blow her a salute on the ship's steam whistle and go out onto the bridge wing and wave at her. Such "meetings" were always bittersweet, a reminder of how much better the Rogers City men had it.

That's one reason Captain Bryan was so happy when one of his mates came into his room during the late-evening hours of November 17, 1958, to tell him that they were almost done unloading at the U.S. Steel mill at Gary, Indiana. As soon as the last of the cargo of limestone was dumped onto the shoreside pile, Rollie Bryan would head his ship up Lake Michigan, bound for the winter layup dock at Rogers City. It was his ship's forty-sixth and final trip of the 1958 season. In a couple of days, he would be finished for the season and finally free to visit *his* family and friends . . . especially Florence.

As he made his way up to the pilothouse, Bryan wished that the weather forecast was a little better. Storm warnings had been posted, and a pretty good wind had already kicked up out of the southwest. If they weren't on their way to the layup dock, Bryan might have considered staying at the dock in Gary to see what developed with the weather. The *Bradley* was, after all, not a new boat anymore. Thirty-one seasons had passed under her keel. That didn't make her an old boat, for sure, but the *Bradley* was definitely "middle-aged." She was due for her five-year American Bureau of Shipping and Coast Guard inspections before she sailed the following spring, and the company planned to do a lot of work on her over the winter to repair accumulated damage.

She needed it, too! Her cargo holds were in pretty bad shape. There were places where you could actually see through the steel bulkheads that separated them. The sloping floors of the holds weren't in very good condition either, and there were enough little leaks in the ship's hull that they regularly had to pump water out of the ballast tanks.

Florence always worried about him when there was a storm on the lakes, but he'd reassured her that she could rest easy. He knew his ship was "pretty ripe," and he wasn't about to take it out in any bad storms. Even the office had told him to "take it easy" with the old girl that fall.

Despite the gloomy weather forecast, Rollie Bryan decided to head the *Bradley* up the lake. It had been a long season, and the crew was anxious to get home . . . and he was anxious to get off the boat. If he took a delay at Gary, everybody in the crew would be complaining loudly. Besides, with the wind southwest, they could sneak up the west side of the lake and stay in the lee of the Wisconsin shore. When they got up north and had to cut across the lake, the wind would be on their stern, so she ought to ride pretty good. In thirty hours they'd be back in Rogers City, and the season would be over!

After leaving the dock at Gary at 9:30 P.M. on November 17, the *Bradley* steamed northward through the night, beachcombing along the west shore for protection from the wind. By the following afternoon, weather conditions were worsening. Winds had increased to sixty to sixty-five miles an hour, and the surface of the lake had been piled into waves that were twenty to twenty-five feet high. Nearing Cana Island, the point where the *Bradley* would have to turn to the northeast and cut across to the Michigan shore, Captain Bryan called back to the galley and asked Steward John Zoho if he could feed the crew a little early. They might roll some when they made the turn, he explained, and it would be better if Zoho had dinner out of the way and everything secured in the galley before they made the haul. Zoho agreed.

Deckwatch Frank Mays, a twenty-six-year-old Rogers City native, was on the 4-to-8 watch, and he went aft to eat an early supper before he went to work. He hurried back along the port side of the deck, not wanting to stay out in the bitter wind any longer than he had to. If the weather had been much worse, Mays would probably have used the tunnel to go aft. Unlike the straight-deckers that had a walking tunnel just below each side of the spar deck, self-unloaders like the *Bradley* had only a single conveyor tunnel that ran down the center of the ship below the cargo hold. It wasn't as clean or convenient as a walking tunnel, but at least you could get aft if waves were breaking over the deck.

While Mays ate his supper in the crowded and noisy messroom, he talked with Deckhand Alva Budnick, his cousin. Zoho, wanting to get the galley secured before the old man hauled the ship around to head across the lake, hurried the crewmen along. "Eat it, and beat it," was the clear message they got that evening. Not eager to upset the cook, Mays finished his meal and went to work. On his way forward, he went through the conveyor tunnel, stopping to turn on the sump pumps to pump out the water that had accumulated in the tunnel when the cargo hold had been washed down after unloading. With that task finished, Mays continued through the tunnel to the forward end and the assorted cleaning chores that would take up the balance of his watch.

At 5:30 P.M., Mays and Deckhand Gary Price were working in the dunnage room below the main deck in the bow of the ship when they heard what Mays later described as "a loud thud." "You hear a lot of sounds on a boat," Mays remembered, "but we instantly knew this one was wrong."

As Mays and Price hurriedly climbed the ladder to the main deck level, Captain Bryan and First Mate Elmer Fleming, forty-three, were in the pilothouse. When they heard the unusual noise, they both instantly turned and looked aft along the *Bradley*'s deck. What they saw immediately struck terror in their souls: their ship was breaking in half! There was a wide crack all the way across the middle of the deck, and the stern was sagging badly.

Fleming knew intuitively that the ship was going to sink. Picking up the radio mike, he hurriedly broadcast a distress call. "Mayday, mayday, mayday!" Fleming shouted, making no effort to sound calm. "This is the *Carl D. Bradley*. We are breaking in two and sinking. We are twelve miles southwest of Gull Island. The *Bradley* is going down! Any ships in the area, please come to our aid."

While Fleming repeated the message, Rollie Bryan flipped on the general alarm and immediately began blowing the "abandon ship" signal on the whistle. He then reached over and jammed the handle on the engine order telegraph to the "stop" position. "Run, grab your lifejackets," Bryan yelled to the wheelsman and watchman who were in the pilothouse. "Get to the lifeboat!"

In the radio rooms of Coast Guard stations, in the pilothouses of several ships at anchor in northern Lake Michigan, and at the small office of Central Radio near the loading dock at Rogers City, horrified radio operators monitored Elmer Fleming's distress call. In the background, they could clearly hear Rollie Bryan shouting for his men to get their lifejackets and get to the lifeboats. A radio operator at station WAD in Port Washington, Wisconsin, answered Fleming's distress call, requesting confirmation of the *Bradley*'s position. Fleming had no sooner given it to him then the ship broke in half, the radio went dead, and the lights went out. All of a sudden, Elmer Fleming realized that his lifejacket was down in his room, and he ran down the stairs to get it. Despite the experience of the *Steinbrenner* five years earlier, no spare lifejackets were carried in the *Bradley*'s pilothouse.

Mays and Price had looked out one of the rear doors of the forward cabin that led onto the main deck, and they were startled by what they saw. "The aft section sagged so badly that you had to look hard to see it," Mays recalled later. "The ship was humped about 8 feet amidships." With the general alarm bells clanging and the ship's whistle blasting out the "abandon ship" signal, Frank Mays raced to his room to get his wallet and watch.

After Mays and Fleming made quick trips to their rooms, they hurried up to the deck behind the pilothouse, where a pontoon-type raft was located. By then, the *Bradley* was listing heavily to port and rolling badly in the high seas. Mays saw Captain Bryan and several other crewmen trying to work their way along the rail toward the high side of the pilothouse deck. Just then, the ship lurched abruptly to port and Mays and Fleming were both thrown into the forty-degree water. When they surfaced, the raft was floating nearby and they quickly climbed onto it. The bow of the *Bradley* had already sunk out of sight, but they could see the stern of the ship. "We could see right into the cargo hold, and it was filling with water," said Mays. Men were running on deck, trying to free the lifeboats. Then she was gone."

The stern section tipped up, the propeller high in the air, before it, too, dove toward the bottom of the lake. "Then we saw a flash, and heard an explosion as the cold water crushed her hot boilers," said Mays. "It was the most utterly fascinating, horrifying, and unbelievable moment of my life."

Mays and Fleming could hear the shouts of shipmates in the water, but in the pitch blackness, with the raft rising and falling on the huge waves, they couldn't see anyone. Instead, they started shouting, "Over here, over here." Minutes later, the two helped Dennis Meredith, a twenty-five-year-old deckhand, and Gary Strzelecki, a twenty-one-year-old deck-watch, onto the eight- by ten-foot raft. They heard other crewmembers yelling, but those on the raft couldn't see them. In a few minutes the powerful wind and seas pushed the raft away from the wreck scene, and the only noise they heard was the roar of the wind and the pounding of their adrenaline-pumped hearts.

There was a survival kit on the raft, and Fleming dug it out. Inside were a number of parachute-type signal flares, and the mate fired two into the air, which was instantly flooded with an eerie red glow.

Wet and painfully cold, the four survivors huddled together on the raft. Above them, the black sky was filled with the incessant shriek of the wind. Around them, the violent seas slapped at the raft and hurled stinging spray at the men. Suddenly, a huge wave flipped the raft over and spilled them into the water. Mays, Fleming, and Strzelecki climbed back aboard, but Dennis Meredith had disappeared beneath the black sea. Left floating on the water were the lifejacket and sweatshirt that he had somehow slipped out of when he was dumped off the raft.

Not long after, Mays, Fleming, and Strzelecki saw the lights of a ship approaching, its spotlights sweeping the water. Unknown to the three survivors, the German freighter *Christian Sartori* had been downbound on Lake Michigan only about four miles ahead of the *Bradley*. Although those aboard the *Sartori* didn't hear Fleming's distress call, they did see the bright flash of light when the *Bradley*'s boilers blew up. Captain Paul Mueller suspected they were seeing a ship in trouble, and he immediately altered course to steer for the location where they had seen the flash. Laboring badly in the towering seas, it took the *Sartori* two hours to reach the scene. "We could see their spotlights," said Mays, "but it was like looking through a fog or mist. The wind was blowing so hard that the water just filled the air." Fleming scrambled to fire another signal flare, but the flares had been drenched and he couldn't get any to ignite. The three screamed as loud as they could, but the lights of the ship moved slowly past them and disappeared in the distance.

The balance of the night was a nightmare for the three survivors. The raft was upset by the waves many times, and each time the battered and worn sailors struggled back aboard. Just after dawn, Gary Strzelecki had had enough. "He said he didn't want to stay on the raft anymore," Mays said. "He jumped off just after dawn. The last time I saw Gary, he was swimming away in the fog."

About an hour later, a search aircraft spotted the raft twenty miles north of where the *Bradley* had gone down. The position of the raft was radioed to the Coast Guard Cutter *Sundew,* and its crew pulled Mays and Fleming aboard at 8:37 A.M., fourteen hours after they had first been thrown into the water.

In Rogers City, the entire community waited for word that the crew of the *Bradley* had been found. Most tried to carry on as though nothing had happened, as if to do otherwise might be seen as an admission that something horrible had happened. The children of some *Bradley* crewmembers even went to school that morning. Officials from the Calcite plant who had visited the homes of all the *Bradley* sailors the previous evening had been quick to point out to the families that there were many islands in northern Lake Michigan, and it was quite likely that the crew had made it safely to one of them.

54. The steamer *Carl D. Bradley* was the longest and most powerful ship on the Great Lakes when it was launched in 1927. The 639-foot self-unloader's home port was the small community of Rogers City, Michigan, on northern Lake Huron. Most of the sailors who served on the ship over the years were from the area around Rogers City, including twenty-five of the thirty-five men who were aboard the *Bradley* when it broke up and sank in a Lake Michigan storm on November 18, 1958. (Author's Collection)

When word that two survivors had been found was flashed back to Rogers City, it buoyed everyone's spirits. If two men had survived, it was possible that all thirty-five had. Lake Michigan is a huge lake, and it just might take awhile to find all of them. The people of Rogers City clung to hope with the same unswerving tenacity that Frank Mays and Elmer Fleming had clung to the *Bradley*'s life raft.

It was not to be, however. Word soon came that search vessels had found dead bodies. Throughout the day, the children of *Bradley* crewmen who had gone to school were called out of their classes by principals whose anguished faces betrayed the heart-wrenching messages they bore.

By late afternoon, the bodies of eighteen dead sailors had been recovered by the search vessels. Gary Strzelecki was among them. The

55. Captain Roland Bryan took the *Carl D. Bradley* out into a Lake Michigan storm, even though he knew the thirty-one-year-old freighter's hull was "pretty ripe." The *Bradley* soon encountered powerful seas that were from twenty to twenty-five feet high, as shown in this painting by Rogers City artist and merchant seaman Steve Witucki. At 5:30 P.M. on November 18, 1958, the *Bradley* began to break up. Within minutes, it rolled over and sank. While many of the thirty-five crewmembers aboard managed to get off the ship before it plunged to the bottom, only two survived. (Author's Collection)

bodies of Dennis Meredith, Captain Roland Bryan, and thirteen of their shipmates were never found. Rogers City was plunged into mourning. By the time the sun set that tragic day, twenty-three local women had been widowed and fifty-three children lost their fathers. "There was literally a funeral on every street," said the mayor of the little port city. "The town just couldn't hold all the grief."

Using sonar equipment, the Corps of Engineers later located the sunken hull of the *Bradley* in 365 feet of water south of Gull Island. Global Marine Exploration of Los Angeles was later hired by U.S. Steel to examine the wreck using an underwater television camera. They reported that the hull of the *Bradley* was still in one piece, not broken in half as Mays and Fleming had reported. Both stuck to their stories, however. "I will never change my story," said Mays. "I saw the *Bradley* break in half. I saw two distinct pieces of her hull. I saw the severed electrical wiring flash when it broke in half, and I saw two separate pieces of the hull go down."

After an extensive investigation, the Coast Guard concluded that the *Bradley* had sunk as a result of "excessive hogging stresses." In other words, because the ship was empty, each wave passing under the hull tended to lift the midship section. That constant working of the hull in the extraordinary seas she encountered that night on Lake Michigan eventually stressed the hull plates and framing beyond their limits. Hairline cracks had been discovered in some hull plating during an inspection earlier in the season, and investigators concluded that they might have indicated that some weakening of the hull had existed prior to the sinking. The bottom line, according to the members of the Coast Guard board, was that Captain Bryan "exercised poor judgement" when he made the decision to leave the shelter of the Wisconsin shore and head across Lake Michigan that night. The *Bradley* wasn't up to taking such a pounding, and Bryan should have known that.

The investigators were also critical of the cork lifejackets carried aboard the ship, even though they met the Coast Guard standards in effect at that time. Because of the way the lifejackets fit, it was necessary for a wearer to hold the jacket against his body with his arms. If the wearer was unconscious, or lifted his arms over his head for some reason, it was quite easy to slip out of the jacket. They recommended that all lifejackets be required to have a crotch strap to hold it down, and a collar to support the head of the wearer. Despite the findings and recommendations of the *Bradley* board, cork lifejackets remained on the Coast Guard's list of acceptable lifesaving equipment for another twenty-six years, until 1984.

The members of the Coast Guard board also concluded that it would have been virtually impossible to launch the *Bradley*'s two lifeboats, given the high seas and the short time before the ship sank, because of the type of davits and falls she was equipped with. They recommended that the lifeboats on ships like the *Bradley* be equipped with a mechanical disengaging apparatus that would facilitate their rapid launching.

When the board's report crossed the desk of Coast Guard Commandant A. C. Richmond, however, he disagreed with some of the findings. His review of the evidence gathered in the case led him to conclude that the *Bradley* sank due to "undetected structural weakness." Captain Bryan, Richmond added, did *not* exercise poor judgment in taking his ship out onto Lake Michigan that night. There was nothing "unusual or unique" about the sea conditions the *Bradley* encountered in the storm of November 18, 1958, according to Richmond. She had been in many similar storms during her career on the lakes, and both Fleming and Mays had testified that their ship was riding quite smoothly at the time she broke up. It was also pointed out that in addition to the *Sartori,* two U.S. ships—the freighters *Johnstown* and *Charles L. Hutchinson*—were out on the lake that night.

In the light of Captain Bryan's own reservations about the condition of the *Bradley,* Vice Admiral Richmond's conclusions are hard to understand. He seemed to be saying that since the *Bradley* had weathered storms with winds of sixty to sixty-five miles an hour in the past, it was reasonable for her captain to conclude that the ship could *always* weather such storms. Richmond apparently believed that ships don't get less seaworthy with age.

Commandant Richmond also seemed to be suggesting that a captain on the Great Lakes could almost never be faulted for taking his ship out into a severe storm. If the sea conditions on Lake Michigan the evening the *Bradley* sank weren't "unique or unusual" enough to compel ships to stay in port, then Richmond was giving captains almost carte blanche Coast Guard authorization to take their ships out in *any* weather conditions. The fact that the *Bradley* sank seems to suggest there's something questionable about Richmond's logic.

When Rollie Bryan headed his ship across Lake Michigan in the storm, there were eight other freighters lying at anchor in sheltered waters on northern Lake Michigan. Their captains obviously thought the storm was "unique and unusual" enough that they didn't want to take their ships out in it.

Most captains on the lakes were used to hearing arguments like those made by Richmond, but not from the Coast Guard. Management personnel in their company offices often used the very same arguments—"Your ship's been through worse storms before" and "Other ships are going out"—to discourage them from going to anchor during bad weather.

The families of the thirty-three dead crewmen definitely didn't think the *Bradley* should have been out in the storm. They sued the owners of the ship for a total of $16,490,000. The claimants eventually received a total of $1,250,000.

When the 1959 shipping season began, Elmer Fleming went back to the boats, as he had for many years. Before he retired, Fleming eventually rose to the rank of captain.

Frank Mays never sailed again. After working at a local lumberyard for a few years, he took a job at the Medusa Cement plant in Charlevoix,

Michigan, the port that he and Elmer Fleming had been brought to after their rescue. He later took a position in Brooksville, Florida.

In the late summer of 1995, Mays had an experience that is unparalleled in the annals of shipwrecks on the lakes. Thirty-seven years after the sinking of the *Bradley*, he had an opportunity to go down to the wreck in a two-person submarine. Visibility was poor, but there was no mistaking the familiar gray hull of the long lost *Carl D. Bradley* . . . sitting on the bottom in two distinct pieces.[147]

Daniel J. Morrell, 1966

Six years after the sinking of the *Bradley*, Art Dobson, chief dispatcher for Bethlehem Steel's Great Lakes Steamship Division, spent most of the afternoon and evening of November 29, 1966, trying to locate his company's *Daniel J. Morrell*. Nobody had heard from Captain Art Crawley on the *Morrell* since about midnight on November 28 when the ship was upbound in a severe storm on Lake Huron. Dobson had asked crewmembers on the company's *Edward Y. Townsend* and *Arthur B. Homer*, both of which were also on Lake Huron, to try to raise the *Morrell* on the radio, but neither was able to make contact. Captains on both ships told Dobson they thought the *Morrell* might be having radio problems, or its radio antenna could have been damaged by the storm.

Dobson also put in a call to WLC, the marine radio station at Rogers City, Michigan, located along the shore of northern Lake Huron. WLC radio operators said they had heard no radio traffic from the *Morrell*, even though they had been constantly monitoring both AM and FM bands. They did mention, however, that AM transmissions had been interrupted by heavy snow squalls throughout much of the storm. The *Morrell* was equipped with both AM and FM radios.

On the morning of November 30, Dobson again tried unsuccessfully to contact the *Morrell* after the ship had again failed to call in their "morning report," required of all Bethlehem ships during the fall sailing season. He did hear from Captain Tom Connelly on the *Townsend*, and the word was not good. While taking on fuel at Lime Island in the lower St. Marys River, crewmen had discovered that some rivets on the *Townsend*'s deck had worked loose during the storm. Worse yet, there was a crack in the deck plating at the corner of number 10 hatch that ran toward the side of the ship, and almost four feet of water was found in the cargo hold.

While the company would have to notify the Coast Guard about the damage sustained by the *Townsend*, Dobson's main concern was still the whereabouts of the *Morrell*. The *Morrell* had been about twenty miles ahead of the *Townsend* as the two freighters worked their way up the lakes, so it should have reached the sheltered waters of the St. Marys River first. But nobody had seen or heard from the ship.

Shortly after noon on November 30, Bethlehem officials finally called the Coast Guard's rescue coordination center in Cleveland and reported that the *Morrell* was overdue. Coast Guard staff immediately began to launch a coordinated search for the missing freighter. Less than an hour after hearing from personnel at Bethlehem, however, they received word that the steamer *G. G. Post* had sighted a body wearing a lifejacket stenciled with the name *Daniel J. Morrell* about eight miles north of Harbor Beach, near the tip of Michigan's "thumb." At 4 P.M., Coast Guard vessels and helicopters searching the area off Harbor Beach notified the Cleveland rescue coordination center that they had found more bodies floating in Lake Huron. Then, just a few minutes later, the Coast Guard staff in Cleveland was notified that one of their helicopter crews had found a life raft washed up on the beach fifteen miles above Harbor Beach. The raft held the dead bodies of three *Morrell* crewmen . . . and Dennis Hale, a twenty-six-year-old watchman, who would prove to be the only survivor of the shipwreck.

Hale, suffering badly from exposure, frostbite, and hypothermia, was rushed to a nearby hospital. There he told Coast Guard investigators that the 601-foot *Morrell* had begun to break in half about 2 A.M. on November 28. Hale and the other deck crew who lived in the ship's forward cabin climbed aboard the life raft located between hatches on the forward deck. From there they could see that the deck was riding higher amidships than it was at the bow or stern, and there was a crack running across the deck that gave off sparks as the ship worked in the high seas. Then the ship broke cleanly in two and the bow began to settle rapidly in the water. Within minutes, waves rolled up the deck and washed the raft off the ship, spilling the crewmen into the frigid waters.

Hale and three others—a wheelsman and two deckhands—managed to swim back to the raft and crawl aboard. With the temperature hovering around the freezing point, the four wet seamen huddled together on the raft in an effort to stay warm. The two deckhands on the raft died at about 6 A.M. on the morning of November 29. That afternoon, the wheelsman quietly told Hale that he was going to "throw in the sponge," and he rolled over and died. Hale burrowed beneath the bodies of his dead shipmates for some protection from the cold. Sometime on the morning of November 30, waves pushed the raft onto the beach, but by then Hale was too weak to do more than yell for help. That afternoon, when Hale heard the Coast Guard helicopter hovering overhead, he summoned the little energy he had left to lift his head and wave an arm.

Coast Guard investigators eventually concluded that the *Morrell* had broken in half because the steel used in her hull tended to be brittle, especially in cold weather. Coast Guard officials said it was a "common problem" with ships built before 1948. They had apparently done nothing to correct the problem, however, or to prohibit ships built with brittle steel from operating during periods of cold weather. The same problem was blamed for the cracks that had been discovered on the deck of the *Townsend*. While it had made it through the storm of November 28–29, 1966, it never operated again.

More of the *Morrell*'s crewmen might have been saved if the ship had been able to broadcast a distress call before it went down. Based on testimony from Dennis Hale and an examination of architectural plans for the ship, investigators decided that the electrical cables running from the generators in the engine room at the stern of the ship to the pilothouse at the bow had probably parted when the *Morrell* first began to break up. Since there was no emergency power backup for the radios in the pilothouse, there was no way a distress call could have been broadcast. The Coast Guard soon changed their regulations to require a backup power supply on the forward end of ships like the *Morrell*.

The board also recommended that inflatable, covered life rafts be required on Great Lakes vessels so that occupants would have at least some protection against hypothermia. "Under the existing sea conditions, the lifeboats could not have been lowered and launched successfully," they concluded. They also suggested that consideration be given to requiring cargo hold compartmentation on newly constructed Great Lakes ships, "so that in the event any one main cargo hold should be flooded, the vessel will have sufficient buoyancy to remain afloat."

As in the case of the *Bradley*, Captain Crawley was not faulted for being out on Lake Huron that night, even though gale warnings had been posted when he left the sheltered waters of the St. Clair River. In fact, the *Morrell* had anchored below Detroit the previous night because of adverse weather. When the *Morrell* was off Saginaw Bay on the evening of November 28, Captain Crawley talked with Captain Connelly on the *Townsend*. He said that the wind was then blowing out of the north at thirty-five miles an hour, and both the wind speed and wave height were increasing rapidly. At that point, the two ships could have sought shelter in Saginaw Bay, or turned around and returned to the St. Clair River. In the face of the worsening storm, they chose to continue on. That decision ended the careers of two ships, and killed twenty-eight sailors.

"Whether a ship should or should not proceed in heavy weather conditions is a command decision," the Coast Guard board wrote. "There is no clear showing that either the master of the *S.S. Daniel J. Morrell* or the masters of the other vessels who proceeded into the face of the storm were negligent for doing so."[148]

Looking Back

While some ships sank after their hulls were crushed or holed by ice, and the *Eastland* capsized because it was top-heavy and overloaded, when we think of founderings on the Great Lakes we generally think about vessels lost in storms. In the strictest sense, however, it's important to note that no foundering was ever *caused* by a storm. Storms were a factor, that's for sure, but never the cause.

In order for a ship to founder, either it has to capsize, like the *Eastland,* or it has to take enough water into its hull to lose buoyancy and sink. That water can find its way into the hull in a lot of ways. The hull can come apart, like the *Western Reserve, Carl D. Bradley,* or *Daniel J. Morrell.* On ships with planked wooden hulls, the seams can work open, as happened on the old *Idaho.* Water can also find a way in through the hatch openings, which was the case with the *Cyprus, Henry Steinbrenner,* and probably the *Edmund Fitzgerald.* Water can also flood in through doorways, portholes, or sea gates, like the one on the *Milwaukee.* It's not the storm that sinks the boat, but the flooding. A "seaworthy" ship, one that has been properly designed, properly built, and properly maintained, should be capable of safely coming through virtually any storm it encounters. Unfortunately, many of the ships that have been lost on the lakes over the years simply weren't seaworthy.

From 1838 on, passenger steamers were required to undergo annual hull inspections to ensure that they were seaworthy. That requirement was extended to include steam-powered cargo ships in 1871. Sailing vessels were never subject to inspections, however, and hundreds of aging and poorly maintained sailboats foundered over the years. The last to go was the 182-foot *Our Son,* lost during a Lake Michigan gale in 1930 while downbound for Muskegon, Michigan, with a load of pulpwood.

Her rotten sails were ripped out by the strong winds and, caught in the troughs, the hull of the fifty-five-year-old schooner began to come apart. Fortunately, the seven crewmembers aboard the antique ship were able to abandon the sinking schooner and row to a steamer that was nearby.[149]

Even ships that were inspected weren't always seaworthy, though. That's most obvious in the tragic case of the *Eastland,* but it was also true of the *Western Reserve.* Between the time the big freighter was built in 1890 and when she broke up and sank on Lake Superior in 1892, steamboat inspectors were unaware that steel made in the Bessemer process wasn't strong enough to be used in ship construction. Few, if any, steamboat inspectors at that time had the technical expertise to make such a determination. Their agency also didn't have the power to review construction plans for ships until 1936.

Even after they had their badly needed "corps of experts" and the legal authority to review plans prior to construction, the agency wasn't always able to ferret out problems that made ships unseaworthy. During World War II, for example, the Coast Guard approved plans for the construction of sixteen virtually identical Maritime-class freighters to augment the fleets on the lakes. One of those was the 621-foot *George A. Sloan,* which came out in July 1943 for U.S. Steel's Pittsburgh Steamship fleet. In late September, the *Sloan* was heading up Lake Huron in moderate seas when crewmembers going aft for dinner discovered a crack running three-quarters of the way across her deck. The *Sloan* went into the shipyard where she had been built, and a steel strap about three feet wide and more than two inches thick was riveted along each side of her hull to strengthen the ship.[150] The incident was reported to Coast Guard inspectors, who approved use of the steel strapping to strengthen the *Sloan*'s hull.

Although the Coast Guard inspectors were well aware that all sixteen Maritime-class ships had been built from basically the same plans, it apparently didn't occur to them that the hulls of other ships in the class might also be too weak. Just a few days after the incident with the *Sloan,* the Maritime-class *Robert C. Stanley* was launched for the Pittsburgh Steamship fleet. Less than two months later, the *Stanley* was crossing Lake Superior in ballast during a November gale when she, too, cracked. Three to four inches wide, the crack ran all the way across the freighter's deck and twelve to fourteen feet down the sides of her hull.

Fearing their ship would break in half as it continued to work in the seas, crewmembers lashed the deck together with mooring cables. The heavy steel cables were run fore and aft across the deck and secured over bollards. When the mooring winches snugged up on the cables, the crack in the deck was pulled together. The *Stanley* then turned around and slowly steamed back to Sault Ste. Marie, accompanied by two other ore boats. Temporary repairs were made at the Soo and, interestingly, the Coast Guard allowed the ship to make one more trip despite the damage to its deck.[151] All sixteen Maritime-class ships eventually had their hulls strapped to prevent cracking.

After the 1958 loss of the *Carl D. Bradley* and the 1966 sinking of the *Daniel J. Morrell*, both of which cracked in half while out in severe storms, the Coast Guard admitted that the steel used in ships built before 1948 had a "high transition temperature, and [was] therefore susceptible to brittle fracture." All but a handful of U.S. and Canadian ships on the lakes, of course, had been built prior to 1948, but while the Coast Guard had apparently been aware of the brittleness of pre-1948 steel since at least 1958, there is no record that the problem was ever brought to the attention of the shipping companies or the masters of those ships. After the loss of the *Morrell*, Coast Guard inspections of sixteen freighters built before 1948 turned up two that needed to have hull strapping installed. The balance were allowed to continue operating, even though Coast Guard Commandant Willard Smith admitted that the problem could be difficult to detect.[152] A number of pre-1948 ships are still in service on the lakes today, and they regularly go out in storms during cold weather— the exact conditions blamed for the loss of the *Morrell* more than thirty years ago. Whether the captains of those ships, their owners, or current Coast Guard hull inspectors are aware of the potential hazard of brittle steel is questionable. The painful lessons of the past often tend to be forgotten over time.

Many generations of Steamboat Inspection Service officers and Coast Guard personnel were also aware of the ongoing problem of Great Lakes ships flooding through their hatches, yet no effective solution was ever forced on the industry. Of course, many generations of shipowners were also aware of the problem, yet they didn't come up with any solution either. As better hatch closure systems were developed, government inspectors didn't force owners to update their vessels, and owners seldom took the initiative themselves. Ships with dangerous wooden hatch covers were allowed to operate well into the 1970s,[153] and there are still a number of vessels in both the U.S. and Canadian fleets with telescoping hatch covers.

At the same time, the Steamboat Inspection Service and the Coast Guard allowed the use of tarpaulins to be discretionary on ships with wooden and telescoping hatch covers from the first of April until the end of August, despite the fact that flooding through their hatches had been a factor in the sinkings of a number of ships during those very months. The *S. R. Kirby* and *Henry Steinbrenner* were two of those.

Captains, too, need to share the blame for ships lost because they didn't have their deck crews put tarps on before leaving port. Many, like Al Meswald of the *Wocoken*, went out one time too many without tarps on, and they lost their ships and all or most of their crews as a result.

Many ships on the lakes—including the *Niagara* and *S. R. Kirby*—were also lost because of overloading before load lines were finally required in 1936. Several generations of politicians, marine inspectors, shipping company executives, and captains share the blame for the hundreds of deaths that occurred over the years as the result of unconscionable overloading. At the same time, the continual opposition to load lines by the shipping companies could only have been motivated by greed and a pathetic disregard for the welfare of the sailors who crewed their ships.

There's also solid evidence to show that shipping companies have regularly pressured their captains to take ships out into storms, although the Steamboat Inspection Service and Coast Guard seem to have shied away from the issue. The investigation into the 1929 sinking of the *Milwaukee* was quite revealing, however, and today's captains regularly complain about pressure from "the office" to go out in bad weather.

The Coast Guard has also shown no interest in taking on the volatile issue of whether or not it's safe for ships to go out on the lakes when heavy weather is predicted. Their position is that only the captain can decide when it's safe to sail. The historical record clearly shows, however, that captains have frequently made the wrong decision about whether or not it was safe for their ship to be out in bad weather—and not just *a few* captains, mind you, but *hundreds* over the history of the industry. As a result, at least 1,077 ships have been wrecked during storms on the lakes since the loss of the *Griffon* in 1647 . . . and the lives of many hundreds of sailors and their passengers have been snuffed out, most needlessly.[154]

Two significant factors account for most of the deaths as a result of founderings. First, those aboard were often not aware that their ship was going to sink, or they were hoping it wouldn't. It's the nature of founderings that ships have buoyancy and are afloat one second, then lose buoyancy and sink the next. Second, in cases where those aboard had advance warning that their ship was going to sink, many died because lifeboats couldn't be launched, or they capsized, or those in the boats died from hypothermia because they were exposed to the elements. People knowledgeable about the industry have been complaining about lifeboats since at least 1901.[155]

Despite that, the problem has persisted. The only solution the Steamboat Inspection Service and Coast Guard ever came up with was to require vessels to carry life rafts that would float free when a boat sank. The only survivors from the 1958 loss of the *Bradley* and the 1966 sinking of the *Morrell* were on such rafts, in fact. The Coast Guard boards that investigated the loss of those two ships said it would have been virtually impossible to launch their lifeboats given the sea conditions that existed when they went down. The same conclusion was reached after the 1975 loss of the *Fitzgerald* (see Chapter 5), and many of the sailors who testified during the Coast Guard hearings indicated they had no confidence in the lifeboats carried aboard their ships. Despite that, all but a handful of the newest ships on the lakes are still equipped with the same basic types of outmoded lifeboats and davits that were on the *Bradley, Morrell,* and *Fitzgerald.* The next time a ship founders on the Great Lakes, it's likely that more sailors will die because of the lack of adequate lifeboats.

The death roll of victims in founderings is a long one, but so is the list of those who must accept some measure of blame for their deaths. It includes the names of countless politicians, officials of regulatory agencies, insurance underwriters, shipping company executives, captains, and crewmembers who have in their own ways contributed to the continuing carnage on the lakes.

>>5<<

A COMMONSENSE POSTMORTEM:
The Sinking of the *Fitzgerald*

A T 7:10 ON THE EVENING OF NOVEMBER 10, 1975, the steamer *Edmund Fitzgerald* could be seen on the radar screen in the pilothouse of the *Arthur M. Anderson*. At 7:20 it was gone. It happened that fast.

Bernie Cooper, captain of the *Anderson*, refused to believe his eyes. The heavy snowfall that had been limiting visibility on the east end of Lake Superior let up a little at 7:20, and Cooper asked Morgan Clark, his first mate, to look for the *Fitzgerald*'s silhouette on the horizon, thinking that the freighter might have had a power failure. Clark said he could see the lights of three ships about seventeen or eighteen miles ahead, but he was sure they were the saltwater ships *Nanfri, Benfri,* and *Avafors* that had just come out of Whitefish Bay. The *Fitzgerald* had been running along about nine miles ahead of the *Anderson,* but the mate could see no lights or silhouettes in that area.

Captain Cooper adjusted the *Anderson*'s radar and took another look. The saltwater freighters showed up clearly, but there was no target in the area where the *Fitzgerald* had been. Cooper then tried to call the *Fitzgerald* on the radio: "*Edmund Fitzgerald, Edmund Fitzgerald,* this is the *Arthur M. Anderson.*" There was no response.

The *Anderson*'s first mate then tried to contact the *Fitzgerald* on the radio: "*Edmund Fitzgerald, Edmund Fitzgerald, Edmund Fitzgerald,* this is the *Arthur M. Anderson,* the *Arthur M. Anderson* on Channel 16." Again, no reply. Morgan Clark then called the *William Clay Ford,* which he knew was anchored behind Whitefish Point because of the storm. The *Clay Ford* immediately answered the radio call, informing the mate that he was coming in loud and clear.

After trying unsuccessfully to contact the Coast Guard station at Sault Ste. Marie, Captain Cooper then called the *Nanfri,* one of the three salties that was leaving Whitefish Bay and heading across the lake. The U.S. pilot aboard the *Nanfri* answered Cooper's call and said that he couldn't see any targets on his ship's radarscope that could be the *Fitzgerald.*

At 8:32 P.M., Cooper talked to a Coast Guard radio operator at the Soo. "I'm very concerned with the welfare of the steamer *Edmund Fitzgerald,*" said Cooper. "He was right in front of us experiencing a little difficulty. He was taking on a small amount of water, and none of the upbound ships have passed him. I can see no lights as before, and don't have him on radar. I just hope he didn't take a nose dive." Despite his understatement, Cooper later told Coast Guard investigators that by that time "it was pretty evident that the *Fitzgerald* was gone," he just couldn't bring himself to say it that bluntly over the radio. It was hard for Bernie Cooper to admit, even to himself, that the *Fitzgerald* had sunk.

The radio operator at the Soo couldn't believe it either. He tried to call the *Fitzgerald* on his radio, but with no success. He then called WLC, the marine radio station at Rogers City, Michigan, and asked the radio operator there to try to raise the *Fitzgerald.* The WLC operator called back several minutes later to report that he'd had no luck contacting the *Fitzgerald.* In the face of growing evidence that the *Fitzgerald* may have taken "a nose dive," as Captain Cooper had put it, the Coast Guard station at the Soo alerted the Coast Guard's rescue coordination center at Cleveland that "there was an uncertainty concerning the *Fitzgerald.*"

At 9:03 P.M., Cooper again called the Coast Guard station at the Soo. This time he was emphatic: the *Edmund Fitzgerald* is missing!

By 9:15, the rescue coordination center in Cleveland had contacted the Coast Guard Air Station at Traverse City, Michigan, and directed them to dispatch a helicopter to the last known position of the *Fitzgerald.* As the helicopter crew at Traverse City's Cherry Capital Airport was scrambling to launch their chopper, the rescue coordinators in Cleveland also directed the cutter *Naugatuck,* at Sault Ste. Marie, and the *Woodrush,* at Duluth, to get under way.

At 10 P.M., the commanding officer of the Coast Guard's group headquarters at the Soo personally called Captain Cooper on the *Anderson* and asked him to turn his ship around and assist in the search. Without hesitation, Cooper agreed. By then, the *Anderson* was safely within the sheltered waters of Whitefish Bay. Cooper was agreeing to again go out onto Lake Superior, where the wind was blowing more than sixty miles an hour and waves were twenty to twenty-five feet high.

56. The steamer *Edmund Fitzgerald* encountered thirty-five-foot waves and winds that gusted to one hundred miles an hour when she tried to outrun a Lake Superior storm on November 10, 1975. Seen here in a painting by artist Steve Witucki, the 729-foot onetime Queen of the Lakes suffered some damage to her deck and began taking on water at about 3:30 in the afternoon. At 7:10 P.M., the *Fitz* suddenly plummeted to the bottom in more than five hundred feet of water, taking twenty-nine crewmen down with her. (Author's Collection)

At 10:30 P.M., the group commander called seven ships that were at anchor in Whitefish Bay, asking them to go out on Lake Superior and search for possible survivors from the *Fitzgerald*. The seven vessels included three U.S. freighters—the *William Clay Ford, William R. Roesch,* and *Benjamin F. Fairless*—and four Canadian ships—the *Frontenac, Murray Bay, Hilda Marjanne,* and *Algosoo*. Only Ford Motor Company's *Clay Ford* and Upper Lakes Shipping's *Hilda Marjanne* agreed to get under way. The other captains felt that to go out onto Lake Superior that night would put their ships and crews in jeopardy.

Perhaps they were right. After only twenty or thirty minutes out in the violent storm, the captain of the *Hilda Marjanne* turned his ship around and returned to Whitefish Bay.

The *Anderson* and *Clay Ford* searched through the night without sighting anything. Then, at 8 A.M., the *Anderson* sighted the severely battered forward two-thirds of a lifeboat with the words "*Edmund Fitzgerald* No. 1" on it, about nine miles east of where the steamer was believed to have gone down. An hour later, the *Fitzgerald*'s other lifeboat, intact but badly damaged, was sighted by the *Anderson* about four miles south of the first one. Close inspection suggested that the boats had been ripped loose from their davits as the ship sank, rather than having been launched by the crew of the *Fitzgerald.*

As the storm died down on November 11, other commercial and Coast Guard vessels, and aircraft from both the U.S. and Canadian Coast Guards, joined the search. Both of the *Fitzgerald*'s twenty-five-person, inflatable life rafts were recovered near the Canadian shore. The rafts appeared to have inflated themselves as the ship went down. They were slightly damaged, and missing some equipment they carried, but both were judged to have been serviceable.

The intensive search was finally suspended at sundown on November 13. By that time, all that had been recovered, in addition to the two lifeboats and two life rafts, were twenty cork-type life preservers, eight oars, a piece of sounding board used to record ballast tank soundings, eight flotation tanks from lifeboats, a wooden fender block, two propane cylinders, thirteen life rings and a piece of another, several pieces of line, two wooden planks and some other pieces of wood, a wooden stool, two ladders, half a lifeboat cover, a lifeboat rudder, an empty boat box from a lifeboat, a large floodlight, and a plastic spray bottle marked "pilothouse window."

Twenty-nine men had been aboard the *Edmund Fitzgerald* when she sank, but no bodies were ever recovered. Coast Guard investigators later concluded that "the end was so rapid and catastrophic that there was no time to warn the crew, to attempt to launch lifeboats or life rafts, to don lifejackets, or even to make a distress call."

What was believed to be the sunken hull of the *Fitzgerald* was located by sonar on November 14 in 530 feet of water, about seventeen miles north of the entrance to Whitefish Bay. The following May, the Coast Guard brought in an unmanned Navy submersible to photograph and videotape the wreckage.

The hull of the 729-foot *Fitzgerald* was found to be in two pieces. The bow section, about 276 feet long, is upright on the bottom. A 253-foot stern section lies about 170 feet away, upside down. Between the two pieces of the hull there is a debris field that includes pieces of the crushed midsection of the ship and spilled taconite pellets. The bow is holed and its thick steel plating is badly distorted, as is the steel of the deck cabin and pilothouse. Almost all of the pilothouse windows are gone, and the steering pole bent back against the pilothouse hard enough that it left a crease in the steel plating.

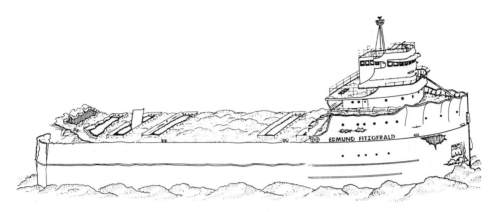

57. When the 729-foot *Edmund Fitzgerald* plunged to the bottom, the freighter's bow was driven deep into the mud and the ship broke into two pieces. Shown here in a Coast Guard drawing is the heavily damaged bow section as it rests on the bottom of Lake Superior. The *Fitzgerald*'s hatch covers were blown off by air pressure as the ship sank, and the taconite pellets it was carrying spilled over the deck. There were no survivors, and no bodies were ever recovered, but a body in a lifejacket was seen alongside the wreck during a 1995 survey by a submarine, suggesting that crewmembers were concerned their ship might sink. (Author's Collection)

From the evidence, it appeared that the *Fitzgerald* had gone to the bottom in one piece, bow first. The bow collided with the muddy lake bottom with such force that the center cargo hold area of the ship collapsed and the stern section twisted away and landed upside down. It's very similar to the wreckage pattern seen when commercial airliners crash into the ground nose-first.[1]

The investigation into the sinking of the *Fitzgerald* was, at that time, the longest and most exhaustive in the history of the U.S. Coast Guard. The three-member board of inquiry spent eighteen months exploring every element that could have been involved in the loss of the big freighter and her crew. Without any survivors, though, it was impossible for them to determine conclusively what caused the ship to sink.

What they did know was that the *Fitzgerald* was owned by the Northwestern Mutual Life Insurance Company of Milwaukee, and named for the man who had been president of the company when the *Fitzgerald* was built in 1959. After her launching, the classic Great Lakes straight-decker was operated under charter by the Columbia Transportation Division of Oglebay Norton, one of the largest fleets on the lakes.

On Sunday, November 9, 1975, the *Fitzgerald* had loaded 26,116 long tons of taconite pellets at the Burlington Northern Railway dock in Superior, Wisconsin. She finished loading and departed for Detroit at about 2:15 that afternoon, following the normal eastbound course. Weather reports at that time showed a storm over Kansas that was predicted to move across the lakes the following day.

That same day, U.S. Steel's *Anderson* had loaded taconite at Two Harbors, Minnesota, northeast of Duluth and Superior. She departed the ore dock at Two Harbors at about 4:30 P.M. and headed east on Lake Superior, some ten to twenty miles ahead of the *Fitzgerald*. Because the *Fitzgerald* was the faster of the two ships, she eventually overtook and passed the *Anderson*.

The National Weather Service posted gale warnings for the lakes at 7 P.M. on November 9, predicting east to northeast winds of twenty-nine to forty-three miles an hour that night. Winds were expected to shift to northwest to northerly at thirty-five to forty-six miles an hour on Monday. When the forecast was issued, the storm center was over Iowa. Barometric pressure readings were dropping, showing that the storm was intensifying, and its speed had increased significantly as it moved toward the northeast.

On the regular 10:30 weather advisory that night, the forecast was revised. It then called for easterly winds of thirty-seven to forty-eight miles an hour that night, with forty- to fifty-two-mile-an-hour winds on Monday afternoon. The wind was expected to have gone around to the west or southwest by then, and rain and thunderstorms were predicted. Waves eight to fifteen feet high were anticipated on Monday on Lake Superior.

At 2 A.M. on November 10, the National Weather Service issued a special advisory, posting storm warnings for the lakes. With the storm then centered over central Wisconsin, barometric pressures were still dropping as the low-pressure system intensified. Winds later in the day were expected to shift from the northeast to northwest at forty to fifty-eight miles an hour—just shy of hurricane strength.

Sometime after Captain Cooper on the *Anderson* got the 2 A.M. weather report, he called the *Fitzgerald* and discussed the forecast with Captain Ernest McSorley. The *Fitzgerald* was almost neck and neck with the *Anderson* at that time. The captains were definitely concerned about the deteriorating weather report, and they agreed to continue heading northeasterly in the lee of the Canadian shore, rather than turning to the southeast on the direct course to Whitefish Bay and the Soo.

At about 4 A.M., the two freighters were closing on the Canadian shore at the east end of the lake, and they both turned to the southeast, heading down toward Whitefish. Winds were then out of the southeast, so the *Fitzgerald* and *Anderson* were heading almost directly into the moderate seas.

Around 2 P.M. the ships passed just west of Michipicoten Island. The weather was then overcast. The wind was recorded on the *Anderson* as only about five miles an hour, but it had swung around to the northwest, as predicted. By 2:45 the wind had increased to forty-eight miles an hour and it started snowing. The *Fitzgerald* was then about sixteen miles ahead of the *Anderson*. A little later, Captain Cooper and Second Mate Roy Anderson watched on the radarscope as the *Fitzgerald* passed north and east of Caribou Island. There is a shoal north of Caribou that has only about thirty-six feet of water over it, and Cooper commented to Anderson that the *Fitzgerald* was closer to the shoal than he wanted to be. Winds were then blowing at forty-nine miles an hour, seas had built to twelve to sixteen feet, and it was still snowing heavily.

Morgan Clark relieved Roy Anderson in the *Anderson's* pilothouse at 3:20 P.M., and the two mates and Captain Cooper stood around talking. At 3:30 their conversation was interrupted by a radio call from Captain McSorley on the *Fitzgerald*.

McSorley told Cooper that the *Fitzgerald* had sustained some topside damage—she had a fence rail down, two vents lost or damaged, and a list. McSorley said that he was going to check down to let the *Anderson* catch up a little. "Do you have your pumps going?" Cooper asked. "Yes," McSorley replied, "both of them." The officers on the *Anderson* testified later that when the conversation ended they weren't left with the impression that there was any need to be overly concerned about the *Fitzgerald*. McSorley seemed to be talking about some relatively insignificant damage.

At 4:20 the *Anderson* logged wind speeds of sixty-seven miles an hour out of the northwest, the highest sustained winds they recorded during the voyage. It was still snowing, and seas had built to twelve to eighteen feet. The waves were striking the *Anderson* and *Fitzgerald* on their stern quarters. Loaded as they were, both ships had about ten feet of freeboard—ten feet of their hulls was out of the water—so waves two to eight feet high were regularly rolling over their decks and crashing against the aft side of their forward cabins. The *Anderson* was rolling pretty good at that time, and it's likely the *Fitzgerald* was, too.

The *Fitzgerald* called again at around 4:30 P.M. Their radars weren't working, and they asked if the *Anderson* would provide some navigational assistance. Clark agreed that he would keep track of them. Over the next several hours, Clark talked to the *Fitzgerald* on at least two other occasions, providing information on the *Fitzgerald*'s position.

Between 5:00 and 5:30 P.M., Captain Cedric Woodard, the pilot aboard the upbound Swedish *Avafors,* called Captain McSorley to tell him that the Whitefish Point light was on, but the radio beacon wasn't working. Someone from the *Fitzgerald* had called the *Avafors* about an hour earlier to determine the status of the light and beacon. At that time, both were out as a result of a power failure. After Woodard told McSorley that the Whitefish Point light was back on, the two continued to chat on the radio. At one point during the conversation, McSorley paused, apparently to answer a question from someone in the *Fitzgerald*'s pilothouse. "Don't allow nobody on deck," Woodard overheard McSorley say, followed by something about a vent that Woodard was unable to understand. McSorley then went on to tell Woodard that the *Fitzgerald* had a bad list and was taking heavy seas over her deck. McSorley said it was one of the worst seas he had ever been in.

Captain Cooper later said that the *Anderson* regularly had as much as twelve feet of water on her deck during the late afternoon and early evening hours. Around 6:30 P.M., two waves which he estimated were at least thirty feet high overtook the ship from the northwest. One buried the after cabins and damaged a lifeboat by smashing it down into its saddle. The second wave was reportedly so high that it washed over the *Anderson*'s bridge deck, thirty-five feet above the ship's waterline. The waves continued on toward the *Fitzgerald,* and Cooper estimated that they would probably have hit the already damaged ship at about 7:15.[2]

At 7:10 P.M., Morgan Clark called the *Fitzgerald* to tell them that there was a radar target about nine miles ahead of the *Fitzgerald.* "Well, am I going to clear?" the person on the *Fitzgerald* asked rather testily. "Yes," replied Clark, "he is going to pass to the west of you. He then asked how the *Fitzgerald* was making out with their problems. "We're holding our own" was the blunt response from the *Fitzgerald.*

A few minutes later, the *Fitzgerald* dropped off the *Anderson*'s radarscope. The sixteen-year-old *Fitzgerald,* the "Queen of the Lakes" when she was launched in 1959, had simply "gone missing."

The images of the wreck provided by the Navy submersible in the spring of 1976 showed that air trapped inside the hull when she sank had blown the *Fitzgerald*'s hatch covers off. The Coast Guard investigators were surprised to see that few of the hatch clamps that had held the heavy steel hatch covers in place had been bent or broken when the hatch covers were blown off. After interviewing many seamen who had previously served on the *Fitzgerald*, they concluded that it was likely that not all of the hatch clamps had been put on when the ship left Superior. There was also evidence to support a conclusion that many of the clamps that were on were probably not on as tight as they should have been, and that the heavy rubber gaskets on the hatch coamings that were supposed to seal any gaps between the covers and the coamings had not been maintained very well.

After careful analysis of the information available on the size and frequency of the waves that were breaking over the *Fitzgerald* in the hours before she went down, the Coast Guard board reached the conclusion that "the most probable cause of the sinking of the *S. S. Edmund Fitzgerald* was the loss of buoyancy and stability which resulted from massive flooding of the cargo hold. The flooding of the cargo hold took place through ineffective hatch closures as boarding seas rolled along the spar deck."

The Lake Carriers' Association and many others in the industry strongly disagreed with the board's conclusions. They argued that while it might have been theoretically possible for the cargo hold to flood through the small openings that would have resulted if hatch clamps weren't put on, or if gaskets on the hatches weren't properly maintained, that scenario was highly unlikely. The LCA theorized that the *Fitzgerald* had struck bottom in the shallow water over the six-fathom shoal north of Caribou Island, probably unknowingly, and tore her bottom open enough to eventually cause her to sink. The Coast Guard acknowledged that grounding was a reasonable alternative explanation for the sinking of the *Fitzgerald*, as was the topside damage that had been reported by McSorley at around 3:30 P.M..

Coast Guard investigators surmised that the damage to the fence rail and vents could possibly have been caused by a heavy floating object, such as a log, carried aboard by the high seas. A much more plausible explanation is that something broke loose on the *Fitzgerald*'s deck, such as the hatch crane, a hatch cover, or the spare propeller blade that was carried in a saddle amidships. At the same time, the damage, particularly the loss of the two vents, could *not* have been the result of hitting bottom on the six-fathom shoal.

The loss of the vents McSorley reported would almost certainly have resulted in the flooding of two ballast tanks, or a ballast tank and one of the walking tunnels. That would have caused the ship to take on a list, but the resulting loss of buoyancy wouldn't have been sufficient to sink the *Fitzgerald*. There is virtually universal agreement that water was somehow getting into the *Fitzgerald*'s cargo hold during the hours before she sank.

Unfortunately, there would have been no way for Captain McSorley and his crew to know how much water was getting into the hold. It's also unlikely that they would have been able to pump the water out of the cargo hold. Sailors and naval architects testified that it is virtually impossible to pump water out of the hold of a loaded lake freighter. At the same time, since the bulkheads separating the cargo holds on the *Fitzgerald* were not watertight, any water that got in would eventually have migrated throughout the entire hold.

Captain McSorley's decision to slow down and allow the *Anderson* to catch up with his ship was taken by the Coast Guard board members as a *possible* indication that he "knew or sensed that his problems were of a more serious nature" than he had let on during his conversation with Captain Cooper. Actually, *there is no other reasonable explanation for McSorley's decision to slow down.*

Slowing down meant prolonging the *Fitzgerald*'s exposure to the seas that were hammering McSorley's ship, delaying their arrival in the sheltered waters of Whitefish Bay. At the same time, since the waves were on the *Fitzgerald*'s stern, McSorley knew that slowing down would increase the force of the waves crashing against the hull and cabins of his ship. Given those circumstances, no captain would have slowed down—unless he feared his ship was going to sink. When McSorley called Captain Cooper on the *Anderson* to tell him about the topside damage the *Fitzgerald* had sustained, he said he was going to slow down. Even then, at 3:30 in the afternoon, McSorley must have felt there was a possibility that his ship was going to sink. McSorley wanted the *Anderson* nearby to pick up survivors. The topside damage to the *Fitzgerald* may have been much more serious than he let on.

The Coast Guard board's conclusion that the sinking of the *Fitzgerald* "was so rapid and catastrophic that there was no time to warn the crew, to attempt to launch lifeboats or life rafts, to don lifejackets, or even to make a distress call" was probably an overstatement. A videotape of the *Fitzgerald*'s sunken hull made in 1995 shows the body of a crewmember lying alongside the bow of the ship. *The body is clad in a lifejacket.*[3]

That's clear evidence that at least one crewmember was concerned enough about the possibility of sinking that he put on a lifejacket. It's quite possible that Captain McSorley, aware that the *Fitzgerald* was on the verge of sinking, ordered everyone in the crew to put their lifejackets on. Such a scenario is completely consistent with McSorley's decision to check down and allow the *Anderson* to catch up.

McSorley's comment about not letting anyone on deck, overheard by Captain Woodard during their late-afternoon radio conversation, also suggests that at least some crewmembers may have been aware that their ship was close to foundering. With waves two to eight feet high rolling over the deck, there are only two logical explanations for why someone would consider going out on deck. One would be to attempt to repair damage that was threatening to sink the ship. The other would be to abandon ship, or prepare to abandon ship.

As in the case of the *Morrell* and *Bradley,* there was strong testimony from experienced Great Lakes seamen that it would have been virtually impossible to launch the *Fitzgerald*'s lifeboats in the huge seas overtaking the ship on the evening of November 10. Then, too, none of the crew had any experience in launching the ship's two inflatable life rafts. When the Coast Guard began requiring ships to carry the enclosed inflatable rafts after the 1966 loss of the *Morrell,* they simultaneously required that crewmembers be trained on how to use the new lifesaving equipment. When questioned during the *Fitzgerald* hearings, however, seamen said that they had received no training. All the companies had done was put up posters that explained how to launch the rafts.

In general, safety training was found to have been very lax aboard the *Fitzgerald* and other ships on the lakes. Fire and boat drills that were supposed to be held weekly were not, even though entries were made in the ship's log each week indicating that the requirement had been met. Many sailors interviewed by the Coast Guard during their investigation felt that the lifeboats and life rafts were useless in a storm like the one that claimed the *Fitzgerald.* Most doubted if either could have been launched successfully, and one longtime sailor seemed to speak for many in the industry when he said that if his ship was sinking he would just climb into bed and pull the covers over his head.

On the evening the *Fitzgerald* went down, the high winds and waves would have made it very difficult to launch the inflatable life rafts. If a raft canister was thrown over the side, the raft could easily have been blown away, or been tipped upside down by the fierce wind. Even if it inflated right-side up, crewmembers would still have had to jump into the bitterly cold water to board the raft. Such an undertaking is risky, and any captain worth his salt would have avoided putting such a plan into motion until there was no alternative left.

And, Captain McSorley did have an alternative: right up until the instant the *Fitzgerald* plummeted below the surface, he and his men were high and dry on their ship. If those aboard the *Fitzgerald* were at all aware of what happened when the *Morrell, Bradley,* and *Steinbrenner* sank, and they probably were, they would have anticipated having at least a few minutes' warning before their ship went down. Until then, the safest thing for Captain McSorley and his crew to do was to stay right where they were—with their lifejackets on.[4]

Unfortunately, the *Fitzgerald* didn't sink like the *Morrell, Bradley,* or *Steinbrenner.* While McSorley and his crew watched and listened for some sign that the ship was going to sink . . . it just went. Either McSorley or Morgan Clark was standing in the front window, right next to the radio, yet when the *Fitzgerald* plunged to the bottom there wasn't even time to pick up the microphone and shout "Mayday!" There wasn't time to do anything—no radio call, no hastily scribbled note, no race for the lifeboats, probably not even time to murmur a final prayer.

It's both interesting and puzzling that the Coast Guard board, the Lake Carriers' Association, and a number of private groups that subsequently studied the *Fitzgerald*'s sinking, including the crew of Jacques Cousteau's *Calypso,* all discounted the most obvious explanation for why the ship went down—the topside damage experienced at 3:30 in the afternoon. While the damage reported by Captain McSorley would not have been sufficient to cause the ship to sink, the actual damage could easily have been more extensive than McSorley could detect from his position in the pilothouse . . . or more serious than he wanted to let on to a captain from another fleet. Whatever heavy object damaged the fence rail and sheared off the two sturdy steel vents could easily have stove in several hatch coamings, allowing water to flood into the cargo hold as the huge waves incessantly rolled across the deck of the *Fitzgerald.*

In the face of incontrovertible evidence that the ship had sustained topside damage, it doesn't make sense to try to contrive some other explanation for the sinking of the *Fitzgerald.* To do so is analogous to theorizing that the *Titanic* was sunk by a German U-boat or rammed by a mystery ship, even though she reported striking an iceberg.

Based on the evidence they had available to them, the members of the Coast Guard board said there was no evidence of misconduct, inattention to duty, negligence, or willful violation of the law or regulations on the part of the crew of the *Fitzgerald.* What they had found, however, was "complacency, and an overly optimistic attitude concerning the extreme

58. A group of VIP passengers in survival suits pose for pictures during a fire and boat drill aboard the *Edgar B. Speer*. The suits provide both flotation and protection from hypothermia, and have been required aboard ships on the lakes since shortly after the 1975 sinking of the *Edmund Fitzgerald*. Crewmembers are frequently required to put their suits on during drills, but few have ever had an opportunity to actually wear them in the water. (Author's Collection)

weather hazards which can and do exist." That attitude was reflected in "deferral of maintenance and repairs, in failure to prepare properly for heavy weather, and in the conviction that since refuges are near, safety is possible by *running for it*." The problems weren't limited to the *Fitzgerald*; they appeared to be pervasive throughout the Great Lakes shipping industry.[5]

About the only significant changes that came out of the loss of the *Fitzgerald* and all the months of hearings that followed were a new requirement by the Coast Guard for ships on the lakes to carry exposure suits, commonly referred to as "survival suits," for each crewmember, and emergency position indicating radio beacons (EPIRBs). The rubber suits are designed primarily to protect crewmembers from hypothermia if they have to abandon ship. If the crewmembers have to go into the water, the suits also provide excellent flotation. An EPIRB is a radio transmitter that is designed to float free from a sinking ship. Once activated by being in the water, it broadcasts a continuous signal to satellites that the Coast Guard can use to pinpoint the location of the sunken ship.

The *Fitzgerald* was the last ship lost in a storm on the Great Lakes. The "gales of November" keep rolling, however, and there have been lots of close calls since 1975. Unfortunately, logic tells us that the *Fitzgerald* will eventually lose her dubious distinction as the last storm loss to some other hapless ship and its unlucky crew.

>>6<<
BEAN COUNTERS, BUREAUCRATS, AND COWBOY CAPTAINS:
The Human Factor in Shipwrecks

URING THE CIVIL WAR, ONE HISTORIAN SAID THAT while shipping losses on the lakes varied greatly from year to year, there were times, especially late in the season, when the weekly reports resembled reports from a battlefield.[1] Unfortunately, the carnage on the lakes was just beginning in the 1860s. There were just over 200 hundred serious shipping casualties during that entire decade. How would the Civil War–era historian have reacted to the 568 serious wrecks that occurred during the 1880s, or the more than 600 that took place during the first decade of the twentieth century?

When we look closely at the thousands of shipwrecks and deaths that have occurred on the lakes, it seems obvious that many of them could have been avoided. Government regulators have just been too timid, shipowners too callous, captains too reckless, and crews too complacent to correct the problems that led to shipwrecks.

In studying the history of groundings and strandings, for example, it's clear that most occurred while ships were operating during fog, snow, or rain. At the same time, the shipping companies expected their ships to keep running during periods of limited visibility, and government regulators allowed them to do so. Even after navigational aids like radio direction-finding and radar became available, many shipowners didn't install the equipment on their ships until they were forced to do so.

Between 1870 and 1940, many of the most serious groundings involved unpowered barges that were driven aground in storms after being cut loose or breaking loose from the steamers towing them. Many wrecks and deaths could have been avoided if companies had simply abandoned the dangerous practice of having their steamers tow barges. Because the barges didn't have engines, they were "uninspected vessels," not covered under the various marine safety laws. Government regulators, however, had to be well aware of the terrible toll being taken on barges and their crews, yet there's no evidence that officials of the Steamboat Inspection Service ever tried to have them prohibited, or at least brought under their control.

Fires were a natural consequence of having wooden ships, or iron- or steel-hulled ships with wooden bulkheads and fixtures in their cabin areas, and many sources of ignition present—sparks and ashes from boilers, kerosene lamps, heat stoves and galley ranges fueled with wood or coal, and cigars and cigarettes smoked by passengers and crewmembers. Devastating shipboard fires provided the impetus for many of the marine safety regulations put into effect from 1838 to the present, yet fires continued to be a serious problem until wooden ships disappeared and the extensive use of wood in outfitting cabins and galleys was finally banned in 1962. Many of the wooden ships that burned, especially after the turn of the century, were more than forty years old. Little more than floating tinderboxes of questionable seaworthiness, they were still running only because of the greed of their owners and the laxness of the steamboat inspectors.

While marine safety laws and regulations dating back to 1838 required ships to be equipped with fire-fighting equipment, and crews were eventually required to hold regular fire drills, there is no evidence that any fire-fighting training was provided until the 1980s, and then only for new officers. In a pattern that would become familiar, government regulators implemented requirements for fire drills, then failed to follow up to ensure that meaningful drills were actually being held. At the same time, there is also no evidence that shipowners were committed to ensuring that their crews were prepared to fight a fire if one broke out.

Like fires, collisions between ships took a heavy toll, particularly in the days when there were many passenger steamers operating on the lakes. Almost all collisions were the result of either poor visibility or pilot error. While the rules of the road that were in effect after 1864 required ships to slow down when visibility was limited, there's ample evidence that most ships continued to run along at full speed. Shipping companies either encouraged or tolerated that dangerous practice. With the exception of the river patrol that was established in the St. Marys River in 1897, there is no evidence that either the Steamboat Inspection Service or the Coast Guard ever aggressively enforced the rule requiring ships to reduce speed during periods of limited visibility. Banning ships from operating in congested areas during poor visibility would undoubtedly have dramatically reduced the number of collisions, but there is no record that government agencies ever sought that power.

Persons applying for licenses as deck officers on Great Lakes ships have been tested on their knowledge of the rules of the road since shortly after those rules first went into effect during the Civil War. Despite that, many collisions have resulted from violations of the rules by the pilots navigating the vessels involved, or mistakes in handling their ships. Neither shipowners nor government regulators apparently ever reached the rather obvious conclusion that those operating the ships needed additional training or testing on the rules of the road and shiphandling. Even today, the Coast Guard doesn't test deck officers on their actual ability to handle a ship. The only shiphandling training that's available is through schools run by the American Maritime Officers, the union representing most officers who work on the Great Lakes.

Storms were a factor in the vast majority of the founderings that have occurred on the lakes since the dawn of navigation. They've also led to many of the more serious groundings, and even some fires and collisions. Many ships were simply out on the lakes when they should have been in port. Although shipping companies lobbied to have better weather forecasts available to their captains, there is also overwhelming evidence that the "bean counters" in the company offices regularly pressured captains to take their ships out in bad weather. At the same time, there is no evidence that any government regulatory agency ever fought for the power to control vessel movements when dangerous weather was predicted. Only a captain can legitimately decide if it's safe to take his ship out, they argue.

After thousands of ships were wrecked because their captains went out in storms, you'd think the steamboat inspectors or Coast Guard personnel would have reconsidered their position. If the historical record is clear on anything, though, it is that safety margins are cut too thin and risks exceed acceptable levels when ships head out onto the lakes in severe storms. It's as though the government agencies keep hoping that the captains will eventually get it right. But they haven't.

Even if the Steamboat Inspection Service and Coast Guard didn't want to infringe on a captain's prerogative to take his ship out, you'd think they would have moved swiftly to correct some of the other obvious deficiencies that cause founderings. There, too, the government regulators and shipping companies failed to act.

Hatch covers have always been a problem, for example, and many ships that have foundered over the years did so because they took on water through their hatches. "Hatches are and have always been, the most vulnerable part of the vessel," said Captain James Watts of the steamer *J. F. Durston* after the tragic storm of 1913. While steel telescoping hatches had been invented in 1904, most ships were still equipped with wooden hatch covers in 1913. "For many years, no thought was given to improvements," said Captain Watts, "because the hatches were easy to repair or renew, since wood could be obtained easily at any and every port. But during heavy weather, tarpaulins were easily torn off, and many times the first smashing wave over the decks did the worst damage. It struck the side coamings, deflected, and forced them upward, and the wooden covers just floated overboard or fell into the hold."[2] Watts, who took the *Durston* up Lake Huron during the storm, was convinced that wooden hatch covers were to blame for many of the founderings that occurred during the 1913 storm.

For some reason, neither shipbuilders, shipowners, nor the Steamboat Inspection Service ever came up with a satisfactory system to secure wooden hatch covers. In fact, when a steamboat inspector in Duluth pressed his bosses for authority to work on the problem, he was bluntly told to drop the subject.

Telescoping hatch covers were much stronger than the wooden ones, and they could be secured quite effectively with a system of clamps, but they weren't much more watertight than wooden hatch covers. To keep water from leaking into the cargo hold, both had to be covered with canvas tarpaulins. A ship that took seas over its deck in a storm simply wasn't seaworthy without tarps.

While the Steamboat Inspection Service eventually began requiring ships with wooden or telescoping hatches to put tarpaulins on during those months when storms were most likely, use of tarps between the first of April and the end of August was generally left to the discretion of the captain. If bad weather was anticipated, the captain was supposed to see that tarps were in place over the hatches. Unfortunately, the requirement to put tarps on has been regularly ignored by captains, and many ships have been lost as a result. It takes time to put on the heavy and unwieldy sheets of canvas, and it's something that has to be done at the dock, because the tarps are extremely difficult to handle if there's much wind. Putting on tarps means a delay in getting under way after loading or unloading, and most captains cringe at the prospect of taking a delay, regardless of how minor it might be. When their ship is loaded or unloaded, they want to head out onto the lake.

Based on the industry's track record, it would have been reasonable for the Steamboat Inspection Service and Coast Guard to simply require tarps to be used at all times on ships with wooden or telescoping hatch covers. Inspections of ships entering the Detroit, St. Clair, or St. Marys Rivers would also have been a foolproof means of discovering when captains were violating tarping requirements. A system of fines or license suspensions for violators might have helped put a stop to the dangerous practice . . . and saved many ships from sinking.

When single-piece steel hatch covers were introduced in 1925, the Steamboat Inspection Service or Coast Guard could also have forced shipowners to retrofit boats that had wooden or telescoping hatches with the newer and safer equipment. That, too, could have eliminated some founderings, including the 1953 loss of the *Henry Steinbrenner*. That wasn't done, of course, and we still have a few old ships out on the lakes with telescoping hatch covers today.

After single-piece hatch covers came into use, government inspectors seem to have assumed that personnel on the ships would see to it that the covers and coamings would be well maintained, that their rubber seals would be replaced when necessary, and that hatch clamps would be put on and tightly secured. Although the single-piece hatch covers began to be used in 1925, it wasn't until after the loss of the *Edmund Fitzgerald* in 1975 that Coast Guard officials caught on to the fact that those things weren't always being done. While there was every reason to believe that the crews on the ships couldn't be trusted to properly maintain and use the hatch cover systems, Coast Guard officials generally only inspected them at fit-out in the spring and during their pre-November inspections. If the *Fitzgerald*'s hatches were poorly maintained in the fall of 1975, as was later asserted by the board that investigated the ship's sinking, then Coast Guard inspectors failed to discover that fact in the pre-November inspection they performed only weeks before the ship went down.

In addition to hatches, overloading was also a major cause of founderings. While Samuel Plimsoll got the British Parliament to enact a load-line law in 1876, opposition from the shipping companies and lukewarm enthusiasm on the part of the Steamboat Inspection Service delayed implementation in the United States until 1936. In the fifty years between 1876 and 1936, dozens of ships were lost on the lakes because they were overloaded. That included the *Eastland,* the most deadly shipwreck in the history of the lakes.

Shipowners and steamboat inspectors must also share responsibility for the loss of dozens of old wooden ships that probably should never have been allowed to go out on the lakes. At least 97 wooden steamers and 185 wooden sailing ships were lost on the lakes between 1900 and 1930. Of those, 142 grounded and 135 foundered—came apart, seams opened up, swamped, or capsized. It couldn't have gone unnoticed by the steamboat inspectors that more than two-thirds of those wooden ships were more than thirty years old. In fact, 73 were more than forty years old and 24 had been around for fifty years or more.[3]

The frequency of strandings or founderings of aging wooden ships is clear evidence that either they were not seaworthy or, at the least, they shouldn't have been allowed to operate during those periods of the season when stormy weather was most likely to be encountered. The steamboats had all been inspected and found to be seaworthy by the steamboat inspectors, however, which brings into serious question their judgment, or the standards they were using, or both. The wooden sailing ships, on the other hand, weren't required to be inspected, and there is no evidence that the Steamboat Inspection Service ever fought to get such authority, even though regulation of sailing ships might have significantly reduced the number of shipwrecks on the lakes.

The unseaworthiness of many of the wooden ships on the lakes seems to have been apparent to just about everyone except their owners and the steamboat inspectors. "After the first September gale, the 'lame ducks' are numerous," one observer noted in 1882. "All the old rotten hulks from everywhere have poked out during the fair weather, and the first real blow cripples them, often fatally. It must be said for the hardiness of lake sailors that they will go to sea in craft of amazing craziness," he added.[4]

The *Idaho* was fairly typical of the wooden ships lost. Built in 1863, the aging steamer foundered in a November storm in 1897. She had been taken out of commission several years before that, but when freight rates went up in the fall of 1897 her owners fitted out the thirty-four-year-old ship and put her back into service. Just over a month later, she came apart during a storm on Lake Erie and took nineteen crewmembers down with her.[5]

Similarly, the 1890-built wooden package steamer *North Star* was laid up when the Great Depression settled over the country in 1929. When her owners had a chance to haul some cargoes of fresh fruit the following fall, however, they put the forty-year-old ship back into service on Lake Michigan. She disappeared off Milwaukee during a gale on September 26, 1930, taking her entire crew with her.[6] Before she went out that season, the *North Star* was inspected and certified as seaworthy by the local steamboat inspectors. Apparently she wasn't quite as seaworthy as they thought.

It wasn't just wooden ships that went down because their hulls and

59. Samuel Ward Stanton's drawing of the 220-foot steamer *Idaho* that foundered in a November storm on Lake Erie in 1897. The thirty-four-year-old ship hadn't operated for several years, but her owners brought her out of layup when freight rates soared. She sank just over a month later. Two of the twenty-one crewmembers aboard the ship survived the sinking by clinging to the *Idaho*'s tall forward mast, which was sticking out of the water. (Author's Collection)

machinery weren't up to snuff. After the *Andaste* disappeared in a Lake Michigan storm on September 9, 1929, persons familiar with the thirty-seven-year-old freighter said she was suffering from a lack of maintenance. She had never been equipped with electricity, had no radio, and her lifeboat davits were reportedly so rusted that the boats couldn't be lowered.[7] You don't have to look far to find many cases similar to those of the *Idaho, North Star,* and *Andaste.*

Underpowered ships were yet another major factor in both strandings and founderings on the lakes until the end of the 1930s. In particular, many of the big iron and steel ships built between the 1880s and the early years of the twentieth century were seriously underpowered. Caught out in storms, they often didn't have enough power to keep from broaching or being driven ashore, as in the case of the *E. W. Oglebay* in 1927. More powerful engines were available, but many shipowners skimped on horsepower to save on construction and operating costs. The problem might

**60. Bethlehem Steel's 600-foot *Daniel J. Morrell* broke in half and sank during a
storm on Lake Huron on November 29, 1966. Coast Guard investigators later
determined that the ship had been built of steel that became brittle when it was
cold. They had known for some time that steel used to build ships before 1948
was inferior, but despite the fact that Coast Guard officers had inspected the
Morrell on numerous occasions, they had never tested the steel in her hull or
warned her owners about possible problems. (Author's Collection)**

have been solved if the Steamboat Inspection Service had been given the
power they wanted to approve plans prior to construction. Unfortunately,
the shipping companies and shipyards were able to block giving that
power to the steamboat inspectors until after the inspection service was
merged with the Coast Guard in 1936. A second alternative, however,
might have been for the Steamboat Inspection Service to severely limit
when low-powered steamers could operate in order to ensure that they
were unlikely to get caught out in a storm. That might also have provided
an incentive for shipowners to repower their ships, or see to it that they
stayed in port when the weather got bad.

The Steamboat Inspection Service was well aware that poor design and
construction were factors in the losses of many ships over the years, the
Eastland being a prime example. When steamboat inspectors did have an
opportunity to limit the activities of poorly designed ships, such as when

they were considering how many passengers the *Eastland* could carry, they often failed to take a tough stand. The inaction by the steamboat inspectors was often blamed on their cozy relationships with shipowners, but their lack of technical expertise was undoubtedly also a factor, and that was clearly evident in their handling of the *Eastland*'s instability problems.

Even after the Steamboat Inspection Service was merged into the Coast Guard and they were finally given the authority to establish a technical division with powers to approve or disapprove construction plans, they often proved unable to ferret out serious structural problems. After the *Carl D. Bradley* sank in 1958, Coast Guard technical experts were aware of the shortcomings of the notch-sensitive and brittle steel that was used to build many ships prior to 1948, but there doesn't seem to have been any program in place to warn the owners or crews of such vessels. That led to the loss of the *Daniel J. Morrell* in 1966, and may have been a factor in many other shipwrecks.

The hulls of the Maritime-class freighters built during World War II proved to be too weak, even though the Coast Guard had signed off on their building plans. The decks of both the *Robert C. Stanley* and *George A. Sloan* cracked the first time they went out in even a moderate seaway, and the Coast Guard eventually had to order all the boats in that class to have strapping added to strengthen their hulls.

Looking back, it's also obvious that the shipowners and regulatory agencies could have done a great deal more to prevent deaths as a result of shipwrecks. Most obvious is the fact that passenger steamers were not required to carry enough lifeboats and life rafts to be able to get everyone off safely in the case of a casualty. From the very earliest days of the industry on the Great Lakes, the lack of an adequate number of lifeboats was a key factor in the losses of hundreds of lives in the wrecks of ships like the *Erie, Phoenix, Atlantic, Lady Elgin, Pewabic,* and *Morning Star.* As obvious as the problem was, the political power of the shipping companies was great enough that neither Congress nor the Steamboat Inspection Service did anything to correct the situation until after the 1912 loss of the *Titanic,* and then they delayed implementing "boats for all" as long as possible. If the steamboat inspectors had been strongly motivated to save the lives of persons traveling on steamers on the lakes, or on any other U.S. waters, they would have been complaining to Congress *daily* about the deficiencies in lifeboats. Nothing else they did had the potential to save as many lives as simply providing enough lifeboats on passenger ships.

The second most significant thing they could have done to cut the number of deaths in shipping accidents would have been to find a solution

61. The *George A. Sloan* was one of sixteen Maritime-class ships built on the lakes during World War II. She was launched in July 1943, and in September of that year her deck cracked when the ship was heading up Lake Huron in moderate seas. The *Sloan's* hull had to be strengthened with steel strapping that was three feet wide and two inches thick. Even though the Coast Guard was aware of the problem, they didn't require strapping to be installed on the other Maritime-class boats until after the deck of the *Robert C. Stanley* cracked in November 1943. (Author's Collection)

to the ongoing dilemma of how to safely launch a metal lifeboat in high seas. Tragically few crewmembers from ships lost in storms have been saved by metal lifeboats. The problem goes back at least to the loss of the *Western Reserve* in 1892, yet neither the Steamboat Inspection Service nor the Coast Guard ever forced the industry to come up with a workable solution.

While today's ships are still required to carry lifeboats and to hold boat drills each week, the general consensus seems to be that if sailors have to abandon ship during a storm it would probably be safer to use one of the self-launching, inflatable life rafts they've had to carry since after the loss of the *Morrell*. Given the choice between a traditional metal lifeboat and one of the new life rafts, rafts are definitely the way to go. Despite their weekly boat drills, most sailors today have virtually no experience in rowing the big and unwieldy lifeboats. If they did manage to launch one in high seas, it would probably broach and fill with water or capsize.

Many lives were also unnecessarily lost because most shipping companies were averse to equipping their ships with radios that would have allowed crewmembers to call for assistance if their boat was experiencing difficulties. Radiotelegraph equipment was first tested on the lakes as early as 1905 on the passenger steamer *Indianapolis.* The Lake Michigan car ferries of the Ann Arbor Railroad were equipped with transmitters and receivers the following year. Although the Wireless Ship Act required U.S. passenger steamers to be equipped with radios in 1910, and ocean cargo vessels came under the law in 1912, Great Lakes shipping companies operating cargo ships were successful in having themselves exempted. Many U.S. and Canadian shipping companies didn't install radios on their boats until the time of World War II.

In fact, in 1912 a rift developed between the Lake Carriers' Association and companies operating passenger steamers over the issue of radios. In testimony before a Senate committee, A. A. Schantz, vice president of the Detroit & Cleveland Navigation Company, expressed the opinion that freighters on the lakes also needed to be equipped with radios. Harvey Goulder, attorney for the LCA, was quick to respond. "I wonder if he would be ready to bear a part of that expense," Goulder asked the senators on the committee. "We cannot do it out of our freight returns."[8] Equipping ships with radiotelegraph equipment was a fairly expensive proposition at the time. It wasn't that the transmitters and receivers were that expensive, but one or two radio operators had to be employed to operate the complicated equipment and broadcast and receive messages in Morse code.

During the early 1920s, a number of bulk fleets on the lakes began experimenting with radiotelephone equipment that allowed transmissions to be sent and received in voice rather than by telegraph. Tests of radiotelephone were conducted during the 1922 shipping season using equipment installed on the *Carl D. Bradley* of the Bradley Transportation fleet from Rogers City, Michigan. Bradley Transportation was a subsidiary of Michigan Limestone and Chemical Company, which also operated its own marine radio station. By 1924 there were about twenty ships on the lakes equipped with radiotelephones.

If officers on Great Lakes ships were lukewarm about having radiotelegraph equipment on their ships, they were vehemently opposed to radiotelephones. Captains, in particular, were almost unanimous in their opposition to radiotelephone, fearing that it would give "too much control over the operation of the ships to the home office."[9]

It was probably for exactly that reason that shipping companies began to warm toward the idea of being able to communicate with their ships by radio. Despite opposition from captains, two hundred U.S. and Canadian ships had been equipped with radiotelephone sets by 1937, about a third of all ships operating on the lakes.[10] While it had been demonstrated very early on that radios could help reduce deaths resulting from marine casualties, it wasn't until 1954 that the Coast Guard finally required all U.S. ships to be outfitted with radiotelephone equipment.[11]

When ships in distress called for help, it was most often personnel from the U.S. Life-Saving Service that responded. From the time the first professionally manned lifesaving stations were established on the lakes in 1876 until their agency was merged with the Revenue Cutter Service in 1914, crews of the Life-Saving Service responded to 9,763 vessels in distress. Of the 55,639 persons aboard those vessels, only 275 died during the entire thirty-nine-year period.[12] Of all the various efforts to reduce the number of deaths resulting from shipwrecks on the lakes, nothing was more effective than the gallant performance of the "storm warriors."

Bean Counters

While the crews of the Life-Saving Service established an enviable record in saving the lives of sailors and their passengers who were shipwrecked on the lakes, the historical record suggests that executives of most shipping companies and their trade associations have tended to put profits ahead of safety. They seem to have had an overriding commitment to maximizing profits, a business attitude that was fairly pervasive throughout much of our country's history. The recipe for maximum profits was quite simple: spend as little as possible on ships and crews, make sure that each boat carried as much cargo as possible each trip, and see that each ship made as many trips as possible each season. One historian has said that the shipping companies exerted "insidious pressures" on their captains. "Many owners piously issued orders to take no chances, but still judged the man and his opportunity for advancement on the basis of trips completed and tonnage carried."[13]

The shipowners and managers established a tradition of opposition to programs that would undoubtedly have reduced the number of shipwrecks and resulting deaths, such as "boats for all," load lines, and radios. They were aided in those efforts by political allies in Washington. Shipowners were a powerful political force throughout much of our nation's history, and none more than those on the Great Lakes. Many of the early passenger steamers on the lakes, for example, were owned by eastern railroads that cultivated immense political muscle early on.

Nowhere was that more obvious than in the passage by Congress in 1851 of the Harter Act, the "limited liability law" that has undoubtedly been responsible for saving the shipping companies hundreds of millions of dollars. The law, still in effect today, limits the damages that a shipping company can be made to pay to the value of the ship and its cargo *at the time of the liability award.* Obviously, a ship that has sunk or burned is worth virtually nothing. The limit applies to all shipwrecks, unless it can be proven that the shipowners knew the vessel wasn't seaworthy or that its crew was inadequate.

As much clout as the railroads had during the nineteenth century, it was eventually eclipsed by the power of shipowners from places like Buffalo, Cleveland, Detroit, Milwaukee, and Chicago. In fact, legislation was eventually pushed through Congress that forced the railroads to liquidate their fleets of passenger and freight steamers on the lakes.

After the Civil War, a new breed of shipowners emerged on the Great Lakes as a result of opportunities created by the growing demand for the movement of bulk cargoes. Many of those shipowners became immensely wealthy, and they had strong political allies in the burgeoning iron and steel industries they hauled for. When they needed to exert their political muscle, they could usually count on support from New York financiers like J. Pierpont Morgan, Jay Gould, and John D. Rockefeller, who were heavily invested in the steel industry.

The shipping executives also developed close ties to the American automobile industry that developed in Detroit just after the turn of the century. Automakers quickly became the main consumers of the raw materials hauled by freighters on the lakes, and they supported many of the shipping industry's lobbying efforts. In time, Henry Ford would start his own fleet and thereby join the ranks of Great Lakes shipowners.

Among the most powerful and influential of the shipping executives was Marcus Alonzo Hanna, founder and owner of M. A. Hanna Company. His firm owned and managed coal and iron mines, shipyards, and one of the major fleets on the lakes. Headquartered in Cleveland, Hanna was active in both Ohio and national politics. A Republican, he was an early and ardent supporter of William McKinley, an Ohio congressman. With the aid of Hanna's powerful political machine, McKinley was elected governor of Ohio in 1891, and went on to become the twenty-fifth president of the United States in 1897. Credited with orchestrating McKinley's election, Marcus Hanna soon become national chairman of the Republican Party, and he was later elected to the U.S. Senate from Ohio. He was still serving in the Senate when he died in 1904.[14]

Shipowners like Marcus Hanna ensured that the Great Lakes shipping industry had enough political muscle to see that most decisions made in Washington favored their positions. Unfortunately, by caving in to political pressure from shipping company lobbyists, many of the decisions made by the Congress deprived crews and passengers on Great Lakes ships of badly needed improvements in vessel safety.

The written or unwritten policies of the shipping companies also put many ships in harm's way. They allowed—"encouraged" is probably more accurate—their captains to operate in fog and to take their ships out in bad weather. They sent out tired old ships and barges that were of questionable seaworthiness, and there is no evidence to indicate that they ever made a strong commitment to seeing that their crews were well trained to deal with emergency situations.

Quite a number of informed observers share the sentiment expressed about the shipping companies by John Disturnell in his book *The Great Lakes, or Inland Seas of America,* published in 1857. "Were it not for the almost criminal carelessness or recklessness of many of the owners and masters navigating these lakes, whereby hundreds of valuable lives have been lost and millions of property destroyed," wrote Disturnell, "no more safe, instructive, or grand excursion could be found on the face of the globe."[15]

Shipowners and shipping company executives have been targets of similar harsh criticism in the wake of virtually every shipping disaster in the long history of commerce on the lakes. Through their actions and attitudes, they often appeared to exhibit a callous disregard for the safety of their crews. From the "captains of industry" who ran the fleets to the accountants, or "bean counters," in the company offices who entered the revenues and expenses in the ledger books, the management of shipping companies often seemed to be motivated by a single overriding objective—to maximize profits. In many instances that was precisely the case.

The effectiveness of managers was measured by how profitable the company was. Because of the availability of marine insurance, the number of sailors or ships that were lost during a season didn't necessarily have a negative impact on a fleet's profitability.

The first marine insurance company in the United States was formed in 1792. For much of their history, the insurance underwriters did little to help reduce the number of shipwrecks that occurred each year. In fact, it could be argued that the availability of insurance probably *resulted in* many vessel casualties.

If the price was right, the marine insurance underwriters would provide coverage for any old hulk. Shortly after the devastating storm in November 1913, for example, an insurance underwriter told a newspaper reporter, "When you read in the current reports of storms on the lakes that such and such vessels have been wrecked and are a total loss, don't get the impression that the owners will suffer a material financial loss. As a matter of fact," he added, "it is quite generally considered that when a vessel is lost on the lakes she is as good as sold."[16]

It was undoubtedly often less expensive for a fleet to pay a high insurance premium than to incur the costs of improving the seaworthiness of a vessel. At the same time, the availability of insurance reduced the risks the fleets subjected themselves to by expecting their ships to continue operating in fog or storms.

Combined with the limited liability law of 1851, the ready availability of insurance coverage guaranteed shipowners that their losses would be minimal if one of their ships went down. In fact, there were undoubtedly many instances where a ship paid higher dividends to its owner by sinking than it did by hauling cargo.

In fairness, however, it should be noted that the businessmen who owned and managed the ships and fleets weren't any different from their counterparts in other sectors of the economy. There is ample evidence that owners and managers in the mining, timber, railroad, and manufacturing industries were similarly slow to make the safety of their employees a priority—and not just in the United States, but throughout the industrial world. According to one historian, "Few industrialists showed any concern for those they employed who were exposed to danger . . . from the unguarded machines—one writer reported that in a walk around Manchester [England] a person would see so many maimed operatives that it was like being in the midst of an army just returned from a campaign."[17]

Worker safety didn't become a significant issue in the United States until workers' compensation laws were enacted during the first half of the twentieth century. Until then, hazards in the workplace were widely accepted as a *fait accompli*, not just by business owners and managers, but by many employees as well.

For the most part, the owners and managers of shipping companies, mines, lumber camps, and manufacturing plants weren't callous and indifferent profiteers. Many were actually highly respected leaders of their communities. They simply acceded to the prevailing business standards of the day.

Bureaucrats

There's also plenty of evidence to suggest that steamboat inspectors were often in the pockets of the shipowners they were supposed to be regulating. The first steamboat inspectors were appointed by federal judges. Many of those judges were undoubtedly friends of shipowners in their communities. Not being experts on what it took to be a competent hull or boiler inspector, it's likely that judges commonly sought advice from friends who owned ships. It's also not unreasonable to assume that some shipowners encouraged judges they knew to appoint friends or family members to positions as steamboat inspectors.

Regardless of how they got their appointments, however, from 1838 until 1852 steamboat inspectors depended on shipowners for their pay. The first steamboat inspectors were compensated solely through the fees that shipowners paid to have their ships inspected. If an inspector was perceived as being too tough in his inspections, many shipowners wouldn't have used him a second time, and they'd have taken their boats elsewhere for their inspections. As a result, it's likely that most steamboat inspectors did their best not to antagonize local shipowners. We have no way of knowing the extent to which that impinged on the way they did their jobs, but it was unquestionably an influence.

After 1852, steamboat inspectors were paid salaries by the Steamboat Inspection Service, lessening the extent to which they could be influenced by shipowners. That didn't put an end to charges that inspectors had been corrupted by those they were supposed to regulate, however. It seems as though the issue of corrupt steamboat inspectors was raised after virtually every major shipping casualty on the lakes, such as the 1915 capsizing of the *Eastland.* Many people thought that corruption was the only reasonable explanation for the often-questionable performance of the steamboat inspectors.

We have no way of knowing the extent to which the seemingly poor judgment of the steamboat inspectors was the result of their having been influenced by shipowners or merely a consequence of their incompetence. There is no question that many inspectors lacked the technical knowledge necessary to make sound decisions about hulls and boilers. Nowhere is that clearer than in the succession of errors made by steamboat inspectors who were involved with the *Eastland* between her launching in 1903 and when she finally foundered in 1915.

It's safe to say that from 1838 until the period after the *Eastland* disaster, steamboat inspectors were often less than aggressive in their efforts to improve marine safety. They seemed to be extraordinarily tolerant of dangerous conditions in the shipping industry, many of which had relatively simple solutions. Leaders of the Steamboat Inspection Service weren't outspoken advocates for "boats for all," the establishment of load lines, eliminating flammable materials in ship construction, or requiring ships to be equipped with radios. While it was obvious by 1905 that inadequate hatch covers were a contributing factor in the founderings of many ships on the lakes, for example, top officials of the service shied away from taking the initiative to develop a safer system of hatch closures.

Some of the reluctance by the heads of the Steamboat Inspection Service to lock horns with shipowners may have resulted from their awareness of the tremendous political power that groups like the LCA had in Washington. They had seen the shipping industry lobbyists block enough marine safety legislation to know that their perennially under-staffed and underfunded agency could only remain viable if it had at least tacit support from the shipowners. In head-to-head confrontations with the shipping industry, the Steamboat Inspection Service almost always came out second best. Nowhere was that more apparent than in the agency's ongoing attempts to get authorization to establish a technical division with powers to approve ship's plans before construction. First recommended in 1914, and brought up again right after the *Eastland* debacle the following year, the proposal was successfully blocked by the industry until 1936.

The Steamboat Inspection Service was stung by widespread public criticism in the aftermath of the devastating fire on the *General Slocum* in 1904, the needless deaths of so many due to the lack of lifeboats when the *Titanic* sank in 1912, and the incomprehensible *Eastland* tragedy in 1915. That finally led to the appointment of Dickerson Hoover to head the agency, with orders from President Woodrow Wilson to clean things up. Hoover was aggressive, and willing to take on volatile issues like overloading that had been largely ignored by his predecessors. His efforts were roundly scuttled at almost every juncture by the opposition of the shipping companies, however. With steamboat inspectors under a constant barrage of criticism from 1914 on, the often-frustrated Hoover found that his agency was simply impotent in its attempts to act on many major safety problems in the industry. Whenever a serious marine casualty occurred, steamboat inspectors were often forced to spend more time defending their actions than investigating the shipwreck.

When the Coast Guard inherited the Steamboat Inspection Service in 1936, it also seems to have fallen heir to that agency's tarnished reputation. The policies and performance of the Coast Guard have often been called into question after marine casualties, in the same way the Federal Aviation Administration commonly spends much time defending its actions following airline crashes. After the 1975 sinking of the *Edmund Fitzgerald,* for example, an attorney representing the families of two crewmembers who went down with the ship asked whether the three Coast Guard officers appointed to the board of investigation could be impartial judges when their agency may have been guilty of careless conduct. "Should they judge themselves on the competency of the rescue attempt, if safety equipment in the ship was adequate, or if the ship should have been even sailing in such rough weather?" he asked. "They may be passing judgment on their own actions and negligence in similar tragedies in the past."[18]

It's hard not to hold the Coast Guard at least partially responsible for the sinking of the *Fitzgerald.* Before the *Fitz* was even built, Coast Guard officials had begun jawing about the need for watertight subdivision of the cargo holds on Great Lakes ships. While a parade of Coast Guard brass had cited the lack of watertight subdivision as a contributing factor in the loss of numerous ships and the deaths of dozens of sailors, they were all talk and no action. For one reason or another, they never implemented administrative rules to require the use of watertight bulkheads in the cargo holds of Great Lakes freighters. Even after the loss of the *Fitzgerald,* when it was obvious to virtually everyone that the ship would probably have had enough buoyancy left to limp into Whitefish Bay if there had been watertight bulkheads in its cargo hold, the Coast Guard still didn't implement the necessary rules. They proposed them, to be sure, and they had strong support from the labor unions representing Great Lakes sailors. In the face of vehement opposition from the shipping companies, though, they backed off.

Perhaps the most embarrassing aspect of the *Fitzgerald*'s sinking for the Coast Guard, however, was the fact that from the time the ship was built in 1959 until its loss in 1975, they had reduced the ship's required freeboard during the dangerous months of the late fall by a total of thirty-nine inches. In November 1975 the Coast Guard actually allowed the *Fitzgerald* to load more than three feet deeper than it could when it first went into operation sixteen years earlier. That means it had more than three feet less reserve buoyancy than it had been required to have when it came out in 1959.

On three occasions, in 1969, 1971, and 1973, the *Fitzgerald*'s load line during the critical late-fall sailing season had been raised. It went up about six inches in 1969, another thirteen inches in 1971, and twenty inches in 1973.

The 1969 increase in the load line was available to all ships the Coast Guard considered as "having superior design and operational features." In 1971 the Coast Guard approved an across-the-board load-line increase for Great Lakes ships during the period from November 1 until the end of the season. To qualify for the 1973 load-line increase, ships had to make a number of safety improvements, such as strengthening watertight doors, increasing the height of the deck railings at the bow and stern, increasing the height of tunnel vents, and covering the chocks at the bow through which the mooring lines and anchor chains pass.[19]

The members of the *Fitzgerald* board of inquiry and Admiral O. W. Siler, then commandant of the Coast Guard, made the point very clearly that the ship might have survived if there had been "even a minimum degree of watertight subdivision within the cargo hold." They conveniently failed to mention, however, that Captain McSorley and his crew also might have made it across Lake Superior on November 10, 1975, if their ship would have had three more feet of freeboard.

By blaming the sinking of the *Fitzgerald* on complacency that appeared to be industry-wide, the Coast Guard laid bare their own complacency. Coast Guard personnel experienced in dealing with the Great Lakes shipping industry must have been aware of the dangerous attitudes and behaviors that were so common aboard the ships, yet they did nothing to correct the situation. On October 31, 1975, less than two weeks before the *Fitzgerald* sank, Coast Guard personnel performed one of their pre-November inspections on the ship while it was unloading in Toledo. If the hatch coamings, gaskets, and clamps were poorly maintained, why wasn't it discovered at that time? Why wasn't corrective action taken? For the Coast Guard to plead that they were unaware of the problems is to admit that they hadn't been doing their jobs very well.

The Coast Guard did its best to avoid the issue of whether the *Fitzgerald* should have been out on Lake Superior in the storm of November 10, 1975. Like a broken record, they once again took the position that only the captain of a ship can make a sound decision about whether to sail or not.

For a number of years, however, the Coast Guard had already been operating a vessel traffic control system on the St. Marys River, known as Soo Control. All vessels transiting the St. Marys are required to check in with radio operators at Soo Control at a number of predefined checkpoints along the river. That helps Coast Guard personnel to ensure that vessels are complying with the speed limits, and allows Soo Control operators to keep the ships informed of other traffic in the system. During inclement weather that could make navigation hazardous, such as periods of high winds or limited visibility, Coast Guard personnel at Soo Control are also empowered to order ships to go to anchor in the river.

While the traffic control system in the St. Marys has worked effectively in reducing the number of collisions and groundings, the Coast Guard has balked at the prospect of deciding when ships can, or cannot, sail on the open lakes. Whenever the issue is raised after the loss of another ship, they always fall back on their historic position that only a captain knows when it's safe to take his ship out. Of course, one could ask why that logic applies on the lakes but not on the St. Marys River.

Cowboy Captains

While the shipping companies, insurance underwriters, Washington politicians, and bureaucrats from the Steamboat Inspection Service and Coast Guard all share varying degrees of responsibility for the ongoing cycle of shipwrecks and deaths on the Great Lakes, there is no group that must bear more of the blame than the generations of captains who have commanded ships on North America's freshwater seas. Through their incompetence, recklessness, errors in judgment, and taciturn willingness to go along with shipping company policies that put their ships, passengers, and crews in jeopardy, captains have been responsible for most of the shipwrecks and deaths on the Great Lakes. In the graveyard of the lakes, it is the captains who have been the grim reapers.

Among the most deplorable are the "cowboy captains" who willingly, even enthusiastically, have taken their ships out in dangerous storms. Some of them are portrayed as colorful, almost laughable, characters, like Captain Emerald Malone. It's said that Malone "used to fiddle to work up a higher wind during a storm. When his uneasy crew would beg him to shorten sail for fear the masts might be shattered, he'd keep sawing away and tell them, 'Let her blow, boys, let her blow, just so she's blowing for home!' Then he'd dance a jig on the reeling deck and bend his fiddle against the roar of the gale."[20] Malone's antics might put a smile on the face of a landlubber, but it's unlikely his crews took much pleasure in the wild rides he gave them.

Others cowboy captains are generally described in macho, seemingly laudable, terms. Captain Jimmy Owen of the steamer *Henry B. Smith*

62. Heavy weather still represents the most serious threat to ships operating on the Great Lakes. The awesome power of the waves can be seen in this photo taken during the 1990s by a crewmember aboard Oglebay Norton's *Buckeye*. Waves rolling aft down the deck of the 699-foot freighter can be seen crashing into the stern cabin. (Dave Cook, *S.S. Buckeye*)

was described by his sister as being "perfectly fearless," for example. "My brother laughed at danger," she said. Like Malone, though, Captain Owen seemed to get some twisted pleasure out of taking his ship out in a storm. "He laughed when he went into a storm," recalled his sister, "and he laughed when he came out of it."[21] She was speaking of her brother in the past tense, of course. He and twenty-four crewmembers were lost when the *Smith* sank somewhere off Marquette during the November storm of 1913, under circumstances that forever cast a pall over Captain Owen's reputation.

Captain Owen and the *Smith* had arrived at the ore docks in Marquette on Friday, November 7, about the same time that storm warnings were being posted for all the lakes. Loading of the ship proceeded at a snail's pace because dockworkers were having great difficulties getting the frozen iron ore out of the railcars that had been sent down from the mines under a freezing rain.

When the storm worsened on Saturday, the dock boss sent his crews home, feeling that the strong winds made it too dangerous for them to be working up on the high dock. As loading of the *Smith* ground to a halt, the weather report in that day's *Marquette Mining Journal* didn't look at all promising. "Marquette and the entire Upper Peninsula will today be swept by one of the most severe storms expected this year," the Weather Bureau predicted. "The wind is to come from the southwest, accompanied by rain and followed with snow."[22] Given the weather forecast, it looked as though there really wasn't any rush to load the *Smith* and the other ships waiting at the Marquette dock—they weren't going anywhere anyway.

Captain Jimmy Owen had other plans, however. As the storm continued to worsen Saturday evening, he pleaded with the managers of the dock to load his ship on Sunday. It's said that "the urgency of his manner and some knowledge of the pressures Captain Owen was under apparently moved the officials, for [the] dock superintendent . . . was ordered to finish loading the *Smith* on Sunday."[23]

Because of the adverse weather conditions, dockworkers didn't finish loading the *Smith* until about 5 P.M. on Sunday. Almost before they had raised the last chute on the dock, however, Captain Owen had his deckhands on the dock to throw off the mooring cables. Minutes later, the 525-foot freighter pulled away from the dock and picked up speed as it headed out onto the frenzied waters of Lake Superior. Crewmembers aboard the other two freighters waiting out the storm at the Marquette dock were shocked to see the *Smith* leaving—the *Smith*'s deck crew hadn't even had time to get all the hatch covers and tarps back on!

On the deck of the *Choctaw*, Captain Charlie Fox watched in disbelief as the *Smith* steamed out onto the stormy lake like a rabbit attacking an angry elephant. After twenty minutes of pitching and rolling in the towering seas, Captain Fox saw the *Smith* make a hard left turn. Fox knew instantly that Captain Owen had realized he'd made a serious mistake and had seemingly decided to turn and run for shelter behind the Keweenaw Peninsula, rather than continue on toward the Soo. As the *Smith* turned, it fell into the trough between the huge swells and the angry waves broke over her decks, at times covering it with water ten feet deep. It was going to be a long, wet, uncomfortable trip to the Keweenaw, Captain Fox thought to himself.

Long, indeed. That was the last anyone saw of the *Henry B. Smith* or its crew.

After the storm blew itself out and it became obvious that the *Smith* was one of the many ships wrecked by the hurricane-strength winds and explosive seas, there were a lot of different explanations for why Captain Owen had taken his ship out in the storm. Some of those who knew the "fearless" Captain Owen thought his courage might have been of the liquid variety.

There were reports that Jimmy Owen had been drinking heavily right up until the time he had taken his ship out. Some said that he was so drunk that it had taken two men to get him aboard his ship. Of the volumes that have written about shipwrecks on the lakes, it's one of very few instances where the specter of drunkenness was offered as an explanation for why a captain went out into a storm.

There was also a rumor that Captain Owen had received orders from the *Smith*'s owners to sail "or else." Jimmy Owen hadn't been having a good year. The *Smith* had taken a lot of delays that season due to fog or because other ships had beaten it to the loading or unloading docks. As a result, the tonnage they'd hauled was way below what they would usually have carried. Captain Owen knew his bosses in the Hawgood fleet's offices in Cleveland weren't happy with his performance, and with the season rapidly drawing to a close, he was intent on resurrecting his tarnished image.[24]

Like Jimmy Owen, most heavy-weather sailors and cowboy captains probably weren't really fearless, and it's unlikely they derived any perverse pleasure from taking their ships out in storms . . . but they did anyway. In reality, many were probably motivated more by fear than bravado. Fear of the front office has always been a powerful motivator for captains on the lakes.

Captain John Brown of St. Clair, Michigan, seems to have been one of those. One of four brothers who became captains, John Brown was on the little steamer *Margaret Olwill* during the 1899 season. The ship was running back and forth from Kelleys Island to Cleveland on Lake Erie, hauling limestone for a harbor breakwater project.

On an evening in late June, under rapidly decaying weather conditions, Captain Brown pulled the *Olwill* away from the stone dock at Kelleys Island and headed east for Cleveland. The holds of the 175-foot ship were filled to their hatch coamings with 300 tons of limestone. Another 600 tons had been piled high down the center of the wooden steamer's deck.

By the time the *Olwill* was only a couple hours out of Kelleys Island, winds had increased to fifty miles an hour and the overloaded steamer's seams began to open up. From there on, nothing went right for Captain Brown. As water leaking into the cargo hold mixed with the limestone, the ship soon took on a dangerous list. Off Lorain, he tried to bring the boat around to run for cover, but the steering chains parted and the *Olwill* slipped broadside to the powerful seas. Knowing that his ship was doomed, Captain Brown ordered all those aboard to the lifeboats. Before the boats could be launched, though, a monstrous wave struck the *Olwill* and it capsized and sank. Only four of the eleven persons aboard managed to survive. Among the dead were Captain Brown's wife and eleven-year-old son, who were making the trip with him.[25]

Captain Brown "knew only one thing, and that was to follow orders," said Captain Russel Jones, a longtime friend. "If the owners had told him to put the boat on the beach, he would have done it."[26]

In trying to understand why Captain Brown would have overloaded his ship and then taken it out in bad weather with his wife and young son aboard, one historian said, "It was a period when it was not only unfashionable but unwise to question the judgment or decisions of owners, no matter how unreasonable or unrealistic they might be. Overloading, safety procedures, and dangerous weather considerations were quite properly the legal province of captains, but often these decisions were made by men ashore, many of whom had little or no sailing experience themselves."[27]

Even today, captains continually feel pressured by office personnel to sail during inclement weather. Many go out when other captains are ducking for cover, not because they're fearless and macho, but because, down deep, they're worried about their standing with the office. The self-confident captains go to anchor, while the timid, weak, and uncertain ones don't have the fortitude to stand up to the bean counters.

One of the last heavy-weather sailors to lose a ship on the lakes was Ernest McSorley, master of the *Edmund Fitzgerald* when it went down on November 10, 1975. George "Red" Burgner, longtime steward on the *Fitz,* said later that McSorley regularly "beat hell out of the *Fitzgerald*" and "seldom ever hauled up for weather."[28]

Storm warnings for Lake Superior were issued at 2 A.M. on November 10, while the *Fitzgerald* and *Arthur M. Anderson* were still in the shelter of the north shore. The storm warning predicted winds of forty to fifty-eight miles an hour from the northeast, going to the northwest, accompanied by waves eight to fifteen feet. Shortly after the storm warnings were broadcast, Captain McSorley talked to Captain Jesse Cooper on the *Anderson* about the worsening weather, and they decided to take a conservative approach and stay in the lee of the Canadian shore, rather than follow the normal courseline that cut down the middle of the lake.

Eight hours later, at between 10:00 and 10:30 in the morning, the two ships neared the eastern end of the lake and changed their courses to the southeast, heading down toward Whitefish Bay. Winds continued to blow out of the east at the time, so the ships were still in the lee of the Canadian shore at the east end of the lake. If the winds made the predicted shift to the north or northwest, however, both captains should have known that their ships would be left in an exposed position. Turning southeast was the critical decision made by Captain McSorley and Captain Cooper on November 10, 1975, and, in the case of the *Fitzgerald,* it proved to be a fatal one.

The conservative approach would have been to haul around and backtrack along the Canadian shore, where they would be sheltered from winds out of any quadrant of the north. We have no way of knowing for sure what went through Captain McSorley's mind when he decided to leave the safety of the north shore and run the risk of tangling with north or northwest winds of up to fifty-eight miles an hour. Either he felt that his ship could handle winds of fifty-eight miles an hour, and the powerful waves they would generate . . . or he was hoping that the Weather Service's prediction was wrong and the winds would never go that high . . . or he was simply "running for it," hoping that his ship could make it down to the sheltered waters of Whitefish Bay before the winds shifted around.

Whatever his thinking, there was some risk involved in the decision to head down the lake in the storm. It was the type of decision Captain McSorley had been called on to make many times during his long career, and he'd probably gambled many times before. Always before, things had come out fine. He and his ships had always come through alright. On November 10, 1975, however, McSorley's lucky streak finally ran out. The winds went to the northwest only a few hours after his ship had turned to the southeast. The wind speed topped the predicted fifty-eight miles an hour during the afternoon, with some gusts as high as one hundred miles an hour. When the winds went to the northwest, the seas quickly built to eighteen to twenty-five feet. When he talked on the radio with Cedric Woodard on the *Avafors* between 4:00 and 4:30 in the afternoon, McSorley himself said that the seas were among the worst he'd ever seen. He probably wished he'd stayed along the north shore.

It's interesting to note that at least two other Columbia ships were out in the storm that night, and both sustained some damage. The *Armco* encountered the storm while upbound on Lake Superior. When she arrived at the ore dock at Silver Bay, Minnesota, crewmembers reported that the couch in the chief engineer's room had broken loose during the storm. Even worse, fifty-five-gallon oil barrels tore loose in the engine room. Thankfully, they were secured before they damaged any of the equipment. As soon as the *Armco* finished loading, it went right back out into the storm.

On the night of November 10, at about the same time the *Fitzgerald* was sinking on Lake Superior, Columbia's *Middletown* was going down the St. Marys River. When the captain reached the mouth of the river at Detour, he sailed right out into the storm on Lake Huron. Crewmembers later said that lights and wooden crash blocks broke loose on the deck in the high seas. Most of the rungs on an aluminum boarding ladder were also ripped away.

The fact that at least three Columbia ships were out in the storm when so many other vessels were tied up in port or at anchor raises the specter, as was true in the case of the *Milwaukee,* that captains in the fleet felt pressured to sail regardless of weather conditions. Like the reluctant Grand Trunk ferry captains, though, captains in the Columbia fleet aren't likely to divulge such feelings in front of a Coast Guard board of inquiry. It could be bad for their careers.

Stephen Nolawski, a spokesperson for the union that had represented the unlicensed crewmembers on the *Fitzgerald,* had a slightly different explanation for why some captains took their ships out into the violent storm. To support his view, Nolawski told the story of what happened aboard the steamer *G. A. Tomlinson* during the November 10 storm.

The *Tomlinson* had unloaded cargo at Fairport, Ohio, and by the time they finished, fierce winds were blowing and tremendous seas were crashing over the breakwall at the entrance to the harbor. Despite that, as soon as they were unloaded, the captain started to turn the boat around so they could head out onto Lake Erie. The process of "winding" the boat around—keeping the bow securely against the dock and using the engine to drive the stern around in a 180-degree arc—would normally have taken fifteen to thirty minutes. On November 10, however, it took an hour and a half to swing the stern around into the wind. In fact, the engineers had to open up the bypass on the engine to increase power, or they might never have gotten the ship turned around. After all that, you'd think the captain might have put out the mooring lines and stayed there at the dock. The *Tomlinson* was no spring chicken. She had been built in 1907, and after more than sixty seasons on the lakes, her best years were definitely behind her. If there was a ship that could easily justify staying in port, it was the *Tomlinson*.

But on that day, in the midst of one of the worse storms in memory, her captain sailed her out of the Fairport harbor and onto the riled waters of Lake Erie, bound for Detroit. With the wind blowing at near-hurricane force out of the northwest, the captain soon found that his tired, old ship couldn't make any headway. Ducking behind an island for shelter, he had the bow anchors dropped, finally conceding that it was best for them to wait out the storm. Unfortunately, the anchors wouldn't hold, and the captain had to run the engine at full speed simply to hold the *Tomlinson* in position.

Some crewmembers on the *Tomlinson* were scared, and they put their lifejackets on. "Upon seeing this," Nowalski recounted, "one of the mates informed them if he were the skipper, he'd fire every goddamn one of them!"

Nowalski felt the judgment of the captains who took their ships out into the storm "was unduly influenced by a compulsion to competitive performance beyond prudence and ordinary good sense." In some cases, the behavior was probably the result of innate "machoism," while other captains undoubtedly felt pressured by the shipping companies to compete with their peers.

Nowalski was one of many in the industry who felt that the Coast Guard should regulate navigation during the late-fall storm season. He called for implementation of an "all-craft warning," when ships of any size would have to remain in port or seek shelter. Daniel Smith, a representative of the union that represented the officers on the *Fitzgerald* and most other Great Lakes ships, called for similar action.[29]

The extent to which some captains will go in order to keep the company office happy would be laughable if it hadn't resulted in disasters so many times over the years. One of the lucky ones was Captain Jim Phillips of the steamer *Charles S. Hebard* in the Wilson Transit fleet.

While on its way from Duluth to Fort William, Ontario, to load grain in late November 1931, the 504-foot *Hebard* strayed into shallow water and struck bottom. One of the wheelsmen later said that the pilothouse compass hadn't been working right for three months, but Captain Phillips hadn't done anything about it.

When the *Hebard* struck, the wheelsman quickly swung the wheel to the right and headed the ship out into deep water. Once they were safely offshore, an investigation showed that the ship was taking water into its number 5 ballast tank. Captain Phillips had the tank pumped out, then sent crewmen into the dark tank to pack the tears with dunnage to stop the leaks. They all assumed that he would make the required report to the Steamboat Inspection Service and have more permanent repairs made once the ship put in at the Canadian lakehead. They were in for a big surprise.

At the grain elevator at Fort William, Captain Phillips warned crew-members not to say anything about the damage to anyone. To make sure none of them got loose tongues after having a few beers up the street, he had the ladder pulled up and wouldn't let anyone off the boat during the almost twenty-four hours it took to load. As soon as they were loaded, Phillips headed the wounded *Hebard* down the lake, bound for Buffalo. It was later learned that Phillips wanted to get under way before insurance rates went up at midnight on November 30.

After unloading at Buffalo, the *Hebard* went to Cleveland to be dry-docked and repaired. After the graving dock had been pumped dry, shipyard workers found a one-ton boulder sticking through the hull. The rock and the dunnage jammed in around it had kept the flooding to a minimum, but if it had dropped out on the way down the lake, it could have spelled catastrophe for those aboard the *Hebard*.[30]

While Captain Jim Phillips abandoned common sense and ignored Steamboat Inspection Service regulations in what appeared to have been an attempt to appease the managers of the Wilson Transit fleet, the motivations of some other captains aren't quite as easy to understand. At about noon on April 30, 1940, for example, the canal-sized Canadian steamer *Arlington* left Port Arthur, Ontario, on Thunder Bay with 51,466 bushels of wheat. The little steamer's captain was Fred "Tatey Bug" Burke, brother of the two men who owned the ship. Those who sailed with him described Captain Burke as big, florid, rough-talking, erratic, stubborn, impulsive, moody, and intemperate—characteristics not at all unusual in the ranks of Great Lakes captains. He also had a reputation for running a "happy ship." In Great Lakes parlance, that usually means that there was little or no discipline.

After sailing for twenty-five years, Captain Burke had left his old job with Canada Steamship Lines at the end of the 1939 season to go to work with his brothers, so the *Arlington* was a new command for him. None of the crew had sailed with him before, but most were from Midland, Ontario, where Captain Burke lived, and they were certainly familiar with his reputation. They liked the idea that he wasn't a strict disciplinarian, but were less excited by his apparently well-earned and much-deserved reputation as a heavy-weather sailor.

Shortly after leaving the dock at Port Arthur, Captain Burke went to his stateroom, leaving the ship in the able hands of Junus Macksey, first mate. The weather was supposed to be moderate, but shortly after leaving the shelter of Thunder Bay, the *Arlington* encountered a severe spring storm. Because the *Arlington* had just over three feet of freeboard when loaded, Macksey set a course to run along in the lee of the north shore instead of heading across Lake Superior. Minutes later, Captain Burke stomped into the pilothouse and ordered the wheelsman to head the ship out into the lake and steer for Whitefish Point. With that, he retired again to his room.

When Macksey came back on watch again shortly after midnight, the storm had worsened considerably and the deck was continually awash. The conscientious mate decided to turn the *Arlington* before the wind so he could inspect the ship's hatches. Macksey told the wheelsman to swing the boat around, but when the mate started to go out on deck to take a look at the wooden hatches and the canvas tarps that protected them, Captain Burke again stormed into the pilothouse, obviously displeased.

"We're never going to get anyplace going in the wrong direction," he said harshly, then he ordered the wheelsman to get back onto the course for Whitefish. When the ship was again headed across the lake, Burke once more retreated to his room.

By about 3:30 A.M., seas ten feet high were rolling down the deck of the *Arlington,* and Macksey was sure he could see where tarps had been torn off the hatches. Worried, he sent the watchman down to wake the captain. The watchman returned a short time later, reporting that Captain Burke wouldn't answer his door. Angry, Macksey then went down and hammered on the captain's door, shouting that he needed Burke to come to the pilothouse so he could try to secure the hatches.

By the time Captain Burke made his appearance in the pilothouse, Macksey could see that several tarps had definitely been blown away. Even worse, the number 5 hatch had burst and water was flooding into the cargo hold. Almost immediately, the *Arlington* took on a five-degree port list. Without discussing the ship's dangerous situation with his mate,

Captain Burke had the wheelsman swing the ship around and head for the north shore.

The engine room started to flood about that time, and the watch engineer woke up Chief Engineer Fred Gilbert around 4:30 A.M. It took Gilbert only a second to conclude that their pumps couldn't handle the amount of water coming in. They were sinking!

Gilbert ran topside and sounded five short blasts on the ship's whistle to arouse the crew, then went below to make sure that everyone was up and preparing to abandon ship. By then the list had increased to thirty degrees. Up in the pilothouse, Macksey sounded a distress signal on the forward whistle. The call for assistance was heard by crewmembers aboard the *Collingwood*, a larger Canadian freighter that had left Thunder Bay at about the same time as the *Arlington* and was following along behind them.

Captain Burke remained in the pilothouse while Macksey and the other deck department crewmembers hurried aft to the lifeboats, which had already been swung out by Chief Gilbert and his men. The boats were dropped into the water and pulled around under the stern where they were sheltered from the pounding seas. The men waited there for the captain, but when it became obvious that he had no intention of joining them, they climbed down into the boats. Those in the pilothouse of the *Collingwood* noted the time in their log as 5:15 A.M. Day was just breaking on Lake Superior.

As the men in the lifeboats pulled toward the *Collingwood*, which was standing by between a quarter mile and a half mile from the foundering *Arlington*, several of the men caught a glimpse of Captain Burke. He had come down from the pilothouse, stood in the doorway to his room for a few seconds, then waved his arm and disappeared inside. Moments later, the *Arlington* rolled over on her port side and sank.[31]

Much was later made of Captain Burke's inexplicable decision to stay on the sinking ship. Contrary to popular myth, captains don't often voluntarily go down with their ships. In fact, in addition to Captain Burke, historians are only aware of two other cases on the Great Lakes. In 1883, Captain John McKay reportedly chose to go down with the steamer *Manistee* after three of the ship's four lifeboats were destroyed and there wasn't enough room in the remaining boat to evacuate all those aboard. In 1903, Captain William Morse reportedly chose to stay aboard the sinking *William F. Sauber* and was lost when the ship went down. We'll never know why Captain Burke refused to abandon his dying ship. Perhaps it was because he knew that his choleric actions and inattention to his duties had caused the ship to be lost. Maybe he saw death as being preferable to the dishonor that surely awaited him.

Jimmy Owen, John Brown, Jim Phillips, and Tatey Bug Burke are part of the lore of the lakes now, remembered long after their deaths because they lost their ships. They provide us with what may be extreme examples of ways in which the actions of captains have sunk ships and sentenced those aboard to watery deaths. Other captains have achieved the same result simply by ignoring storm warnings, running in fog, not seeing to it that hatches were battened down, making navigational errors, taking out ships that were of questionable seaworthiness, and . . . the list is virtually endless.

Often, the captains are aided by co-conspirators—the very crews that sail with them. A ship and its crew are in a hostile environment when they're out on the lakes. The margin between safety and disaster is often surprisingly small, yet the actions of crewmembers sometime whittle that margin down even further.

In the day-to-day routines aboard the big freighters, safety isn't taken seriously by many sailors. The problem may be worse today than it has ever been in the past. In large part, that's a reflection of the relatively sterling safety record of the industry in recent years. Many of today's sailors were still struggling to learn their ABCs and ride two-wheel bikes without training wheels when the *Sidney E. Smith, Jr.* collided with the *Parker Evans* and sank below the Blue Water Bridge, the *Fitzgerald* disappeared in a Lake Superior storm, the *Cartiercliffe Hall* burned, and the *Frontenac* tore its bottom out trying to go into Silver Bay—all during the 1970s. They're well aware of the industry's history of disasters, but in many respects they associate shipwrecks only with an earlier era, like reciprocating steam engines, wooden hatch covers, magnetic compasses, and taffrail logs.

Because they don't expect to be shipwrecked, today's crewmembers aren't always conscientious when it comes to things that could affect the seaworthiness of their ship. Hatch clamps aren't always tightened down, for example, and watertight doors intended to seal off various parts of the ship in case of flooding are commonly not dogged shut. Few take the fire and boat drills seriously. The quicker a drill is over the happier they are, even if they don't know how to launch a lifeboat or life raft, or what to do in case of a fire. They're apparently convinced that someone else will take care of those things in the unlikely event that their ship is wrecked. That complacency will someday exact its toll, just as it always has in the past.

Looking Back, Looking Ahead

In 1995 the Coast Guard conducted a comprehensive review of its programs and the extent to which the agency was effective in reducing marine casualties. They found that while their programs tended to concentrate on engineering and technical solutions to safety problems, an analysis of shipwrecks over the previous thirty years showed that 80 percent were the result of human error, with only 20 percent attributable to "hardware failures," such as steering systems, navigational equipment, and hull fractures. "Governments and operating companies have, in other words, been devoting most of their attention to fixing problems that account for only about 20 percent of the overall safety picture," concluded Admiral James Card, then head of marine safety for the Coast Guard.[32]

Many other studies of marine casualties reviewed by the Coast Guard showed similar results, with human error blamed for 75–96 percent of all accidents. The mistakes made by shipboard personnel fell into three main categories: first, inattention, carelessness, and fatigue, what the Coast Guard termed "operator status"; second, "knowledge," including inadequate technical knowledge, or knowledge of shipboard operations; and third, failures in "decision-making," such as those resulting from poor judgment or inadequate information.

Human error in shipping accidents wasn't limited just to the crewmembers aboard the ships, however. The Coast Guard study also identified "management errors," including faulty standards and legislation, inadequate communications or coordination, poor equipment design, and hazards in the natural environment, as major causes of marine casualties.

According to Admiral Card, four primary factors accounted for the persistence of marine casualties. First on his list was the Coast Guard's failure to conduct "root cause" investigations of shipwrecks, thereby making it impossible to identify the specific human errors that caused the casualties. Second, the Coast Guard had failed to identify and systematically analyze high-risk operations. Third, marine safety programs generally failed to focus on preventing the specific types of human error that were causing accidents. And fourth, the marine industry as a whole had failed to analyze problems, share analyses, and share lessons learned.[33]

This review of the history of shipwrecks on the lakes clearly supports Admiral Card's conclusions. The categories generally used to classify shipwrecks—strandings and groundings, fires and boiler explosions, collisions, and founderings—are both inaccurate and misleading. In reality, most of the accidents and deaths that have occurred over the long history

63. Despite being equipped with the most sophisticated navigational equipment of any ship operating on the Great Lakes, The *M/V Buffalo* smashed into the fifty-five-foot-tall Detroit River Lighthouse early on the morning of December 12, 1997. Traveling at about eleven miles an hour at the time, the ship collided with the massive concrete base of the lighthouse, crushing a thirty-foot-by-twenty-five-foot section of the bow. The damage, clearly visible in this photo taken at a dock in Toledo, Ohio, shortly after the accident, was estimated at more than $1 million. An ensuing Coast Guard investigation attributed the casualty to human error, the primary cause of 80 percent of all accidents involving U.S. vessels. Investigators concluded that the mate who was navigating the ship failed to make a critical turn in the river because he was both distracted and suffering from fatigue at the time. (James R. Hoffman)

of the shipping industry on the Great Lakes have been the result of human errors that span the spectrum from simple mistakes to gross incompetence; from misfeasance, malfeasance, and nonfeasance to gross negligence. Those who have erred include generations of shipping executives, government officials, captains, and crews who share responsibility for the abysmal record of shipwrecks and deaths on the Great Lakes.

Chiseled into the stone over the Pennsylvania Avenue entrance to the National Archives in Washington is the motto "What's Past Is Prologue," taken from a line in Shakespeare's *The Tempest*.[34] It's a simple but elegant concept, and one that has been repeated and paraphrased many times over the years by historians, philosophers, and politicians, from Henri Bergson and George Santayana to Patrick Henry and Harry Truman. In fact, it's the primary reason we study history. Studying history solely for the sake of history can be immensely entertaining, but it has little utility outside of Trivial Pursuit or Jeopardy. That's probably why there are so few "help wanted" ads for historians.

Our real interest in studying history grows out of our knowledge that the ideas and events of yesterday set the stage for what will transpire today and tomorrow. We study the past, then, to better understand what's happening today . . . to make our lives a little better . . . and to help us avoid repeating our previous mistakes.

When Dana Thomas Bowen wrote in 1952 that "shipping quickly turns its losses into lessons" and "almost all of the disasters recounted could not have happened even a few years later," he was simply *wrong*. The historical record shows that all too vividly. The shipping industry has consistently failed to effectively address the major causes of shipwrecks and deaths on the lakes.

Statistical analysis of the relationship between the number of ships on the lakes and the number of casualties from 1830 through 1979[35] yields a correlation of .86. That suggests that 86 percent of the change in the number of accidents can be explained merely by taking into consideration the number of ships in service. As the number of ships operating on the lakes increased during the eighteenth century, the number of shipwrecks kept pace. When the number of ships began to decline in the twentieth century, so did the number of wrecks. Statisticians will tell you that .86 is a *very strong* correlation. At the same time, it suggests that whatever efforts were made by government agencies and shipping companies weren't very effective in altering the trend in the number of vessel casualties on the Great Lakes.

The correlation for the period 1830–1909 is even higher, at .90, while it drops to only .68 for the years 1910–79. It's impossible to determine with any precision why there is less of a correlation between the number of ships and the number of accidents after 1910. We know, however, that the nature of the shipping industry changed dramatically after 1910. In addition to the major reduction in the number of ships operating on the lakes, steel ships that were stronger and less likely to catch fire replaced wooden vessels; sailing ships were replaced by steam-powered vessels that were less likely to be driven ashore during storms; navigational equipment became much more sophisticated with the advent of radio direction-finders, gyrocompasses, radar, and LORAN, significantly reducing groundings and collisions; weather forecasting improved, making it less likely that ships would get caught out on the lakes in storms;

and radio made it possible for ships to get updated weather forecasts and, eventually, traffic reports in the often-congested river systems. Such technological advancements clearly played a major role in reducing vessel casualties on the lakes after 1910.

It's impossible to confer credit for the reductions in casualties that resulted from those technological improvements on either the shipping companies or government regulators, however. The shipping companies didn't develop the new technology, and they were often slow to embrace it. Shipowners didn't shift from wooden to steel ships unless it was economically advantageous to them, for example, and most didn't install radios or improved navigational systems until they were required to do so by the government. In the case of radio, for example, the bulk shipping companies that belonged to the LCA mounted an aggressive, ongoing, and highly successful campaign against government proposals that would have required them to install transmitting and receiving equipment on their ships.

At the same time, Washington politicians and bureaucrats in both the Steamboat Inspection Service and the Coast Guard have been recalcitrant in forcing shipowners on the lakes to adopt new technology that would reduce the number of shipwrecks and resulting deaths.[36] Sail-powered cargo ships and tow barges were never regulated, and old wood-hulled sailboats and steamers were allowed to continue operating despite clear evidence that they were highly vulnerable to sinking the first time they encountered even a moderate storm. The politicians and bureaucrats didn't force shipbuilders and shipowners to stop using flammable materials in their ships until the 1960s, and even then they didn't force shipowners to retrofit older ships to reduce the likelihood of fires. Cargo ships weren't required to have radios until 1934, and even then, small freighters that were probably the most likely to encounter difficulties were excluded from the requirement. The same was true in the case of radio direction-finding equipment.[37]

Despite the poor track records of the shipping companies, politicians, and officials in the various government regulatory agencies, the number of shipwrecks and deaths on the lakes has steadily declined since 1910. That phenomenon is largely a result of the continuing downsizing of the fleet, combined with a wide array of technological developments.

Today, serious casualties are rare. When accidents do occur, however, they are very often the result of the same sorts of problems that have plagued the industry since its earliest days—problems that haven't been dealt with effectively by the shipping companies, the politicians, or the government bureaucrats. "Disasters are often years in the making," noted one knowledgeable observer. "Sometimes they occur as the result of cumulative error . . . and sometimes they result from long-term ignorance of technical realities."[38]

If the past is prologue, then it only follows that the present is also prologue. The conditions that exist when the sun sets on this day will help shape the events of all our tomorrows.

The head of the Coast Guard's marine safety office recently called upon the shipping industry to help instill a "culture of safety" throughout the marine transportation system.[39] There is certainly no culture of safety in the Great Lakes shipping industry today. Despite the industry's incredible efficiency and its vastly improved safety record over the past two decades, many dangerous safety problems have not been eliminated.

While the industry is safer today than it has been at any time in the past, numerous dangerous conditions persist that almost guarantee that the roll of sunken ships and dead sailors is not yet complete. If we don't act to correct the problems today, there *will* be more needless shipwrecks and deaths on some tomorrow that lies just over the eastern horizon.

Talk to the sailors who crew the ships out on the Great Lakes, and you'll find that they aren't at all bashful about telling you that from their bird's-eye view it's not a question of whether or not there'll be another shipwreck. As they see it, it's only a question of which ship, and when.

You might also be surprised to learn that most of today's sailors aren't at all optimistic about their chances of surviving a shipwreck. Despite state-of-the-art communications, lifeboats, life rafts, survival suits, EPIRBs, and other safety equipment, most sailors are alarmingly fatalistic on the subject. It they happen to have the bad luck to be aboard the next ship that goes down, many feel they're likely to suffer the same fate as the crew of the *Edmund Fitzgerald.*

At the same time, many of those same sailors have excellent ideas about things that could be changed to both lessen the likelihood of casualties and improve the chances for crewmembers to survive if their ship sinks. For example, as the Coast Guard looks for ways to improve safety within the shipping industry, it might be wise for them to do the following:

- Implement a traffic control system that will keep ships off the lakes during severe storms.
- Require greatly improved safety training.
- Demand that new ships have watertight bulkheads within their cargo holds.

- Require new Great Lakes ships to be equipped with the same motorized enclosed lifeboats now required on ocean ships.
- Advocate repeal of the 1851 Harter Act that limits the liability exposure of shipping companies.
- Increase regulation of the growing number of tugs and barges operating within the maritime industry.

An excellent first step would be for the Coast Guard to expand their "ship-rider" program. Because Coast Guard inspectors seldom have a chance to spend any significant amount of time aboard operating vessels, they simply don't know what's going on within the industry. That's possibly one reason why they're always in for surprises in the aftermath of casualties.

After the *Fitzgerald* went down, for example, the Coast Guard investigators discovered that hatch clamps weren't always maintained, or even put on, and that crewmembers hadn't been trained in how to launch their inflatable life rafts. Any ordinary seaman with more than thirty days of service in the industry could have told them those things *before* the *Fitzgerald* sank.

The more time Coast Guard personnel can spend aboard the ships and getting to know crewmembers, the better they're going to understand what their agency needs to do to make the boats safer. A marine board of investigation is a less-than-optimum forum for Coast Guard staff to become educated about the industry they're supposed to be regulating.

Unfortunately, the Coast Guard has experienced significant budget cuts in the years since the beginning of the Reagan presidency. Those cuts in personnel and resources have undoubtedly undermined the agency's ability to perform its historical functions. One reflection of that was implementation of a self-inspection program that now allows shipping companies to perform many of the inspections previously conducted by Coast Guard personnel. Budget cuts have also led to a reduction in the Coast Guard's search-and-rescue capabilities. Today, it could take Coast Guard rescue vessels six to twelve hours to reach the scene of a vessel casualty, particularly on Lake Superior or Lake Huron. Given the Coast Guard's current fiscal situation, it's questionable whether they have the resources necessary to adequately monitor safety issues within the shipping industry.

While this book has focused only on shipwrecks and safety issues within the Great Lakes shipping industry, there is every reason to believe that the same sorts of problems that exist on the lakes are also common on ships

64. Despite the availability of enclosed lifeboats and gravity davits, most ships on the Great Lakes are still equipped with open lifeboats that have to be launched from outdated quadrantal or sheath-screw davits. Here, crewmembers aboard the *Calcite II* struggle to crank a lifeboat davit out during a fire and boat drill. It has long been the consensus within the shipping community and Coast Guard that it would be virtually impossible to launch a boat like the *Calcite*'s in high seas. (Author's Collection)

operating on the oceans, including those of U.S. and Canadian registry or ownership. In fact, the recent record shows that it's far more dangerous to sail on ocean ships than on those on the lakes. Between 1980 and 1997, 259 bulk freighters sank on the oceans. Many disappeared, with all hands lost.[40] By comparison, only one ship was lost on the lakes during that period—the tanker *Jupiter*—and only one sailor died in that casualty. The abysmal record of shipwrecks on the oceans demands the immediate attention of the international shipping community.

The Great Lakes shipping industry can point with a great deal of pride to its comparatively safe record during recent years, but there have been too many close calls, and there are too many lingering problems for the industry to become any more complacent than it already is. If changes along the lines of those that have been suggested here aren't put into effect, the day will eventually come when people in downtown Detroit will again hear the bells at Mariner's Church tolling plaintively in sad remembrance of ships and sailors lost on the lakes.

NOTES

Preface

1. Thompson, *Steamboats and Sailors,* 150.

Introduction

1. Telephone conversation with Pastor Richard W. Ingalls, June 2, 1994.

2. Gordon Lightfoot, "Wreck of the *Edmund Fitzgerald,*" Moose Music, Ltd., 1976.

3. Havighurst, *Great Lakes Reader,* 287.

4. Hatcher and Walter, *Pictorial History,* 53.

5. La Salle went on to explore the Mississippi River all the way to its mouth and claim Louisiana for the French.

6. Hennepin, *New Discovery,* 120–21. My friend Rev. Richard Nelson of Duluth, a student of Native American history in the Great Lakes region, called my attention to a second possible explanation for the loss of the *Griffon.* There is an oral tradition within the Algonquin Nation that members of several tribes, fearing the encroachment of Europeans into their region, killed the crew of the *Griffon.* Further information can be found in Ives Goddard, "Reflections of Historical Events."

7. Wolff, *Lake Superior Shipwrecks,* 3.

8. Mansfield, *History of the Great Lakes,* 595–96.

9. Ibid.

10. Hatcher and Walter, *Pictorial History,* 95.

11. Capron, *U.S. Coast Guard,* 41.

12. Mansfield, *History of the Great Lakes,* 439.

13. Hall, *Marine Disasters,* 20.

14. Mansfield, *History of the Great Lakes,* 439.

15. Wolff, *Lake Superior Shipwrecks*, ix.

16. Wolff, *Lake Superior Shipwrecks*, 3.

17. Stonehouse, *Keweenaw Shipwrecks*, 1–315.

18. Stonehouse, *Lake Superior's "Shipwreck Coast,"* 1–365.

19. Parker, *Shipwrecks of Lake Huron*, 80–89.

20. Ibid., 50–61.

21. Swayze, *Shipwreck*, 21.

22. Parker, *Shipwrecks of Lake Huron*, 65–77.

23. Ibid., 93–102.

24. Harold, *Shipwrecks of the Sleeping Bear*, 1–17. Harold's total does not include the *Francisco Morazon*, which ran aground on the southern tip of South Manitou Island during a Lake Michigan storm in 1960.

25. Greg Reisig, "Gravesites of the Manitou Passage," *Elk Rapids (Mich.) Gazette*, September 2, 1994, 1–19.

26. Havighurst, *The Long Ships Passing*, 259.

27. Mansfield, *History of the Great Lakes*, 110.

28. Ibid., 439.

29. Swayze, *Shipwreck*, 5–6.

30. Oleszewski, *Ice Water Museum*, iii.

31. From a 1940 newspaper article in the vertical file of the Traverse Area District Library, Traverse City, Michigan. The newspaper from which the article was clipped is not identified, nor is its exact date.

32. Bowen, *Shipwrecks of the Lakes*, 67, says that between 60 and 101 people died aboard the *Alpena*.

33. Ibid., 67–70.

34. Extracted from the newspaper clipping previously cited.

35. Ratigan, *Great Lakes Shipwrecks and Survivals*, 242.

36. Pitz, *Lake Michigan Disasters*, 56.

37. Wolff, *Lake Superior Shipwrecks*, 98.

38. Hansen, "The Christmas Tree Schooner," 309–14.

39. Pitz, *Lake Michigan Disasters*, 62.

40. Donahue, *Terrifying Steamboat Stories*, 184–86.

41. Bowen, *Lore of the Lakes*, 177–79. Some reports say there were only forty-seven crewmembers aboard the *Milwaukee* when it went down.

42. Gebhart, "Reluctant Acceptance of Wireless," 150.

43. Van Der Linden, *Great Lakes Ships We Remember II*, 261–62.

44. *Marine Casualty Report: S.S. Daniel J. Morrell*, 1–34.

45. *Marine Casualty Report: S.S. Edmund Fitzgerald*, 26–32.

46. Mansfield, *History of the Great Lakes*, 507.

47. Ibid., 439.

48. Hall, *Marine Disasters*, 5.

49. Mansfield, *History of the Great Lakes*, 439.

50. Ibid.

51. Ibid., 507.

52. Stonehouse, *Wreck Ashore*, 144–49.

53. The history of the evolution of ships on the lakes is taken from Thompson, *Steamboats and Sailors*, 13–57.

54. Bowen, *Shipwrecks of the Lakes*, 1–2.

Chapter 1

1. Sivertson, *Once Upon an Isle*, 86–87.

2. Stonehouse, *Wreck Ashore*, 3.

3. Ibid., 86.

4. Stonehouse, *Isle Royale Shipwrecks*, 32–36.

5. Wolff, *Lake Superior Shipwrecks*, 74.

6. Stonehouse, *Isle Royale Shipwrecks*, 32.

7. Sivertson, *Once Upon an Isle*, 86.

8. Wolff, *Lake Superior Shipwrecks*, 3–4.

9. Ibid., 27–28.

10. Stonehouse, *Isle Royale Shipwrecks*, 43

11. Ibid., 72.

12. There are conflicting reports on the number of persons aboard the *Monarch*. In *Shipwrecks of Lake Superior*, 121–22, Wolff doesn't give a total, but he

reports that there were thirty crewmembers and "a few passengers." In Stonehouse's *Isle Royale Shipwrecks*, 186, the number is given as thirty-two crewmen and twelve passengers. Van Der Linden, *Great Lakes Ships We Remember*, 295, says there were sixty-one persons aboard. For the sake of expediency, I've decided to use Stonehouse's figures.

13. According to Gill, "Sound and Radio Aids to Navigation," 255, "Before the radio direction-finding system was so generally used there was a tendency on the part of Lakes' pilots to maintain their full speed in low visibility in order to keep their dead reckoning accurate. They relied on their reckoning when going at their normal full speed, but they were unable to rely on their reckoning when going at reduced speed. The tendency to maintain full speed resulted in some very serious collisions."

14. Barry, *Wrecks and Rescues of the Great Lakes*, 30–31.

15. Information for this section has been extracted from accounts in the three works previously cited in footnote 12.

16. Van Der Linden, *Great Lakes Ships We Remember II*, 74.

17. Stonehouse, *Isle Royale Shipwrecks*, 84.

18. Van Der Linden, *Great Lakes Ships We Remember II*, 74.

19. *Pilot Rules for the Great Lakes*, 3.

20. Wolff, *Lake Superior Shipwrecks*, 192.

21. Wakefield and Wakefield, *Sail and Rail*, 61–62.

22. Woodford, *Charting the Inland Seas*, 12–13.

23. Stonehouse, *Munising Shipwrecks*, 16.

24. Hatcher and Walter, *Pictorial History*, 277.

25. Stonehouse, *Munising Shipwrecks*, 16.

26. Charts in the series are most often referred to as "the Bayfield charts" in honor of Henry W. Bayfield, a young naval lieutenant who was deeply involved in the surveys and subsequent development of the charts.

27. Brown, "The Great Lakes," 162.

28. Woodford, *Charting the Inland Seas*, 31.

29. Morrison, "Feat of Long Point Heroine 100 Years Ago Is Recalled," 18; reprint, *London (Ontario) Free Press*.

30. Wolff, *Lake Superior Shipwrecks*, 6–7.

31. Ibid., 19–20.

32. Ibid., 21.

33. O'Brien, *Guardians of the Eighth Sea,* 30.

34. Wolff, *Lake Superior Shipwrecks,* 21.

35. Mansfield, *History of the Great Lakes,* 378.

36. Stonehouse, *Keweenaw Shipwrecks,* 317.

37. Ibid., 318–22.

38. Captain Bob Massey and I were on our way out to the wreck of the *Nordmeer* in the spring of 1975 when a heavy fog settled over northern Lake Huron. Our little tug wasn't equipped with radar, but we got a firm fix on our position when we passed Thunder Bay Island Light and were able to set a compass course to the wreck. As we neared the wreck, we could clearly hear the ringing of the bell buoy that sat just off the *Nordmeer*'s stern. Even though we crisscrossed the waters for two hours, we never did locate the bell buoy or the wreck. At times the bell had sounded so close you would have thought you could literally reach out and touch it.

39. "Canadians Disconnecting Foghorns on Great Lakes Lighthouses," 20.

40. Barry, *Wrecks and Rescues of the Great Lakes,* 39–41.

41. Lewis, "Curious History of the Infamous *Fame.*"

42. Barcus, *Freshwater Fury,* 126.

43. Walton, "Developments on the Great Lakes," 128–30.

44. Wolff, *Lake Superior Shipwrecks,* 176–80.

45. "1927 *Lambton* Disaster Recalled," 1–3 (reprint of an article that appeared in the *Canadian Echo* of Wiarton, Ontario, December 15, 1927).

46. Wolff, *Lake Superior Shipwrecks,* 181–83.

47. Ibid., 192.

48. *Bulletin of the Lake Carriers' Association,* July 1947, 17.

49. Wolff, *Lake Superior Shipwrecks,* 199–200.

50. Ibid., 207–13.

51. Ibid., 240–41.

52. "Canadians Disconnecting Foghorns on Great Lakes Lighthouses," 20.

53. "Great Lakes Calendar," 52–57.

54. Jack Storey, "Navigation Woes for Kinsman," *Sault Ste. Marie (Mich.) Evening News,* December 2, 1990, B-4.

55. "Canadian Tugs Refloat Vessel," *Sault Ste. Marie (Mich.) Evening News,* November 26, 1990, 1.

56. "Grounded Ship Damaged," *Sault Ste. Marie (Mich.) Evening News*, November 28, 1990.

57. "Ore Carrier Smashes into Lighthouse," 43.

58. "Ore Ship Runs Aground in St. Mary's River," 58.

59. Mansfield, *History of the Great Lakes*, 439.

60. Swayze, *Shipwreck*, 14–253.

61. Ibid.

62. Ibid.

63. Lake Carriers' Association [LCA], *1910 Annual Report*, 115.

64. Stonehouse, *Wreck Ashore*, 199.

65. Swayze, *Shipwreck*, 14–253.

66. Ibid.

67. Mansfield, *History of the Great Lakes*, 439; and LCA, *1900 Annual Report*, 24; *1910 Annual Report*, 28; *1920 Annual Report*, 23; and *1930 Annual Report*, 59. The totals include both U.S. and Canadian ships.

Chapter 2

1. Hatcher and Walter, *Pictorial History*, 252.

2. *Chronicle of America*, 317.

3. Havighurst, *The Long Ships Passing*, 127.

4. Mansfield, *History of the Great Lakes*, 439.

5. Kaplan and Hunt, *This Is the Coast Guard*, 153.

6. Mansfield, *History of the Great Lakes*, 610.

7. Kaplan and Hunt, *This Is the Coast Guard*, 153.

8. Capron, *U.S. Coast Guard*, 41.

9. Ibid.

10. Bowen, *Shipwrecks of the Lakes*, 13–16.

11. Barry, *Ships of the Great Lakes*, 51.

12. Ibid.

13. Bowen, *Shipwrecks of the Lakes*, 13–16.

14. Barry, *Ships of the Great Lakes*, 52.

15. Havighurst, *The Long Ships Passing*, 128.

16. Pitz, *Lake Michigan Disasters*, 2–12.

17. LCA, *1914 Annual Report*, 24.

18. Boyer, *True Tales of the Great Lakes*, 107–32.

19. Ibid., 112.

20. Ibid.

21. Ibid.

22. Stefoff, *U.S. Coast Guard*, 46.

23. Capron, *U.S. Coast Guard*, 41–42.

24. Wolff, *Lake Superior Shipwrecks*, 6.

25. Ibid., 6

26. "Splendid Trips," *Portage Lake Mining Gazette*, August 5, 1865, 3.

27. "Steamboat Races," *Portage Lake Mining Gazette*, August 5, 1865, 3.

28. "Burning of the *Meteor*," *Portage Lake Mining Gazette*, August 19, 1865, 3.

29. Gjerset, *Norwegian Sailors*, 31.

30. Capron, *U.S. Coast Guard*, 43.

31. Hall, *Marine Disasters*, 20.

32. Donahue, *Terrifying Steamboat Stories*, 30–31. The *Alaska* ended its career cut down for service in the Canadian lumber trade. It was destroyed by fire in 1910 at Tobermory, Ontario, on Georgian Bay.

33. For an interesting account of the race, see Boyer, *Great Stories of the Great Lakes*, 1–22.

34. Shipley and Addis, *Wrecks and Disasters*, 30; Wolff, *Lake Superior Shipwrecks*, 53.

35. Donahue, *Terrifying Steamboat Stories*, 60–61.

36. Stonehouse, *Munising Shipwrecks*, 106; Wolff, *Lake Superior Shipwrecks*, 101–2.

37. Wolff, *Lake Superior Shipwrecks*, 104.

38. Capron, *U.S. Coast Guard*, 44.

39. Stonehouse, *Wreck Ashore*, 196.

40. Shipley and Addis, *Wrecks and Disasters*, 36–37.

41. Donahue, *Terrifying Steamboat Stories,* 60–61.

42. Extracted from LCA annual reports from 1920 to 1949.

43. Bowen, *Shipwrecks of the Lakes,* 322–35.

44. Donahue, *Terrifying Steamboat Stories,* 232–33.

45. A "mechanical assistant" is the Canadian equivalent of an oiler or QMED on a U.S. vessel.

46. *Marine Casualty Report: M/V Cartiercliffe Hall,* 1–17.

47. Based on conversations with Marty Tice, who was serving as an engineer on the *Barker* at the time of the fire.

48. Mike Magner, "Dock Caused *Jupiter* Disaster," *Bay City (Mich.) Times,* October 30, 1991, 1.

49. Ted Kleine, "Sparks Seen at Total Dock," *Bay City (Mich.) Times,* September 27, 1990, 1–2.

50. "Tanker Explodes, Burns," *Detroit Free Press,* September 17, 1990, 1–9.

51. Ted Kleine, "Buffalo's Actions Called Hit and Run," *Bay City (Mich.) Times,* September 19, 1990, 4A.

52. "Tanker Explodes, Burns," 1.

53. Elizabeth McKenna, "Blast Sounded Like a Sonic Boom," *Bay City (Mich.) Times,* September 18, 1990, 4A.

54. Kathy Petersen, "Fire and Cleanup Cost $6.1 Million," *Bay City (Mich.) Times,* September 15, 1991, 5A.

55. Ibid.

56. Elizabeth McKenna, "*Jupiter* Not First to Burn," *Bay City (Mich.) Times,* September 21, 1990, 8A.

57. "Engineer Complained of Fire Equipment," *Bay City (Mich.) Times,* September 30, 1990, 12.

58. Kleine, "Sparks Seen at Total Dock," 2.

59. Magner, "Dock Caused *Jupiter* Disaster," 1.

60. Petersen, "Fire and Cleanup Cost $6.1 Million," 5A.

61. Extracted from Swayze, *Shipwreck.* The other tankers included the *Blue Comet, Roy K. Russel, J. Oswald Boyd, Transiter, Transoil, Morania #130,* and *Norman P. Clement.*

62. *Lake Log Chips,* February 7, 1987, 5. The news item quotes Captain John Leonard on the subject of methane explosions on Canadian canallers.

63. Ibid. The report was attributed to W. R. Oehlenschlager, who had been the second assistant engineer on the *Hulst* when the explosion occurred.

64. Ibid.

65. *Lake Log Chips,* October 18, 1986, 4.

66. *American Ship Building Company and Predecessors,* 1–18.

67. Gatewood, "Construction of a Fireproof Excursion Steamer," 1.

Chapter 3

1. Van Der Linden, *Great Lakes Ships We Remember,* 42.

2. Both the weather conditions and the number of passengers aboard the *Atlantic* are the subject of conflicting reports. Van Der Linden, *Great Lakes Ships We Remember,* 42, gives the number of passengers as 600 and reports that "the night was hazy but not foggy." Havighurst, *The Long Ships Passing,* 140–41, says there were 500 aboard and the ship was running in "dense fog." I've attempted to reconcile the conflicting reports. It must be remembered that passenger lines operating on the lakes in 1852 were not known to keep accurate passenger manifests, as would have been the case on ocean vessels. Since the voyages on the Great Lakes were relatively short, they seem to have been treated largely as "day cruises"—you paid your money and you went aboard, without a lot of paperwork.

3. Mansfield, *History of the Great Lakes,* 507.

4. "Further Particulars of the Loss of the *Atlantic,*" *Detroit Free Press,* August 23, 1852, 3.

5. "The Loss of the *Atlantic,*" *Detroit Free Press,* August 23, 1852, 2.

6. Van Der Linden, *Great Lakes Ships We Remember,* 42.

7. Havighurst, *The Long Ships Passing,* 141.

8. "Further Particulars of the Loss of the *Atlantic,*" 3.

9. Barry, *Ships of the Great Lakes,* 80.

10. Ibid., 80–82.

11. Another report in Barry, *Ships of the Great Lakes,* 82, says that there was one oar in the lifeboat.

12. An account of the sinking attributed to a survivor reports that "on this extempore raft not less than 300 persons were collected, the majority of whom clung to their places until nearly daylight. The raft was mostly under water from the weight of the living burden, and very few who clung to it

but were above the waist in the turbulent sea" (ibid., 83). It is impossible to determine the accuracy of this report.

13. Boyer, *True Tales of the Great Lakes*, 199–200.

14. Van Der Linden, *Great Lakes Ships We Remember*, 247.

15. Boyer, *True Tales of the Great Lakes*, 200.

16. Ibid. Barry, *Ships of the Great Lakes*, 83, sets the figure at 350.

17. The same would hold true under today's rules of the road.

18. The general details of the sinking of the *Lady Elgin* and *Mojave* have been taken from Boyer, *True Tales of the Great Lakes*, 177–208.

19. Hayler, *American Merchant Seaman's Manual*, 191.

20. Landon, *Lake Huron*, 272.

21. Ibid., 275.

22. Wolff, *Lake Superior Shipwrecks*, 6.

23. Ibid., 4–5.

24. Bowen, *Memories of the Lakes*, 44.

25. Wolff, *Lake Superior Shipwrecks*, 6.

26. Ibid.

27. LCA, *1911 Annual Report*, 113–20.

28. Mansfield, *History of the Great Lakes*, 702.

29. Mason, *Copper Country Journal*, 311.

30. Ibid.

31. "Appalling Calamity," *Detroit Free Press*, August 12, 1865, 1.

32. Douglass, "The *Pewabic* Disaster," 433.

33. Busch, *Lake Huron's Death Ship*, 11.

34. Dorothy Gheen, "The *Pewabic:* Lake Huron's Mystery Ship," *Alcona County (Mich.) Review*, November 17, 1981, 7.

35. Ibid.

36. "Appalling Calamity," 1.

37. Busch, *Lake Huron's Death Ship*, 17.

38. Ibid., 16.

39. "Appalling Calamity," 1.

40. "Burning of the *Meteor*," *Portage Lake Mining Gazette*, August 19, 1865, 3.

41. "The Late Marine Disaster," *Detroit Free Press*, August 16, 1865, 1.

42. Quoted in ibid.

43. "Chapter of Marine Disasters: Three Steamboats Lost," *Portage Lake Mining Gazette*, August 19, 1865, 3.

44. Busch, *Lake Huron's Death Ship*, 19.

45. Wolff, *Lake Superior Shipwrecks*, 22.

46. "Two from the Lakes," 151.

47. Bowen, *Memories of the Lakes*, 44.

48. Bowen, *Shipwrecks of the Lakes*, 53.

49. Ibid., 52–57.

50. Hall, *Marine Disasters*, 20.

51. Dunham was president of Dunham Towing and Wrecking, Chicago Steamship, and Chicago Transit Company. He was elected president of the Lake Carriers' Association in 1898.

52. Mansfield, *History of the Great Lakes*, 504.

53. "Father's Arrival in Nick of Time Saves Runaway Boy from *Cowle* Disaster," *Detroit News*, July 14, 1909, 1.

54. Wolff, *Lake Superior Shipwrecks*, 131.

55. "Eleven Men Drown When Boats Crash at Whitefish Point," *Detroit News*, July 12, 1909, 1.

56. Wolff, *Lake Superior Shipwrecks*, 131.

57. Mansfield, *History of the Great Lakes*, 465–83.

58. Ibid., 490–94.

59. LCA, *1914 Annual Report*, 171.

60. Thompson, *Queen of the Lakes*, 80–82.

61. Swayze, *Shipwreck*, 27–93.

62. "Battled for Lives in Small Yawl Boats," *Sault Ste. Marie (Mich.) Evening News*, December 7, 1909, 1.

63. "Vessels Clash in St. Marys River," *Sault Ste. Marie (Mich.) Evening News*, December 6, 1909, 1.

64. Van Der Linden, *Great Lakes Ships We Remember II*, 328.

65. Oleszewski, *Sounds of Disaster,* 69–77.

66. "Woman Survivor Describes Wreck," *Detroit News,* May 24, 1910, 1.

67. Oleszewski, *Sounds of Disaster,* 69–77.

68. "Warned to Flee, Engineer Stuck to Sinking Boat," *Detroit News,* May 25, 1910, 1.

69. Ibid.

70. LCA, *1914 Annual Report,* 210.

71. Stonehouse, *Wreck Ashore,* 198

72. Mansfield, *History of the Great Lakes,* 504; LCA, *1915 Annual Report,* 25; and *1926 Annual Report,* 49.

73. "No Trace Found of Crew of Lake Wreck," *Detroit Free Press.* August 22, 1920, 1.

74. Ibid.

75. Boyer, *Ships and Men of the Great Lakes,* 113–15.

76. "Str. *Steinbrenner* Gets a Hole Smashed in Its Bow," *Sault Ste. Marie (Mich.) Evening News,* October 12, 1923, 3.

77. "Ship Sunk off Whitefish," *Detroit Free Press,* October 12, 1923, 1.

78. "Str. *Steinbrenner* Gets a Hole Smashed in Its Bow," 3.

79. LCA, *1940 Annual Report,* 47.

80. "Freighter Sinks Near Mackinaw after Collision at Night in Fog," *Cheboygan (Wis.) Daily Tribune,* June 15, 1943, 1.

81. Dick, "Fishing for a Million," 1.

82. Wolff, *Lake Superior Shipwrecks,* 196–97.

83. "Divers Busy on Sunken Wreck," *Cheboygan (Wis.) Daily Tribune,* November 1, 1943, 1.

84. Dick, "Fishing for a Million," 1–2.

85. "9,000 Tons of *Humphrey* Ore Is Removed," *Cheboygan (Wis.) Daily Tribune,* December 6, 1943, 1

86. Doner, *The Salvager,* 36.

87. "Second Barge Will Help to Raise Vessel," *Cheboygan (Wis.) Daily Tribune,* August 23, 1944, 1.

88. Dick, "Fishing for a Million," 5.

89. "*Humphrey* May Leave Sunday," *Cheboygan (Wis.) Daily Tribune,* August 31, 1944, 1.

90. "*Humphrey* Is Refloated Sunday," *Cheboygan (Wis.) Daily Tribune*, September 11, 1944, 1.

91. Dick, "Fishing for a Million," 5.

92. "*Humphrey* is Refloated Sunday," 1.

93. "Salvaged Vessel Leaves Mackinaw," *Cheboygan (Wis.) Daily Tribune*, September 16, 1944, 1.

94. Kemp, "The Ship with Two Lives," 20–21.

95. "No One Panicked. Everyone Knew Their Job and Did It Automatically," *Presque Isle Advance*, May 13, 1965, 7.

96. Ibid.

97. Unless otherwise indicated, all details related to the sinking of the *Cedarville* have been taken from *Marine Casualty Report: S.S. Cedarville*.

98. *Marine Casualty Report: S.S. Parker Evans and S.S. Sidney E. Smith, Jr. Collision*, 1–9.

99. Barry, *Wrecks and Rescues of the Great Lakes*, 93–95.

100. Swayze, *Shipwreck*, 14–253.

101. Hall, *Marine Disasters*, 20.

102. Swayze, *Shipwreck*, 14–253.

103. Ibid.

Chapter 4

1. Swayze, *Shipwreck*, 78.

2. Ryan, "Enhancing Weather Forecasting," 99–100.

3. Clary, *Ladies of the Lakes II*, 125.

4. A storm is often referred to by the name of a particular ship that was lost during the blow, even though the storm may actually have claimed many vessels. The *Alpena* storm, for example, wrecked ninety ships, while at least seventeen vessels were lost or damaged in the Big Storm of 1905.

5. Combining lists of shipwrecks from Swayze, Wolff, Parker, and Bowen. To the extent possible, shipwrecks used represent only the most serious casualties, generally involving the loss of a ship.

6. Clary, *Ladies of the Lakes II*, 116.

7. Mansfield, *History of the Great Lakes*, 101.

8. Ibid., 630.

9. Extrapolated from the data in ibid., 439.

10. Ibid., 630.

11. Clary, *Ladies of the Lakes II*, 116.

12. Mansfield, *History of the Great Lakes*, 718.

13. LCA, *1920 Annual Report*, 125.

14. Hall, *Marine Disasters*, 20.

15. Clary, *Ladies of the Lakes II*, 116.

16. Wolff, *Lake Superior Shipwrecks*, 19–21.

17. Clary, *Ladies of the Lakes II*, 117.

18. Donahue, *Terrifying Steamboat Stories*, 51.

19. Stonehouse, *Went Missing*, 15.

20. Donahue, *Terrifying Steamboat Stories*, 51.

21. Stonehouse, *Went Missing*, 15.

22. Wolff, *Lake Superior Shipwrecks*, 37–38.

23. Donahue, *Terrifying Steamboat Stories*, 50–51.

24. Wolff, *Lake Superior Shipwrecks*, 38.

25. Clary, *Ladies of the Lakes II*, 118.

26. "Fatal Fall Gales," *Sault Ste. Marie (Mich.) Evening News*, September 9, 1887, 1.

27. "The Captain's Family Safe," *Sault Ste. Marie (Mich.) Evening News*, September 9, 1887, 1.

28. Ibid.

29. Wolff, *Lake Superior Shipwrecks*, 50–51.

30. "Overloading on the Lakes," *Sault Ste. Marie (Mich.) Evening News*, September 13, 1887, 2.

31. Historians generally refer to the *Onoko*, launched on February 16, 1882, as the first iron bulk freighter on the lakes. It was not, however, the first iron ship. That honor belongs to the USS *Michigan*, launched at Erie, Pennsylvania, in 1843. The *Michigan* was also the U.S. Navy's first iron ship. The first iron-hulled freighter was actually the *Merchant*, built in 1862 and lost on Lake Erie in 1875.

32. Barry, *Ships of the Great Lakes*, 146.

33. Ibid.

34. "Marine Notes," *Sault Ste. Marie (Mich.) Evening News,* September 30, 1891, 3.

35. Mansfield and Wolff both write that the *Western Reserve* actually anchored in Whitefish Bay for a short time before heading out onto Lake Superior. No other accounts refer to the ship's anchoring, however, including the deposition given by Harry Stewart, the sole survivor of the sinking. In addition, Stewart said the *Western Reserve* went through the locks in the early afternoon, passed Whitefish Point at 4 P.M., and sank at 9 P.M. If those times are reasonably accurate, and they appear to be, the ship would not have had time to reach the point of its sinking, sixty miles northwest of Whitefish, if it had gone to anchor.

36. Boyer, *Great Stories of the Great Lakes,* 57.

37. Ibid., 57–58.

38. "Wrecks and Deaths," *Detroit Free Press,* September 2, 1892, 1.

39. Boyer, *Great Stories of the Great Lakes,* 58.

40. "The Wrecked Steamer," *Detroit Free Press,* September 3, 1892, 1.

41. Ibid.

42. Stonehouse, *Lake Superior's "Shipwreck Coast,"* 66.

43. Barry, *Ships of the Great Lakes,* 147.

44. "Wrecks and Deaths," *Detroit Free Press,* September 2, 1892, 1.

45. *Sault Ste. Marie (Mich.) Evening News,* September 24, 1892, 8.

46. Boyer, *Great Stories of the Great Lakes,* 66.

47. Donahue, *Terrifying Steamboat Stories,* 73–75.

48. Wolff, *Lake Superior Shipwrecks,* 70.

49. Swayze, *Shipwreck,* 33.

50. Barry, *Wrecks and Rescues of the Great Lakes,* 46–49.

51. Swayze, *Shipwreck,* 77.

52. Historian Ralph Roberts pointed out to me that the James E. Davidson Shipyard in Bay City, Michigan, was one of the last major Great Lakes yards to build wooden ships. Between 1895 and 1900 the yard turned out at least twenty-three wooden boats, including some of the largest ever built on the lakes at that time.

53. Calculated from the data available in Swayze, *Shipwreck,* 14–253.

54. Wolff, *Lake Superior Shipwrecks,* 112.

55. Ibid., 115.

56. Ibid., 115–16.

57. Pieced together from accounts in Barry, *Wrecks and Rescues of the Great Lakes*, 49–53; Wolff, *Lake Superior Shipwrecks*, 116–18; and Havighurst, *The Long Ships Passing*, 245–47.

58. Wolff, *Lake Superior Shipwrecks*, 124–25.

59. Havighurst, *Vein of Iron*, 112.

60. Mansfield, *History of the Great Lakes*, 478.

61. Weather conditions and details on the sinking of the *Louisiana* were extracted from Barcus, *Freshwater Fury*, 9–10, 141–48.

62. With telegraph lines down to many ports around the lakes, officials of Merchant's Mutual Line, owners of the *Turret Chief*, were unaware that their ship had passed up through the Soo and onto Lake Superior on the morning of November 7, before the storm had started. About 4 A.M. on November 8, however, the little Canadian freighter had been driven ashore on Keweenaw Point at the tip of the Keweenaw Peninsula.

63. Clary, *Ladies of the Lakes II*, 214–16.

64. Barcus, *Freshwater Fury*, 85–92.

65. Ibid., 133–37.

66. Boyer, *True Tales of the Great Lakes*, 312.

67. Ibid., 314.

68. Ibid., 316.

69. Barcus, *Freshwater Fury*, 117.

70. Ibid., 75.

71. Ibid., 149.

72. Eichenlaub, *Weather and Climate*, 290–97.

73. Boyer, *True Tales of the Great Lakes*, 313.

74. Ibid., 314.

75. Mansfield, *History of the Great Lakes*, 467.

76. Ibid., 316–20.

77. Barcus, *Freshwater Fury*, 125.

78. Boyer, *True Tales of the Great Lakes*, 68.

79. LCA, *1914 Annual Report*, 183.

80. Capron, *U.S. Coast Guard*, 41.

81. Ibid., 45.

82. LCA, *1914 Annual Report*, 192.

83. Mansfield, *History of the Great Lakes*, 439.

84. LCA, *1919 Annual Report*, 164.

85. A total of 1,653 persons died as a result of the 1865 boiler explosion and fire on the Mississippi River steamer *Sultana* near Memphis. The accident occurred just two days before the formal end of the Civil War, and over 1,400 of the dead were Union soldiers who had just been freed from Confederate prisoner-of-war camps and were being returned to their homes in the North. In the nation's second-worst maritime disaster, 957 were killed in the 1904 fire on the *General Slocum* on Long Island Sound.

86. Hilton, *"Eastland": Legacy of the "Titanic,"* 29.

87. Donahue, *Terrifying Steamboat Stories*, 157–58.

88. Hilton, *"Eastland": Legacy of the "Titanic,"* 25–40.

89. Ibid., 42.

90. Boyer, *True Tales of the Great Lakes*, 54.

91. Ibid., 46.

92. Ibid., 48–49.

93. Ibid., 52.

94. Bowen, *Lore of the Lakes*, 204.

95. Ibid., 57–61.

96. Boyer, *True Tales of the Great Lakes*, 52–53.

97. Hilton, *"Eastland": Legacy of the "Titanic,"* 1–12.

98. Barry, *Ships of the Great Lakes*, 190.

99. Hilton, *"Eastland": Legacy of the "Titanic,"* 113–15.

100. Ibid., 124–26.

101. Ibid., 137.

102. Boyer, *True Tales of the Great Lakes*, 37.

103. Ibid., 64–65.

104. Hilton, *"Eastland": Legacy of the "Titanic,"* 271–81.

105. LCA, *1925 Annual Report*, 103.

106. LCA, *1915 Annual Report*, 214.

107. Ibid., 141.

108. Ibid., 215.

109. Ibid., 216–17.

110. Stonehouse, *Went Missing*, 103.

111. LCA, *1909 Annual Report*, 33.

112. Ibid.

113. Van Der Linden, *Great Lakes Ships We Remember II*, 172–73.

114. "Search Without Success for Twenty Members of Steamer *Kirby* Crew," *Sault Ste. Marie (Mich.) Evening News*, May 9, 1916, 1.

115. "Believe *Kirby* Loaded Greatly Over Capacity," *Sault Ste. Marie (Mich.) Evening News*, May 10, 1906, 1.

116. Wolff, *Lake Superior Shipwrecks*, 156–57.

117. Benford, "Samuel Plimsoll," 77–80.

118. Mansfield, *History of the Great Lakes*, 465–67.

119. Bowen, *Lore of the Lakes*, 209–17.

120. LCA, *1916 Annual Report*, 139–40.

121. Boyer, *Ghost Ships of the Great Lakes*, 80–90.

122. "Third Tragic Blow Falls on Stricken Grand Haven," *Detroit News*, October 25, 1929, 36.

123. Boyer, *Ghost Ships of the Great Lakes*, 94–95.

124. Van Der Linden, *Great Lakes Ships We Remember*, 290–91.

125. Dickerson Hoover was the brother of J. Edgar Hoover, director of the FBI.

126. Boyer, *Ghost Ships of the Great Lakes*, 98.

127. Ibid.

128. Ibid., 94–98.

129. Ibid., 96–97.

130. Ibid., 97–98.

131. Van Der Linden, *Great Lakes Ships We Remember II*, 261.

132. LCA, *1929 Annual Report*, 45, and *1930 Annual Report*, 44–45.

133. The Bureau of Navigation and the Steamboat Inspection Service had been merged into the Bureau of Navigation and Steamboat Inspection in 1932

as an economy measure during the depression. The new agency was part of the Department of Commerce.

134. Capron, *U.S. Coast Guard,* 130–70.

135. Donahue, *Terrifying Steamboat Stories,* 222.

136. Ibid., 224.

137. *Marine Casualty Report: S.S. Henry Steinbrenner,* 1–4.

138. Ibid.

139. Stonehouse, *Isle Royale Shipwrecks,* 162–63.

140. *Marine Casualty Report: S.S. Henry Steinbrenner,* 4.

141. It's actually possible to get a Coast Guard "Lifeboatman" endorsement on your merchant seaman's card without ever rowing a lifeboat. The test covers only the parts of the boat, procedures to launch it, and rowing commands.

142. Ships in the Pittsburgh Steamship fleet were often referred to as "tin stackers." Their smokestacks were painted silver and looked to some like tin cans.

143. Geoffrey Howes, "Ten Minutes and She Was Gone," *Detroit Free Press,* May 12, 1963, 1.

144. "Bitter Survivors Call Ship Too Old," *Detroit Free Press,* May 15, 1953, 1.

145. *Marine Casualty Report: S.S. Henry Steinbrenner,* 7–12.

146. Wolff, *Lake Superior Shipwrecks,* 203.

147. The details on the sinking of the *Carl D. Bradley* are taken from *Marine Casualty Report: S.S. Carl D. Bradley;* "Here Is What Happened," *Presque Isle County Advance,* November 27, 1958, 2; Tom Greenwood, "The *Bradley's* Final Gasp: 'Fascinating, Horrifying,' " *Detroit News,* November 13, 1988, 1–2; "Mayday!" *Alpena (Mich.) News,* November 19, 1988, 6B; Clary, *Ladies of the Lakes,* 145–55; and the personal recollections of the author.

148. *Marine Casualty Report: S.S. Daniel J. Morrell,* and *Sinking of the S.S. Daniel J. Morrell in Lake Huron with Loss of Life.*

149. Thompson, *Queen of the Lakes,* 27–28.

150. *Lake Log Chips,* March 7, 1987, 5. The report on the crack in the deck of the *Sloan* was from W. R. Oehlenschlager, who had been the second assistant engineer on the ship at the time.

151. *Lake Log Chips,* December 27, 1986, 5. The report on the hull failure on the *Stanley* was attributed to Leo Gallagher, a wheelsman on the ship when the incident occurred.

152. *Marine Casualty Report: S.S. Daniel J. Morrell,* 5.

153. According to Great Lakes historian and merchant seaman Robert Vance, the last U.S. ship on the lakes with wooden hatch covers was Columbia Transportation's *Wyandotte,* built in 1916, and the last Canadian freighter with wooden hatches was the *Pic River,* operated at the end of her career by the Quebec and Ontario Transportation Company. The ship had been launched in 1896 as the unpowered barge *James Nasmyth.* The *Nasmyth* was the consort of the *Mataafa* when that ship was lost in 1905.

154. Swayze, *Shipwreck,* 14–253.

155. See *Marine Review,* May 8, 1901.

Chapter 5

1. The fact that the *Fitzgerald* lies in two pieces on the bottom led some, including the crew of Jacques Cousteau's *Calypso,* to conclude that the ship broke in half on the surface and that it sank *as a result of* breaking in half in the high seas. Such a conclusion is totally unsupported by the historical record. The two halves of ships that break in half generally have sufficient buoyancy left to float for some period before sinking, as was the case with both the *Carl D. Bradley* and *Daniel J. Morrell* (see Chapter 4). In fact, I have been unable to find a single report of a ship breaking in half and instantly plummeting to the bottom. If the *Fitzgerald* had broken in half on the surface it is almost inconceivable that those in the pilothouse wouldn't have been able to issue a distress call.

2. Wolff, *Lake Superior Shipwrecks,* 222–23. According to Hatcher and Walter, *Pictorial History,* 107–8, Forrest Pearse, a retired captain of the *Carl D. Bradley,* suspected that a "tidal wave" might have caused the *Bradley* to break in half and sink during the November 18, 1958, storm. "On the Great Lakes," said Pearse, "there are certain small areas during a storm that have a lower barometric pressure than the surrounding area. Because of the differences, a few waves often build up to twice the height of other waves. Usually there are two or three such giant waves in succession." During the storm that claimed the *Bradley,* waves were twenty-five to thirty feet high. Pearse surmised that a few waves might have been from forty-five to sixty feet high. These unusual series of exceptionally high waves are sometimes referred to as "the three sisters." In *The Perfect Storm,* Sebastian Junger provides an excellent explanation of how "rogue waves" form. According to Junger, "Rogue waves . . . are thought to be several ordinary waves that happen to get 'in step,' forming highly-unstable piles of water. Others are waves that overlay long-distance swells from earlier storms. Such accumulations of energy can travel in threes—a phenomenon called 'the three sisters'—and are so huge that they can be tracked by radar" (123–24).

3. *Expedition to the "Edmund Fitzgerald"* (Great Lakes DeepQuest Organization, Ltd., 1995), videotape.

4. If the captain had ordered the crew to put their lifejackets on and prepare to abandon ship, those housed in the forward cabin would have undoubtedly gathered in the forward recreation room and those living aft would have congregated in the messroom.

5. *Marine Casualty Report: S.S. Edmund Fitzgerald,* 1–109.

Chapter 6

1. Gjerset, *Norwegian Sailors,* 80.

2. Barcus, *Freshwater Fury,* 125.

3. Swayze, *Shipwreck,* 1–253.

4. Stonehouse, *Wreck Ashore,* 21.

5. Mansfield, *History of the Great Lakes,* 179–80.

6. Swayze, *Shipwreck,* 171.

7. Donahue, *Terrifying Steamboat Stories,* 184.

8. Gebhart, "Reluctant Acceptance of Wireless," 150–52.

9. Parker, *Shipwrecks of Lake Huron,* 40–41.

10. Walton, "Developments on the Great Lakes," 130.

11. Boyer, *Ghost Ships of the Great Lakes,* xxi.

12. Stonehouse, *Wreck Ashore,* 199. The figures cited include *all* casualties responded to by the Life-Saving Service, including pleasure boats.

13. Boyer, *True Tales of the Great Lakes,* 250–51.

14. "Marcus Alonzo Hanna," *Encarta 98 Encyclopedia* (Microsoft, 1998).

15. Quoted in Hatcher, *Lake Erie,* 168. Interestingly, Samuel Plimsoll would make a similar comment about British shipowners a decade later in his campaign to enact legislation to outlaw dangerous practices in his country's maritime industry: "If a small number of well-known ship owners were put aboard one of their own vessels when she was ready for sea, we should, in the event of bad weather, see that with them had disappeared from our annals nine-tenths of the losses we deplore" (quoted in Benford, "Samuel Plimsoll," 79).

16. Barcus, *Freshwater Fury,* 111.

17. Rooke, *The Industrial Revolution*, 67.

18. Wolff, *Lake Superior Shipwrecks*, 222.

19. *Marine Casualty Report: S.S. Edmund Fitzgerald*, 69–72.

20. Ratigan, *Straits of Mackinac*, 92.

21. Boyer, *True Tales of the Great Lakes*, 259.

22. Ibid., 251.

23. Ibid., 252.

24. Ibid., 251–54.

25. Boyer, *Ships and Men of the Great Lakes*, 14–25.

26. Ibid., 28.

27. Ibid.

28. Wolff, *Lake Superior Shipwrecks*, 226–28.

29. *Vessel Traffic Control Hearings*, 355–57.

30. Wolff, *Lake Superior Shipwrecks*, 190–91.

31. Ibid., 101.

32. Card, "The Coast Guard's Role," 14–15.

33. Ibid., 11–16.

34. It's somewhat ironic that the first scene in *The Tempest* is about a ship ravaged by a storm at sea.

35. Results were produced using multiple regression analysis.

36. The same holds true for politicians in Quebec and bureaucrats in the Canadian Coast Guard. In general, regulation of the Canadian shipping industry on the lakes has lagged behind that on the U.S. side of the lakes.

37. Byrnes, "Radio Communication and Equipment," 210–27.

38. "More Eyes on Ore," 26.

39. Card, "The Coast Guard's Role," 15.

40. "More Eyes on Ore," 26.

BIBLIOGRAPHY

Altobello, Peter David. *Lakers: Ghost Ships of the Great Lakes.* Montreal: Eden Press, 1988.

American Ship Building Company and Predecessors, 1867–1920. Bowling Green, Ohio: Libraries and Learning Resources, Bowling Green State University, 1988.

Amos, Art, and Patrick Folkes. *A Diver's Guide to Georgian Bay.* Toronto: Ontario Underwater Council, 1979.

Anderson, Charles M. *Isle of View: A History of South Manitou Island.* Frankfort, Mich.: J. B. Publications, 1979.

———. *Memo's of Betsie Bay.* Manistee, Mich.: J. B. Publications, 1988.

Appleton, Thomas E. *Usque Ad Mare: A History of the Canadian Coast Guard and Marine Services.* Ottawa: Department of Transportation, 1968.

Arnott, David. "Load Line Regulations, with Special Reference to the International Load Line Convention—1930." *Transactions of the Society of Naval Architects and Marine Engineers* 38 (1930): 77–102.

Baker, Catherine C. *Shipbuilding on the Saginaw.* Bay City, Mich.: Museum of the Great Lakes, 1974.

Barcus, Frank. *Freshwater Fury.* Detroit: Wayne State University Press, 1960.

Barry, James P. *The Fate of the Lakes.* Grand Rapids, Mich.: Baker, 1972.

———. *Ships of the Great Lakes.* Berkeley: Howell-North Books, 1973.

———. *Wrecks and Rescues of the Great Lakes: A Photographic History.* San Diego: Howell-North Books, 1981.

Beasley, Norman. *Freighters of Fortune.* New York: Harper & Brothers, 1930.

Beaton, Horace L. *From the Wheelhouse: The Story of a Great Lakes Captain.* Cheltenham, Ontario: Boston Mills Press, 1979.

Benford, Harry. "Samuel Plimsoll: His Book and His Mark." *Seaway Review,* January–March 1986, 77–80.

Bowen, Dana Thomas. *Lore of the Lakes.* Daytona Beach: Dana Thomas Bowen, 1940.

———. *Memories of the Lakes.* Cleveland: Freshwater Press, 1969.

———. *Shipwrecks of the Lakes.* Cleveland: Freshwater Press, 1952.

Boyer, Dwight. *Ghost Ships of the Great Lakes.* New York: Dodd, Mead, 1968.

———. *Great Stories of the Great Lakes.* New York: Dodd, Mead, 1966.

———. *Ships and Men of the Great Lakes.* Cleveland: Freshwater Press, 1977.

———. *True Tales of the Great Lakes.* Cleveland: Freshwater Press, 1971.

Brown, Andrew T. "The Great Lakes, 1850–1861, Part I." *Inland Seas* 6 (Fall 1950): 161–63.

Busch, Gregory James. *Lake Huron's Death Ship.* Saginaw, Mich.: Busch Oceanographic Equipment Co., 1975.

Bush, Captain Eric. *The Flowers of the Sea.* Annapolis, Md.: Naval Institute Press, 1962.

Butler, Hal. *Abandon Ship.* Chicago: Henry Regnery Company, 1974.

Byrnes, Irving F. "Radio Communication and Equipment." *Transactions of the Society of Naval Architects and Marine Engineers* 48 (1940): 210–27.

"Canadians Disconnecting Foghorns on Great Lakes Lighthouses." *Professional Mariner,* June–July 1995, 20.

Capron, Walter C. *U.S. Coast Guard.* New York: Franklin Watts, 1965.

Card, Admiral James. "The Coast Guard's Role in Marine Safety Issues." *Professional Mariner,* December 1995–January 1996, 11–16.

Channing, Edward, and Marion F. Lansing. *The Story of the Great Lakes.* New York: Macmillan, 1909.

Chronicle of America. Mount Kisco, N.Y.: Chronicle Publications, 1989.

Clark, William H. *Ships and Sailors.* Boston: L. C. Page & Company, 1938.

Clary, James. *Ladies of the Lakes.* Lansing: Michigan Department of Natural Resources, 1981.

———. *Ladies of the Lakes II.* West Bloomfield, Mich.: Altwerger and Mandel, 1992.

Davenport, Don. "The Great Storm of 1913." *Great Lakes Travel and Living,* December 1988, 12–23.

Dayton, Fred Erving. *Steamboat Days.* New York: Tudor, 1925.

Dick, Ross M. "Fishing for a Million." *Popular Mechanics,* December 1944, 1–5.

Donahue, James. *Terrifying Steamboat Stories.* West Bloomfield, Mich.: Altwerger and Mandel, 1991.

Doner, Mary Francis. *The Salvager: The Life of Captain Tom Reid on the Great Lakes.* Minneapolis: Ross and Haines, 1958.

Douglass, Samuel T. "The *Pewabic* Disaster." *Michigan History* 17 (August 1932): 431–38.

Dunsmore, Deena J. *Shipwrecked on the Great Lakes.* Goodells, Mich.: Grand Isle Press, 1994.

Eichenlaub, Val. *Weather and Climate of the Great Lakes Region.* Notre Dame, Ind.: University of Notre Dame Press, 1979.

Ellis, Gary D. *Historic Context: Marine Cultural Resources, Indiana Territorial Waters of Lake Michigan.* Notre Dame, Ind.; University of Notre Dame, 1989.

Engman, Elmer. *Shipwreck Guide to the Western Half of Lake Superior.* Duluth: Innerspace, 1976.

Expedition to the "Edmund Fitzgerald." Great Lakes DeepQuest Organization, Ltd. 1995. Videotape.

Feltner, Dr. Charles E., and Jeri Baron Feltner. *Great Lakes Maritime History: Bibliography and Sources of Information.* Dearborn, Mich.: Seajay, 1982.

———. *Shipwrecks of the Straits of Mackinac.* Dearborn, Mich.: Seajay, 1991.

Fleming, Robert M. *A Primer of Shipwreck Research and Records for Skin Divers, Including an Informal Bibliography Listing over Three Hundred Sources of Shipwreck Information.* Milwaukee: Global Manufacturing, 1971.

Folkes, Patrick. *Shipwrecks of the Saugeen, 1828–1938.* Willowdale, ON: Patrick Folkes, 1970.

———. *Shipwrecks of Tobermory, 1828–1935.* Willowdale, Ontario: Patrick Folkes, 1969.

Frederickson, Arthur C., and Lucy F. Frederickson. *Frederickson's History of the Ann Arbor Auto and Train Ferries.* Frankfort, Mich.: Gulls Nest Publishing, 1994.

Frimodig, Mac. *Shipwrecks off Keweenaw.* Copper Harbor, Mich.: Fort Wilkins Natural History Association, 1975.

Gatewood, William. "Construction of a Fireproof Excursion Steamer." *Transactions of the Society of Naval Architects and Marine Engineers* 14 (1906): 1–14.

Gebhart, Richard. "The Reluctant Acceptance of Wireless Use on the Great Lakes." *Inland Seas* 49 (Summer 1993): 149–53.

Gill, Commander I. L. "Sound and Radio Aids to Navigation." *Transactions of the Society of Naval Architects and Marine Engineers* 48 (1940): 228–57.

Gillham, Skip. "The Last of the Consorts." *Telescope* 25 (November–December 1976): 155–61.

———. *Ships along the Seaway.* Vol. 2. Fonthill, Ontario: Stonehouse Publications, 1975.

———. *Ten More Tales of the Great Lakes.* St. Catharines, Ontario: Stonehouse Publications, 1989.

Gjerset, Knut. *Norwegian Sailors on the Great Lakes.* Northfield, Minn.: Norwegian-American Historical Association, 1928.

Goddard, Ives. "Reflections of Historical Events in Some Traditional Fox and Miami Narratives." In *Papers of the Sixteenth Algonquian Conference,* ed. William Cowan, 47–59. Ottawa, Ontario: Carleton University, 1985.

"Great Lakes Calendar." *Inland Seas,* Spring 1995, 52–57.

Greenwood, John O. *The Fleet Histories Series.* Vol. 2. Cleveland: Freshwater Press, 1992.

———. *Namesakes of the Lakes.* Cleveland: Freshwater Press, 1970.

———. *Namesakes II.* Cleveland: Freshwater Press, 1973.

———. *Namesakes of the '90's.* Cleveland: Freshwater Press, 1991.

———. *Namesakes, 1900–1909.* Cleveland: Freshwater Press, 1987.

———. *Namesakes, 1910–1919.* Cleveland: Freshwater Press, 1986.

———. *Namesakes, 1920–1929.* Cleveland: Freshwater Press, 1984.

———. *Namesakes, 1930–1955.* Cleveland: Freshwater Press, 1981.

———. *Namesakes, 1956–1980.* Cleveland: Freshwater Press, 1978.

Gutsche, Andrea, Barbara Chisholm, and Russell Floren. *The North Channel and St. Mary's River.* Toronto: Lynx Images, 1997.

Hall, Captain J. W. *Marine Disasters on the Western Lake during the Navigation of 1871.* Detroit: Free Press Book and Job Printing Establishment, 1872.

Hansen, Harry. "The Christmas Tree Schooner." In *The Great Lakes Reader,* ed. Walter Havighurst, 309–14. New York: Macmillan, 1969.

Harold, Steve. *Shipwrecks of the Sleeping Bear.* Traverse City, Mich.: Pioneer Study Center, 1984.

Hatcher, Harlan. *The Great Lakes.* New York: Oxford University Press, 1944.

———. *Lake Erie.* New York: Bobbs-Merrill, 1945.

Hatcher, Harlan, and Erich A. Walter. *A Pictorial History of the Great Lakes.* New York: Bonanza Books, 1963.

Havighurst, Walter. *Land of Promise.* New York: Macmillan, 1947.

———. *The Long Ships Passing.* New York: Macmillan, 1942.

———. *Vein of Iron.* New York: World Publishing, 1958.

———, ed. *The Great Lakes Reader.* New York: Macmillan, 1969.

Haws, Duncan. *Ships and the Sea.* New York: Crescent Books, 1975.

Hayler, William B., ed. *American Merchant Seaman's Manual.* Centreville, Md.: Cornell Maritime Press, 1994.

Hemming, Robert J. *Gales of November.* Chicago: Contemporary Books, 1981.

———. *Ships Gone Missing.* Chicago: Contemporary Books, 1992.

Hennepin, Father Louis. *A New Discovery of a Vast Country in America.* Chicago: A. C. McClurg & Co., 1903.

Hilton, George W. *"Eastland": Legacy of the "Titanic."* Stanford, Calif.: Stanford University Press, 1995.

Hulse, Charles Allen. "A Spatial Analysis of Lake Superior Shipwrecks: A Study in the Formative Process of the Archaeological Record." Ph.D. diss., Michigan State University, 1981.

Johnson, Robert Erwin. *Guardians of the Sea.* Annapolis, Md.: Naval Institute Press, 1987.

Johnston, Paul F. "Downbound: Exploring the Wreck of the *Indiana.*" *Michigan History* 77 (September–October 1993): 24–30.

Junger, Sebastian. *The Perfect Storm: A True Story of Men against the Sea.* New York: Norton, 1997.

Kaplan, H. R., and James F. Hunt. *This Is the Coast Guard.* Cambridge, Md.: Cornell Maritime Press, 1972.

Kemp, William C. "The Ship with Two Lives." *Michigan History* 77 (May–June 1993): 20–21.

Labadie, Patrick C., Brian Agranat, and Scott F. Anfinson. "Minnesota's Lake Superior Ship-Wrecks, A.D. 1650–1945; Historical Contexts and Property Types." In *Archaeological and Historical Studies of Minnesota's Lake Superior Shipwrecks,* ed. Scott F. Anfinson, 17–33. St. Paul: Minnesota State Historic Preservation Office, Minnesota Historical Society, 1993.

Lake Carriers' Association. *Annual Reports.* Cleveland: Lake Carriers' Association, 1905–95.

Landon, Fred. *Lake Huron.* New York: Bobbs-Merrill, 1944.

Larson, John W. *Essayons: A History of the Detroit District, U.S. Army Corps of Engineers.* Detroit: U.S. Army Corps of Engineers, 1981.

Larson, Phil, and Paul Schmitt. "Regina Yields Her Secrets." *Great Lakes Travel and Living,* December 1988, 18–22.

Lewis, William D. "The Curious History of the Infamous *Fame.*" Unpublished manuscript, Alpena Public Library, 1989.

Lyons, Captain S. A. "Ordeal on Sunday." In *The Great Lakes Reader,* ed. Walter Havighurst, 329–34. New York: Macmillan, 1969.

MacInnis, Dr. Joseph. *Fitzgerald's Storm: The Wreck of the Edmund Fitzgerald.* Holt, Mich.: Thunder Bay Press, 1998.

Mansfield, J. B. *History of the Great Lakes.* 1899. Reprint, Cleveland: Freshwater Press, 1972.

"Marcus Alonzo Hanna." *Encarta 98 Encyclopedia.* Microsoft, 1998.

Marine Casualty Report: M/V Cartiercliffe Hall. Washington, D.C.: U.S. Coast Guard, 1979.

Marine Casualty Report: M/V Indiana Harbor. Washington, D.C.: U.S. Coast Guard, 1996.

Marine Casualty Report: S.S. Carl D. Bradley. Washington, D.C.: U.S. Coast Guard, 1959.

Marine Casualty Report: S.S. Cedarville. Washington, D.C.: U.S. Coast Guard, 1967.

Marine Casualty Report: S.S. Daniel J. Morrell. Washington, D.C.: U.S. Coast Guard, 1968.

Marine Casualty Report: S.S. Edmund Fitzgerald. Washington, D.C.: U.S. Coast Guard, 1977.

Marine Casualty Report: S.S. Henry Steinbrenner. Washington, D.C.: U.S. Coast Guard, 1953.

Marine Casualty Report: S.S. Kinsman Independent. Washington, D.C.: U.S. Coast Guard, 1990.

Marine Casualty Report: S.S. Parker Evans and S.S. Sidney E. Smith, Jr. Collision. Cleveland: Ninth Coast Guard District, 1972.

Marine Casualty Report: S.S. Sidney E. Smith, Jr. Washington, D.C.: U.S. Coast Guard, 1972.

Martin, J. R. "Preliminary Comparative and Theme Study of National Historic Landmark Potential for Thunder Bay, Michigan." In *Proposed Thunder Bay National Marine Sanctuary: Draft Environmental Impact Statement— Draft Management Plan.* Vol. 2. Washington, D.C.: National Oceanic and Atmospheric Administration, 1997.

Mason, Philip P., ed. *Copper Country Journal: The Diary of Schoolmaster Henry Hobart, 1863–1864.* Detroit: Wayne State University Press, 1991.

McCormick, Jay. *November Storm.* Garden City, N.Y.: Doubleday, Doran, 1943.

McKee, Russell. *Great Lakes Country.* New York: Crowell, 1966.

Meyer, Balthasar Henry, ed. *History of Transportation in the United States before 1860.* Washington, D.C.: Peter Smith, 1948.

Micketti, Gerald F. *The Bradley Boats.* Traverse City, Mich.: Gerald F. Micketti, 1995.

Mills, James Cook. *Our Inland Seas.* 1910. Reprint, Cleveland: Freshwater Press, 1976.

"More Eyes on Ore." *Surveyor,* September 1997, 26–31.

Morrison, Dr. Neil F. "Feat of Long Point Heroine 100 Years Ago Is Recalled." *Bulletin of the Lake Carriers' Association,* July 1955, 18.

A Most Superior Land. Lansing: Two Peninsula Press, 1983.

"1927 *Lambton* Disaster Recalled." *Nor'easter* 12 (January–February 1987): 1–3.

Noble, Dennis L., and T. Michael O'Brien. *Sentinels of the Rocks.* Marquette: Northern Michigan University Press, 1979.

Nute, Grace Lee. *Lake Superior.* New York: Bobbs-Merrill, 1944.

O'Brien, T. Michael. *Guardians of the Eighth Sea: A History of the U.S. Coast Guard on the Great Lakes.* Washington, D.C.: U.S. Government Printing Office, 1976.

Oleszewski, Wes. *Ghost Ships, Gales, and Forgotten Tales.* Marquette, Mich.: Avery Color Studios, 1995.

———. *Ice Water Museum.* Marquette, Mich.: Avery Color Studios, 1993.

———. *Sounds of Disaster.* Marquette, Mich.: Avery Color Studios, 1993.

———. *Stormy Seas.* Marquette, Mich.: Avery Color Studios, 1991.

"Ore Carrier Smashes into Lighthouse on Lake Michigan." *Professional Mariner,* February 1994, 43.

"Ore Ship Runs Aground in St. Mary's River." *Professional Mariner,* April–May 1996, 58.

Parker, Jack. *Shipwrecks of Lake Huron.* AuTrain, Mich.: Avery Color Studios, 1986.

Pilot Rules for the Great Lakes and Their Connecting and Tributary Waters. Washington, D.C.: U.S. Government Printing Office, 1909.

Pitz, Herbert. *Lake Michigan Disasters.* Manitowac, Wis.: Manitowac Maritime Museum, n.d.

Plimsoll, Samuel. *Our Seamen, An Appeal.* London: Virtue and Co., 1873.

Quaife, Milo M. *Lake Michigan.* New York: Bobbs-Merrill, 1944.

Ratigan, William. *Great Lakes Shipwrecks and Survivals.* Grand Rapids, Mich.: Eerdmans, 1960.

———. *Straits of Mackinac.* Grand Rapids, Mich.: Eerdmans, 1957.

Rock, Rear Admiral George H. "The International Conference on Safety of Life at Sea, 1929, with Special Reference to Ship Construction." *Transactions of the Society of Naval Architects and Marine Engineers* 37 (1929): 89–100.

Rooke, Patrick. *The Industrial Revolution.* New York: John Day Company, 1971.

Ryan, George J. "Enhancing Weather Forecasting on the Great Lakes." *Seaway Review,* July–September 1984, 99.

Shipley, Robert, and Fred Addis. *Wrecks and Disasters.* St. Catharines, Ontario: Vanwell, 1992.

Sinking of the S.S. Daniel J. Morrell in Lake Huron with Loss of Life. Washington, D.C.: National Transportation Safety Board, 1968.

Sivertson, Howard. *Once Upon an Isle: The Story of Fishing Families on Isle Royale.* Mount Horeb, Wis.: Wisconsin Folk Museum, 1992.

Stefoff, Rebecca. *The U.S. Coast Guard.* New York: Chelsea House, 1989.

Stonehouse, Frederick. *The Great Wrecks of the Great Lakes.* Marquette, Mich.: Harboridge Press, 1973.

———. *Isle Royale Shipwrecks.* AuTrain, Mich.: Avery Color Studios, 1983.

———. *Keweenaw Shipwrecks.* AuTrain, Mich.: Avery Color Studios, 1988.

———. *Lake Superior's "Shipwreck Coast."* AuTrain, Mich.: Avery Color Studios, 1985.

———. *Munising Shipwrecks.* AuTrain, Mich.: Avery Color Studios. 1983.

———. *Shipwrecks of Thunder Bay.* Alpena, Mich.: B&L Watery World, 1986.

———. *Went Missing.* AuTrain, Mich.: Avery Color Studios, 1984.

———. *Wreck Ashore.* Duluth: Lake Superior Port Cities, 1994.

———. *The Wreck of the "Edmund Fitzgerald."* AuTrain, Mich.: Avery Color Studios, 1977.

Stories of the Great Lakes. New York: Century Co., 1893.

Strobridge, Truman R. *Chronology of Aids to Navigation and the Old Lighthouse Service, 1716–1939.* Washington, D.C.: U.S. Coast Guard, 1974.

Swayze, David D. *Shipwreck!* Boyne City, Mich.: Harbor House, 1992.

Tawresey, Rear Admiral J. G. "The International Conference of 1929 and the New Convention for Safety of Life at Sea." *Transactions of the Society of Naval Architects and Marine Engineers* 37 (1929): 101–20.

Telescope. Detroit: Great Lakes Maritime Institute, 1952–90.

Thomas, Gordon, and Max Morgan Witts. *Shipwreck: The Strange Fate of the Morro Castle.* New York: Dell, 1972.

Thompson, Mark L. *Queen of the Lakes.* Detroit: Wayne State University Press, 1994.

———. *A Sailor's Logbook.* Detroit: Wayne State University Press, 1999.

———. *Steamboats and Sailors of the Great Lakes.* Detroit: Wayne State University Press, 1991.

Turpin, Edward A., and William A. MacEwen. *Merchant Marine Officers Handbook.* Cambridge, Md.: Cornell Maritime Press, 1965.

"Two from the Lakes." *Seaway Review,* June–August 1985, 151.

United States Coast Pilot. Vol. 6. Washington, D.C.: U.S. Department of Commerce, 1988.

Van Der Linden, Rev. Peter, ed. *Great Lakes Ships We Remember.* Cleveland: Freshwater Press, 1979.

———. *Great Lakes Ships We Remember II.* Cleveland: Freshwater Press, 1984.

———. *Great Lakes Ships We Remember III.* Cleveland: Freshwater Press, 1994.

Vessel Traffic Control Hearings before the Subcommittee on Coast Guard and Navigation of the Committee on Merchant Marine and Fisheries, U.S. House of Representatives. Washington, D.C.: Committee on Merchant Marine and Fisheries, U.S. House of Representatives, 1976.

Vrana, Kenneth J. *Inventory and Maritime and Recreation Resources of the Manitou Passage Underwater Preserve.* East Lansing: Center for Maritime and Underwater Resource Management, Department of Park, Recreation and Tourism Resources, Michigan State University, 1995.

Wakefield, Lawrence, and Lucille Wakefield. *Sail and Rail* Traverse City, Mich.: Lawrence M. Wakefield, 1980.

Walton, Ivan H. "Developments on the Great Lakes, 1815–1943." *Michigan History* 27 (1943): 72–141.

Warner, Thomas D., and Donald F. Holecek. *The Thunder Bay Shipwreck Survey Report*. Lansing: Recreation Research and Planning Unit, Department of Park and Recreation Resources, Michigan State University, 1975.

Weborg, Captain Elmer. "Ice-bound." In *The Great Lakes Reader*, ed. Walter Havighurst, 335–37. New York: Macmillan, 1966.

Whitlark, Frederick Louis. *Introduction to the Lakes*. New York: Greenwich, 1959.

Williams, Elizabeth Whitney. *A Child of the Sea, and Life Among the Mormons*. Ann Arbor, Mich.: Edwards Brothers, 1905.

Wilson Marine Transit Company. Cleveland: Wilson Marine Transit Company, 1966.

Wolff, Julius F., Jr. "Grim November." In *The Great Lakes Reader*, ed. Walter Havighurst, 315–20. New York: Macmillan, 1966.

———. "In Retrospect." *Inland Seas*, Summer 1976, 122–24.

———. *Lake Superior Shipwrecks*. Duluth: Lake Superior Port Cities, 1990.

Woodford, Arthur M. *Charting the Inland Seas: A History of the U.S. Lake Survey*. Detroit: U.S. Army Corps of Engineers, Detroit District, 1991.

INDEX

Titles in the Great Lakes Books Series

Freshwater Fury: Yarns and Reminiscences of the Greatest Storm in Inland Navigation, by Frank Barcus, 1986 (reprint)

Call It North Country: The Story of Upper Michigan, by John Bartlow Martin, 1986 (reprint)

The Land of the Crooked Tree, by U. P. Hedrick, 1986 (reprint)

Michigan Place Names, by Walter Romig, 1986 (reprint)

Luke Karamazov, by Conrad Hilberry, 1987

The Late, Great Lakes: An Environmental History, by William Ashworth, 1987 (reprint)

Great Pages of Michigan History from the Detroit Free Press, 1987

Waiting for the Morning Train: An American Boyhood, by Bruce Catton, 1987 (reprint)

Michigan Voices: Our State's History in the Words of the People Who Lived It, compiled and edited by Joe Grimm, 1987

Danny and the Boys, Being Some Legends of Hungry Hollow, by Robert Traver, 1987 (reprint)

Hanging On, or How to Get through a Depression and Enjoy Life, by Edmund G. Love, 1987 (reprint)

The Situation in Flushing, by Edmund G. Love, 1987 (reprint)

A Small Bequest, by Edmund G. Love, 1987 (reprint)

The Saginaw Paul Bunyan, by James Stevens, 1987 (reprint)

The Ambassador Bridge: A Monument to Progress, by Philip P. Mason, 1988

Let the Drum Beat: A History of the Detroit Light Guard, by Stanley D. Solvick, 1988

An Afternoon in Waterloo Park, by Gerald Dumas, 1988 (reprint)

Contemporary Michigan Poetry: Poems from the Third Coast, edited by Michael Delp, Conrad Hilberry and Herbert Scott, 1988

Over the Graves of Horses, by Michael Delp, 1988

John Jacob Astor: Business and Finance in the Early Republic, by John Denis Haeger, 1991

Survival and Regeneration: Detroit's American Indian Community, by Edmund J. Danziger, Jr., 1991

Steamboats and Sailors of the Great Lakes, by Mark L. Thompson, 1991

Cobb Would Have Caught It: The Golden Age of Baseball in Detroit, by Richard Bak, 1991

Michigan in Literature, by Clarence Andrews, 1992

Under the Influence of Water: Poems, Essays, and Stories, by Michael Delp, 1992

The Country Kitchen, by Della T. Lutes, 1992 (reprint)

The Making of a Mining District: Keweenaw Native Copper 1500–1870, by David J. Krause, 1992

Kids Catalog of Michigan Adventures, by Ellyce Field, 1993

Henry's Lieutenants, by Ford R. Bryan, 1993

Historic Highway Bridges of Michigan, by Charles K. Hyde, 1993

Lake Erie and Lake St. Clair Handbook, by Stanley J. Bolsenga and Charles E. Herndendorf, 1993

Queen of the Lakes, by Mark Thompson, 1994

Iron Fleet: The Great Lakes in World War II, by George J. Joachim, 1994

Turkey Stearnes and the Detroit Stars: The Negro Leagues in Detroit, 1919–1933, by Richard Bak, 1994

Pontiac and the Indian Uprising, by Howard H. Peckham, 1994 (reprint)

Charting the Inland Seas: A History of the U.S. Lake Survey, by Arthur M. Woodford, 1994 (reprint)

Ojibwa Narratives of Charles and Charlotte Kawbawgam and Jacques LePique, 1893–1895. Recorded with Notes by Homer H. Kidder, edited by Arthur P. Bourgeois, 1994, co-published with the Marquette County Historical Society

Strangers and Sojourners: A History of Michigan's Keweenaw Peninsula, by Arthur W. Thurner, 1994

Win Some, Lose Some: G. Mennen Williams and the New Democrats, by Helen Washburn Berthelot, 1995

Sarkis, by Gordon and Elizabeth Orear, 1995

The Northern Lights: Lighthouses of the Upper Great Lakes, by Charles K. Hyde, 1995 (reprint)

Kids Catalog of Michigan Adventures, second edition, by Ellyce Field, 1995

Rumrunning and the Roaring Twenties: Prohibition on the Michigan-Ontario Waterway, by Philip P. Mason, 1995

In the Wilderness with the Red Indians, by E. R. Baierlein, translated by Anita Z. Boldt, edited by Harold W. Moll, 1996

Elmwood Endures: History of a Detroit Cemetery, by Michael Franck, 1996

Master of Precision: Henry M. Leland, by Mrs. Wilfred C. Leland with Minnie Dubbs Millbrook, 1996 (reprint)

Haul-Out: New and Selected Poems, by Stephen Tudor, 1996

Kids Catalog of Michigan Adventures, third edition, by Ellyce Field, 1997

Beyond the Model T: The Other Ventures of Henry Ford, revised edition, by Ford R. Bryan, 1997

Young Henry Ford: A Picture History of the First Forty Years, by Sidney Olson, 1997 (reprint)

The Coast of Nowhere: Meditations on Rivers, Lakes and Streams, by Michael Delp, 1997

From Saginaw Valley to Tin Pan Alley: Saginaw's Contribution to American Popular Music, 1890–1955, by R. Grant Smith, 1998

The Long Winter Ends, by Newton G. Thomas, 1998 (reprint)

Bridging the River of Hatred: The Pioneering Efforts of Detroit Police Commissioner George Edwards, 1962–1963, by Mary M. Stolberg, 1998

Toast of the Town: The Life and Times of Sunnie Wilson, by Sunnie Wilson with John Cohassey, 1998

These Men Have Seen Hard Service: The First Michigan Sharpshooters in the Civil War, by Raymond J. Herek, 1998

A Place for Summer: One Hundred Years at Michigan and Trumbull, by Richard Bak, 1998

Early Midwestern Travel Narratives: An Annotated Bibliography, 1634–1850, by Robert R. Hubach, 1998 (reprint)

All-American Anarchist: Joseph A. Labadie and the Labor Movement, by Carlotta R. Anderson, 1998

Michigan in the Novel, 1816–1996: An Annotated Bibliography, by Robert Beasecker, 1998

"Time by Moments Steals Away": The 1848 Journal of Ruth Douglass, by Robert L. Root, Jr., 1998

The Detroit Tigers: A Pictorial Celebration of the Greatest Players and Moments in Tigers' History, updated edition, by William M. Anderson, 1999

Letter from Washington, 1863–1865, by Lois Bryan Adams, edited and with an introduction by Evelyn Leasher, 1999

Father Abraham's Children: Michigan Episodes in the Civil War, by Frank B. Woodford, 1999 (reprint)

A Sailor's Logbook: A Season aboard Great Lakes Freighters, by Mark L. Thompson, 1999

Huron: The Seasons of a Great Lake, by Napier Shelton, 1999

Wonderful Power: The Story of Ancient Copper Working in the Lake Superior Basin, by Susan R. Martin, 1999

Tin Stackers: The History of the Pittsburgh Steamship Company, by Al Miller, 1999

Art in Detroit Public Places, revised edition, text by Dennis Nawrocki, photographs by David Clements, 1999

Brewed in Detroit: Breweries and Beers since 1830, by Peter H. Blum, 1999

Detroit Kids Catalog II: The Hometown Tourist, by Ellyce Field, 2000

"Expanding the Frontiers of Civil Rights": Michigan, 1948–1968, by Sidney Fine, 2000

Graveyard of the Lakes, by Mark Thompson, 2000

Enterprising Images: The Goodridge Brothers, African American Photographers, 1847–1922, by John Vincent Jezierski, 2000

New Poems from the Third Coast: Contemporary Michigan Poetry, edited by Michael Delp, Conrad Hilberry, and Josie Kearns, 2000

Arab Detroit: From Margin to Mainstream, edited by Nabeel Abraham and Andrew Shryock, 2000

The Sandstone Architecture of the Lake Superior Region, by Kathryn Bishop Eckert, 2000

Looking Beyond Race: The Life of Otis Milton Smith, by Otis Milton Smith and Mary M. Stolberg, 2000

Mail by the Pail, by Colin Bergel, illustrated by Mark Koenig, 2000

Great Lakes Journey: A New Look at America's Freshwater Coast, by William Ashworth, 2000

A Life in the Balance: The Memoirs of Stanley J. Winkelman, by Stanley J. Winkelman, 2000

Schooner Passage: Sailing Ships and the Lake Michigan Frontier, by Theodore J. Karamanski, 2000

The Outdoor Museum: The Magic of Michigan's Marshall M. Fredericks, by Marcy Heller Fisher, illustrated by Christine Collins Woomer, 2001

Detroit in Its World Setting: A Three Hundred Year Chronology, 1701–2001, edited by David Lee Poremba, 2001

Frontier Metropolis: Picturing Early Detroit, 1701–1838, by Brian Leigh Dunnigan, 2001

Michigan Remembered: Photographs from the Farm Security Administration and the Office of War Information, 1936–1943, edited by Constance B. Schulz, with Introductory Essays by Constance B. Schulz and William H. Mulligan, Jr., 2001

This Is Detroit, 1701–2001, by Arthur M. Woodford, 2001

History of the Finns in Michigan, by Armas K. E. Holmio, translated by Ellen M. Ryynanen, 2001

Angels in the Architecture: A Photographic Elegy to an American Asylum, by Heidi Johnson, 2001